a Young American in Iran

TOM KLOBE

A PEACE CORPS WRITERS BOOK

A Young American in Iran
A Peace Corps Writers Book
An imprint of Peace Corps Worldwide

© 2014 Tom Klobe
All rights reserved.

Printed in the United States of America
by Peace Corps Writers of Oakland, California

No part of this book may be used or reproduced in any manner whatsoever
without written permission except in the case of brief quotations contained
in critical articles or reviews.

For more information, contact peacecorpsworldwide@gmail.com
Peace Corps Writers and the Peace Corps Writers colophon are trademarks
of PeaceCorpsWorldwide.org

ISBN: 978-1-935925-46-0
Library of Congress Control Number: 2014957198

First Peace Corps Writers Edition, December 2014

This book is dedicated to
the people of Alang
who helped me to see
and understand.

"Plant the tree of friendship for its fruit will be the desire of your heart…" *

—Shah Ismael Safavid, 1510, passage from letter to Uzbek leader Shaibani Khan whose forces were raiding the cities of eastern Persia

* Mirza Haidar, Tarkh-i Rashidi, *A History of the Moghuls*, trans. E. Denison Ross (Patna: Academica Asiatica, 1973), 232.

CONTENTS

Schoolyard Wall, Alang 1965

ACKNOWLEDGEMENTS

THIS BOOK IS A TRIBUTE to the people of Alang and Iran—to their love and goodness. It strives to capture the essence of life in a specific village and Iran in the mid-1960s. It is also the story of an individual attempting to understand others and their culture, and of his attendant initial frustrations trying to fit in. Ultimately he realizes the depth of his love for the people and for a country in which he was always the outsider. It is an account of growing in a special kind of wisdom that cannot be learned within the context of formal education, of knowing you can be an idealist—always— but that you must have your feet firmly planted on the ground.

The idea of writing about the nearly two years I lived in Alang in northern Iran as a Peace Corps Volunteer never occurred to me until 2011 when my wife and I attended an Iran Returned Peace Corps Volunteer reunion in Portland, Oregon. There, I realized my connection to the village and its people was profound and long-lasting. While all Peace Corps Volunteers have unique and meaningful experiences, I finally understood the singular importance of my situation. Few other volunteers in Iran had lived in a remote village and thus missed the opportunity to encounter isolation from American norms and experience cultural assimilation to the degree I had. I left the reunion still not aware of the need to document what happened in those years and how it influenced my life. However, before I reached home, my determination to record this story was set.

My parents saved my letters, and it is from those ramblings that I am able to recollect and reconstruct the stories within these pages. Some dates are exact; others are approximate.

The names of most of my Iranian friends are real and presented with my utmost respect. Some names have been changed intentionally, and the vicissitudes of time no longer allow me to remember all. With few exceptions, I have used only first names of American friends and Peace Corps Volunteers and staff. Locations retain the names and spellings most commonly used during the period.

My deepest gratitude goes to my wife Delmarie who served as a Peace Corps Volunteer in Malawi while I was in Iran. She lovingly encouraged me in this endeavor and worked closely with me to edit a much larger manuscript. My appreciation also goes to M. R. Nikou for his advice as Persian editor and consultant. To those who critiqued the manuscript, in part or in whole, you have my sincerest thanks. Any errors in the book are solely mine.

PROLOGUE

I GREW UP ON A SMALL FARM in an all-white community near Young America, Minnesota. So, in a way, I was a Young American through and through. My parents taught my brother and me to believe in the American ideals of freedom and democracy, in the rights and privileges of being an individual, and, most importantly, that "all men are created equal."

Life was an endless whirlwind of dizzying dichotomies. We were quiet liberals in a conservative community, staunch Catholics, but from early on I was apprehensive of the clergy. We respected our parents because they deserved our adulation, but they taught us to question authority. We were fiercely independent and proud of it, even if it hurt. "Always do the right thing, no matter how difficult it is," they would tell us.

When we moved to Hawaii in 1959, a year after I finished high school, I could freely live the American ideals my parents had instilled in us. Freed from the American norm, and realizing that democracy thrives on pluralism and diversity, I could now truly be an individual. Foremost, I saw and understood the necessity of equality for all people, and I knew I had to work to ensure that all would have the same opportunities. Yet my aptitudes and interests were in art, and I would strive to find ways to mesh my chosen career with my philosophical thought.

Iran and the Peace Corps were a diversion, a solidifying element that provided my life with professional, intellectual, emotional, and spiritual depth. To say my adopted country of Iran and the Peace Corps were life-changing cannot adequately describe the significance of both. They, along with my parents, formed my very life.

TO LIVE THE LEGACY

FRIDAY, NOVEMBER 22, 1963 "Oh, c'mon, let's play one game before you go," Randy pleads.

Bill and Lily, who wait for me to walk with them to campus, roll their eyes with that knowing look—*here we go again.*

"No, I have to get the printing done today."

"Oooh, just one! Then you can go. It won't take long."

Everyone knows it doesn't take much to beat me at ping-pong, but they also are aware I'm easily tempted. Anytime, I can be coaxed into one more game before I leave for class. One game leads to another and another. I have a reputation for turning up at a two-hour art class an hour and a half late. One professor even confided that he thought I was an unusually conscientious student as I often showed up in the printmaking studio about fifteen minutes before his class ended. Impressed that I was arriving early for the next class, it wasn't till the end of the semester, when he found my name on his roll sheet, that he woke up to the fact I was in *his* class!

"No. It's imperative I get this assignment done."

"One game will only take ten minutes."

"Lily, Bill . . . Randy is right. Wait while I play one game."

Lily gives her habitual obstinate pout. "No. Let's go *now*. It's always this way—just one more game! We need to get to the library. Bill, let's go without him."

"No. Wait for me! Then we can walk together. Besides, Randy always beats me in no time at all."

"Oh, you. Always making us late," Lily retorts, decidedly irritated.

Randy wins. He begs for another game. I already pushed Lily to the limit, so I say, "No. You always win anyway. This afternoon, when the gang is here, let's play mahjong. I'll beat you at that." Even though Randy and many of my friends are Chinese, I triumph at mahjong.

"See you later," we call out to Randy as we leave the Newman clubhouse shortly before 8:30am. The bright Hawaiian sun shines over St. Louis Heights. To our right, in the valley, a gentle rain casually drifts toward us.

"See? Just because of you we're going to get wet," Lily complains.

What can I say? I try to ignore it. Fortunately, as we walk to the center of campus, the rain dissolves into a fine mist, and a faint rainbow frames the fountain at Varney Circle and old Hawaii Hall behind it. Parting I say, "See you at the Snack Bar for lunch."

Alone, I trek across the quad to the art department in George Hall, get my supplies and grubby painting clothes from my locker on the third floor, and descend the back stairs to the screen-printing room. My silk screen is a design inspired by the vertical and horizontal strokes of Arabic calligraphy I saw in a book in the library. Del comes by between her history classes in nearby Crawford Hall. She knew I planned to print this morning and she wanted to say hi and see how I was doing. Her dark hair glistens with sparkling droplets of the light rain she's come through. We chat a few minutes and then she departs for her nine o'clock class.

I return to my task, pinning the three yards of fabric to the table, slowly pulling it as taut as youthful skin. Someone pokes his head in the door.

"The President was shot!"

I recoil in disgust. "Don't joke about something like that."

"It's true."

"Don't be ridiculous."

He leaves me in my disbelief. Continuing to stretch the fabric, I try to put what he said out of my mind, but cannot rid my thoughts of the possibility it could be true. As I assemble the printing inks, I struggle to concentrate. Finally, recognizing I'm too distracted to start printing, I put the inks and screen away, pull the pins out of the fabric, fold it, gather my supplies, and ascend the stairs to my locker. The sound of a transistor radio in a nearby classroom stops me in my tracks.

BULLETIN:
PRESIDENT JOHN F. KENNEDY DIED AT APPROXIMATELY
1PM CENTRAL STANDARD TIME TODAY HERE IN DALLAS. HE DIED
OF A GUNSHOT WOUND IN THE BRAIN.

IT IS 9:30. I heard the first official word of this black moment in America's history. I grab the staircase railing and bite my lower lip in a half-hearted effort to suppress the tears that make it hard for me to see. My feet are heavy and my legs almost immovable. I stagger to the top and stare emptily into the classroom. The lone student with the radio and I look at each other and say nothing. I turn, lumber to my locker, deposit my things, and leave the building. My body aches and it is hard to breathe. Still, I trudge to the library as fast as I can. I reach the second floor, see Lily, then Bill.

"Lily, President Kennedy was killed."

She looks at me in dismay. Others nearby heard. All are stunned.

"It's not true," she utters, but she can tell from the look on my face I'm shaken. I look away, out the open windows to Waikiki and the magnificent blue Pacific beyond—water meeting water—so she can't see the tears I attempt to conceal. At that moment the American flag in front of Bachman Hall descends to half-mast. I look at Lily again.

"See the flag?"

Immediately, everyone gathers around. Del arrives, her woe readily apparent. Her class disbanded when news of the assassination was announced. She went to George Hall to find me, but I had already left. She knew where I would be. Together, in silence, we leave the library to go to the Newman clubhouse. Many have already assembled there. We look at each other in anguish, listen to the unfathomable news on the radio, and talk in hushed tones. I call Father Dever, our chaplain.

"Father, could you come and say Mass at noon?"

"Of course, I'll be there."

Father does what he can to console us. His words at this time of national mourning help to explain the meaning of death—and life, to reassure us individually, and restore our faith in the mission of America. Gradually we come to terms with what occurred.

Arriving home with my brother Alan, Mom meets us at the door, hugs each of us, and says nothing. Dad resolutely stands behind her. I look into his eyes. They, too, are red around the rims. *Why do we have to endure things like this?* I brood. Dad's visible grief—evident in such a stoic and stalwart man—makes me feel even worse. I have never seen him cry.

Over the days that follow, we watch on television the unfolding events in Dallas and the manifestations of the unthinkable sadness that grips our nation and the world. All is black and white, but mostly gray.

MONDAY, NOVEMBER 25, 1963 The day before my 23rd birthday three men are laid to rest: Dallas police Officer J. D. Tippitt who was killed in his pursuit of the suspected assassin Lee Harvey Oswald; Oswald, who had been killed by Jack Ruby; and John F. Kennedy, 35th President of the United States.

MONDAY, DECEMBER 2, 1963 Among the collage of posters that covers the walls of the Snack Bar—a dilapidated remnant of a World War II barrack on campus—one announces, "Peace Corps Placement Test, 8:30am, December 7, 1963, Old Post Office Building, Honolulu." Somewhat embarrassed, I admit to Del, "I've often thought of joining the Peace Corps, but they wouldn't want me."

She looks at me surprised. "I've thought of it too, but I'm just a history major. What use could I be? Growing up on a farm and now your role in student activities make you exactly the kind of person they want."

I'm not persuaded. "But you know history so well, and you know the grades I got in history. I'm only an art major. They'd never want me."

"Yes, they would. You should try it."

"Well, would you take the exam on Saturday? If you take it, I will too."

Lily, Bill, and Jerry are already at a table when we join them in the noisy, rather dark interior of the Snack Bar.

"How have you guys been? Did you have a nice Thanksgiving?"

"Good as could be expected," Lily responds.

Abruptly I say, "Del and I are going to take the Peace Corps exam on Saturday."

Their faces light up. All agree they had often thought of it too, but were afraid to tell anyone for fear they wouldn't make it. Regardless, we are idealists, convinced we might be able to change the world, even if only in our own little way. Now with Kennedy's death, it is important to show the world what Americans are really like and keep Kennedy's legacy alive.

SATURDAY, DECEMBER 7, 1963 I'm scared. Probably Del, Lily, Bill, and Jerry are too. None of us lets on. I'm afraid I won't pass the exam.

I'm sure I want to join the Peace Corps, especially after what had so recently happened in America. But, I also reflect that this is a rather auspicious day to be taking an exam for peace. It is the 22nd anniversary of the bombing of Pearl Harbor—so close by—a day that plunged America into a dreadful war.

The exam, specifically the Spanish-language exam, heightens my anxiety that I won't make it. I had taken Spanish in high school and indicated on my application I preferred to go to South America or the Philippines, but was open to going anywhere. I particularly liked the prospect of the Philippines as the Newman Club had hosted the Bayanihan National Folk Dance Company at the clubhouse one evening and we had so much fun together—and the Filipina women are *so* beautiful!

OMINOUS NEWS! I see the overwhelming anxiety on my parents' faces when I return home. What is their son doing? They hand me the *Honolulu Star-Bulletin*. Headlines: "Hawaii Man Held Hostage in Bolivia." I feel sick as I read. Robert Fergerstrom was President of Newman Club when I joined and among the first Peace Corps Volunteers from Hawaii to go into the field. Now Communist rebels hold him and three additional Americans hostage at a mine in Bolivia. The four had gone on a friendly mission to offer schools to the mining villages high in the mountains. In a horrifying turn of events, they and others became hostages in a ransom deal that threatens to push Bolivia into civil war and prompts President Johnson, a little over two weeks in office, to deliberate over sending in US troops.

For ten agonizing days America and Hawaii watch and wait as the hostages are held above a roomful of dynamite and angry miners and their women brandish guns and sticks of explosives. In a desperate bid to end their weary captivity, the hostages descend the stairs from their second-story confinement, ignoring the shrill protests of their lady guards. They step out into the crowded plaza to a moment of uncertain silence. Then, a spatter of applause breaks the deafening stillness. A smattering of miners surges forward to shake the Americans' hands.

LATE 1963–EARLY 1964 My parents' unease over my decision to join the Peace Corps is evident, but they don't express it. Surely, to them, the other option—joining the military—is even worse.

While I still hope somehow I might make it, I try to put the Peace Corps out of my mind. I don't talk about it, especially around my parents—the silence of love. I don't want to worry them and, for me, it is mental protection from the inevitable letter of rejection.

The fall semester ends in January with my predictable Herculean effort to finish all my art projects and study for exams. No more ping-pong, mahjong, or going out and having fun. Procrastination is not my one and only problem. Invariably I have overambitious plans, and everything has to be perfect, so it takes longer than I anticipate. Often, at the end, I am so exhausted from lack of sleep I doze off in final exams!

My last semester at the university starts. Besides the work for my classes, I am co-editor of the yearbook and president of Newman Club—not too much time to think about anything else. I never consider the possibility of graduate school. There is always the army, and I'm prime draft age. The idea of war bothers me, but if it has to be, it has to be.

Things go differently for my brother. He is sworn into the Army Reserves at Fort DeRussy on March 10. Mom takes it hard. Vietnam looms. No outright war; but news is depressing. The thought that he might be going to war obsesses her. Dad says nothing; his silence says everything. Alan leaves for training at Fort Ord, California on April 29, Dad's birthday.

Mid-March a letter arrives from the Peace Corps. Mom eagerly meets me at the door.

"Hurry up, open it."

"I'm afraid to. I can't bear the disappointment."

Finally . . . "It's not the Philippines or South America. It's Iran."

Mom asks, "Are you happy it's Iran?"

"I don't know. Any place will be fine."

I think, *What do I know about Iran? Only its rich and glorious ancient history from my art history classes. There are deserts, oil, and the Shah. That's it.*

I feel like someone hit me very hard in the stomach. But it is also exciting. I want to call Del, Lily, Bill, and Jerry to see if they have received letters, but then I don't want them to know I have been accepted in case they haven't. I figure they'll call me as soon as they find out. Then I'll tell them I had a letter too.

I sit, stunned, thinking. Mom quietly utters, "I'm losing both my sons." I look at her. Tears run down her face. I turn away. It's hard to comprehend what a mother feels, but her statement and sadness stab at my soul.

The next day I go to the library to get books on Iran. I become more enthusiastic, but I'm also scared. *I'm going to a faraway place. I'll be leaving my family and friends and all that is familiar to me. I don't know the language. What will it be like in this strange place? What if I don't make it through training? How will I face my friends?*

The following week, when I arrive home, Mom is all smiles. "Del called a little while ago. She's excited. She got a letter from the Peace Corps to train for French West Africa."

"Did you tell her I'm going to Iran?"

"No, I wanted you to be able to tell her. Give her a call. She's waiting."

Del is thrilled and I am happy to inform her of my invitation for Iran. What adventures are ahead for both of us! This seems like dreams come true. I'll be living the pages from *National Geographic* I pored over as a kid. It was my way of seeing the world vicariously. Now I'll actually be doing it!

SUNDAY, JUNE 14, 1964   Graduation is just graduation. Something you go through for others, mainly your parents. They are proud to have a son who graduated from university, and I am resigned to give them this sense of accomplishment.

Del's parents and brother came from Hilo for graduation and are staying to see her off for Peace Corps training. Our families go out for a Chinese dinner at McCully Chop Sui. Afterwards we see Elia Kazan's film *America, America* at Varsity Theater. This poignant film of a young Turk's striving desire to reach the land of opportunity seems an odd send-off for two young Americans who will be doing the opposite, departing for Peace Corps training this week, and ultimately leaving America.

Are we crazy to be doing this? Others want to come here and we want to leave. But there's a big difference. We are Americans. We will be gone for only two years. We will return and everything will be the same—we think.

WEDNESDAY, JUNE 17, 1964 Del's family and a large crowd from Newman Club gather at the airport to give Del her send-off for training at Oberlin, Ohio. In the tradition of Hawaii, she is covered with lei. Not enough time to be together any more. Boarding is announced. One final hug and kiss goodbye.

"All the best. Keep in touch." I turn away.

She says a tearful farewell to her parents and brother as I stand in the background. She looks back and we all wave as she enters the aircraft. We continue waving as the plane taxis onto the runway and, in the dark, becomes airborne. Somberly we walk out of the terminal.

Tom and Del

TWO MORE DAYS AND ONE NIGHT—one more going-away party. Mom wants me at home. I want to be with friends. I want to spend a little more time with Lily. She, too, is special, always so much fun—especially fun to tease. But she has her own persnickety way of giving it back. Recently I had been with Del a lot, and I liked that, but I had always taken my father's sage advice rather earnestly: "There is safety in numbers," he would tell me. So when somebody commented I was getting serious about a certain person I asked someone else out. I wasn't ready to settle down and, per Dad's words of wisdom, I wanted to "keep the playing field completely open."

FRIDAY, JUNE 19, 1964 Friday night comes too quickly. Exhausted and anxious about leaving home and friends, tears cloud my eyes as each gives me a lei and wishes me well. *Do I truly want to go?* There's no turning back now. One more hug for everyone. I wait till the end to say goodbye to Mom and Dad. All look on in subdued silence. I turn and walk to the plane, stop, turn and wave, then press on. It's difficult, but I'll be back in three months.

SATURDAY, JUNE 20, 1964 Eight hours later the plane touches down in San Francisco. Aunt Catherine, Uncle John, and my cousin George are there to meet me at the gate. Determined to fatten me up, my aunt plies me with food the entire weekend.

MONDAY, JUNE 22, 1964 My eyes smart as I step from the plane into the intensely bright and warm Salt Lake City sunshine. Per Peace Corps instructions, I catch a Greyhound bus for the two-hour trip to Logan, Utah.

I'm assigned a room with another guy in Kappa Delta sorority house. We're disappointed not to find a sorority girl in our closet, but it's double disappointment. There are no women in this training group. Just 76 guys!

TESTING THE METTLE

SUMMER 1964 *"In ketab ast."* Our instructor holds up a book. He places the book on the table and points. *"Un ketab ast."* He holds up a pen. *"Man qalam doram."* He hands me the pen. *"Shoma qalam dorid.* Repeat after me. *In ketab ast. Un ketab ast. Man qalam doram. Shoma qalam dorid.* Again."

Seven of us struggle to repeat what he says. My head is spinning. *What's going on?*

"Again. *In ketab ast....*"

What is this all about? He doesn't write anything on the board. When we ask him what this means, he simply holds up the book and says, *"In ketab ast.* Repeat."

Then, *"In ketab ast?"*

Do I detect an inflection? Is that a question? Same arrangement of words. Strange.

Again, *"In ketab ast? Baleh."*

What is baleh? Could it be yes?

An hour later, maybe—just maybe—some of this is sinking in. We look around the room at each other, eyes glazed, exhausted. A short break. A new Iranian teacher enters. Same thing—just more of it! More new words. By noon our brains are fried. Great to get away for lunch. But our Iranian instructors join us at the tables. And they speak only Farsi! I am lost. Frustrated! *How will I survive this? I can't wait to get out of here—back to Kappa Delta. Any kind of break before it starts over!* The other guys flee too. We laugh about how ridiculous this seems. But the fact we are together in the same sinking boat makes us feel a little better.

The 7am to 9pm regimen of classes concentrates heavily on Farsi. Our teachers rotate classrooms each hour so we hear different accents. Though we have lesson books, we are not allowed to open them. We aren't being taught to read. We are learning to *speak* Farsi. As the summer wears on, things begin to make more sense, but each day brings new vocabulary, new tenses, and more complex sentences. I never get ahead. One day we learn the curious squiggles of the alphabet and that you read backwards—arrogant of us to think there is solely one correct way to read! Most importantly, our Iranian teachers are becoming our friends. We like their stories of Iran. They bring reality to our classes in Iranian cultural studies and history, and our desire to make it through training becomes more imperative.

Many mornings at 7am, the 37 community development trainees load onto a bus. Groups of two or three are dropped off in little towns surrounding Logan. Charged with unveiling the social structure of the community, for most of us it is a lark, a chance to see how quickly we will be invited into a home for garden-fresh strawberries, raspberries, or gooseberries and newly baked goods; and the big challenge—to see how long we can stave off the inevitable spiel about Mormonism. We scrupulously time how long it takes for religion to surface as the subject of discussion. Usually it is simply a matter of minutes. When we pile into the bus to return to Logan, those that fended off the subject longest score for the day. And, we compare notes on what we had to eat. Not that we needed to eat; we already had a big breakfast in true Mormon fashion. But it's fun to partake of the gentle Mormon hospitality. I begin to appreciate their sincerity and zeal. This is becoming an unforgettable opportunity to learn about a unique microcosm within the rich tapestry of American culture.

The resolve of my Aunt Catherine to fatten me up in the two days I visited is now reversed. I retreat to my old ways of eating only as much as I want. "Please don't put so much on my plate," I tell the cooks. They oblige and remove a bit. But the food is appetizing. As the days go on, I request more. I eat it all. More the next time. I begin to take two pieces of cheesecake for dessert. My clothes appear to be shrinking. Eventually I am eating four pieces of cheesecake a day. I even take one piece to Kappa Delta House to have as a snack before going to bed.

ON THE 4ᵀᴴ OF JULY four other guys and I set off to conquer Logan Peak (9,710 feet). We follow the ridgeline trail and reach the summit by late afternoon. To pick up time before darkness descends, we take an easier way down. As the sun stretches its course across the sky, we hit an area where an avalanche had recently gone through. *Now what?* To retrace our steps to the summit would put us on the mountain overnight. We have no warm clothes, no food, and no more water. The hum of cars on the highway in the valley far below reassures me there is civilization somewhere.

"We need to go straight down from here," I suggest. "It's the only way we'll get off this mountain before dark."

"You're crazy! There's no trail, an avalanche has gone through here, there are loose boulders everywhere, and you don't know if the mountain will suddenly drop off in a thousand-foot vertical cliff. Besides there could be rattlesnakes in any crevasse and we don't have a snakebite kit."

"But we've got to get off this mountain and back to Kappa Delta before our housemother and the other trainees alert the Peace Corps we're missing. If we don't get back there tonight, we're out of the program for sure." Gene, the youngest guy in our group, agrees.

"OK, Gene, let's go down from here." We start off, figuring the others will follow. They don't. I never consider they could be right.

They yell to us, "That's a bad idea." We look back. They turn and head up the mountain. Gene and I push on.

We descend fast. Rocks slip from under our feet and tumble down the mountain. We listen as they rumble along for several hundred feet before they lodge somewhere. We keep going. I look carefully before I grasp anything; I don't want to grab a rattlesnake that might be lurking on a ledge.

The sound of the cars on the highway gets louder. The sun is still shining on the peaks around, but the shadows of the valley are swiftly rising above us. This is definitely a rush against time. There are at least a thousand feet to go before the valley floor. The mountainside gets steeper. Suddenly it's straight down for about fifty feet. I look up. There's no way we can go back. We look at each other. I begin to shake—cold, but mostly terribly scared.

"Gene, there's only one way to go—down. We have to do it. It ain't that much farther."

Painstakingly we ease our way over the cliff, aiding each other as best we can, trying to withstand the bloodsucking flies that swarm about us. They are big as quarters and they just sit on us. And, they bite! We try to swat them off, but we have to hang onto anything now—trees, rocks, bushes— as we lower ourselves over ledges. We make it! We're in the valley; the road is on the other side. We forge our way fitfully through the trees and brush in darkness, the drone of flies diminishing as we progress. A river halts us—not that big. Off with our shoes and socks. We wade in. The water is freezing—melt from the snow high above—not that deep. Quickly we put on our shoes and scramble up the embankment to the road. One of the first cars stops to give us a ride—even two bedraggled guys found in the dark in the middle of nowhere in Utah.

Mom Jones, our housemother, is relieved to see us. She was concerned, particularly after it got dark. "Where are Mike, Jim, and Steve?"

"We don't know. Still trying to get down the mountain."

"Well, at least two of you are here." It comforts her somewhat.

We discuss with Mom Jones what we should do. We don't dare inform the Peace Corps. Guaranteed, it'll knock the guys out of training. But what if they need help? Anyway, how could they be found in the dark? What if they aren't back by morning? Do we notify the Peace Corps then?

Each time we hear guys coming up the walkway we expect it to be Mike, Jim, and Steve. Each time we are disappointed.

About midnight, Mom Jones reaches her limit. "Let's drive out in the canyon to see if we can find the guys. We can call for them. If they hear us, they will answer, and we'll know they're OK." I had never lived in a frat house, so it never crossed my mind a "mom" could worry about her "sons" as real moms do. From that night on, Mom Jones becomes very special.

THE STILLNESS OF THE DARK CANYON is only broken by the incessant screech of crickets and the intermittent roar of an oncoming truck.

"Mike-ike-ike-ike-ike-ike." The echo fades away as it bounces off the canyon walls.

"Steve-eve-eve-eve-eve-eve. Jim-im-im-im-im-im."

Each time we listen and anticipate a response. Nothing.

We drive deeper into the valley. More calls. More listening. Nothing; only the diminishing echo. We drive farther and farther, stopping and calling each time. An hour goes by. We drive back to Logan, the three of us silent, thinking, worried.

"You two are exhausted. Go get some sleep. I'll rest here in the chair. I have to know they got back OK."

We bid her goodnight. I look back from the top of the stairs. Her large frame appears small sitting there alone. I hope her vigil will not be long.

IT'S SUNDAY. No alarm to wake us at 5:50am to shower, shave, be at breakfast at 6:30, and in class by 7:00. I wake late, startled by the time— guilty I had slept without regard for my friends. The house is still. Mom Jones is no longer in the chair by the door.

I check to see if the guys have returned. They are asleep. I'm relieved and now aware that my whole body aches from the ordeal the day before.

Later I hear the tale of their frigid and hungry night on the mountain. They ascended almost to the summit one more time and then started down the trail. However, in the dark they unwarily took a wrong turn. Blindly they groped their way down the mountain. About 3am they happened upon a farmhouse. Cautiously they knocked on the door. After a while, a disheveled man appeared and shined a flashlight in their faces.

"Yeah?"

"Can you tell us the way to Logan?"

"Logan!" the man growled. "That's on the other side of the mountain, nearly an hour from here over these roads. Where's your car? Did you run out of gas? How did you get here?"

They explained. "Would you mind taking us to Logan? We're Peace Corps Volunteers."

"It's the middle of the night and you want me to take you all the way to Logan?"

"Yes," they pleaded hesitatingly. "Please."

He turned, leaving the door ajar. They saw the trail of the flashlight disappear inside. They heard muffled tones. "Have to take these guys, three of them, to Logan. Something about peace something or other."

They piled into his ramshackle truck with broken shocks and bumped along a jeep trail down the mountain and off to Logan. Tired and hungry, they dragged their nearly broken tailbones into Kappa Delta about 4am. Mom Jones rose from her chair and breathed a sigh of relief. They apologized for keeping her up.

DREADED TUESDAYS! "Lower your pants. Which cheek do you want it in?"

It's the gamma globulin shot. We all stagger away with a stiffened leg. There are umpteen shots for virtually everything. Most are in our arms. It doesn't make any difference which arm. Often it is both!

Then there are appointments with the psychologist. This is always unnerving. We are convinced he holds the key to our de-selection. So we psych out how best to answer his questions. It is truly mind against mind!

I briefly sweat one of them. He asks me a question that takes me aback. It's oblique, but I know the reference. *How did he get this information? Doubtlessly a professor with whom I had serious disagreements has squealed.*

I respond, "Well, I've had many teachers in my years. Some were excellent. Some not. There was one I learned a lot from. That is, if I ever become a teacher, I'll know what not to do."

He seems satisfied and goes on to other questions. But I leave the session troubled that he's aware of my confrontations with this professor. *Obviously the Peace Corps knows more about me than I thought they did. To whom had they talked? What had they found out? This is unsettling. This is twenty years before 1984, but "Big Brother" is already watching me!*

The FBI had been at the University of Hawaii checking on me. One of my colleagues told me I was in the yearbook office working with him when an agent was interviewing our advisor. But I didn't know how extensive their investigation had been. *What have they learned and how will this affect my future? What kind of files does the government have on me?*

Our former neighbors, Ruben and Nora Goede, reported that an agent had also poked around the farming community near Young America where I grew up. He showed up unannounced at their door. Politely, but hesitantly, they let him in. Certainly he detected the comforting smell of freshly baked bread mingled with the strong odor of clothes saturated with the stench of the barnyard that I vividly remember from my childhood. Nora offered him a cup of coffee, bread, butter, and some of her homemade strawberry jam. He obliged.

They sat around the kitchen table, Ruben and Nora on one side, the agent on the other. As he questioned them about my family and me, Ruben and Nora deliberated in German how they should respond to each question. When they agreed upon an answer they replied in English. This process went on for nearly an hour. As the agent rose to leave he thanked them in impeccable German for the information they provided. Ruben and Nora looked at each other wide-eyed in disbelief.

STRESS! MID-TERM DE-SELECTION! In Peace Corps "speak," there is no such word as rejection—just de-selection. Earlier, some guys had opted out of the program; now, it's not our choice. Someone else is determining our fate. We suspect the psychologist is the one who has a big, evil hand in this, but there could be an informant anywhere. We constantly have to be on guard.

Then it happens, and suddenly guys just disappear. No goodbyes. Gone—there's an empty bed in somebody's room. Those of us who make it are relieved we aren't going home as failures yet. There are another six weeks to final de-selection.

Mom Jones is grateful so many of "her" boys made it to the halfway mark. "Let's celebrate. There's a rodeo in Pocatello, Idaho Saturday night. Would you like to go?"

She knows I am always ready to get out of Logan for a new adventure. Barkley, three other guys, and I pile into Mom's olive-green Chevy. It doesn't take much to get Barkley spinning yarns of backcountry Kentucky—places with names like Goose Creek, Deer Lick, Hooker, Mill Pond, Pigeonroost, and Hog Hollow. Only, with Barkley's hillbilly twang, it sounds more like "Hog Holler." We laugh all the way to Pocatello.

We'd come to sample local color, but with Barkley's non-stop talking, we get double bill. He's wound up. He regales us with stories of life in

Appalachia while the rodeo crowd around us eavesdrops. They are as engrossed in Barkley and his anecdotes of the free and untrammeled people of the Kentucky mountains as we are in the rodeo. Barkley is truly a storyteller in what I would discover is the tradition of the celebrated storytellers of Iran and the Middle East. I am in awe of his philosophical wisdom and human compassion—honored to be in the presence of a man of this singular stature.

IN AUGUST, A NEW SATURDAY PROGRAM for community development trainees begins—building a simulated Iranian village at Hardware Ranch in Blacksmith Fork Canyon. It's a relief to escape Farsi classes and cut loose for a day. The task: to make sun-dried bricks. We get mud and water from the nearby stream and straw from bales that had been delivered, then mix them together, mud oozing between our toes as we stomp up to our knees in the muck. But one vital ingredient is missing—the binder. No cow manure! But we make hundreds of square bricks anyway. We return to Logan sunburned and tired, and speculate if we will ever make mud bricks in Iran.

We can't wait to get to the ranch the following Saturday to see our bricks and start building a privy and an oven. Disappointment! Nearly all the bricks are severely cracked, most unusable. *What went wrong?* No cow manure! Well, since there's no cow manure, we'll simply make a lot more bricks to beat the odds. Nothing can stop future Peace Corps Volunteers! Undaunted, we go to work.

What a sight—thousands of bricks are drying in the sun when we finish.

Saturday after Saturday we survey our ostensible failure, sort out the few usable bricks, and make more. It doesn't dawn on our community development instructor that we need to get a load of "farmer's gold" delivered. We loosen up a bit, have mud fights, and start the foundation and walls of an oven; not that we are ever going to bake any bread out here, but an oven is small and takes fewer bricks.

The ultimate test of our mettle comes one weekend when our Peace Corps endurance is tested on a two-day hike and camp-out in the mountains. Can we withstand the grueling hike and sleeping in the wild?

By midafternoon of the first day my feet are so sore, I almost can go no farther. I'm not alone. Others, too, can hardly walk. I stop, take off my shoes, and look at my sorry feet. It is heavenly to feel cool, fresh air flowing between my toes. *OK, time to put on my rubber slippers.*

"Not in this terrain," our Peace Corps instructor tells me. "Besides, there are rattlesnakes here. You're not in Hawaii."

I'm aware of that. We passed a rattler sunning itself beside the trail this morning. However, I am not deterred. Off I go, my shoes tied to my backpack. I feel refreshed. Most limp along till early evening and our arrival at the campsite deep in the mountains. At least sixty tough guys look like they are at death's door. Some quickly crawl into their sleeping bags. I find a spot somewhere in the middle. Safer that way, I calculate— any snake, bear, mountain lion, or other wild animal would have to pass over my buddies before it gets to me.

I don't sleep well. Never mind the possible animals; the ground is hard. No soft bed. But worse is the cold. I shiver most of the night. My Hawaii blood is still too thin. At long last I see a sliver of daylight. Rising, I put on my shoes just to get my feet warm, breakfast, packing up, and out of here. I go back to my rubber slippers.

Back in Logan on Sunday evening, the sorority houses are quiet. There is no partying tonight. We are sore all over, but my feet are in better shape than most.

We drag ourselves into classes the next morning. More and more Farsi. I seem to be falling behind. I fear this will prevent me from going to Iran. But I keep trying. Besides, others are struggling too. I still have hope. More than anything, I am gaining a deep and abiding love for Iran.

WEDNESDAY, SEPTEMBER 9, 1964 This is it—de-selection! In our minds, the alternative isn't even a word in the English language. Our stomachs are twisted in knots as we gather in the large lecture hall. The usual noisy, jovial banter is absent. Many sit alone in silence. I close my eyes and pray. I can't look as guys are called to the front of the room and handed an envelope. Klobe is in the middle of the alphabet. I wait, heart pounding.

"KLOBE, THOMAS M."

I rise. My knees shake. I can barely make it to the front of the room. Nonetheless, with extreme difficulty I strive to put on an air of composure. I am handed the feared envelope. I fumble and drop it, my life and fate sealed inside, there on the floor. I retrieve it and walk far away. I can't open it. But the agony of not knowing is driving me mad. I peer into the envelope with trepidation—merely a small strip of paper inside, "CONGRATULATIONS ON BEING SELECTED TO GO TO IRAN!" I say a quick prayer of thanks and look around. Others have small strips of paper too, and their faces emit a look of circumspect assurance as they watch the remainder receive their envelopes. For some, there is a larger sheet of paper. They leave the room. We never see them again. Their things are gone when we return to the sorority houses before lunch.

Immediately, I send a postcard to Del. She is now in training at Syracuse, New York with a group for Malawi, in southeast Africa. She had been reassigned midway through her training at Oberlin. I hope she will make it to Africa.

Now I feel a little sorry about leaving Logan. It has been an incredible summer in Mormon Utah. I will miss Mom Jones and our Iranian language instructors. But a whole new world is opening. It is both frightening and exciting.

LAST FLING

THURSDAY, SEPTEMBER 10, 1964 Aunt Catherine, Uncle John, and George meet me as I enter the terminal in San Francisco. I am all smiles.

"You look great. See, I knew. I was right. Your mother never took care of you well. You put on weight. You look rested. You have good color."

I am now unequivocal evidence of my mother's incompetence and neglect. Aunt Catherine undoubtedly is taking pride in the thought she had a little to do with this physical transformation. After all, she laid the foundation during those two days I spent with them. I am twenty pounds heavier than the emaciated and haggard individual my mother sent off to the mainland two-and-a-half months ago.

John wants to know what I learned about Iran; Catherine, if I will be safe. "Where will you be living? What is it going to be like?" I promise them the Peace Corps will make sure we are safe, but I have no idea where I'll be in Iran or about the living conditions. Aunt Catherine hands me a box of Almond Roca when my Pan Am flight to Honolulu is called. Obviously she thinks I'll need it since I'm going home.

The plane touches down in Honolulu minutes before midnight. The familiar warm, humid air envelops me as the fuselage doors open. I stride to the terminal humbly pleased I am a returning son of whom my parents can be proud. They are there—Mom and Dad—waiting for me. They, too, are astonished at how I look.

"What about Alan? Will he be home before I leave?" I do want to see my brother before I head for Iran and his possible departure for Vietnam.

"He wrote he plans to be home by the 22nd."

I'm relieved. He *is* my brother. Even though we fought like Bantam cocks as kids, our bond had been forged, and then cemented as adults.

"I made your favorite . . . pecan pie. We can have a piece before we go to bed. Girlie will have some with us." Girlie is our next-door neighbor and Mom's sidekick. They are always together, and stand on quiet Ohana Street yakking for hours late at night, each leaning on her mailbox. I used to say, "Anyone would think you two are hookers." Girlie's eyes would sparkle devilishly and she'd kick her leg high in the air at me.

Girlie is there as soon as we stop in the driveway. She gives me a big hug. Dad goes to bed; he has to get up early for work. We have our pie. Mom is right. I love pecan pie, and she makes the best. Tired, I excuse myself. It seems strange to be in my own bed, hearing the trade winds rustling through the palm branches outside. As usual, Mom and Girlie gab half the night at the mailboxes.

I AM UP AT THE CRACK OF DAWN—a lot to do, but I can't wait to start calling my pals. Even so, I must get my footlocker off to Washington or it won't go with the shipment to Iran. Warm clothes and gloves are hard to find in Hawaii. Neighbors and friends bring what they have to see if it will fit me, and we buy two years' worth of supplies—shoes, underwear, toilet paper, shaving cream, toothpaste and brushes, and deodorant. I pack in a few art books and some novels I never had a chance to read when I took World Lit—twice!

My social calendar fills quickly. Mom is disappointed when she finds I won't be spending all my time at home.

Monday I get my airfreight off. One week to tear the town apart. The TV is on as Dad and I talk and he savors his routine slow beer before dinner. Mom is in the kitchen. There is a knock on the door. She looks out the window and detects the outline of a man in a military uniform. I hear her sigh. I look toward her as she hesitantly goes to the door. I rise to follow. She screams as she throws open the screen door.

Alan grabs her. Dad comes running. We stand there in one great family embrace. "This is the happiest day of my life," she sobs. "Both my boys are home. We are all together again."

Tuesday night, my "last fling" begins—dates, parties, coming home late—night after night, sometimes not getting home at all. I pass out on the floor somewhere. One morning, I wake up, look in the bathroom mirror, and discover long red streaks on my forehead, on my cheekbones, and down my long nose. *What's going on? It isn't lipstick. It won't rub off.* I wander out. My friends are strewn all about. Though they are justifiably tired, I suspect they are feigning sleep.

"OK, I can tell you're just pretending. What's this all about?"

No response. As I look closely, Lily's face twitches, a hint of a smile. She turns so I can't see. "All right, I know you're awake. You might as well stop faking it. What's this stuff all over my face?"

They all express shock and have many theories, each one more preposterous than the former. "You must have caught some exotic disease. You won't be able to go into the Peace Corps now."

At last the truth emerges. Lily and Janice had painted nail polish on my face after I fell asleep in the middle of the floor.

Though I complain vociferously, they know it's an act. I'm comforted they felt they could play this trick on me.

THURSDAY I GO TO THE UNIVERSITY to say goodbye to my professors, especially Mr. Kingrey. I regret he was on sabbatical my senior year. He's like a father to me. Like my parents, he taught me crucial life values, but he also instilled within me professional principles of design and a conceptual way of thinking that, even at this early stage in my life, I knew would remain with me forever. We talk about his recent travels and the designers and artists he met, even some of the works of art he bought—a Picasso drawing for which he pawned his overcoat, and a medieval Spanish Madonna. I am astounded. He asks what I will be doing in Iran. I try to explain the nebulous nature of community development—that we will have to find our own work. He smiles. "You should have no problem."

He perhaps detects my anxious smile. What's ahead of me is like nothing I am familiar with. I am still plagued by doubt. However, the Peace Corps and going to Iran are what I truly want and believe in.

"What do you intend to do when you get out of the Peace Corps?"

"I have no idea." I never thought beyond getting out of the university; then, it was joining the Peace Corps. I took one step at a time. I lived in the present. There was no long-term life plan.

"What about grad school?"

I don't tell him I never thought of it, that I just feel fortunate to have completed my undergraduate education.

"I think you should consider going to Yale or the Art Institute of Chicago."

I am stunned, speechless. I can't comprehend what I am hearing. *Yale, with my grades?* I think. I had done very well in my art classes, but my academic record was not stellar. As my advisor, he knows. Throughout my undergraduate education, on the first day of classes, I determined what grade I would get in a class, and then I worked for it. I was realistic. There was a finite amount of time in life. I put my priorities where I thought they were important. A "C" was fine in some classes; others were worth an "A." There also needed to be plenty of time for fun.

"Have you ever thought of becoming a teacher? You have qualities that would make an excellent teacher."

"Mr. Kingrey, from the time I was a kid, I always said there are three professions I would *never* take up—being a doctor, a dentist, or a teacher. I never want to be any of them."

Once I say it, I realize Mr. Kingrey is a teacher. I regret I uttered such a thing to a professor whom I admire so much and to whom I am so grateful.

He looks at me intently, "Never say *never*. You would make a good teacher."

I put my head down apologetically, chagrined. I rise to say goodbye, embarrassed to let him see my feelings.

"Write. Let me know how you're doing in Iran. I'm interested."

"Yes, Mr. Kingrey." I slip away.

TUESDAY, SEPTEMBER 22, 1964 I spend my last day at home. I owe it to Mom. I'm uneasy all day. I go through my stuff, give some things to her, and throw away much of my artwork. When she objects to the discarding of my work, I tell her, "I don't want to burden you by having my junk around." I'm insensitive to what this purging is doing to her. I never look at her carefully or I might see how much this is hurting her—this, added to my departure this evening. It never occurs to me a mother might be depressed over a son going to a faraway—and in her mind, dangerous—land for two years, and any connection to her son might be very meaningful.

It's hard for sons to understand what a mother goes through in life. We are men, and, we feel things differently. Mom had been emotionally fraught all summer, but no one told me everything—again, the silence of love. She had lost both her sons, almost concurrently. She was in tears most of the time. Dad escaped to the backyard to cope. Then he bought an old car—a fixer-upper. Now Mom was also a "car widow." Her letters to me in training never disclosed her inner feelings—or perhaps I was too oblivious, self-indulgent, and preoccupied to notice. I was a young man on the loose, undeniably out of the nest.

We go to Aunt Dodo's, Mom's sister, for dinner. Uncle Hugh is his typical witty self, making light conversation. He plainly sees I am tied in knots. My cousins, Debbie and Denise, bounce around, so cute with their toothless grins. I force myself to eat a bit of my last family-familiar meal for nearly two years. They look at me, sad and distressed over how much I have changed in the twelve days of my leave. Again, I look gaunt, tired, and thin. There are dark bags under my eyes and I lost the twenty pounds I put on in training. It wasn't Mom's fault—too much "burning the candle at both ends."

At the airport I am smothered in lei and happy to have everyone around. The flight is called. One final hug. Now it is time to say goodbye to my brother and Mom and Dad. Even Dad is crying. Seeing him cry shakes me. I can hardly see through my squelched tears as I turn toward the plane. I stand briefly at the door, look back, wave, and bravely enter. I have a window seat on the terminal side of the aircraft, but as I sink down I break into nearly uncontrollable grief. *This is it! What have I done?* Try as I might, I can see no one in the terminal through my tears. The plane lifts off. I watch the Honolulu city lights vanish in the distance, and the inky blackness of the vast Pacific engulfs me. I am alone and on a new and scary adventure. My family will be there, always, but I also recognize a lot will change in two years—my friends might always be friends, but somehow I am aware it will never be the same.

What I don't know is that the unthinking years of my American youth—the Age of Innocence—ended when I boarded this plane. Nothing will ever be the same.

I drift into a long and much-needed sleep. The stop in San Francisco is brief; now, another eight hours across America. It is late afternoon as the plane circles over New York Harbor. The Statue of Liberty and ships plying the harbor come into view. I am experiencing the essence of America, a land I love so much—a land I am leaving.

Being with the guys again, we seem so unconcerned and animated. This is not the heavy, somber departure in Honolulu. We board the Pan Am flight to Frankfurt. The volunteer next to me stuffs his duffle bag in the space in front of him; there's no room for his long legs. He settles in, knees in his face. He is half in my space as well. I'm already tired and sore from traveling 5000 miles across the Pacific and America. I do not look forward to sitting next to a clod like this for at least another 6000 miles—well over one day—to Tehran, but I make the best of it.

We land in Frankfurt—only time to stretch. Another short stop in Munich, and then on to Istanbul. It is raining as we descend over the isthmus that separates two great continents. Minarets and domes of renowned Ottoman mosques crown the many hills of the city. We are on the threshold of another world, a world wondrously foreign—one that will become the passion of my life.

The airport terminal is strangely familiar, but like nothing I have ever experienced. It has the same appearance of intimacy as the old terminal in Honolulu where families gathered together on the floor, speaking softly, someone strumming a ukulele as others sing along, children running around, and the sweet smell of plumeria wafting on gentle breezes. Here in Istanbul, men in baggy pants huddle on the floor around a hookah, conversing in an incomprehensible language; women with hennaed hands and covered in long, dark veils slide by with children in tow; and the pungent smell of stale tobacco and old clothes permeates the air. It is like being inside an intimate 19th century Orientalist painting.

Fuel workers strike in Beirut, our next stop! The gas tanks have to be filled here in Istanbul so we can make it all the way to Tehran—but the plane will be too heavy to land in Beirut. A second plane is found. Half of us are loaded onto it. I rush to board, grab three seats, spread myself out, and go to sleep—the first I've had in a day and a half. Selfish or not, I traveled the farthest, and I had the bad luck of a passenger with too much luggage next to me.

It's dark when we land in Beirut. Wait. Wait. Wait. Wait for the other plane to arrive. Then transfer to the other aircraft. Wait again. The King of Jordan arrives in his private jet. We watch the red carpets being spread out on the darkened tarmac. Ceremony! At length we are cleared for takeoff.

BAPTISM

FRIDAY, SEPTEMBER 25, 1964—1:30AM Iran! Too tired to absorb anything, I absently follow the other guys, see my passport stamped, pick up my luggage, and board the waiting bus. I lean my head against the window and close my eyes. Each of the others slumps into a seat too. The door closes. The engine races. We start moving.

INSTANT ALERT! We aren't just moving—we're going at break-neck speed—horn tooting. Cars skitter out of the way. Our driver aggressively fights for every inch of highway with the drivers of large transport trucks, each blasting his horn at the other as they race along the streets. Red lights mean nothing! Lanes mean nothing! The other side of the road means nothing! Is the driver trying to scare these fifty-two "tough" Americans? We sit there, wide-eyed, in stunned silence, hanging on for dear life as the bus swerves among vehicles rushing in all directions. Nick starts a "Hail Mary." A good Italian is not going to take any chances. I silently join him. Finally, the Palace Hotel in central Tehran! Thankful we have not already met our untimely ends, we find our rooms and turn in for the night, too exhausted to be kept awake by our recent scare.

Late in the morning, I peer out the window at the street below. Everything is tan—only bits of green are visible on the underside of the leaves of a few scrawny trees. The tops are thick with dust. A woman, *chador* wrapped around her, crouches beside the gutter on the other side of the street. She is washing dishes. A few feet away a man squats next to the wall. That explains why the wall is wet and decayed at the bottom; he is relieving himself. Obviously he is not the first to do it. Repulsed, I turn away from the window. *What was I thinking wanting to join the Peace Corps? This is central Tehran, the capital city. We're going to villages in the provinces!*

Lunch, then off to Karaj, fifty kilometers west of Tehran, for three days of in-country orientation—another hair-raising bus ride—like the erratic movement of a 1920s silent film. In towns we zigzag among cars, trucks, buses, bicycles, and peasants leading slow-moving donkeys laden with huge bundles of straw. Women in *chadors* with children in hand jump aside as vehicles careen past. Chickens take wing, squawking vehemently as they narrowly miss being made into hash. On the open highways we pass strolling camels and play "chicken" with oncoming traffic—horns blaring, lights flashing, cars taking to the ditches. We, too, escape becoming hash by a large transport truck when our driver skillfully maneuvers a return to our lane as we pull in front of a village bus burgeoning with passengers hanging out the windows. There are only inches to spare on each side. Fifty-two guys noiselessly heave sighs of relief. We hang on, mouths agape. That's just the first of our close calls—there will be more.

Desert everywhere, as far as the eye can see—everything the color of dust. Dust-colored walls, many half-standing, some seeming to enclose nothing, define treeless villages. Dust envelops a troop of boys chasing a tired soccer ball. Dust devils swirl upward in the distance. A rising line of dust marks the path of a vehicle somewhere out there. *This is Iran. We came here voluntarily. What were we thinking?*

Finally, Karaj. As we pass through town, idle men converse on the dirt sidewalks, *chador*-covered women scurry about shopping for the evening meal, tired donkeys with garlands of blue beads around their necks are burdened with five-gallon cans of merchandise strapped to their backs, and a shopkeeper washes a basket of apples in the *jub*, the open drainage ditch that lines both sides of the streets in Iran. I recall the woman I saw washing dishes in the gutter in Tehran earlier in the day. *Will I ever be able to eat an apple during these two years in Iran? Will I be able to eat anything? If I'm thin now, what will I look like at the end of two years?*

Our destination, Karaj Agricultural College, is the reassurance we all need, a sure sign Iran is on the path to becoming a modern nation. Beds of softly scented roses and colorful petunias, zinnias, and marigolds border grand, sweeping lawns and spectacular reflecting pools. The campus reveals a unified design concept, one distinctly contemporary and restrained, yet Persian in its use of pattern and materials. This is an oasis of hope, a proverbial paradise garden.

Karaj Agricultural College

Hope manifests itself even more strongly in the Iranians we meet. Here, a group of Sepah-e Danesh—Literacy Corpsmen—is training. The Sepah-e Danesh is an enlightened program begun by the Shah whereby, instead of the mandatory two years of military service, intelligent high school graduates receive three months of training to become teachers. These young men will be sent to isolated villages throughout the country where no one knows how to read or write. They will be charged with building a school and teaching the village children. I immediately feel a special sentiment with these youthful Iranians. We are Sepah-e Solh— Peace Corps—and they are Sepah-e Danesh—our Iranian equivalent. We all are going to live and work in places very foreign to us.

The Iranians are eager to make our acquaintance. They gather outside our dorms, waiting for us. I am guardedly enthusiastic about meeting them. Few know English well, and my Farsi seems to have regressed now that I'm in Iran. But, I want to get to know them and this is the way I will learn the language. I and a few others venture out.

"Salaam, hale shoma chetoreh?"

I return the greeting inquiring about their health. At least fifteen Iranians surround me, looking me up and down, each greeting me with *"Salaam, hale shoma chetoreh?"*

Now what? What if they ask me a question? This is scary.

They do ask questions. I understand some. Many I don't. They want to know what state I come from in America. I reply, "Hawaii."

Their eyes light up, a smile beams on their faces. "Elvis Presley! *Blue Hawaii!*" With both hands, they trace the shape of a Coke bottle in the air.

I grin. There is a universal language among men in this world. In fact, I'm already beginning to miss not seeing what men like to look at—and Hawaii has a reputation for the best, even in Iran.

We use a lot of sign language. We laugh. We awkwardly stumble through a conversation and I grow more comfortable trying to communicate.

SATURDAY, SEPTEMBER 26, 1964 We are given our provincial appointments. I get Mazandaran, a large area along the southeastern Caspian Sea. It doesn't mean much. It is like being told you're going to California.

In our training as community development volunteers, it was relentlessly emphasized we needed to be flexible. In Utah we trained to work in villages—after all, why did we make all those mud bricks? Our real work would be to inspire and initiate change. The metaphorical bridge we would build between Iranians and Americans is the most important goal.

Now the Peace Corps has a change of plans. We will be living and working at the regional level, an area that encompasses about thirty towns and many villages. Many of us feel misled, but it really makes no difference. This is just the way it is. *Be flexible.* And, to be deemed successful, we must complete at least three major projects, like building a school, mosque, bathhouse, or roads, or putting in new water systems.

Wow! A new and unexpected burden has been unleashed upon me. I'm not an engineer. I have no idea how to do this. I look around at the other volunteers. Their bridled concern is apparent as well. Although we complain among ourselves, we feel obligated to accept this challenge as part of our responsibility having joined the Peace Corps. It's the way it is.

SUNDAY, SEPTEMBER 27, 1964 No time to lie in bed! Grab the roll of toilet paper I brought with me! Run! Down with my pants! Squat over the hole in the floor! Made it precisely in time! Use the *aftabeh* (ewer) to wash the paper and everything down. Return to my room. Another urgent call. Run, toilet paper in hand.

I am not the first, nor the last. About half of us woke up with the "Tehran Trots" this morning.

The Peace Corps gives us some pills, "It will bind you up." But I'm smart. I keep a handy supply of TP in my pants pocket, just in case.

A day-and-a-half in this remote place and we are already crawling the walls, longing for the big city. Nick has an idea. It's Sunday, and Catholics are required to go to church. The closest church is in Tehran. *Perfect!* Surprisingly, there is a large Catholic contingent within our group, more than I knew were Catholic in training. Fourteen of us squeeze and fold ourselves into a station wagon for the hour-long trip to Tehran. I don't relish traveling over these roads in an over-loaded vehicle, but if a car is leaving, I'm in it. After all, we *should* be safe. *Most* of our intentions are worthy.

The guys are finishing dinner when we return. Without delay, we join in. Everyone is curious about what Mass was like in this Muslim country. Nick is quick. He quips, "Just like back home. But I was shocked to see *chadoris*"—what we already call women—"there."

"*Chadoris!* They even wear a *chador* in a Catholic church?" they query.

I'm puzzled. I'd missed them.

Nick puts on a very solemn air. "Yeah, solid black, with white around the head, and a white bib."

Some of us begin to grin as it registers he is referring to the devout nuns in the front row of the church.

TUESDAY, SEPTEMBER 29, 1964 We return to Tehran for several more days of orientation and receptions. Every chance I get I roam the streets, looking in shops and meeting young Iranians who want to practice English. They are eager to show me the city, stroll its gardens and fine shopping areas, glimpse through trees the Shah's palace with its tiled dome, and investigate the crowded and noisy corridors of the grand covered bazaar. I am seeing a great city, and experiencing the proverbial Persian graciousness and hospitality. One evening, a high school student and his chauffeur meet me at the hotel for a tour of the city. I am enthralled with the thousands of lights and the kinetic neon signs that line Khiaban-e Takht-e Jamshid—like nothing I have ever seen before. We circle Meydan-e Toopkhaneh—more lights; the Majles, the center of government; and up to exclusive Shemiran in the hills high above the city.

SATURDAY, OCTOBER 3, 1964 Dust storm! Visibility—almost zero! I venture out, fighting the wind and blowing sand, barely able to open my eyes. I am determined to get some supplies before we depart for Mazandaran.

Rain! Only a few big drops—brown spots all over my clothes. I look like I contracted some exotic communicable disease.

Train station, Tehran—shortly after 7pm. I tentatively follow the other volunteers. Strange sounds, strange language—I've never been in a train station or on a train before. I am uneasy.

The train departs at 7:30. We are on our way to Sari, the capital of Mazandaran. The darkness outside is disorienting. I try to get some sleep, but am kept awake by the clickety-clack and scream of the metal wheels on the tracks and, each time the train stops momentarily in a little town, the monotonous, one-word wail of vendors scurrying up and down the platform with their large trays. *"Nan, nan, nan…"* (Bread, bread, bread…), *"Miveh, miveh, miveh…"* (Fruit, fruit, fruit…), *"Seeb, seeb, seeb…"* (Apple, apple, apple…), *"Portoqal, portoqal, portoqal…"* (Orange, orange, orange…), "Fanta, Fanta, Fanta…" (a soft drink). Their tired eyes grow wide when they see the compartments filled with foreigners. They stare in stunned silence. The train begins to move. The vendors' swinging kerosene lanterns cast long and ghostly shadows about the platform as we pick up speed. I can hardly wait for dawn to get a bearing in this alien world.

SUNDAY, OCTOBER 4, 1964 Mercifully, dawn arrives—gray and overcast.

But the countryside is green. 6:30am—the conductor appears at our compartment door.

"Sari."

We gather our bags. The train rolls to a stop. It has taken eleven hours to cover 250 kilometers (155 miles). It is cool, but the humidity must be in the high 90s. We look around. It had rained overnight. There is mud everywhere—pretty dismal for a provincial capital. Speechless, we look at each other.

Nick brings us back to reality. "Who's Sari now?"

We smile reluctantly. No one has a witty comeback.

As I look around, I'm quietly calmed. Here, at least, luxuriant fields stretch to the base of cloud-draped mountains. Humble buildings and people working evoke Kauai and the Big Island of Hawaii.

We meet our Iranian community development counterparts—the men we will be working with. They are well-educated, many engineers. They recently have been appointed to head community development programs in regional areas of the provinces. It is a new program instituted by the Shah to initiate change at the village level. Villages will establish their own governing councils, assess and collect a two percent annual income tax, and develop yearly project priorities such as building schools, bathhouses, mosques, or improving roads. The Iranian government will provide technical assistance and match the funds raised by the villages.

In turn, we introduce ourselves and tell of our backgrounds. My studies in art and work in the design offices of a contractor in Honolulu draw much interest from the head of community development in Mazandaran. Before lunch he takes me and another volunteer, who had construction experience, to his office. We meet his staff and see some of the projects they are working on. He eagerly tells me he will teach me technical skills, like how to survey. I become excited about the prospects of using my education and abilities and of learning new skills.

More meetings, then a little time to prowl the streets and see Sari before our reception with the governor in the evening. Several of us head off together. The streets contain much the same hustle and bustle of frenzied activity we saw in Karaj and Tehran. As we saunter along, three middle-aged women turn silent, stealthily staring at us from under their carefully clutched *chadors*.

Nick turns it on. "Come on girls, cover it up! All up! I don't want to see anything showing. Not even an eyeball!"

We quickly separate, each one of us busting a gut, knowing if we hang together we'll lose it all. Nick remains deadpan. The women keep peering curiously at these strange Americans.

MONDAY, OCTOBER 5, 1964 "Kennedy good." Beside a picture of the Shah, is one of President Kennedy—both hang in the new pump house in the village of Rostam Kola. Everywhere we go—Karaj, the streets of Tehran, now the small villages of Mazandaran—everyone expresses condolences over the death of our President, now almost a year ago. They talk about him as if for them, too, he was the light and the hope of the world—a glowing lamp snuffed out too soon.

In the three villages we visit with the Iranian community development officials, we, ordinary young Americans, are received as dignitaries. The entire village of Rostam Kola comes out to welcome us. Crowds of men follow through the streets as the village leaders proudly show us their new school and water system, and enthusiastically tell of future objectives. Women scatter as we enter the enclosure where they wash clothes. We are impressed with the ambition of the people and the cleanliness of the village. With genuine Persian hospitality they serve tea, cookies, and fruit. We pile into the waiting jeeps for our journey to the next village. As we drive away our hosts cheer and clap. We wave and shout goodbye— *"Khodahafez."*

Our reception in Tabaqdeh is equally exuberant. We see more community projects that have made the people's lives healthier, more productive, and easier. Lunch has been prepared—this is a banquet in true Persian fashion! Multiple colorful oilcloths are spread upon the sumptuous carpets on the floor of a long room in the headman's home. Plates, spoons, and forks line the perimeter of the cloth. We are invited to take our place at this feast; we watch our Persian hosts, and, like them, cross our legs, sitting before a plate.

Trays upon trays of rice are brought and placed on the cloth. Then several large trays with bowls of chicken fixed at least a dozen ways are ushered in. Then come bowls of lamb and beef stews, plates of kebab, yogurt, salads, fresh warm breads, soft drinks, and *doogh* (a drink of water and yogurt). Servers walk down the center of the cloth and fill our plates with huge mounds of rice—more than I would eat in several days. I hastily take some of the stews, kebab, and yogurt to avoid being served. My efforts prove futile. I hadn't put enough on my plate. A server loads on what he determines is sufficient for my slim frame. The food is spectacular. I patiently struggle to eat it all. (I still am tormented by thoughts of the "starving children in China" from my childhood.) I nearly manage to clear my plate, but the server is observant. He piles on more rice and serves me chicken and stew. I am distraught. Not to insult our host, I make a valiant attempt to conquer this plate. After a while my cross-legged posture and the pressure of a full stomach on a belt now cinched too tight curtail further consumption. I sit there looking at what I didn't eat. Our plates and the bowls of uneaten food and rice are carried away. We all lean back against the perimeter walls, legs still politely crossed. The lower portion of my body is becoming numb. I look at the other guys. They appear uncomfortable too. We stoically suffer through it. The 60s fashion of tight jeans is decidedly detrimental to health in this part of the world.

Conversation quiets as the Iranians and Americans digest their food. The servers enter with more plates, forks, and knives and two huge trays overflowing with fresh fruit. Our eyes pop! Our Iranian colleagues project an attitude of, *Well, what did you expect?* A third tray laden with fruit is brought in, then a fourth, and a fifth!

Finally we rise. Many of us almost fall over from lack of circulation in our legs. We thank our host for his gracious hospitality. He beams politely and wishes us well.

We briefly stop at another village to observe their recent achievements to improve the living conditions within their community. Again we are grandly received, but the Iranian development officials courteously decline any offers of tea and sweets.

TUESDAY, OCTOBER 6, 1964 More rain. Today we learn our assignments, but first, there are meetings that impart valuable information about the customs and people who live in the provinces of Mazandaran and Gilan.

I sense an urgent need to leave. I whisper, "Patrick, do you have any toilet paper I could borrow?"

"Borrow! I suppose you plan to return it after you use it? No." He grins wickedly.

How mean, I think. Obviously, I'm not going to get any of that vital stuff from him, even if he has a supply in his pocket. We all know it's worth far more than its meager weight in gold.

I rise to leave the room, wondering if I can make it to the hotel across the street to get the roll in my suitcase. I had forgotten to replenish my pocket supply when I left the room this morning. As I delicately approach the door, there is only one option—the *mostarah* (toilet) down the hall. I move as swiftly as humanly possible under the circumstances. I get there, rip down my pants, and squat—just in time.

As I precariously balance myself over the hole in the floor, I deliberate. *Now what do I do? I could use my handkerchief. But then what do I do with that? The plumbing won't take it. Besides—what if the mess is too big for one handkerchief?*

My gut begins to ache some more. This isn't the end of it. I balance there longer. I start to sweat, looking at the *aftabeh* (ewer) and water spigot in front of me. They told us in training this would happen—sooner or later. We would learn the "Persian method." We all vowed we wouldn't.

I begin to shake. Balancing in this position is difficult. I grab the *aftabeh* and the spigot for stability. Merely touching them seems abhorrent. Though my stomach feels a bit better, I have to do something. Again, it crosses my mind, *You wanted to join the Peace Corps.*

I put the *aftabeh* under the spigot, fill it with water, and hesitate for a long time. I hold out my left hand, pour some water on it, tightly close my eyes, and gingerly put my hand back there. *Yuk!* I feel a mess. My eyes widen and I sharply pull my hand away. I take a deep breath and look at my hand. *Disgusting.* I had barely touched myself—the work still had to be done!

I pour more water on my hand and proceed to do what people do in the greater part of the world. I am initiated—baptized. I keep pouring more water on my hand, wiping more and more.

Now what do I do? I'm totally wet. What do Iranian's do? I can't balance here until I dry off. Frustrated, I pull up my underwear and pants. *This feels revolting.*

I exit the little room with the hole in the floor and go to wash my hands with soap. Suddenly, I have another urgent call. I make a beeline and endure a second baptism. I wash my hands again, and as I walk down the hall to the conference room my underwear feels soaked. I hope my pants aren't wet too. Patrick looks my way, grins, and quietly chuckles. I say nothing. Inwardly I wish him retribution—*soon!*

This was unquestionably my first step toward assimilation. Toilet paper would lose all the perceived value I had accorded it. In fact, it would prove to be a liability rather than an asset—how does one dispose of it? The roll in my suitcase would languish there, and all the rolls in my airfreight would become padding in my freight when I leave Iran.

Barkley is the first to be assigned. He is going to Gonbad-e Kavus, Turkoman territory, more than six-and-a-half hours away over treacherous dirt roads. To reach Gonbad before dark, Barkley is immediately whisked away. In the few days of orientation at Sari, our Iranian counterparts warned us about the formidable Turkomans. We fear for Barkley, and wonder if we will ever see him again in one piece.

I am posted to Gorgan, at the edge of Turkoman territory, four hours east. I will be the nearest to Barkley. I am excited, but apprehensive. I will be on my own. The other volunteers will be stationed in cities of western Mazandaran and Gilan provinces. They will be in easy reach of each other. *Why wasn't I assigned to the central offices in Sari where the head of community development showed such an interest in my background?* I ponder. *Who or what determined our assignments? It's as if someone, somewhere, mysteriously pulled straws that decided our future.*

Now, however, everything is too uncertain for me to be disappointed. *I'm ready for anything.*

I will be working with Mr. Vahdati, a brilliant man of commanding stature, striking countenance, and impeccable attire. My slight, nearly six-foot frame seems diminutive next to him. He is head of the community development office in Gorgan. I surmise there must be some bigger plan.

TEMPTATIONS

WEDNESDAY, OCTOBER 7, 1964 Heavy skies underscore the nervousness and foreboding I feel as I part from my Peace Corps friends. I crawl into the back of the canvas-topped jeep, my bags next to me. I glance back and, with resignation, wave. Mr. Vahdati and the driver are in the front. The paved highway through town ends. Our driver maneuvers around huge puddles and deep ruts, crossing the road from side to side like a pinball in an often vain attempt to find high ground. There are few other vehicles, but when we meet another, our driver swerves to avoid being enveloped in a splash of thick brown mud.

The road skirts the base of the cloud-shrouded Alborz Mountains on our right. We pass villages with houses made of mud and sticks—their terra cotta tile roofs a welcome, warm accent amid the green citrus groves and fields of rice.

Mr. Vahdati's English is excellent. He points out interesting sights along the way and discusses the agricultural and economic basis of the areas we pass through. The exceedingly narrow expanse of land between the Alborz and the Caspian is the breadbasket of Iran. I naively wonder why we have been assigned to an area so economically well off. The citrus groves give way to rice, then cotton and other grains. Flocks of sheep with solitary shepherds and their dogs dot the countryside. Gradually, as we proceed east, the clouds rise higher on the mountains, then melt away. Sun bakes the land and our lonely little jeep. The mud ends. Now we bounce along between deep, hard, axle-breaking ruts. It is still dreadfully humid. We disappear inside brown billows of dust whenever we meet oncoming vehicles. I hope nothing is following in this blinding murk. The canvas-covered jeep sucks in the dust—like riding inside a vacuum cleaner. Conversation ceases as the choking grit churns around us.

We push eastward across a plain that becomes ever bleaker. Between fields of cotton and harvested grain, isolated large tree trunks punctuate the landscape. They have been stripped of their branches, save a few spindly spikes. Nevertheless, the mountains to the south look lush and green.

CRASH! The windshield shatters in front of us. We are covered with fragments of glass. We stop abruptly. Two little boys run through the cotton field. The driver and Mr. Vahdati pursue them, but the boys quickly disappear. I sit there wondering what kind of world I have come to. In the debris we find the rock the boys hurled at us.

SCRAWNY TREES LINE THE STREETS of Gorgan, each gaining its water from the *jub* that separates the dirt pathway from the paved but dust-choked thoroughfare.

Fruit vendors, Gorgan

Mr. Vahdati recommends I not stay at the Hotel Miami, the big hotel on the main square in Gorgan, where all the tourists go. "Too expensive," he says. That's fine with me. I trust his advice.

He checks me into a little hotel on the west end of town, the Hotel Chahar Fasl. My room is about five feet by seven. It has a bed, and a window that overlooks the street. The *mostarah* and sinks for cleaning up and shaving are down the hall. It's Spartan, but I didn't come here for luxury, I conclude.

"The driver will return to show you where the public bathhouse is so you can get a shower. He'll be here at 8:30 tomorrow morning to bring you to the office. We have a full day ahead, meetings in the morning. In the afternoon we'll be going out to villages."

"See you in the morning," I offer cheerfully.

I close the door, sit on the bed, and reflect on the day—saying goodbye to the other PCVs, the rock incident, the suffocating dust, this room. Once more, I remind myself I didn't join the Peace Corps to find the comforts of home. There is a knock on the door. It is the driver. I grab my soap, towel, rubber slippers, and clean clothes. Together we descend to the street. He points to the hotel sign. It is in Farsi. It is evident he is genuinely concerned that I am able to find my way back and recognize the hotel. Awkwardly, he indicates that the woman waiting near the entrance is his wife. It is not really an introduction. I nod to her. She clutches her *chador* more tightly to conceal her face. We head off to the bathhouse—walking. I'm uncomfortable as the woman follows about ten paces behind. I slow my pace so she will catch up. She dutifully slows down as well.

We say little. The driver probably suspects I know no Farsi at all.

The *hammam* (bathhouse) is identifiable by the bottoms of bottles that serve as skylights and poke out of its concrete domes, and the distinctive frieze of red-and-black cloths put out to dry in front. "*Aghaye* (Mr.) Mister, can you find your way back to the hotel?"*

I assure him I know exactly how to return. I tell him, *"Khodahafez. Fardow, hasht-o-neem"* (Goodbye. Tomorrow, 8:30). I briefly watch them

---

* Unless indicated otherwise, all conversations with Iranians are in Farsi.

continue along the street. His wife still follows about ten paces in back. *Strange,* I think.

The bathhouse smells of stagnant, backed-up sewer water. It is hot and steamy. I enter the cubical assigned to me and lock the door. It's even hotter in here. My clothes are so sticky from the heat and humidity I have to peel them off. Naked except for my slippers, I venture into the next chamber. It is even hotter. Steam fills the air. I turn on the cold water; I've got to cool this place down. I adjust the water to the lukewarm temperature I like, and soap myself. I hear pounding on the door of the outer chamber. *What's that all about?* I turn off the water, wrap the towel around me, and warily open the door. A man with a red cloth wrapped about his lower extremities wants to come in. Alarmed, I say, *"Na,"* and try to push the door closed. He keeps saying something and making hand gestures. *Oh, I get it. He is the masseur.* I tell him, *"Na, nemekham"* (No, I don't want). I shove the door closed, lock it, and return to the shower to rinse off.

Although I had cooled the place down a lot, it is impossible to dry myself in this steaming humidity. With difficulty, I pull clean clothes over my body. It feels like nothing is on properly, but I have to get out of here. I pay the few rials and hasten into the fresh air.

I find the hotel with no problem, go to my room and sit there. Again there is a knock at the door. I open it. A man is there. *"Salaam,"* I say hesitantly.

The greeting is reciprocated. We shake hands. *"Hale shoma khoobeh?"*

I ask about his health, too. He was passing by on the street and heard there is a foreigner, an American, at the hotel. He was curious and ventured up to make my acquaintance. I motion for him to sit on the bed. I move to the other end. The door is open. Many more visitors gather, greeting me, staring, and joining in the limited discourse. My room is filling up. None of them knows English, but we learn about each other; we use a lot of animated sign language, and they grin when I figure out something new. *This is one way of learning the language,* I say to myself. As conversation exhausts itself, they begin to excuse themselves. I bid each *khodahafez.* Then I quickly lock the door and rush down to the street before another stranger shows up.

Heading east to the central part of town, contrasts abound. Mercurys and Mercedes-Benzes jostle with donkeys and wooden carts. Awesome-looking Turkomans garbed in long coats and tall astrakhan hats stride impassively among ambling Iranians dressed in drab suits. Their women, wearing colorful floral shawls and embroidered headdresses that display dozens of long, finely braided tresses, submissively follow ten paces behind. Except for the last-minute shopper covered in a dark *chador*, few women are on the street.

Near the main square with the Shah's statue in the center, the sidewalk is paved with stone tiles. I see the sign for the Hotel Miami on the opposite side. On another quadrant is the imposing Bank-e Melli. The graceful curve of the buildings surrounding the circle and the beds of flowers around the Shah's statue impart grandeur to the city.

"Hello," two guys greet me cautiously. I return their greeting. Americans! They are Peace Corps teachers who arrived in Gorgan a week ago. Jack is from New York City, tall, thin, and self-assured. I notice the pocket on his jacket is torn. Dave is short and soft-spoken, from California.

"Where are you from?"

"Hawaii."

Dave smiles kindly. Jack smirks. "How provincial!"

I bristle, but slough it off.

"We're going to dinner at the Hotel Miami. Would you like to join us?"

"Thank you, that would be great." I'm looking forward to getting to know these two Americans who will be in Gorgan while I'll be here.

At dinner, Jack divulges he had never been off Manhattan Island before he left for Peace Corps training in Michigan. *How provincial,* I think, but smile and keep my mouth shut. It's the Hawaiian way—"No make waves."

Later, we saunter the short distance to the Red Lion and Sun, the equivalent of the Red Cross, where they are staying. Dave and Jack introduce me to Iranians they have met. I see they are already warmly accepted in the community.

Their room is large, almost as austere as mine. They have straight-backed chairs, a table, and a sink. The *mostarah* is down the hall. They have been looking at houses, but have made no decisions.

After a long and stressful day, I'm tired, and want to hit the sack. Jack says, "Do you want to meet us for dinner tomorrow evening? Why don't you come here first?"

"Sure, sounds good."

I wander back to the Hotel Chahar Fasl at the other end of town. Random street lights shine through the branches of plane trees beginning to lose their leaves. Most of the light comes from the glare of solitary bare bulbs hanging in shops that line the roadway. The walkways and streets are damp from the *jub* water that vendors sprinkle to quell the dust and break the heat of the day. Families are out for their evening *gardesh* (stroll). The women, covered in their *chadors*, coyly reveal exquisite coiffures, makeup, and fine high heels. Children loudly scurry about. Often they run up to me and shout, "Hello, *Meesteer.*" I smile and respond, "Hello." They giggle and run away. Some just smile shyly and wave, their dark eyes flashing. The men, dressed in suits—usually without a tie—curiously have the backs of their shoes broken down. They walk arm-in-arm, each absently fingering his "worry" or prayer beads, converse, glance stealthily at the women, and stop to greet friends. All stare at my blond hair, blue eyes, jeans, and tennis shoes. Some nod as we pass. I return the acknowledgement. When I stop to look at the fascinating array of merchandise in a shop—fresh vegetables and fruit, or sacks of colorful aromatic spices, canned goods on the shelves in the back—I am greeted with, *"Salaam,* Mister, *hale shoma khoobeh?"* and, with a slight shake of the head, *"Cheh mekhaid"* (What do you want)?

Each time I smile and respond, *"Heechi"* (Nothing). I don't know how to say, "I'm just looking."

"Shoma maleh koja-i" (Where are you from)?

"Amrika."

"Amrika! Bah, bah, bah," they say with unqualified approval.

The limited exchange attracts large crowds. The shop owner beams, proud he is carrying on a conversation with an American. In time, my vocabulary is exhausted. I bow slightly and bid him and the eavesdroppers, *"Khodahafez."* I move on until I see another shop of interest and decide to practice my Farsi again.

Much later I reach the Hotel Chahar Fasl. The proprietor is standing in front, possibly anxious his foreign guest may have gotten lost. He smiles and greets me, then asks, *"Shom khordid"* (Did you eat dinner)?

"Baleh."

"Koja" (Where)?

"Hotel Miami."

I try to explain I met two other American Peace Corps Volunteers and we had dinner together. Another crowd gathers. I answer questions the best I can, mainly applying my skills at sign language. We laugh a lot. The hotel owner interjects in Farsi, "You must be tired. Go upstairs to bed. *Shab bekheyr"* (Goodnight).

I nod courteously, say, *"Shab bekheyr,"* and ascend the stairs to my room. I grab my soap, towel, toothpaste and brush, and my canteen of water with a dissolved halazone purification tablet in it, and head down the hall to the sink. Even brushing teeth with this foul-tasting water is repugnant. But, if this saves me waking up having to run swiftly and cautiously down the hall, it's worth it. Back in my room, I turn out the light, and, though the noise from the street surges through the open window, sleep overcomes me.

THURSDAY, OCTOBER 8, 1964 My entry *salaam* at a nearby teahouse draws similar greetings, but the groggy, early morning chitchat is silenced. Everybody looks at me, staring. I'm brought freshly baked *sangak* (a flatbread baked on hot pebbles), goat cheese, and tea. Someone ventures a more extended greeting. I respond in Farsi. Faces light up. Soon the teashop is abuzz, with me the center of attention. My presence in Iran for the next two years, if nothing else, will provide a source of entertainment for Iranians.

The driver makes a point of showing me landmarks on the way to the office. Mr. Vahdati greets me, inquiring how I slept and where I had dinner. I tell him I met Jack and Dave and that I had fun speaking Farsi on the streets of Gorgan the night before. He approves. He outlines the agenda for the day. He introduces me each time village leaders arrive and tells them about the American Peace Corps. He explains in English the projects the villagers are working on. A man brings in trays with glasses of tea and bowls of sugar lumps. I watch as the Iranians hold the sugar between their teeth and strain the tea through it. Many have only stumps of teeth left in front—from years of straining tea through sugar, I surmise. I drink my tea without sugar. The Iranians find this peculiar. It invariably becomes a subject of momentary conversation.

I absorb very little of the discourse. In weariness, my mind strays. I hear almost nothing. The morning drags along, interrupted only by new visitors and another tray of tea. Shortly after 12:00, the appointments cease.

"We can take you back to the hotel. Do you know where to get lunch?"

"No need to take me back. I saw some places to eat on my walk through town last night. I'll go to one of them and then return to the hotel." I already perceive and appreciate Mr. Vahdati's desire that I be independent. I know he feels this will be the best way of my learning Farsi. Undoubtedly this is why he put me in the Hotel Chahar Fasl rather than the Hotel Miami or the Red Lion and Sun with the other Peace Corps Volunteers.

"*Kheili khoob* (Very good). We'll pick you up at the hotel at 2:00 and go to villages where they are working on new development programs."

"*Khoob*, see you at 2:00."

I head off and find a place where I have kebab and rice and a Pepsi. After lunch, as I approach the hotel, the owner smiles broadly when he sees me. We talk. Others join in. I am buoyed by the interaction. We're still chatting when Mr. Vahdati and the driver pull up.

The hotel owner cheerfully calls to Mr. Vahdati, "Mister *Farsi khoob yad megerad*" (Mister is learning Farsi well). I'm not sure Mr. Vahdati agrees, but he smiles.

Mr. Vahdati's enthusiasm for the work the villagers are doing is justifiable. However, I already wonder about my role in this process. *Am I merely going to sit in the office in the morning and follow Mr. Vahdati around in the afternoon?* I imagine what I might be doing if I had been assigned to the central planning office in Sari. *I might actually have a job if I were there.*

On our return, as we near Gorgan, I suggest, "You can let me off at the Red Lion and Sun. I'm going to meet the other Peace Corps Volunteers for dinner." I detect a vague uneasiness in Mr. Vahdati. I suspect he doesn't want me to become dependent on being with other Americans.

Dinner again is at the Hotel Miami. It's a lot more expensive than the place I had lunch, but that's OK. Jack and Dave have tried no other place.

Jack proposes, "Let's go to the cinema at the Moulin Rouge. It's the hot spot in town. *Trapeze* is showing. It's dubbed into Farsi, a good way to learn the language."

"Sounds great. I'm always ready for a new adventure."

Men are lining up in front of the theater. We get our tickets and join the line. When the doors open, we're swept along in the tide of humanity.

As we sit down Jack warns, "Be careful. When the lights go out, they play the national anthem and show a short about the Shah. Everyone quickly stands. That's how I ripped the pocket on my jacket the first night we came to the cinema. It caught on the arm of the seat when I jumped up, startled."

Seeing an American film in Farsi *is* a novel event. Iranians do an excellent job of dubbing. I am envious of how well Gina Lollobrigida, Burt Lancaster, and Tony Curtis speak Farsi. But I'm also intrigued at the amount of "skin" Iranian men are seeing. It's quite a contrast to what they see on the streets of Gorgan. No wonder there was a long line waiting to get in!

FRIDAY, OCTOBER 9, 1964   Friday, the Islamic day of rest. I lie in bed recollecting all that has happened in the past two days. My world has been transformed. Virtually all I was familiar with is gone. I am rather alone. *Funny, that doesn't bother me. In fact, it's rather exciting. Just wish I knew what I was going to do. And, I need to learn Farsi a heck of a lot better. Well, I'm not learning it lying here in bed. Time to get out and see more of Gorgan.*

The men at the teahouse greet me eagerly. They want to know about me, why I am in Gorgan, and what I will be doing here. I tell them about the Peace Corps, that it was President Kennedy's idea. They express their sympathy for and love of Kennedy. I talk about my family, show them pictures of my parents and brother, and tell about my studies at the university and what America is like.

An hour later the shops along the street are still shuttered so I retreat to the solitude of my room. *Guess I'll write home.* Before I start there's a knock on the door. A visitor.

"*Salaam, hale shoma chetoreh?*" I invite him in. Soon my room *again* is filled, with men standing several deep at the door. Much of the same conversation I had at the teahouse occurs. Sometimes somebody poses a question I don't understand, but together they find ways of getting me to comprehend. I smile, happy to have learned a new word or phrase. They are pleased to be part of my education. The morning passes quickly. Rather exhausted, I indicate I must leave for lunch. If I stay here, the steady stream of guests will keep me occupied the entire day.

Most of the shops are still closed as I head to the Red Lion and Sun to find Jack and Dave. They had a quiet morning. It's stimulating to converse about more complex issues in a language I fully understand. I'm going to enjoy these two guys—Dave's relaxed, easy-going nature and Jack's skepticism and caustic wit. What a contrast!

We have an early dinner before I head back to my hotel. The shops have opened and the streets are filled with people. Tonight, many greet me as they pass. We recognize each other from my walk on Wednesday evening. A few of the young men stop to shake hands; more of the same questions and answers. Many are high school students who want to practice English. Each time, a large crowd gathers, and the conversation shifts to Farsi.

As I pass shops where I stopped two nights before, the owners greet me and shake my hand. They pull me in, offer me a tiny stool among the crowded array of merchandise, and order tea. Instantly the sidewalk in front is filled with onlookers. Obviously, this is sensational—an American conversing in Farsi, limited though it is. I thank the shopkeeper for his hospitality, rise, and progress down the street to the next one.

"Come back tomorrow," they call after me with grand smiles.

I had noticed them before, but tonight the young women—usually three together—are even more aware of me; enticingly, they seem to go out of their way to catch my attention. I feel a rush. *This is encouraging.* I stand taller and make sure they are conscious of my attention as well. I use caution, however, only giving them sideways glances. I certainly can't afford to become a statistic in my first weeks in Iran because of my wayward eyes. Particularly notable are their bright, sparkling, dark eyes, for which I have always had a profound weakness. *Iran may not be the worst place to have been assigned in the Peace Corps. Or am I simply kidding myself? The Peace Corps warned us within an inch of our lives not to get involved.*

As the girls pass, I perceive their high heels and alluring ankles. *Hmmm, their chadors seem to be hiked up higher than anywhere else I've been.* Later I learn that the women of Gorgan have a reputation throughout the country for slender ankles they coquettishly expose beneath their *chador*. I fantasize about what the billowing covering is concealing. My pulse quickens. *Damn. Why does getting to know women have to be so out of the question in this country? And, to make it even more difficult, Gorgan definitely has its share of good-lookers.*

SATURDAY, OCTOBER 10, 1964 When I reach the office, Mr. Vahdati greets me in Farsi and asks about my weekend, which, in Iran, is Friday. Meetings drag on all morning. I sit to the side, trying to follow. Either the villagers talk too fast, or the subject is too technical, or they speak a dialect. I catch almost nothing, but I refrain from interrupting and asking Mr. Vahdati to explain.

Lunch is a delicious Iranian meal, seated at a table, with Mr. Vahdati and his family. His wife is attractive, flawlessly coiffed and dressed, and comfortable entertaining a foreigner in their home. She speaks English and is curious about Hawaii. Their children are puzzled that an adult cannot speak Farsi well. Time passes too quickly.

Mr. Vahdati and I discuss the morning meetings as we bound over dirt roads, clouds of dust rising around us. He wears his suit and tie. I'm the practical young American, dressed in a shirt, jeans, and tennis shoes.

The quaint, picturesque villages with their gentle and hospitable people, enthrall me. I empathize with the people's enthusiasm for the improvements they are bringing about. Here I find encouragement. These field trips become the highlight of the day. I look forward to every afternoon when I can connect the words I hear to concrete things, to work being done—not like the abstract language and thinking process I confront in the office in the morning.

SUNDAY, OCTOBER 11, 1964 Jack and Dave are in a bad mood when I meet them for dinner. Jack is vociferous about his disgust. Dave is desolate but quietly resigned.

The two of them had been called into the office by the school principal and told, "Your evening classes for women have been cancelled."

"Why?" Jack demanded. These classes were his one assurance of lightening the burden of living a nearly cloistered life for the next two years.

"Well, it was decided it would be better not to have them."

Jack detected the principal was being evasive. "Why? I need to know why!" He pressed for a more definitive explanation.

The principal hesitated, "I had a visit from SAVAK (the secret police) this morning. The classes are cancelled."

"SAVAK!" the guys exclaimed. "But why?"

"There was an incident in Dave's class last night. He said something you never tell a woman," the flustered principal informed them.

Poor Dave turns red.

"But it was just an innocent mistake," Jack pleaded.

"I know. But it is better the classes are cancelled. It was a bad idea in the first place. Having a man teach a class of women is just not done in Iran."

"Come on—what happened in class?" I implore.

"Well, Dave made an honest mistake because he doesn't know Farsi well. The women were being noisy, and Dave told them 'Be quiet, please.' They kept chattering, so he put his finger to his mouth and went, 'Shhhhh.' The women thought that was funny and started laughing, so Dave tried to think of some Persian words to tell them to be quiet. He thought he recalled the Farsi word for ear, so he said, '*Gooz bedeh*,' give me your ear, and the women went into hysterics. Well, he got the wrong word. The word for ear is *goosh*, not *gooz*. It was just an innocent use of the wrong word. Now our best classes are cancelled. Our only hope," Jack rants.

"So, tell me what *gooz* means," I entreat.

"It means fart! He told them to give him a *fart!*"

I cover my mouth, desperately trying to conceal my laughter. Still, I feel sorry about their all-too-conspicuous disappointment. Ungraciously I pronounce, "It's going to be a long two years."

Jack sneers. The guys are not consoled.

MONDAY, OCTOBER 12, 1964 Bored by endlessly long, agonizing mornings, my mind wanders thousands of miles away—to sunny Hawaii, to anything. Nothing sinks in. *How am I going to deal with two years of this?*

When the appointments end before lunch, Mr. Vahdati asks, "How are you doing? Are you learning Farsi? Do you understand what is being said?" He probably perceives my daydreaming.

I try to be positive. "I understand some of it." It's almost a lie.

"This afternoon, beginning at 2:00, we have more appointments in the office. We're not going out to villages today."

I'm disappointed, but try not to show it. Then I blurt out, "Mr. Vahdati, I'm wondering if it might be better if I live in a village, at least for a while. I would learn Farsi faster there."

"You may have a point. Let me think about this at lunch."

When I return a few minutes before two o'clock, Mr. Vahdati says, "I telephoned a village, and the people are interested in having you come to live with them. The village leader and his son, along with the *dehyar* (community development worker), and others, will be coming tomorrow morning. After you meet them, you can decide if you want to do this."

My heart starts pounding. *What have I done? That was fast. The Peace Corps doesn't want us to live in villages. How will I tell them? What will they do to me?*

But, I answer, "That's excellent. I look forward to meeting the villagers." Now I can hardly pay attention to anything. My pulse is racing, not to mention my mind.

At the end of the day I nearly run to see Jack and Dave and tell them the news. They are disappointed I won't be in Gorgan, but I promise I'll visit them often.

On my leisurely walk back to the hotel, I attentively check out the "scenery"—ensuring they notice me as well. As I steal surreptitious glances at the women, I think, *I'm going to miss this, but it's best I remove myself from this temptation.*

I'm stopped by acquaintances, introduced to new Iranians, and eagerly pulled into shops to chat. I'm beginning to feel at home in Gorgan.

TUESDAY, OCTOBER 13, 1964 Four people from Alang meet me at the office. They do not speak English, except for a cheerful and practiced hello. Mr. Vahdati tells them about me and the Peace Corps. Then he tells me about them and the projects they are working on.

Tofigh Rahemi, the village patriarch, is a large, rotund man with gentle eyes who smiles shyly as he is introduced. His warm, welcoming face glows with kindness. He is soft-spoken. "Are you enjoying Iran?" he asks.

"Yes, I like Iran very much." I see he is pleased.

His son, Ezetollah, has his father's eyes and many of his humble manners. "We hope you will come to Alang. I want you to be my brother."

I am perplexed by his intimate expression of friendship, one that contains meaning I, as an American, am not used to. I don't know what to say, but smile modestly.

Shaban Ali Rahemi, the *dehyar*, is tall and proper. There is stiffness in his manner. He greets me in a friendly but distant sort of way. No doubt he is apprehensive, and senses the obligation my presence will place upon him. After all, we will be working together closely.

The *kadkhodah* (village headman) is an exuberant man who likely perceives my uneasiness. "We look forward to your coming to Alang and we want to make your stay with us pleasant."

"Thank you. I look forward to being in Alang."

There is truth in what I said, but I am filled with anxiety. Each step I've taken since leaving America three weeks ago has thrust me farther and farther from all I ever knew. Now I will be leaving Gorgan, a place I am becoming accustomed to, and Jack and Dave, my last link to America. *Will I be able to handle this? I don't know, but I have started to push a ball that is swiftly moving out of control. I can't stop it now. I have to go with it. What is the Peace Corps going to do to me? Clearly, I haven't followed directions.*

My mind reels with excitement, doubt, a longing to experience something totally new, fear, curiosity, angst, exhilarating energy, foreboding—I feel like I'm going to burst. But I try to appear cool and in complete control. I have no idea what Alang will be like, or what living there will entail. *Do I have the mettle to survive this? Oh, well, Mr. Vahdati says this is temporary, until I learn the language.*

As I sit there inwardly churning with self-doubt, Mr. Vahdati and the villagers confer. I am too distracted to focus my attention on a language in which, at the very best of times, I'm swimming upstream in a raging torrent.

At the end, he says, *"Kheili khoob.* Tom, our friends are inviting you to Alang on Thursday morning. They are very happy you will be coming to live with them."

"Kheili khoob. Moteshakeram" (Very good. Thank you). I try to utter it with self-confidence and gratefulness. I definitely don't want anyone to think I'm not tough enough.

As my new friends from Alang rise to leave, we exchange *khodahafez.* The rest of the morning meetings become a blur. There is too much to dwell on. Even though I try to remain alert and attentive, I am certain Mr. Vahdati detects my mental distraction. However, I'm sure he understands.

In the evening, Jack, Dave, and I return to the Moulin Rouge to see *West Side Story.* While Tony, Maria, and all the actors are fluent in Farsi, they sing in English. We are transported by memories of seeing this classic American film *in* America. There's only one puzzling disappointment. "Gee, Officer Krupke" has been edited from the film for the Iranian market. The song's satire of and disdain for authority made it a target for Iranian censors, who struck it from the film. It stuns us how subtly thought control occurs in a country such as Iran. We are thankful nothing like this happens in America.

I say goodnight to the guys in front of the theater and trudge alone along the dark streets of Gorgan to the hotel. The lingering melodies and lyrics of "Maria" and "Tonight" swell within me. I am not cheered by their sounds; instead, a dreaded loneliness engulfs me. Now, more than ever, I realize how far away I have put myself. I think of when I saw *West Side Story* with my friends in Hawaii, and of the lovely Maria from Newman Club. I can hardly restrain the dampness that wells in the corners of my eyes. I somberly acknowledge the hotel owner as I approach and ascend the stairs. The bleakness of the room makes me feel even worse. Hurriedly I turn out the light and lie there restless, thinking—not of the future, but of the past.

WEDNESDAY, OCTOBER 14, 1964 I fell asleep at some point, but I don't remember when. I awake refreshed, ready for a new day. Knowing this will be my last morning sitting in the office has me charged. In the afternoon we have appointments in two villages. I will miss this, but really, what's the point of going out only to see picturesque villages?

"Come to Gorgan often. Soon we'll have a place of our own," Jack and Dave tell me when we part in the evening. "Spend the weekends with us." I know their invitation is sincere. I have grown to like these two guys in the one week I've been in Gorgan.

My stroll down main street is the familiar long evening ritual—checking out the young women's flashing eyes and narrow ankles and being satisfied they take note of me, and stopping to talk with guys I have met—many are teachers, even Literacy Corpsmen who escape to Gorgan from their villages to peruse the scenery too—and my friends the shopkeepers. I spend time outside the hotel saying goodbye to acquaintances. They remind me to drop by whenever I come to Gorgan. I affirm I will. They have become my friends.

GOOD OMEN

THURSDAY, OCTOBER 15, 1964 There is a lot to do before the driver picks me up at 8:30. First, off to the bathhouse. This may be the last shower I have for a while. The masseur doesn't bother with me any more. I'm sure he thinks, *Americans are a strange and filthy lot. They never rub all that dead skin off their bodies.* I, however, never fail to be amazed at the bright, lobster-red color of Iranians when they depart the bathhouse.

I deposit my stuff in the hotel room, head to the teahouse for breakfast, and eat quickly, briefly answering the questions of the owner and my new friends. I tell them I'm going to Alang. They are incredulous. "Why are you going there? It is very bad. It is a village. Dirty. There are no teahouses. No cinema. Nothing! Do you understand? You should stay in Gorgan. Gorgan is good! Do you understand?" They look at me despairingly, as if I have lost my mind.

I bid them *khodahafez.* They return the goodbye and emphasize, "Stay in Gorgan. Gorgan is good."

Their attempt to drive some sense into my head detained me longer than I planned. I rush up the street to get my laundry, including the suit I had worn on the flights from Hawaii and at the receptions in Tehran and Sari. Though all can see I'm in a hurry, they stop to shake hands and greet me. I can't be rude, so we chat awhile. Each time I excuse myself and walk even faster, until I'm compelled to stop again.

The driver is waiting in front of the hotel when I return. I surge up the stairs with him behind me. I hand him my carry-on, the Peace Corps medical kit, and a bag containing sheets and a blanket the Peace Corps issued. I carefully fit my suit and clean laundry into the suitcase so nothing will get too wrinkled. The driver instantly reappears. I hand him the suitcase, look around to check that I have everything, and race down the stairs after him. I pay the hotel bill and assure the owner I will come to see him each time I'm in Gorgan. He smiles warmly and wishes me *khodahafez*.

I collapse in the front seat, perspiring. *Good thing Iranians operate on Iranian time.* We speed to the office. Mr. Vahdati is waiting. He is irritated.

"Good morning. Sorry about being late. There were too many delays."

"Yes, we should be there by now instead of just leaving." He looks at me. "You're going dressed like that?"

I'm wearing the usual shirt, jeans, and tennis shoes I wore to the office and on our trips to the villages each day. "I can change quickly," I offer.

"No, we don't have time. We're already too late. Get in. We need to get going. Hurry."

I pile in the back of the jeep. *I wish he had told me I should dress up today. But we're only going to a village. No different from any other day. Besides, over these roads, my freshly cleaned black suit would be tan by the time we got there. I paid a lot of money for that suit, the first one I've ever owned. I can't afford to ruin it going out to villages in Iran.* Aware that Mr. Vahdati is displeased, I perspire even more. *If he had only said something yesterday.*

We bounce along the dirt road heading due west—the same road we traversed eight days before on our trip from Sari to Gorgan. No one says anything. Dust is flying everywhere. *A lot of good that shower did me this morning,* I think.

About thirty kilometers out of Gorgan, the driver slows. By a sign I can't read, he turns right off the main highway. This is a track for two wheels, elevated slightly above the rice and cotton fields on either side. Weeds grow down the center of the path. We follow along for another kilometer before reaching a grove of scraggy trees through which thatch, tin, and tile roofs appear.

"This is Alang's school." Mr. Vahdati points out a structure behind a crumbling brick wall on our right. All is still, even though it is a school day. We turn right immediately. Just ahead is Alang. Our driver stops at the entrance to the village. Dust slowly settles around us, but the powerful roar of a nearby motor disquiets the air. To the left, a long line of men extends down the rutted street. Women and children stand to the side or peer from the second-story balconies of their houses.

"What's happening?" I ask.

"This is your welcome," Mr. Vahdati responds.

He steps out of the jeep and motions for me to come. I climb out the back. My knees are shaking, heart pounding. I have no trouble talking to individuals or even small groups of strangers, but I'm almost pathologically shy when attention is focused solely on me. *Mercifully, if only the ground would open up and swallow me—anything to rescue me from this moment.*

"Come on. Follow me."

We begin at one end of the long line, shaking hands and greeting each man—at least several hundred—young and old. Some are bent with age; others appear nearly blind, but their bearded smiles kindly welcome me. Many bow their heads slightly and kiss their hands after I shake them. I am so moved I can hardly breathe.

As we near the end of the line, I recognize the *kadkhodah*, the village headman. His handshake is hearty and reassuring. Shaban Ali, my co-worker, is next. I am happy to see him. Ezetollah grabs my hand, pulls me toward him, and, in the familial Persian manner, kisses me on each cheek. He says, *"Baradaram"* (My brother). I am overwhelmed, shaken. His father, Tofigh Rahemi, softly takes my hand. He, too, pulls me to him and kisses me on each cheek. Then a little girl with a colorful dress and curly, hennaed hair presents me with a bouquet of flowers.

Mr. Vahdati and I are motioned to ascend a stage built for the occasion. On it are a dozen chairs and a microphone. We are offered the center chairs, and the leaders of Alang sit on either side. The villagers draw forward. I am aghast, confused, embarrassed, astounded, even terrified by what is happening, but there is no escaping. *I am no one special, just a young American—still a Minnesota farm boy in spirit—yet they are receiving me as a dignitary.* I'm dismayed by the chain of events my request to live in a village has triggered, unnerved by the expectations I naively fostered.

Tofigh Rahemi measuredly rises to take the microphone and bestows a gracious welcome on behalf of the entire village of Alang. Then he says,

"Your coming to live with us in Alang is clearly a good omen." He points to the pyramidal rig off to the side, beneath which there is a large metal pipe protruding from the ground. Water gushes from the top of the pipe and splashes around it. "For over a month we have been digging, hoping to strike water that can be used for a new water system in Alang. We have dug over one hundred and ten meters (360 feet) often thinking our effort to find this precious resource was useless. This morning, an hour before you arrived, water sprang forth." His voice cracks with emotion. "You have brought us good fortune. You have restored our hope. We will now have running water throughout Alang. Thank you." The crowd claps. He invites me to the microphone.

I attempt to stand up, but my legs wobble like jelly. Mr. Vahdati rises to give me confidence. I am thankful to have him here. Surely he heard my nervous sighs as he interpreted Mr. Rahemi's speech. I stand at the microphone silently for a while. This would have been hard enough for me to do in English, but having to speak in a language I don't know well seems far beyond my capabilities. *If Mr. Vahdati had told me yesterday I would have to give a speech today, we could have prepared.*

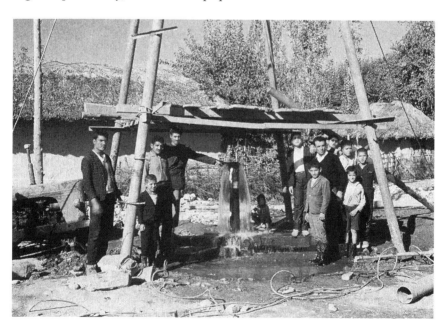

The Well, Alang—October 15, 1964 (Shaban Ali Rahemi, man at right.)

Hesitantly, my voice shaking, I say, *"Salaam."*

The villagers clap. A loud *salaam allekum* rises around us.

"Moteshakeram," I thank them. I want to say more, but emotion and timidity overcome me. Mr. Vahdati takes the microphone and, with poise, introduces me, and eloquently explains President Kennedy's vision and his legacy of the Peace Corps and its work. I am grateful to have someone who can help me through this moment. There is applause when he ends.

TOFIGH RAHEMI AND HIS SON escort Mr. Vahdati and me, along with a throng of men, to their home. *Aghaye* (Mr.) Rahemi moves slowly. There is a pronounced dignity to his carriage, a dignity well-earned, I will discover. Most elderly people in Iran bear this distinction because they live in a culture where age and good deeds command unquestioned respect.

Elegant and meticulously groomed, Mr. Vahdati saunters, appearing as if he were immune to the dust of the vacuum cleaner in which we had ridden. I try to maintain a semblance of self-respect as I embarrassingly follow along in my casual attire.

Women pull their *chadors* around themselves and scurry away as we enter the courtyard. The house is grand—two stories, new, carefully plastered, and painted white on the exterior. Fancy metal grills cover the windows. My grubby tennis shoes are easily identifiable among the dozens of broken-back pairs deposited on the porch. We are stopped at the door by a courteous tussle.

"Befarmayid." *Aghaye* Rahemi gestures for us to enter before him.

"Na. Shoma befarmayid" (No. You first), Mr. Vahdati pleads and takes *Aghaye* Rahemi's arm to guide him inside gently. "You are our host."

Aghaye Rahemi backs away and responds, "Please, you are my honored guest." He attempts to push Mr. Vahdati in. There is an obliging scuffle, but finally Mr. Vahdati steps over the threshold and pulls me with him. *Aghaye* Rahemi follows and the deferential struggle continues as each guest acquiesces to another. This is *taroof,* a protocol at which I would become an expert. Often I am thrown through doorways, not because in my scruffy young American clothes I am dressed properly or am of an age to warrant going first, but because I am the guest and have a university degree. In

Iran, what you wear and your status—defined by age, ancestry, wealth, education, and profession—determine the order in which men enter, sit, and greet each other.

The large room is devoid of furniture and, except for a calendar, the white plaster walls are bare. One of the walls has a seemingly incongruous faux fireplace with empty shelves above. A modern light fixture hangs from the elaborately molded ceiling. White curtains stretched tautly on strings conceal the windowpanes. Covering the floor are several brilliant red Turkoman carpets with traditional black-and-white geometric patterns.

Mr. Vahdati and I are offered a place in front of the ornate false fireplace, obviously a place of honor midway between the door by which we entered and another that I would learn is the servants' entrance. The guests take their places. Some men humbly motion others closer to us. I sense there is a proper hierarchal order that determines where one settles. Mr. Vahdati says, *"Ya Allah,"* sits down cross-legged, and signals for me to do the same. Everyone repeats, *"Ya Allah,"* and sits down as well. Then a curious ritual occurs. Each person in turn holds his right hand to his chest, nods his head, and greets every person from the most distinguished to the most lowly, methodically going around the room. *"Salaam allekum. Chetor hastid? Janeh shoma salamat ast? Khoob hastid? Sehat-e salamat-e shoma khoob ast? Hamechiz beh khair hast? Jur hasti? Khaneh beh khair hast? Zendeh bashi."* (Peace be with you. How are you? Is your soul healthy? Are you well? Are you in good health? Is everything well? Does everything fall in place? Is your household well/prospering? Long life to you.) All acknowledge each greeting and concurrently return it in like manner. Though I don't know all the words, I mumble something.

When Tofigh Rahemi and Ezetollah return, everybody politely stands and greets them. They have changed from their suits to baggy pajamas. There is a shuffling of positions so *Aghaye* Rahemi and Ezetollah can sit next to me. Ezetollah has brought several pairs of pajamas with him. He offers Mr. Vahdati and me each a pair. Mr. Vahdati declines. So do I. But Ezetollah insists. In all likelihood, he is concerned I will suffer a severe case of gangrene in my lower extremities if I sit cross-legged too long in my tight jeans. A few other men take a pair and change in front of everyone.

They wear solid-colored boxer shorts under their pants. The thought of removing my pants in front of all these men causes mental discomfort. *What do I do? Well, there's no graceful way out of this. Just be as cool as you can and do it.* I slip out of my jeans, revealing my briefs, and quickly step into the pajamas and pull them up. *Another moment of acute acculturation,* I rationalize. I recollect my first "no toilet paper" incident and how I lived through that. *Maybe someday I will actually think and act like an Iranian.*

I sit down. Ezetollah sits next to me. He puts his hand on my knee, pats it, and says, *"Behtar, neest"* (Better, isn't it?)

"Baleh," I agree. But, my mind spins. *That hand on my knee is more than I bargained for.* They informed us in training that Iranian men touch each other more than Americans do—it's just cultural. *However, this sure is uncomfortable. It's going to take awhile to get used to this. Cultural assimilation is one thing, but there has to be a limit to what a guy can take.* I reposition myself so the hand will go away, trying to look unconcerned so I won't offend Ezetollah. It works.

A man brings in a tray of tea, cookies, and bowls of sugar cubes. These are cubes, not lumps of sugar. Very special, I conclude.

Mr. Vahdati and I are served first. I refuse the sugar. This provokes interested discussion. Somebody says, "They drink tea with milk and sugar. Maybe he needs milk too."

I understand and say, "No, in Hawaii we drink tea without sugar and milk. Just plain tea."

They are intrigued. "Isn't it too bitter?" someone asks.

"No, we drink it very weak." I don't know how to say "very weak," but Mr. Vahdati says, *"Kam rang."* I realize he is saying little color.

"Baleh, kam rang." I learned another phrase. "There are many people from Asia, especially Japan, China, and Korea, in Hawaii, and that is how they drink tea. They do not use sugar or milk."

Aghaye Rahemi instructs the servant to take my glass of tea and bring me one *kam rang.*

I talk about Hawaii, proud to let everyone know America is not entirely as they imagine it. Most are astonished that a part of America is not all white people. "Yes, only one third of the population of Hawaii is white people. Most of my friends are Japanese and Chinese." The villagers look at each other with surprise, carrying on little conversations together.

To prove it, I go to my bags that the driver brought in and deposited in a corner of the room. I pull out the photos of my departure that I had processed in Gorgan. I pass them around. The men are awe-struck.

"Who is this girl with so many flowers around her neck in this picture with you? She's very pretty."

"She is one of my girlfriends."

"One!" almost everybody exclaims in unison.

Inadvertently I have confirmed their opinions of young people in America. I ignore it. "Yes—she is going to Africa with the Peace Corps. The picture was taken at the airport the night she left."

Their faces register shock. "You are letting her go to Africa by herself? And you came to Iran?"

"Yes."

Conversations erupt around the room. I can only presume what they are saying.

"Who is *this* girl with you in *this* picture? Is she your girlfriend too?"

"Yes. That was taken the night I left for Iran."

"She looks like she is Japanese."

"No, she is Chinese."

Many get up to see the photo. They can't wait till the picture comes to them. They are incredulous.

"And these people in this picture, they are your friends? Most of them are not Americans."

"Oh, they are all Americans. Yes, they are my friends."

"And this picture, is that your mother and father? Is this other person your brother?"

"Yes, they are my mother and father and brother."

"How many brothers do you have?"

"One."

"Do you have any sisters?"

"No."

"Just two of you?"

"Yes." I surmise it is uncommon to have only one sibling in Iran.

"What does your father do?"

"He works at Pearl Harbor. This is where the Japanese bombed America in World War II." I want to convey the historical significance of the place I live in America. Many know about Hawaii and the Japanese attack.

"What does he do there?"

I don't know how to say maintenance man in Farsi, so I say, "He keeps the place clean. He picks up rubbish—paper, bottles, cans, and other things."

They look at each other dubiously. Someone says, *"Kargar."*

"Baleh, kargar." I recognize the word *kargar*. It is the lowest form of laborer in Iran. But I am proud of my father. He has worked hard his whole life, first as a farmer, now at the shipyards, to keep his family together. Besides, it's all right with me to let Iranians know all Americans are not rich. I want them to know the truth about me and about America.

"But you went to the university."

Unmistakably, my education is in doubt. "Yes, I went to the university."

They find it inconceivable. Mr. Vahdati has let me carry the conversation in my own way as I struggle to make myself understood and answer the questions posed to me. Occasionally I ask him for a word. He seems pleased I am trying, and that I know as much Farsi as I do. We had only spoken together in English. Now he explains to the villagers that in America, even the children of poor people can get a university education if they want it.

I join in, "Most of my friends and I worked to put ourselves through university. It's the way it's done in America. I had many different jobs."

"What did you study at the university?"

"I studied art."

"So you are an artist. What kind of artist are you?"

"I studied graphic design." Mr. Vahdati helps me explain that.

In the course of the interaction, our tea glasses have been refilled several times and the cookies passed around. The servant, bearing a tray, gathers the glasses, the bowls of sugar cubes, and the remaining cookies. Cloths are placed the length of the room and plates, tablespoons, and forks are positioned around the edge. We move forward as trays of rice, stews, kebab, yogurt, bread, and salad greens are brought in. It is the standard Iranian feast. Ezetollah piles my plate high with rice. "Not so much," I protest, but it makes no difference. He puts two skewers of kebab on my plate and passes me various stews. I refuse the greens, not knowing where they have been washed. Iranians use the tablespoon to eat. The fork is held in the left hand and used to load the spoon. I do the same. This makes sense— it's easier to get the food from your plate on the floor to your mouth. I sample the yogurt. Some is made with cucumber and garlic. *Hmmm, not bad.* Bottles of Pepsi and Fanta are passed around. To finish up the rice on my plate, I take more of the stews. I'm getting full, straining to eat everything. Without warning, Ezetollah piles on two more huge scoops of rice. I'm perplexed and endeavor to finish it, but cannot.

We all pull back to the edge of the room and the spread is cleared. I am uncomfortable from eating so much. Small plates, knives, and forks are brought in along with trays of melons and other fruit. We eat more.

"*Ya Allah,*" Mr. Vahdati indicates he must be on his way. We all rise. "Well, Tom, I will have the Rahemis and our *dehyar,* Shaban Ali Rahemi, bring you to Gorgan for a meeting. I want to know how you are doing. Also I have a bed, three chairs, some sheets, and pillows for you. When you have a place of your own, we will bring them out. Let me know if you need anything, and stop by the office whenever you are in Gorgan."

"Will do," I respond, with an air of confidence that belies my uneasiness. "And thank you for all you have done for me. I look forward to being with my new friends in Alang. *Khodahafez.*"

AS HE AND THE DRIVER DEPART, my connection with the world I knew vanishes. The villagers bid me *khodahafez* as well. They run off to take a nap. Mr. Rahemi, Ezetollah, and I return to the large room. The servant has brought in a sleeping mat and a large round bolster-like pillow.

"You must be tired. Lie down and rest awhile. Ezetollah and I are going to rest too. Later Shaban Ali and Ezetollah will take you to see Alang and to look at a house you might like. However, Ezetollah and I would be happy to have you stay with us. Our house is yours."

"Thank you. You are very kind, but the Peace Corps wants us to have our own house."

I am tired, but too hyper to sleep. I also feel dreadfully alone. None of my Peace Corps friends is here. *I am a lone American in an unfamiliar place. Really alone. But I have to be tough,* I rationalize. *You brought this upon yourself, and you just have to rough it out.*

I think of the grand reception I was given and how I flubbed it by not being able to give a speech in Farsi—in fact, no speech at all. *I was a failure.* That this event had its origins in the ceremonial pageantry of Achaemenid and Sassanian legacies that survived into Islamic times was not lost on me, for all my naiveté. *I am simply an ordinary American. Yet I was accorded a welcome befitting the President of the United States or a Beatle.*

And I wasn't even dressed properly. What an insult to the villagers. I should have worn my suit and tie and better shoes instead of my jeans and tennis shoes. Never mind that my black suit would have gotten dirty riding in the back of the jeep over those harrowing roads. If Mr. Vahdati had told me, we could have prepared a speech together, even a short one, and I could have dressed properly. What a louse I am. And I'll never be able make it up to them now.

And, they say I am a good omen. Their expectations outweigh my capabilities. I'm hopeless. I don't even know what I am supposed to do here. Why did I ever join the Peace Corps? I love being in Iran, but I need to feel useful. Oh, gosh, what am I to do?

I think and think. It makes me feel worse. Relief comes when Ezetollah enters with tea. Again he says, "You are my brother."

"Yes, my brother. Thank you," I say.

Maybe he has some idea of what I'm going through, but I try not to show I might be uncomfortable in any way.

Shaban Ali arrives. He is full of smiles as he greets me. "Did you sleep?"

"No." I tell him the truth.

Ezetollah pours tea for him as well. We talk awhile. Then we go for a walk. Everyone nods and greets us as we pass. A throng of smiling children tags along, but a boy kicking a limp soccer ball quickly distracts them.

Shaban Ali knocks on the gateway door to a courtyard. The door opens. A woman covering her mouth with her *chador* says, *"Baleh?"*

Shaban Ali tells her something.

"Wait." She runs off.

A man in his pajamas appears. It looks like we woke him up. *"Befarmayid"* (Welcome. Come in). He leads us to the house and shows us some rooms—one on the lower floor and another directly above it. (For safety reasons, the Peace Corps requires that the gas stove they will be providing not be in our living quarters.) I am not satisfied. It would be necessary to walk along an exterior balcony passing two other families' quarters to get to my kitchen on the lower floor.

"Shaban Ali and Ezetollah, I would like to find a place with two rooms next to each other."

Returning home, I hear the powerful sound of a motor as we approach a new brick building, near where the driver stopped when we arrived in the morning. A tall, clean-shaven man with a trim moustache greets us with a broad, toothless grin. He wears a crumpled but clean white shirt, baggy pants, and a felt skullcap. Sparkling, almost mischievous eyes reveal his delight in my visit and the opportunity to shake my hand again.

"Mir Baba Seyed Alangi," Shaban Ali introduces him.

"Salaam, hale shoma chetoreh? I'm happy to meet you," I say.

Mir Baba smiles. He operates the generator that supplies electricity for the village. He enthusiastically shows me the huge motor securely anchored to the floor. Later, I will learn that today was special—the only day in the two years I was in the village that they had electricity all day long. The generator is started at dusk. At 9:45pm the lights flash—the signal to run home and go to bed. The generator stops at 10:00 and darkness engulfs the village.

TEACHING THE CHAIR TO SIT

FRIDAY, OCTOBER 16, 1964 I am awakened by the sounds of activity in the courtyard. I lie there awhile, thinking, not quite ready to rise and face the day—and Farsi. Soon, however, I get up, stretch, and take off my American pajamas. As I grab clean underwear and begin to step into it I hear snickering at the door. Instantly I pull up my briefs, reach for my jeans, slip into them, and put on a shirt. I peer at the door and notice the light through the keyhole is intermittently obscured. I am embarrassed I was caught in my birthday suit. *Well, tomorrow I will have to change in a corner of the room where they can't see me from the door.*

My appearance on the porch silences the busy chatter of the women and children. Not sure I should greet the women, I mumble a cautious, *"Sobh bekheyr"* (Good morning). It is returned in like manner. I head across the courtyard to the *mostarah,* and as I near the outhouse an older woman soberly hands me the *aftabeh,* the ewer. I hadn't intended to use it this time. But, in Iran one always washes oneself off no matter what business is conducted in the *mostarah.*

Washing my face, arms, and hands and brushing my teeth attracts sidelong glances from the women. The children stare and giggle. They are reprimanded, but it does little to satiate their fascination.

Back in the house, the servant brings a bowl of hot water, a mirror, and a towel for me to shave. He has already removed my bed.

Ezetollah appears, greets me, shakes my hand, and asks about my health and if I slept well. He still looks tired, unshaven. We are served breakfast of tea, warm bread, honey, and mild goat cheese.

A walk through Alang with Shaban Ali and Ezetollah, seeing men I met yesterday and experiencing their warm greetings, buoys me. All come to shake my hand. Small mobs of jostling children cheerfully call out, "Hello, *Meesteer. Meesteer*, hello," and trail us until their attention wanes.

We go to see something special—an American bull people in the village are very proud of. The bull was obtained to improve the strain of cattle in the area. It is impressive—even by the standards of an American farm boy.

A large, unglazed ceramic urn nearly four feet tall in an adjoining horse stall attracts my attention. I ask about it. "Oh, it's very old. The farmer unearthed it when he was plowing his field. The fields are full of old broken pottery around here."

"It should not be in the stall with the horse," I say. "It might get broken. It is historically important." Their demeanor, however, indicates it is inconsequential and it won't be moved to a safer place.

We look at another house with rooms overlooking the main street and the new well, the part of town where the ceremony took place yesterday. Both rooms are on the second floor. I like that, especially after my ordeal changing clothes this morning and the many people who have been looking in the open windows at the Rahemis' house. There would be no privacy on the first floor anywhere. But there appears to be an old woman living there, and I have a hunch they intend her to be my servant and live in the one room and I in the other. *There goes my privacy.* Also, I grew up as a humble American from the North, and the thought of being waited on seems odious, even if she is paid. *It smacks of American elitism—not my image of the Peace Corps or America.*

"How much do these rooms cost?"

"Oh, that's all right," Shaban Ali and Ezetollah answer. We were briefed on Iranian *taroof* (politeness) in training, and I'm unsure if this is *taroof* or if they will provide the rooms. In Sari, the Peace Corps had explained to the Iranian community development heads that their regional offices should supply housing for the volunteers, and perhaps Mr. Vahdati had conveyed this to the villagers. Nevertheless, the Peace Corps told us privately, this rarely occurs. The Peace Corps will pick up the costs of rent if a house is not provided.

Ezetollah leaves to work with his father. He extends his hand to shake mine and says to Shaban Ali, "Bring Tom back to the house for lunch."

SHABAN ALI'S HOUSE IS NEARBY, and he wants me to meet his family. We bend and step through the tiny doorway in the large wooden gate into a courtyard enclosed by high mudbrick walls. There are no trees or grass. A few chickens scratch in the dirt. The house is made of unpainted wattle and daub and a tile roof, like many of the buildings in Alang. Three doors issue out to a low and narrow porch. A woman wrapped in a *chador* and two little girls come from the center door. The woman carries a little boy. Shaban Ali is proud to introduce them, though I almost certainly would not recognize his wife again, as she partially covers her face. She nods to me. His daughters shyly cling to the folds of their mother's *chador*. Shaban Ali tells her to make tea. Holding the baby, she goes off to the side of the courtyard to kindle the fire. He asks his daughters to come to him. They do, clutching his legs.

An old man and woman come from the door on the left, along with a young man who is blind in one eye. A woman holding a baby follows him. This is Shaban Ali's father and mother, his younger brother, and the brother's wife and child. The men greet me warmly and shake my hand. His mother says something to me. I interpret it as a greeting. I smile and nod. Shaban Ali explains his parents speak Gilaki, a dialect. His older brother, wife, and children join us from the door on the right. They greet me in Gilaki as well.

Shaban Ali and his family live in a room about nine feet wide and fifteen feet deep. An opening on the back wall reveals a narrow storage area. There are no windows. Light filters through the open door. His older brother's abode appears to be the same size while the room on the left is a bit larger, no doubt because his brother and wife share it with his parents and another brother who is in high school. I begin to comprehend how this village, that one can traverse in less than ten minutes, has a population of 2000. At least sixteen people live in this little building. And I want to find a place with two rooms that will give me some privacy?

The inside is clean but simple. The unpainted daub-coated walls are unadorned. Several large red-and-black felt mats cover the floor. A curtain with embroidery at the bottom is pulled to the side at the door. Another covers the entry to the storage area. Shaban Ali hands me a large bolster-like pillow to lean on and takes one for himself. He spreads a small cloth on the floor and finds a box of cookies. He offers them to me. His daughters are delighted to have some too. His wife silently brings in a tray of tea glasses and saucers, a teapot, another pot of hot water, and a dish of sugar lumps, all the while gripping the edges of her *chador* between her teeth.

Shaban Ali pours the tea. He makes mine *kam rang*.

"Thank you for remembering to make mine weak."

He smiles. "You're welcome."

This is the first time we have had together alone. I ask about his family, his education, and how he became a *dehyar* and got to work in community development. He is 27, three years older than I am, and seems so much more mature. He has a respected career and the responsibilities of a family with three children. I am still unsettled, pretty carefree, with vague aims for the future. The Peace Corps is definitely a diversion—but a welcome one—in any long-range objectives I might have.

We talk about the projects the people are doing in the five villages where he works. I will be going to village council meetings with him and will see what is being done. I discern he is a knowledgeable man. He has been trained well, and he has a sincere desire to find ways to improve the living conditions in the villages. He also wishes to obtain a little piece of property where he can build a house of his own. As I grow tired from the struggle to communicate in this new language, Shaban Ali recognizes our discussion is becoming strained. Even so, he is patient and tries to help me find the right words. For me, this time together is very meaningful.

On our way back to the Rahemi house, we pass by the village tailor, Reza Abtahi. I had met him yesterday. He is a strikingly handsome, good-natured man with several days' stubble. His tiny, dusty shop is a hangout for the young idle men of the village. They sit and jabber—mostly joke around—for hours while he works.

"Beah, beah inja" (Come, come here), he calls gesturing wildly. He comes from behind his sewing machine to shake hands and pull me into his shop.

I am introduced to the other guys standing around. Some I recall seeing before, but I have met so many people, my head is swimming. Shaban Ali and I are offered places on the wooden bench by the door. Reza knows a smattering of English so our dialogue is punctuated with two languages. I enjoy the informal, easygoing atmosphere. Reza encourages me to come back often. "This is the Sherkat-e Sargardon," he says. Everybody laughs.

"Sherkat-e Sargardon? What is that?"

He explains it is the "Do Nothing Company," and all laugh raucously. I realize it is the local hangout for Alang's jolly amateur comedians.

Shaban Ali excuses himself when we reach the Rahemi home. Tofigh and his son are working at a metal folding table with matching chairs— presumably set up specifically to conduct business, as they are using an old wooden abacus. Their preoccupation is my opportunity to resume the letter I started to my parents. In the same room, we have lunch in the Persian manner—on the floor. Obviously the table and chairs are only for business.

About midafternoon, visitors arrive—people from Alang; some are petitioners—poor humble men who come to *Aghaye* Tofigh for his willing assistance and advice. Others are from Gorgan. They want to meet this strange American who has come to live in a village. They ask hundreds of questions. Most I can answer. Sometimes they find another way to say something, or I hand them my Persian/English dictionary so they can find a word I don't know. Quickly I reach overload. Nothing makes any sense. I hope I am responding correctly and not making a fool of myself.

Shortly before I left Alang, nearly twenty months later, a particularly affable older man from Gorgan related a story of this day. It was etched in his memory. He had enjoyed talking with me, but he could tell I was wearing out.

"When we were alone, I asked, 'Are you *rahat* (comfortable) in Alang?'"

"You replied, '*Na*'" (No).

"I was taken aback by your bluntness and lack of politeness, but I knew you were tired and assumed you were guessing at an answer—that you didn't know the Persian word *rahat*. So I asked, 'Are you *narahat* (uncomfortable) in Alang?'"

"'*Na*.'"

"It made me feel better. But I decided to test you again. 'Are you comfortable in Alang?'"

"'*Na*,' you answered to my dismay."

He chuckled apologetically. "So I thought awhile of how I could teach you the meaning of *rahat*. I sat on the chair very properly and said, 'This is *rahat*. Do you understand?' You said, '*Baleh.*' Then I sat on the edge of the chair, almost falling off. I said, 'This is *narahat*. Do you understand?' Again you said, '*Baleh.*' I was satisfied and proud I had taught you some new words. So I asked you one more time, 'Are you comfortable in Alang?' You said, '*Na.*' I gave up! I thought to myself, *nafahm*" (weak-minded).

We both laughed heartily, and I was glad he felt he could tell me the story.

SATURDAY, OCTOBER 17, 1964 Ezetollah asks, "Do you want to go to the fields with me today?"

"Sure, that sounds good. I would like to see the kinds of crops that are raised here."

We spend the morning trekking through fields surrounding Alang and talking with workers, weathered old men—many conceivably only ten years older than I am—stooped from working in the rice fields every day. Everywhere, I observe the respect the workers have for Ezetollah. They are finishing the harvest and opening irrigation ditches. The extensiveness of the Rahemi family's landholdings is staggering to a boy who grew up on a fifty-five acre farm near Young America. No wonder the Rahemi house is so grand in a sea of mud and sticks—even if it is not the largest in Alang.

The sun peeks from behind the heavy morning clouds as noon approaches. Some workers invite us to share a humble lunch under the shade of a few poplar trees at the edge of a field. They spread out a cloth filled with rice mixed with a few vegetables. There are no plates or eating utensils. They politely tell me to begin. I, in turn, suggest they start. I need to learn how this is done so I make no mistakes. They each reach into the pile of rice with their right hand and put it in their mouths, then reach into the rice again. My modicum of American cleanliness leaves me a bit uneasy, but I can't hurt them by not eating. I reach for the rice nearest me and take some, but rather than putting my right hand to my mouth and then putting it back in the rice, I put the food in my left hand and eat from it. There is silence, a few sidewise glances I overlook, and we all continue. They offer me water from a cup that is passed around. I courteously decline and show them the canteen of purified water I brought with me—awful as it is with its halazone tablet.

Ezetollah and I check on more workers and then return to Alang. About 4:00 *Aghaye* Tofigh, Ezetollah and I walk together to a village council meeting. It is in the room overlooking the main street that I was shown as potential lodging yesterday. About a dozen men are there—mostly elders. There is inquisitive discussion about me before the meeting begins, but once they get on to business, I'm pretty lost. Either I'm not familiar with the technical terms, or they are speaking Gilaki. Plus they are talking fast, and not directly to me, so grasping the meaning is very difficult.

Afterwards, Shaban Ali and I go to his house for tea. He reviews the business of the meeting, primarily the new water system in Alang. "The men on the council want you to draw the plans."

Wow, I think, *a pretty tall order for someone with no engineering background. I seem to be getting deeper and deeper over my head.*

But I say, "I'm happy to help. Tomorrow I will send letters to the Peace Corps and USAID to see if they can provide drawings for similar proposals. Then we can work on plans for Alang."

"Did you have a good morning with Ezetollah?" Shaban Ali then asks me.

"*Baleh*, we went out to the fields. It was nice to see how farming is done here. In Minnesota we did not do irrigation. We had lots of rain."

"Ezetollah said you had lunch with the men in the field."

"*Baleh*, we had rice with some vegetables."

"You should be careful about eating just anywhere. It might not be clean. We don't want you to get sick."

I appreciate his concern. He hesitates a bit. "Ezetollah said you put food in your mouth from your left hand. That is not good—not good in Iran. The left hand is dirty."

Immediately I perceive what I did wrong and why it is bad—the left hand is used to clean oneself in the *mostarah*. "I'm sorry," I tell him.

"It's OK, because you used your right hand to take the rice from the cloth, but the workers were appalled you used your dirty hand to feed yourself. Fortunately you didn't put your left hand into the pile of rice. If you had, no one would have eaten."

"Thank you for telling me. I will be more attentive from now on. I didn't want to put the hand I put in my mouth into the rice. I didn't want to spread any germs."

Though Shaban Ali has been uncomfortable telling me, I detect a kind of paternalism in his demeanor. Nevertheless, I am grateful he is teaching me Iranian customs and their significance. "Always tell me what I need to do so I don't make mistakes," I urge him.

I try to recall if the Peace Corps had instructed us about eating with the right hand only. *Had I forgotten? Or maybe no PCVs had ever eaten from a common container without spoons and forks. Maybe I'm the first. It could be an issue that had never cropped up before.*

In the evening, I compose letters to the Peace Corps and USAID requesting their assistance. I mention to the Peace Corps that I'm living in Alang and give them my address.

I never hear from the Peace Corps or USAID. Neither is there any response from the Peace Corps about my moving to a village.

TUESDAY, OCTOBER 20, 1964   As kind as the Rahemis are, the lack of privacy and the incessant Farsi or Gilaki are wearing on me. We look at more possibilities for accommodations. I need my own space, not the busy room where everybody drops by to see the Rahemis—somewhere where I am not constantly observed or waited on.

I like a place at the edge of the village, across from the electrical power generator. It is a small room, about ten feet square, on the second floor of a wattle and daub building with a tin roof. A space about three by ten feet next to it could be my kitchen, but the ceiling is unfinished and it has no door. The fact that the rooms are at the end on the second floor would give me the privacy I long for—nobody would be walking past my rooms. The other large room on that floor is unoccupied. But, Shaban Ali tells me there may be a problem. The owner has a young unmarried daughter. Although the family lives in the main house, they may not want a single male—in particular a foreigner—living in their compound. Unfortunately, the owner is in Tehran now, so we keep looking.

By late afternoon I feel pretty rocky—another case of the "Tehran Trots" is looming on the horizon. I would like to retire to a room of my own, but my room is Entertainment Central in the Rahemi house. Guests keep arriving to see me and the Rahemis. I maintain conversation and civility although I am miserable. A large contingent stays for a late dinner. We take our places at the spread, but when the food is brought in, the odor of pickled garlic overcomes me. I had some for lunch. Now the pungent smell causes me to gag. I grab my handkerchief and run from the room. I seize the ewer. *Darn, it's empty.* Quickly I fill it with water and speed to the *mostarah*. The stench causes me to retch, but nothing comes. My stomach is churning. I stick my finger down my throat in an attempt to encourage what needs to happen. It doesn't. Finally I take down my pants and squat. There is a little relief but I am shaking, sweating, and cold. I feel like I am going to pass out. There is no way I can survive in this dark confined stinking place. I clean myself and pull up my pants.

Outside, the fresh air momentarily revives me. I wash my hands with soap at the basin in the middle of the courtyard. *No way can I go back into the house where those garlic pickles are.* My stomach continues to churn, and the light-headed sensation returns. I bend over the gutter in the courtyard, but can't bring anything up. I retreat to the *mostarah* with the ewer, and my discomfort abates slightly. I spend the rest of the evening in the courtyard and the *mostarah*.

When Ezetollah checks on me, I tell him, "I'm sorry. I can't eat tonight. Don't save anything for me." The smell of the garlic pickles on his breath and hands makes me gag some more.

I regret I am causing him, his father, and the villagers so much distress. When the lights blink at 9:45, everyone leaves, and I return to the house. My bed is made. I stash a flashlight nearby for my nighttime perambulations to the little building at the edge of the courtyard.

THURSDAY, OCTOBER 22, 1964 "This is a book."

With my urging, they struggle to repeat, "This is a book."

A single bare bulb hanging in the center dimly lights the drab schoolroom with its cracked, daub-coated walls. The long wooden desks and benches are filled with boisterous village men. Some stand at the door, others next to the walls. It seems everybody in Alang wants to learn English. This was to be a class for the teachers and a few interested students, but word got around the village that the first class was tonight. Probably most showed up for entertainment. Not much happens in an isolated Iranian village, and an American is clearly a novelty.

I lay the book on the desk and say, "That is a book." They repeat, and I go through a repertoire of objects I find in the classroom, as our Iranian instructors had done in Utah.

"I have a book. You have a book." I go on and on, getting them to repeat. However, pandemonium reigns. Everybody is enthusiastic except the teachers. There is much laughing and talking in Farsi. Unthinkingly, I put my finger to my mouth and say, "Shhhhh." Everyone laughs. Then I remember Dave's misfortune—but in my haste I forget what you're supposed to say, and I don't want to make the same mistake. Flustered, I say, *"Khamoosh kon,"* figuring it was like silence yourself. This brings uproarious laughter. I had ordered them to extinguish themselves.

FRIDAY, OCTOBER 23, 1964 Tofigh Rahemi and Ezetollah invite me to the mosque for prayer. I am startled and a bit apprehensive. I did not expect this so soon after arriving in Iran, but I sense they want me to be truly a part of the village. I am honored.

I try not to stare as the devout recite the words and perform the ritual of their prayer. I am very blessed, I realize, to be able to live in another culture. I pray that my stay in Alang will be a benefit and not a burden to these people.

FRIENDS TAKE ME TO THE CEMETERY at the edge of the village where the Imamzadeh Ibrahim, the tomb of a revered holy man who was martyred here in the early days of Islam, is surrounded by a few large trees. As we stroll across the grass, a gentle breeze plays a game of chase with the first of autumn's curled, rust-colored leaves. To the side, a shepherd tends his flock—the sheep, a most efficient lawn mower as they methodically trim around the tilting tombstones.

The tomb is a stark, octagonal, three-tiered structure topped by a conical tin cupola. Projecting tin roofs define each tier, the bottom roof covering a porch around the building. Inside, a wooden grill encloses a faded, cloth-covered sarcophagus. My friends solemnly kiss the grill and mumble some prayers as we circumambulate the structure.

As we amble among the tombstones, my companions speak longingly of people who are buried here. "Mohammad Yahya was a very generous man, highly respected in the village," they declare as we stand before a leaning slate slab with a weathered inscription. I discern some numbers at the bottom, partially covered with the encroaching earth. We scrape away some of the grass and dirt. The number 132 appears.

"Did you know Mohammad Yahya?" I ask.

"No, but we've heard about him. Everyone talks about him."

"But the number, is that the date he died?"

"Yes, surely."

"That means he died 132 years after the Hijra when Mohammad and his followers fled from Mecca to Medina in 622 of the Christian era. That's over 1200 years ago. Yet you refer to him as if he died recently."

"Oh, no, he died a long time ago, but we all know about him and how good he was. We never realized he lived that long ago. He was a kind and honorable man."

I am puzzled at how my friends talk about a person who died over twelve centuries ago as if they knew him. This is an introduction to a different way of thinking, one very foreign to me as an American. My grandmothers, whom I never knew, are very abstract beings to me even though my parents occasionally mention their mothers. We view history in terms of events: the Pilgrims' arrival in the New World, the Revolutionary War, the Civil War, the bombing of Pearl Harbor, the first man in space. With the exception of George Washington and Abraham Lincoln, our conception of history is based on "what" rather than "who." In Iran, history is connected to persons. They speak about the individual—the man who did something or who was in power and what he achieved at that time. This may be part of the oral tradition of passing on stories of people from generation to generation, so the individual continues to live in the recent past. Here, people seem to be more important than an event in history.

As we meander along, I especially admire the quality of the calligraphic inscription on another stone slab—also centuries old. My friends know nothing of the person who is buried here. Perhaps he was a rich man, I surmise, not known for his benevolence. Still, I am humbled to be standing in the presence of so much history.

CALLERS ARRIVE AT THE RAHEMI HOUSE in the late morning. Again, at lunch I strive to keep conversation going. I'm getting exasperated from the stifling attention and exhausted by having to think and communicate in a foreign language.

When everyone leaves for a nap, I realize I desperately crave some time to myself. I'm starting to crawl the walls! It has been over a week of nonstop Farsi or Gilaki, and no privacy. I have no idea how much longer this will go on before I have a place of my own. They seem to be in no hurry to finalize anything. When Ezetollah comes I tell him, "I want to go for a walk by myself."

"I will go with you. Where do you want to go?"

"Thank you, but I want to go alone."

"That is not possible. You will get lost. It is dangerous. Where do you want to go? We will go together."

"I need to go by myself. I need to walk somewhere alone."

At that moment, Shaban Ali arrives. Ezetollah apprises him of my intention to go for a walk alone. He too finds it incomprehensible.

"We'll go together," Shaban Ali says. "Where do you want to walk?"

"I don't know. I want to go on my own. Please. I need to be alone."

"That is not good. Someone must go with you. Ezetollah and I will go with you. Where do you want to go?"

"If I can't go by myself, I don't want to go anywhere. I will stay here."

"But you said you want to go for a walk. Let's go."

"No, I want to walk alone."

They confer in Gilaki. I suspect they think I don't like them. I feel terrible I am causing them this stress. *They must think I am a very ungrateful person, but I long for some time to myself. Somehow, it seems Iranians don't require time alone.*

"All right, Shaban Ali and I won't go with you. I will get my younger brother Mohammad and some other boys in the village to go with you."

I was right. They think I don't like them. This has turned out so awful. Why did I ever start it? I'm such an ingrate.

Ezetollah goes off and returns with Mohammad and three other boys. I feel obligated to go, even though this is precisely not what I had planned. As we leave the house, I look back at Ezetollah and Shaban Ali. I would rather be walking with them. I worry that I have broken a trust I may never be able to mend. *This Peace Corps job is a lot harder than I ever imagined.*

As we make our way through the village, the men nod and greet me and ask where we are going. Many want to join us, but Mohammad mumbles to them and they excuse themselves. This makes me feel worse. They don't understand I need my space, and I am sure they feel I don't appreciate them. It weighs heavily on my mind. *What kind of Peace Corps Volunteer am I?*

We wander out of the village toward the mountains to the south. The dense forests at their base give way to jagged, gleaming rock walls near the top; the lowering afternoon sun reflects like snow off their surfaces. *Such majesty. I wish I were alone so I could think only of Del and Lily. How I want them to see this too. Even though I am with these boys, I have nobody to share this with—what I see and what I am experiencing. It's as if I'm reaching for the whole world; I see it in all its glory, but it isn't mine, because there's no one to whom I can give what I feel.*

We cross the gravel highway at the end of the path to Alang. Brown clouds rise around us as we wade through the dust-laden weeds in the ditch on the other side and then roam aimlessly through the cotton fields. I am stunned and inspired by the simple beauty of nature.

Mohammad asks, "Where are you going?"

"I don't know. Just walking." He and the boys must find this weird—just walking. Probably Iranians don't do this. They go to a place for a purpose, and my pointless ramble is a cultural aberration.

As we approach the foothills, we meet a shepherd tending his flock. He is a young man dressed in rough-textured handmade clothes. He carries a staff with a curved metal blade at the end. The soles of his shoes are pieces of inner tube—the lacing at the edges is bound around his feet and ankles, that are carefully wrapped with a rough dull-red woolen fabric. He speaks mostly Gilaki, and Mohammad helps us communicate, but I detect he is uncomfortable talking with this peasant.

Shepherd and his flock

We go on, over a bridge crossing a dry ravine. Mohammad informs me this is a bridge of Shah Abbas. I am spellbound. *He was Shah when the Pilgrims landed at Plymouth Rock! I am standing on a 350-year-old bridge. Such history—almost nothing is that old in America!*

I descend to the parched streambed below to see the beautiful pointed arch of the narrow span. A flock of sheep and shepherd pass as I take a photo. It's like I am living a dream.

As we cross a field, I ask the boys if I can take their picture. They pose stiffly, but I tell them to sit in the grass, a gnarled and scraggly tree and the bright haze-shrouded mountains behind them.

This has been a magical time, even if I was not alone.

Four boys from Alang (Mohammad Rahemi second from left.)

SUNDAY, OCTOBER 25, 1964 Tonight the teachers, Shaban Ali, Reza the tailor, Mulla, whom I have gotten to know, and a few others show up for my English class. I presume word got out that I was going to charge for the classes, so only those who truly want to learn have come. I had suggested the teachers collect a nominal fee, and the money be used to buy new volleyball and soccer equipment for the school. They favored the idea, and likely thought it would discourage attendance; I could thus give more attention to their needs and abilities. The outcome was achieved—but no fee was ever collected.

When I decided to start English classes in the village, I wrote to the Peace Corps asking for books on teaching English as a second language. An answer had not yet come, but when it does, it says I was sent to Iran to work in community development and not to be an English teacher. No books are supplied. *Well,* I think, *every time I ask for help, I get nothing. I'll just use my Farsi language books from training as a model for teaching English. I've already started doing that. We were constantly reminded in training, we had to be flexible and resourceful. So I will.*

UNDERSTANDING UNDERSTANDING

MONDAY, OCTOBER 26, 1964 Holiday today—the Shah's birthday. And this is a particularly special day for me. In the morning, I move into my own house—barely moved in, definitely not settled. It is the place I wanted at the entry to the village across from the power station. It happened so fast. I wonder if my wanting to go on a walk alone on Friday precipitated it.

We attend an athletic program at the school in nearby Kordkuy, but I begin to feel stomach cramps. *Oh, no, not another case of the trots.* On the return to Alang, I get the chills and have a temperature.

"Shaban Ali and Ezetollah, I don't feel well enough to eat tonight." They offer to get a doctor from Kordkuy.

"No, I don't need a doctor. I have my Peace Corps medical kit. I will be OK. I promise I will tell you if I ever need a doctor."

I spread my mattress roll, sheets, and blanket out on a straw mat, and make another trip downstairs to the *mostarah*. With my temperature, the many trips downstairs, and the cold air seeping in between the floorboards and through the broken windows, I shiver most of the night.

TUESDAY, OCTOBER 27, 1964 *"Allahu Akbar…Ash-hadu an-la ilaha illa Allah…"* Before dawn, the low, sonorous sound of the call to prayer summons me from my cold, restless slumber. I hadn't noted my room would be only a courtyard away from the mosque; however, the awareness of being awoken each morning by the soft, tranquil reminder of our relationship with God is comforting.

Shaban Ali knocks at my door as the bright early-morning sun streams in the uncovered window of my new abode. His face is ridden by concern. He brings a tray with tea, bread, jam, and cheese. I eat a bit, thankful he has brought me breakfast.

"I want to do some shopping today."

"Just get well. Are you sure you don't need a doctor?"

"No, I am fine. My temperature is gone. I'm getting better."

I make many trips to the *mostarah* all day, often turning around to climb back down the steep stairs as soon as I reach my room. *This is disconcerting. What is my landlord going to think?*

WEDNESDAY, OCTOBER 28, 1964 Mulla, who lives next door, comes to check on me and takes me to lunch at his house. His sincere and mellow, but serious, nature belies his seventeen years. The responsibilities of a wife and baby have made him a man long before he experienced the carefree joys of being a teenager. He has a pleasant way of speaking forthrightly.

"I was not able to finish high school. My father wanted me to get married. I did what he wanted. He arranged my marriage; he selected my wife. She is my cousin," he says this with all respect to his wife and his father, though I perceive he would have liked to complete his schooling.

"I kept going to school at first, but then the baby came and my wife needed help around the home, so I quit. My son, Ismael, is not well. He cries a lot. You must have heard him from your room."

I empathize with him. He is an intelligent young man—one of my better students. "Hopefully you will be able to finish your education someday. I am happy you are in my English class."

"I would like to complete my education and get a job, but I am obligated to help my father oversee the farm. My father owns a lot of land—although not as much as some other men in Alang. There is not much for me to do."

An old woman enters the room with a tray of tea and cookies.

"This is my mother."

She smiles gently and asks in a tone that seems to indicate I might be deaf, *"Ahvalet"* (How are you)? I'm sure she thinks by talking loud I will understand.

"Khoob, moteshakeram" (Fine, thank you).

When she leaves I tell Mulla, "I'm confused. The other day you introduced your mother and I'm positive it was another woman."

"Oh, that woman was my mother too. But, this is my real mother. My father has four wives. They are all my mothers, but this is my real mother."

I try to conceal my shock and consternation. "Your father has four wives?"

"Yes, my mother is his first wife. He took a second wife when his brother died and his widow and their children needed care. Somebody had to provide for them and oversee their land."

"But what did your mother say when he wanted to take another wife?"

"Oh, it was OK. They were good friends and my mother knew her sister-in-law and her children needed help. They are still good friends and help each other a lot. All of my mothers are good friends. They were widows with many children when my father married them. Someone had to support them."

My initial abhorrence turns to compassion and respect. This is not the lecherous desire I had been brought up to believe polygamy purports. In a place where systems of social welfare are nonexistent, human beings have found a manner of caring for each other in a humble and very humane and charitable way.

THURSDAY, OCTOBER 29, 1964 Shaban Ali accompanies me to Gorgan on one of the rickety local buses that prowl the highway, picking up passengers along the way. So far I have not been able to venture out of Alang by myself.

Jack, Dave and I considered going to Tehran, as Saturday is a holiday— Prince Reza Pahlavi's birthday. We thought a "big city" break would be imperative for three young guys who desperately require a change of scenery. There are even Peace Corps women in the capital city. When we stop to see Mr. Vahdati, I mention, "I'm going to Tehran."

"Why?"

"I want to get some supplies I can't get here in Gorgan."

"Like what?"

"Oh, stuff like oatmeal, powdered milk, cocoa, and various spices."

"You can get all of that here in Gorgan. Wait here while I finish what

I'm doing and then I'll take you to an Armenian shop that has all the things you want."

He is right. I can get everything in Gorgan. *Outstanding,* I think, *but I really wanted to get away.*

"Are there other items you need?"

"Well, I need more than the straw mats on my floor, as there is a lot of cold air that comes up through the floor boards at night. Also, I have to get a water container, dishes, and other supplies."

"I will take you to a shop where felt rugs are sold. Then Shaban Ali can take you to get the rest. Gorgan has everything essential."

We bargain for and purchase two deep-red-and-black felt mats made by Turkomans. They will completely cover the floor of my room. Mr. Vahdati says, "You got a good deal on the rugs. The one is exceptional—very thick. They will keep your room warmer." We take the rugs to the bus station.

Shaban Ali leads me up the street to the metalworking bazaar. I stop to see the owner of the Hotel Chahar Fasl as we pass. The radiance of his smile as we shake hands shows his delight in seeing me. I introduce Shaban Ali and say I enjoy living in Alang.

He tells Shaban Ali, "Mister *Farsi khoob yad gerefteh*" (Mister has learned Farsi well). I have made progress in the two weeks I have been in Alang, but I have a long way to go.

The deafening sound of dozens of metalsmiths pounding out objects signals we are approaching the metalworking bazaar long before we get there. Hundreds of copper and tin containers surround the entrance to each shop. Shaban Ali asks about the price of a covered 20-gallon water container with a spigot at the bottom.

"Too much," he says. We turn away.

"How much do you want to pay? What will you give?"

Shaban Ali offers less than half of what the shopkeeper quoted.

"No, do you want me to starve? What about my children?" However, the man brings the price down.

I am surprised. I look at Shaban Ali. He says, "No, too expensive," and he motions for me to come with him.

The shopkeeper calls out, "Wait. How much do you want to pay?"

Shaban Ali offers him a little more. I am abashed. The container is not that expensive and Shaban Ali insists the poor man accept so little.

After prolonged haggling, we agree to half the original price. I pay him. He tells me, "My children will starve." Of course, I am wracked by guilt.

Then Shaban Ali instructs him to take the container to the bus station for Alang. The shop owner agrees. My jaw drops in disbelief.

We venture to another section of the bazaar. Here is shop after shop of housewares—dishes, pots and pans, and silverware. Shaban Ali takes me to a store that has foreign-made dishes and silverware. We inquire about the prices. I feel uncomfortable buying foreign merchandise in Iran. I should be setting an example that Iranian goods are perfectly fine. The whole of Alang is already fascinated by my wristwatch, camera, clothes, and everything else I have from America.

I ask Shaban Ali, "How much would Iranian-made dishes cost?"

"A lot less."

We go to another shop. I select a typical Iranian pattern with small flowers. Shaban Ali negotiates the price. He tells the store owner to wrap them well and deliver them to the bus station.

We buy silverware, pots and pans, a water bucket, a small metal table for my gas stove, a plastic-covered bucket for garbage, and some groceries. Shaban Ali bargains for everything, even the groceries. I tell him, "I am uneasy about bargaining for things you eat."

"It's the way it is done in Iran. You must bargain. You can't pay what they say. They will think you are a foolish foreigner with too much money. Besides, if you pay them what they ask they will wish they had quoted a higher price. You will make them feel bad. You *must* bargain."

We take our purchases to the bus station. Shaban Ali asks, "Anything else before we go back to Alang?"

"I should tell Jack and Dave I won't be going to Tehran with them."

Shaban Ali hails a passing taxi.

The taxi driver asks, *"Koja"* (Where)?

"Manzele Amrika-i" (The American's house). I don't know where Jack and Dave moved when they left the Red Lion and Sun, but this is enough of an address to find the new Americans in Gorgan.

"Get in." But Shaban Ali haggles over the price. There are already people in the taxi. The driver drops them off at their destinations and picks up others on the way to Jack and Dave's.

The guys are glad to see me. They are not going to Tehran either—too far to go for two days—but they are disappointed I won't stay for the weekend.

We wait at the station for the bus that goes into Alang. Other buses only stop on the highway. The driver, Hajireza Savari,* greets me enthusiastically with his gleaming golden grin. He is proud of his front teeth, which have been replaced with gold. He is from Alang. In fact, he parks his bus each night directly below my room. My purchases are loaded on top. Shaban Ali and I are given the seat of honor behind Hajireza. From here he can carry on a running discourse with us while the bus fills, and continue it all the way to Alang. He jokes that his bus is the *Mashini Mashti Mamdali* (The Bus of Mashti Mamdali), an object of ridicule in a popular Iranian folk song. *"Na boogh dareh, na sandali, na motor…"* (No horn, no seats, no motor…).

His assistant solicits potential passengers. Some get off to take another bus and others, remembering they forgot something, run to do more shopping. Slowly, the decrepit vehicle fills. A man with three squawking hens strung together takes a seat behind us. He tucks the hens under the seat. They settle down in silence. Someone with a young goat gets on. An argument ensues. The goat is taken off and unceremoniously dumped on the pile on top of the bus. I cringe and hope it won't decide my things are the perfect place to pee or poop. I don't want to wash the rugs before I use them.

At long last the bus is filled, but somebody is missing. We wait until the man returns. Meanwhile, others have boarded. Short wooden stools are placed down the center aisle for the overflow. Still more arrive. I am given a more exalted place of honor, on a little wooden stool between Hajireza and the driver's side door. Apprehensively, I oblige. He is thrilled to have me right beside him. Belatedly the motor is started, but like an overloaded donkey, the bus revolts and refuses to budge. Men get out

---

* *Haji* is an honorific title given to someone who has made the pilgrimage to Mecca. In this instance, Hajireza is his given name, and I have chosen to write it as one word to signify he has not made the Hajj.

and start pushing. As we chug along, they quickly jump aboard. We go around the corner and pull into a gas station for petrol. *Strange this wasn't done earlier.* The smell of fuel rises around us. Several men are smoking on the bus. I cling to my stool, hoping we won't take off like a rocket. That finished, we sputter off in the direction of Alang, stopping along the way to pick up additional passengers. They disappear into the densely crowded interior behind. Occasionally people are let out. As we gain momentum, I watch them venture down lonely tracks to villages in the distance. The thirty-kilometer journey takes over an hour, but we waited at least two hours to get started. This expedition has taken us the whole day.

FRIDAY, OCTOBER 30, 1964 Silence overcomes the chatter around the well as I approach with fresh bread under my arm and my new water bucket. Only the splash of gushing water breaks the quiet. The women pull their *chadors* around themselves and tuck the edges between their teeth. Some fill their containers and wander off with a wide-based copper vessel balanced on their head while they carry a full bucket in each hand. Others wash their dishes without looking up. I hear their exchange resume as I turn toward my room.

I boil a kettle of water, wash up—a mini bath in an inch of water in the relative privacy of my room with no curtains on the windows—and pray I will have no visitors while I'm trying to do this expeditiously. Yesterday I discovered that the morning light is perfect for shaving on the porch. I wonder if anyone will be offended by my being out here in my T-shirt, which is considered underwear in Iran.

It's almost like being at home to have oatmeal, hot cocoa, the bread I bought on my morning foray, and jam for breakfast.

REZA CALLS OUT, "Rozy, *Amo* Tom *amad*" (Rozy, Uncle Tom came). His little daughter comes running, squealing loudly, *"Amo, Amo."* She throws her arms around my legs. I bend down to hug her. She hugs me back and showers me with kisses. She hangs onto my hand as we step over the threshold into their home and as I sit down she plants herself squarely in my lap, cooing all the while, *"Amo, Amo."*

Reza smiles approvingly. I smile back, blushing a bit, but happy I am his brother. Rozy remembers her *Amo* Tom from my frequenting her father's shop. A bubbly and chattering two-year-old moppet, she is always attired in colorful dresses and pajamas—her father, of course, is the village tailor. Her head is topped with tiny hennaed ringlets. She beams when I admire her hennaed nails as well, jumps up, spins around singing *"Amo* Tom, *Amo* Tom,"* and then bounds into my lap again. We enjoy tea together, followed by lunch with Rozy right beside me.

Rozy in front of the Sherkat-e Sargardon

I RETURN TO MY ROOM to write home while everyone naps; however, a visitor immediately turns up. *So much for that letter!* I make tea and serve cookies and candy. He leaves as I go to class. Dinner is at another person's house. When the lights flash at 9:45, I walk home, exhausted and somewhat exasperated from never having any time to myself and straining to converse in Farsi.

SATURDAY, OCTOBER 31, 1964 Shaban Ali and I bicycle to Chahardeh for a village council meeting. The men are inquisitive about my presence. Shaban Ali and I explain the Peace Corps and my role in community development. Already, in the little more than two weeks I have been in Alang, I have become uneasy explaining that, as a community development volunteer, I am here to help improve living conditions. Somehow this seems to be an affront—a way of America saying Iranians don't know how to live. *Who are we to say? We have been a country less than 200 years and Iran has a civilization that goes back thousands of years.* Mainly, I don't want people in other villages to think Alang is so bad, they need an American to tell them what to do. Thus, we talk about how I am working with Shaban Ali to implement projects the Iranians themselves propose. We also mention that I am teaching a class in English and that Shaban Ali is learning well. The village leaders are envious and want to get a Peace Corps Volunteer in Chahardeh. Now it is evident that Alang *is* very special to be the chosen village, and Shaban Ali feels better about explaining my role as a Peace Corps Volunteer.

Like Alang, Chahardeh plans to put in a water system—even a new bathhouse with showers. We give them encouragement, and Shaban Ali assures them he knows well the methods of getting technical assistance through the Iranian government.

SOMEONE BUTCHERED A WATER BUFFALO in Alang this morning. I bought a hunk of meat to make stew, and was looking forward to cooking my first meal and having an evening to myself. But a friend's son comes to invite me to dinner. He is insistent, so I put the meat away—hoping it will keep until tomorrow, as the temperature at night is very cool.

This is frustrating. I haven't had an evening to myself since I've been in Alang. But as a Peace Corps Volunteer, I must be a gracious guest.

SUNDAY, NOVEMBER 1, 1964 Today I'm going to Kordkuy to pick up my mail and take a shower. I have not been in the bathhouse in Alang, as it is a common pool—no showers—and skin and eye diseases are prevalent in the villages of Iran. The short trip to Kordkuy is worth the precaution. I've been there several times since I arrived in Alang, and the masseur, like the one in Gorgan, already knows about me. Best yet, it is the one place I can have a little time to myself.

I intended to go alone, but Shaban Ali shows up as I finish breakfast. He is accompanying me. While we wait for a bus by the highway, a large transport truck approaches, the driver sees us, and the truck grinds to a halt. We are engulfed in a billowing brown cloud. "Where are you going?"

"Kordkuy."

We crawl in the cab.

"Where are you from?" the driver asks me in Farsi.

"*Amrika.*"

"*Amrika! Amrika khoob* (America good). I thought you were American, your blond hair. That's why I stopped."

At the main intersection in Kordkuy, he says, "I wish you were going farther so we could talk more. *Khodahafez.*"

Shaban Ali is incredulous that an Iranian would stop to give a foreigner a ride just because he has blond hair. I am too, but I had heard about this. Iranians have a reputation for being very hospitable and generous people.

I can hardly wait to read the letters from Mom and Dad, Del, and Lily. However, before we return, I want to peruse the shops of Kordkuy to see what they have, as it would be easier to buy supplies here than going to Gorgan. Somehow Shaban Ali doesn't grasp my desire to window shop. Every time I stop to look or go inside he asks me what I want. I become annoyed but try hard not to show it. I like Shaban Ali, and I know he is a kindhearted guy, but I can't get him or anybody in Alang to understand I need time to myself. I feel like a caged animal. I just need to get away. Yet that seems impossible. I am so tired of all the attention and their kindness. *That really seems ungrateful, doesn't it?* I tell myself.

Shaban Ali insists I have lunch with him. I decline, but it's no use. We take the meat I bought yesterday to his house. *So much for my attempt to cook.* We finish in time to go to class.

VISITORS APPEAR AT MY DOOR for tea as soon as class is over. The landlady sends up a huge bowl of soup. Shaban Ali has given me fresh tomatoes.

That is dinner. Somebody sees the light in my room and comes up. Others arrive as well. I serve tea, cookies, and candy. When the lights flash at the appointed time, my company hurries home. *Wow, time for myself.*

I light my kerosene lantern so I can write my first monthly report to the Peace Corps and finish a letter home and others to Del and Lily. Then I hear a voice.

"Mister Tom, Mister Tom."

I go to the window and peer out into the blackness.

"Ki-eh" (Who is it)?

It is Mir Baba Seyed Alangi, who runs the power plant, and another guy. They had seen the dim light of my lamp through the unconcealed windows. They want to come up. I close the window, go down to open the door in the gateway, and greet them warmly, if insincerely. We have tea and cookies and talk for over an hour. We all grow weary and I usher them downstairs so I can lock the gate behind them.

Now I can get back to my report and letters. The report is difficult because I don't know the Peace Corps' reaction to my living in a village at my own initiative. Nevertheless, I try to be optimistic, telling them about the village council meetings I have been attending and my English classes. Still, I wonder, what I will accomplish in community development—but I can't mention that.

It is after one o'clock when I finally extinguish the lamp. I lie there, comforted by the gentle sounds of the night—water splashing at the well, and the occasional dog barking for some reason unknown.

MONDAY, NOVEMBER 2, 1964 "Mister Tom, Mister Tom." At dawn I wake to knocking and my name being called. It is Shaban Ali.

Groggily I go to the door. *"Baleh?"*

"We have a busy day; council meetings in two of the mountain villages. My brother will lend you his bicycle, but it will take time to get there. We must start out right after breakfast. We will have lunch in one of the villages. Coming back will be easy, as it is downhill."

"Good," I say, even though I can hardly think. I'm still tired from staying up so late.

The trek to the mountain villages by bicycle is grueling. "I hope the Peace Corps will give me a motor scooter," I tell Shaban Ali, huffing as we stop for a much-needed break.

"I hope so too. That would help me get one as well."

"Wow!" I first notice the view—we had not looked back as we struggled up the foothills. It's spectacular at this height, even with the cloud-shrouded skies above. "There's the Caspian Sea! I didn't realize it was so close."

"*Baleh*, and there is Alang. Kordkuy is to the left. And at the southeastern tip of the sea is Bandarshah. Mostly Turkomans live there and in the desert stretching east from the sea. On the horizon, about twenty-five kilometers from Alang, is the Soviet Union. We can't go near there."

Bala Jaddeh, a village about the size of Alang, lies at the very edge of the forest. They also are making plans for running water throughout the village and for a new bathhouse with showers.

At lunch, much the same conversation transpires that ensued my first day in Alang. They want to know about me, and why I would come to Iran to live in a village for two years. They are envious Alang is privileged to have an American Peace Corps Volunteer and would like to get a volunteer in Bala Jaddeh.

Ghalandarayesh is a short distance from Bala Jaddeh, quietly nestled within the coolness of the forest. Shaban Ali had told me it is beautiful. Walking the pathways through the little village is like being transported to another world—a perfect romantic hideaway.

We gather with the councilmen at the headman's house. Trees surround the second-story room; this is such a contrast to the nearly treeless villages on the plain. Now I understand why Shaban Ali likes to come here.

A Literacy Corpsman, who wears his identifying military-style uniform, recently arrived in Ghalandarayesh, and participates in the council meeting. His soft, shy smile is welcoming.

Shaban Ali introduces me and tells about the Peace Corps. The Literacy Corpsman interprets for the villagers. They speak a Turkic dialect—only a few know Farsi. No one is literate. They seem unaffected by my presence and may not know anything about America. This innocence is refreshing following the suffocating attention I receive elsewhere.

Discussion centers around building a school in Ghalandarayesh. The Literacy Corpsman is presently teaching the children in his home, but plans are underway for construction of a little schoolhouse on the edge of the village. I am inspired. This is truly an outstanding program.

As we rapidly descend the mountain by the dirt road, I share Shaban Ali's enthusiasm for Ghalandarayesh. Though I already feel a commitment to Alang, I almost wish I had been assigned there.

Shaban Ali Rahemi and Literacy Corpsman, Ghalandarayesh

TUESDAY, NOVEMBER 3, 1964 Election day in America. I am pissed—my first opportunity to vote in a national election, and I never received my absentee ballot. And this is an important election—Johnson vs. Goldwater. Like the Iranians, I want Johnson to win. However, I strive to imagine the Iranian rationale. They are convinced Johnson killed Kennedy to gain power for himself.

"The fact the assassination occurred in Dallas, in Johnson's home state, is proof he did it," they tell me.

"But if he killed Kennedy, why do you want him to remain President?"

"Because he is a powerful man. He is more powerful than Kennedy was. That is why he had Kennedy killed."

Some even speculate, "It is obviously Lady Bird who instigated it. She didn't want to be 'second fiddle' to Jackie. Women are the practical ones in matters like this."

I am incredulous each time I hear these theories. They are so foreign to our American way of reasoning. Over the next fifteen months, as I live in Iran and study Iranian history, I begin to discern the Iranian way of thinking. They take a very pragmatic view of politics—when somebody stronger comes along, side with him. Always side with whoever is in power. Then you will always be a winner.

"THE LADY DOWNSTAIRS did a very fine job washing my clothes. Thank you for arranging it," I tell Shaban Ali when he arrives.

"Did you pay her?"

"*Baleh.*"

"How much?"

"Ten tomans."

"Ten tomans! That is way too much."

"That's OK. She did an excellent job. Besides, when I had my clothes washed at the laundry in Gorgan, it was much more expensive."

"Yes, but you can't pay her that much. It's not appropriate. Her husband makes three-and-a-half tomans working under the hot sun in the fields all day. This is very bad." He pauses for a few seconds. "I will tell her you didn't have any change and it is for washing three times. Then, after that, you pay her three tomans. Do you understand?"

"*Baleh.*" I am beginning to comprehend the importance of living within the cultural and economic constructs of the place where I am, and that I should not impose my American standards on others. At the bottom of the stairs I hear him stop and speak to the lady.

Shaban Ali is thoughtful. He is teaching me much about life.

I HAVE TIME IN THE MORNING to get curtains made from the gray-and-blue-striped material I bought in Gorgan. Reza sews the sections together and hems up the top and bottom. The guys at the Sherkat-e Sargardon find the material strange for curtains.

"This is pajama material," they say.

I pleat the top like I saw mother do when she made drapes for the house. Now I will have more privacy. No more worrying I'll be caught taking a sponge bath in the morning, and nobody will see my kerosene lantern on after the lights go out. And, the curtains will help insulate the room during cold nights.

A few days later, when I visit my friend Mulla, I see he has new curtains at his windows made from the same material. I muse over the cultural comprehension and assimilation already occurring.

WEDNESDAY, NOVEMBER 4, 1964 The silence that envelops the women at the well when I get water each day is broken this morning by a confident, *"Sobh bekheyr. Hale shoma chetoreh?"* from a kindly looking, bent-over old woman.

Startled I am being addressed, I return the greeting. She speaks a mixture of Farsi and Gilaki, but I have a hunch she is also asking about my mother. Later I will learn her name. For now, she remains a mystery.

Her greeting breaks the icy chill that descends upon the busy gathering at the well every morning as I arrive. From now on, each day the other women greet me—if with reservation.

Later, a friend brings me a bunch of grapes.

"It is from *Haji* Torfeh, the lady who spoke to you at the well this morning."

"Tell me about *Haji* Torfeh."

"All in Alang respect *Haji*. She lives alone. Her husband died many years ago. She never had any children, but she is like the mother of everyone in Alang. She lives over there," he points to the end portion of the house in the next courtyard where Mulla lives.

Haji is on her porch, drinking tea and watching me. I wave and call, *"Moteshakeram."*

She smiles and calls back, "You're welcome."

PRACTICING PATIENCE

THURSDAY, NOVEMBER 5, 1964 Shaban Ali has invited me to go to Gonbad-e Kavus with him. I would have liked to go on my own, but at least I'll have time with Barkley.

The landscape changes abruptly as we head east from Gorgan. Clouds of dust follow our bus. The mountains to the south are lower and the farther we journey the more the desert encroaches around us. Farmers labor to raise a meager crop near tiny, isolated, impoverished villages. About three-and-half-hours out, at Shahpasand, the bus turns off the main highway onto a secondary road to Gonbad. The road we were on was bad, but this is worse. Far off to the north, across the broad, flat desert, a rocket appears to be poised for takeoff.

"What is that, Shaban Ali?"

"That is Gonbad-e Kavus. It is the tower of Gonbad. It is very old. We will be in Gonbad in another half hour. You will like it."

The tower looms larger and larger as we approach the city. Shaban Ali sees I am mesmerized. He smiles approvingly.

As we exit the bus, I almost stumble as I stare at the tower. Its singular power is unimaginable.

"Do you have Barkley's address?" Shaban Ali asks.

"No, but we can find him. We'll tell the taxi driver to take us to the American's house."

He hails a cab; however, instead of finding Barkley, we are delivered to the house of Swedes who are working in the Gonbad area. They know where Barkley lives, and give the driver directions. Barkley is staying with the family of his development director, whom I had met in Sari. Shaban Ali stays awhile before he goes off to be with a colleague he met at a community development conference.

"Come, I want to show you Gonbad," Barkley tells me.

The tower of Gonbad-e Kavus is indeed the focal point of the city—where the townspeople go for an evening stroll—the place to be seen. The mound that serves as the tower's platform is about 35 feet high, well above the highest roofs of Gonbad. The stark brick tower extends in solemn majesty another 167 feet into the sky. I am in awe to be in the presence of such unparalleled and commanding grandeur.

"It is the tomb of Kavus-ibn Vashmgir," one of Barkley's friends tells us. "He ruled this area in the late 10th and early 11th centuries. He was an exceptional man, a scholar, poet, calligrapher, astrologer, linguist, and valiant warrior. But he was excessively suspicious of others and, in the end, his exasperated followers assassinated him. The inscriptions at the top and near the base declare 'Kavus built the tower in 1006.' Would you like to see inside?"

"*Baleh*, I would like to very much."

He tells a boy to run and get the key.

The inside is even bleaker than the simple flanged exterior. A pit drops 35 feet to the natural ground level directly at the door. A circular shaft ascends to the darkened dome, lit by a solitary window in the conical exterior roof.

"The window caught the rays of the rising sun and illuminated the suspended glass coffin that held the body of Kavus. No one knows what happened to the coffin or Kavus' body."

I am humbled before such history. In my studies at the university, and for all the art I have seen in museums, I never had the feeling of actually standing on the ground men of history stood upon. It is as if some of their being has entered my very soul.

Young and old in Gonbad know Barkley already, much like me in Gorgan. His Farsi is halting, but spoken with blind confidence, and with a strong Southern drawl. Most often English and Farsi are generously sprinkled together. I am amazed anyone understands. Barkley truly is a force all his own. Nothing, not even language, daunts him.

Besides his community development work, Barkley too is teaching English. I smile when I hear his students speak English with a Kentucky twang. He gives particular attention to the baby of one of his students. Barkley digs in his pocket for a coin and holds it in front of the child while he waves a book with his other hand. The child reaches for the larger of the two. Barkley says, "See, your son is going to be a scholar. Someday he will be a distinguished man of Iran." The father smiles proudly.

Barkley's fervor is never-ending. At dinner, and for hours into the night, he entertains me with his stories of the places he has been and the things he has done. It's a relief for me, and possibly for him, to be conversing in a language we grew up with. He is surprised to hear I am living in a village. He didn't even know I had been assigned to Gorgan. He resolves to visit me in Alang this coming weekend. I suspect he wants to see what my situation is like.

SUNDAY, NOVEMBER 8, 1964 As I crawl through the gateway door with my bucket of water, my landlord's wife points to the ducks and says, *"Bilbil-i."* I'm confused. I am positive the word for duck is *ordak*.

I point and say, *"Ordak."*

"Na, bilbil-i."

I shrug, have no idea what she is babbling about, and proceed up to my room.

When Shaban Ali arrives I ask him, "Is *ordak* the word for things that go 'quack, quack, quack'?"

He smiles. *"Baleh."*

"Then what is *bilbil-i?* My landlady called them *bilbil-i* this morning. I insisted they were *ordak*. She said, *'Na, bilbil-i.'"*

He smiles more broadly. *"Bilbil-i* is Alangi, the village dialect. Only we call *ordak bilbil-i*. You are learning Alangi too."

MONDAY, NOVEMBER 9, 1964 "Ghalayesh is a very poor village about four kilometers from Alang, out on the barren plain that stretches toward the Soviet Union," Shaban Ali tells me. "Very few of the people speak Farsi. They are from the region of Zabol in eastern Iran, near the border with

Afghanistan. It is imperative you don't eat anything there. It is too dirty. I don't ever eat there. Sometimes I drink tea if I am confident the water is boiled well and the tea glasses are cleaned with hot water.

"A Literacy Corpsman has recently come to Ghalayesh. He is a very amiable guy, but it must be very difficult for him to live in such poverty. He is teaching the children, and the village will be building a school. I am also working with him to find ways of helping the villagers value making their environment cleaner and more sanitary. It is a very big job."

"Thank you for warning me about Ghalayesh. I will watch what you do and then do the same."

Ghalayesh truly is a shock. Shaban Ali's cautionary warning in no way prepares me for what we meet. Most homes are little more than crumbling mud brick walls that support roofs of metal sheets held in place with rocks or old tires. There are no trees. Naked children play in a large stagnant pool of gooey water. Flies crawl over their bodies, especially around their eyes, noses, and mouths. Outhouses empty into the pool.

The Literacy Corpsman greets us warmly, astounded an American is visiting Ghalayesh, and apologizes for the village. He is motivated by the progress he is making in educating the children, and the interest of the village leaders in building a school. As we walk to the headman's house, Shaban Ali discusses issues of education related to sanitation, and the corpsman concurs he has a lot of work to do in this area.

Though the yard surrounding the headman's house is unsightly, inside the humble abode is clean. Felt mats cover the floor and embroidered curtains hang at the windows and over the doorway. The village men are intrigued to meet me, but they seem indifferent to the presence of an American in their village. They have much more important matters to deal with. They are happy their village was assigned a Literacy Corpsman, and show concern that he has to live so far from his family and the comforts of the big cities. They are looking forward to the construction of the school.

Shaban Ali advises the village leaders not to let the children play in the dirty water at the entrance to Ghalayesh, and that the outhouses should be over covered pits. I am impressed how he worked that in. Small steps toward a big problem, I conclude.

Our discussions prior to village council meetings about how to approach the business at hand help me comprehend what is transpiring, and Shaban Ali makes recommendations to the villagers regarding what we talked about. The ideas come from him rather than me—an outsider telling them what to do. In reality, it's his analysis of the situation; he understands the culture and how things are done far better than I do.

"Can we offer you tea?"

"Thank you, but we have to be leaving. It is a long way to Alang. It will be dark before we get there and Mister Tom isn't familiar with the pathway." I sense Shaban Ali schedules his work in Ghalayesh so he can politely say he has to get home before dark.

The Literacy Corpsman departs with us. I express my pleasure at meeting him, and give him encouragement. I cannot get him out of my mind as we pedal back to Alang. The two Literacy Corpsmen I will be working with are definitely top-of-the-line. Not like the ones I met in Gorgan, who troll the streets yearning for some extracurricular night-time activities.

TUESDAY, NOVEMBER 10, 1964   We go to Gorgan to get the furniture—desk, cupboard, and chest of drawers—I had made. Shaban Ali has the carpenter transport each piece to the bus station for Alang.

I stand there breathlessly anticipating catastrophe as a *kargar* (laborer) straps a huge furnishing to his back and ascends the makeshift ladder at the rear of the bus. *He made it! It's unbelievable how strong and adept these people are.* He has no trouble with the other two pieces.

It is dark as Hajireza wends his way along the rutted road to Alang. I have been given the exalted wooden stool beside him, and he engages in an ongoing conversation with "Mister Tom," barely paying attention to the road ahead. Scared, I carefully peer into the blackness for him, praying we will actually make it to Alang. Curiously, Hajireza doesn't use headlights, nor do the drivers of other vehicles. When two drivers meet, they flash their lights. In a state of fright, I think this is a very weird and dangerous custom.

In Alang, each piece of furniture is pulled from the top of the bus over the railing of the balcony. They nearly fill my tiny room, but the cupboard and chest of drawers will be in my kitchen when it is completed.

WE ENJOY AN EVENING of good food and the informality of each other's company, talking and joking around at the home of Reza's older brother Javad, who has invited cohorts from the Sherkat-e Sargardon to dinner. His family lives in a wattle and daub cottage in the Abtahi compound. His little son Abdullah is delighted his *Amo* Tom has come. He competes with his cousin Rozy for my attention. Most often both are in my lap chattering away to me, each pulling my face in his or her direction as they vie for my devotion. Predictably, as the evening wears on, I get very tired.

Reza says, "Tom, *chashmeh shoma mesle koone merg khoorus memoneh."*

Everybody looks at me and laughs.

I'm clueless, squinch my eyebrows, and shake my head slightly back and forth in the Persian manner of questioning. They laugh even more. They love it when I don't understand their jokes, particularly when they are at my expense.

Finally Reza explains, "Your eyes look like a rooster's ass."

I turn red and laugh too. Being a farm boy I know exactly what they look like.

WEDNESDAY, NOVEMBER 11, 1964 Each time I go to goof off with the "Do Nothing" guys at the Sherkat-e Sargardon, everyone shakes my hand, even if I saw him the day before or earlier that day. It is the Iranian way; men shake hands as part of the greeting. Often someone doesn't let go of my hand. I try to pull away. Not wanting to be rude I let my hand hang there limply. Uneasy, I try to free myself. He only pulls me closer. Deliberately I back up to get my space right. He moves closer. I pull my head back stiffly and retreat some more; I don't want to appear discourteous. Suddenly I hit the wall. *Gosh, this is uncomfortable.* I am learning Iranian personal space is very different from American cultural space, but it's hell getting used to it.

THURSDAY, NOVEMBER 12, 1964 Today marks four weeks in Alang, I recollect when I wake up. *What have I accomplished? I'm busy all the time, yet what is the point of this? Also, I'm barely settled in. I still have broken windows, my kitchen shows no signs of ever being finished, and with all this furniture, there's hardly any room to move around.*

I lock up and inform Shaban Ali and my cronies at the Sherkat-e Sargardon I'm setting off for Gorgan to meet Barkley, who is due in from Gonbad-e Kavus about noon. "We'll see you later today," I tell them.

They wish me *khodahafez*.

Surprisingly, I am able to walk unaccompanied out of Alang. The sounds of children reciting their lessons issue over the school wall as I pass. Farther on, I am greeted by a little boy tending flocks of turkeys and geese. Farmers nod and stop to ask where I am going as I trek the narrow path to the main highway. The sun has already burned off the morning clouds illuminating the barren mountaintops. Its warmth is comforting on this glorious mid-November day.

As I wait beside the highway for a passing bus, an old woman, bent with a load of sticks on her back, stops to inquire where I'm going. She has come from the mountain forests with her daily load of firewood for cooking and baking bread. From my room I have seen her and other old women as they pass with their precious cargo each day. She wishes me well and forges on to Alang.

A brightly colored local bus filled with passengers stops.

"Koja" (Where)?

"Gorgan."

"Beah bala" (Come aboard).

I climb in. A peasant is told to give up his seat for me. I insist I can stand—even though my head hits the top if I stand straight. It is no use; everyone is resolute. I take the empty seat.

We disgorge passengers and pick up more. About halfway to Gorgan, most of the bus empties out at Roshanabad, the shrine of two holy men who are buried in the weathered, tile-domed tomb beside the road. Those still on the bus are ordered to get off. An argument between the driver and several passengers ensues. Half my fare is refunded. *What's happening?* The bus loads up people who fulfilled their pilgrimage and heads back in the direction we came. A few of us sit beside the road, waiting for another bus to Gorgan. In due time, one arrives. It makes few stops, and soon we're in the city. *Wow, what freedom to be in Gorgan alone!*

I stop at the teahouse to see my friends.

"How's Alang?"

"Alang is good."

"Alang is good? Gorgan is better."

"*Baleh*, Gorgan is better, but Alang is very good." I don't want to imply I don't like Gorgan, but certainly I'm not going to be critical of Alang. They question me about life in the village, and still are skeptical over my decision.

As I saunter up the street, I greet the owner of the Hotel Chahar Fasl and shopkeepers along the way. I gaze in the glittering windows of the tiny jewelry shops ablaze with gold bracelets, necklaces, and earrings. It is the objects on the lowest shelves that attract me—antique silver Turkoman jewelry inlaid with carnelian. Some of the jewelers ask, "Can I help you?" Convinced everything is very expensive, I reply, "I'm just looking."

BARKLEY WAVES as the bus from Gonbad-e Kavus pulls into the station. We take a taxi to Jack and Dave's, and I suggest we go to lunch at the usual place in Gorgan—the Hotel Miami. We spend a portion of the day together swapping Peace Corps stories, but Barkley's top all of ours put together. The guys are amazed by Barkley too.

"Barkley, it's time we get to Alang. I want you to see it before dark. We won't have a lot of time tomorrow before you return to Gonbad." He could have rattled on the entire afternoon and far into the night if we let him.

On the way to the bus station, many greet us, and I introduce Barkley from Gonbad-e Kavus. Most are surprised the Peace Corps is in Gonbad too. They know Gonbad-e Kavus does not have the amenities of Gorgan.

We board the first bus heading west. The *kadkhodah* (headman) from Alang is on the bus too. He is happy to meet Barkley, and insists we come to dinner this evening.

It's always pleasant walking the path above the fields from the road to Alang, particularly as the sun lengthens the shadows of the poplar trees that line the parcels of the farmers' tracts.

Friends from the Sherkat-e Sargardon are out for their evening stroll, so they meet Barkley before we reach my room. We all head to Reza's house for tea. I am embarrassed to explain to over-achieving Barkley that Sherkat-e Sargardon means "Do Nothing Company." My friends tell

Barkley, "Reza is the *rais-e* (head of) Sherkat-e Sargardon and Tom is the *moallem-e* (teacher for) Sherkat-e Sargardon."

At least I have a job and title, I rationalize, *dubious as they may be.*

"Hello, *Meesteer, salaam,*" village children greet us along the path. They are excited to see two Americans in Alang.

"Salaam," Barkley and I respond. One of the little boys smiles shyly. He has a special bond with me. He realizes he is different from the other dark-haired, dark-eyed children in the village; his blond hair and blue eyes were, until my arrival, unique in Alang.

Reza smiles and, as he looks at the boy, struggles to say in English, "Tom was in Alang about five years ago." His eyes sparkle devilishly. I blush and don't know what to say in front of my Kentucky Baptist friend.

Barkley observes the boisterous informality of my friends as they joke around. "It's evident they've already accepted you as part of the village. You're one of them. They're comfortable with you," he says to me.

After dark, a messenger from the headman's house comes to get us, Reza, Shaban Ali, and others. The jovial disposition of the headman makes conversation easy. Barkley entertains us with stories of growing up in Kentucky. Together we figure out ways of telling his tales.

We rush to my little room when the lights blink. Quickly we spread the bedroll and blanket Mulla lent me for Barkley on the floor and I light the kerosene lamp before the electricity goes off.

Barkley wants to know more about the people in Alang. I recount the day of my arrival, my reception, and that they consider me a good omen. I had not told Barkley this in Gonbad, as I was more interested in hearing his stories. Besides, when Barkley is wound up, there's no way to stop him.

"Have you informed the Peace Corps about being in a village?"

"Yes, I told them."

"What did they say?"

"I haven't heard from them."

"Did you tell them about the reception you received?"

"No."

He seems somewhat disgusted with me. "You must write to them about the day you arrived and that to the villagers you're a good omen."

I promise him I'll do it, even though it's out-of-character for me. I also tell him that, while I like it very much in Alang and the people are wonderful, it is very difficult to have no privacy or time for myself.

"Today is the first day I've been able to go anywhere unescorted. I have no time to read and I'm hardly able to write letters home. I haven't even been able to spend time with Jack and Dave since I left Gorgan four weeks ago. It was so good to be with you last weekend, and it's great you came today. I need to be able to speak English once in a while and discuss issues that go beyond my capabilities in Farsi.

"As much as I like it here, I'm also distressed that I won't achieve anything significant—those three big projects the Peace Corps requires—in the two years we're here. Shaban Ali is very capable of doing the community development work himself. In fact, sometimes I feel I'm an extra responsibility for him. I suggested I live in a village, as I could see I would be sitting in the office and following Mr. Vahdati around for two years. I thought I might have more of an impact in the village. Now I'm not sure if that was the right decision."

"Certainly you're having an impact on the people in Alang. Remember, building bridges between people is one of Kennedy's goals for the Peace Corps. Don't forget, in training we were told it might be hard to measure our successes in community development."

SUNDAY, NOVEMBER 15, 1964 Musicians lead the procession of a bride and her retinue up the main street to the bathhouse. Women bear large trays of soaps, oils, and perfumes on their heads. Singing and chanting continue outside as the bathing ceremony takes place inside.

"The bride is thoroughly cleaned, massaged, and scrubbed. Then she is rubbed with oils and perfumes so she is enticing to the groom. It is also essential her virtue be confirmed," I am told.

At dinner, as usual, I am the center of attention, and given the place of honor next to the bridegroom. In fact, we have been celebrating for four days already—lunches, dinners. When men of unequal rank and age are together, we silently sit around the edge of the room, drink tea, and nibble on sunflower seeds and cookies. I exhaust myself trying to keep conversation going, only to be relieved when trays overflowing with plates of rice and stews and kebabs are brought in.

Tonight, the men solemnly stand around shivering in the late-night cold in the courtyard of the girl's home while the women revel inside. Sounds of music, singing, and laughter emerge. They appear to be having far more fun than the men. About 11:00, some of us depart. I'm cold and exhausted and happy to crawl into bed.

Nearly drowned out by the noise of the generator (the electricity is on late because of the wedding), I hear pounding on the gate below my room.

"Mister Tom! Mister Tom!"

I pull the curtains aside, open the window, and peer down into the subdued blackness. *"Baleh?"*

"Mister Tom, *beah*." Someone insists I come, but I don't understand why.

Reluctantly I dress, climb down the stairs, and open the small doorway in the gate.

"Beah, beah." I follow him along the lonely, nearly dark street to the bridegroom's house.

I am one of the privileged few to attend a ceremony at which the groom's hands are washed with henna. When finished, his hands and fingernails are a dull red color. They will stay that way for several weeks, the color on his hands fading away slowly. His nails will be red until they grow out.

When I ask about the significance of this or of other ceremonies, they simply say, "That's the way it is done." Then I think, *Why do the bride and groom feed each other cake at our weddings, or why do we tie old shoes and cans on the back of the cars of newlyweds?* The meaning is lost in the tradition.

MONDAY, NOVEMBER 16, 1964 As I open the curtains overlooking the main street, the groom and his friends pass by on their way to the bathhouse for his prenuptial bath. There is no singing, no dancing, and no ceremony in the square as there was for the girl the day before.

Lunch at the groom's house is the customary long-drawn-out affair. Afterwards, the men gather in the courtyard for a wrestling match in the groom's honor. Again I am accorded the distinction of sitting next to him and, embarrassingly, garner more attention than he.

Wrestling match, Alang

Later, while the groom waits at home, we assemble at the bride's house and wait for her to emerge. Musicians play a flute, *tonbak* (drum), and an old *kamancheh* (a three-string instrument held vertically and played with a bow). Children dance as men snap their fingers and clap to the rhythm of the music. Excitement erupts as the bride appears at the doorway of her father's house, her face covered with a veil. One of the bridesmaids holds a mirror before her as she descends the steps and proceeds across the courtyard. The women ululate an eerie, high-pitched quivering sound. The bride ascends into a waiting jeep at the courtyard gateway. The crowd follows as the jeep takes her to the groom's family home.

"In the old days, the bride would have ridden on a horse," someone tells me, "but today it is more prestigious to go in a jeep."

Shyly the groom meets her at his courtyard gateway. She is still veiled. The bride's attendant carries the wedding mirror before them as they process to the house amid the noisy fervor of the exuberant crowd. The attendant enters their room and, I am told, before she leaves, she places the mirror prominently in the center of the *Sofreh-e Aghd* (wedding cloth) decorated with lighted candles, flowers, sweets, bread, grain seeds, colored eggs, pomegranates, coins, the Quran, and incense. All have symbolic significance for a happy and fruitful marriage. When the attendant leaves, the bride and groom will sit before the spread. She will remove her veil and, in the mirror, they will have their first intimate glimpse of each other.

Abruptly the celebration outside ends, and we all go home.

At sunset friends call, "Tom, *beah*. Come to the mosque with us." There, the *mullahs* and village leaders break a large sugar cone and send half of it to the newly married couple.

"What is the meaning of this ceremony?" I ask.

With difficulty they try to explain. I presume it is to sweeten the marriage.

WEDNESDAY, NOVEMBER 18, 1964 *Will I survive?* My Farsi has reached a point at which not much gets past me, but by the end of the day I'm exhausted from operating in a language that remains foreign—that I continually have to decipher.

Also, Iranian customs are baffling. Men can sit around the edge of the room for hours at a party and stare blankly at the floor. To me this is unnatural and unfathomable, so I struggle to keep a conversation going.

And, I'm annoyed being the center of attention. I'm unaccustomed to and frustrated by the constant adulation accorded me. I can't stop to talk to anyone on the street without having a crowd assemble around me. I have no time for myself. Someone is always with me—from sunup till the lights go out. I don't even get time to write a letter or read when everyone else naps because someone comes to see me. When the villagers learned I did not take a nap each day, they assigned a different person to keep me company, for it is a cultural aberration to be alone. Someone makes the supreme sacrifice of foregoing his nap to entertain me! They mean well, but I need my own space.

THURSDAY, NOVEMBER 19, 1964 I decide to escape, pack my Pan Am bag, walk to the dusty highway, and catch a bus to Gorgan. It's a pleasure to wander the streets, discover new things, and see friends on my way to Mr. Vahdati's office.

"How is Alang? Do you feel more settled in?"

"*Baleh*, I'm always busy. Shaban Ali and I have been going to village council meetings, and I have my English classes. There was a wedding this week, and another one has begun—endless parties. The Peace Corps has given us four days off for Thanksgiving. I plan to go to Tehran with the Peace Corps Volunteers from Gorgan. I will be stopping by the Peace Corps office to discuss a poultry project they've informed us about.

"Oh, and the Peace Corps has approved my getting a bicycle. So far I've borrowed a bike from somebody in the village. If Shaban Ali will be getting a motor scooter through your office, I will advise the Peace Corps I require a scooter too."

"Shaban Ali won't be getting a scooter. It is best you get the bicycle."

I don't let on I am disappointed, nor do I tell him I'm going crazy from all the attention in Alang. Most of all, I don't want to hurt the villagers. They are doing what they feel is proper. It is their culture, and I have to get used to it. So, I rationalize that the problem is mine, not theirs. I have to be patient and accepting and . . . let things happen as they will.

JACK AND DAVE SMILE when I show up at their door. "I see you brought your bag. You're going to stay the night," Dave says casually.

"If you guys will have me. I need to get away from Farsi. I just need to have a more intelligible conversation for a change."

"We've been wondering when you were going to come. You've been in Alang quite a while now."

"Five weeks today. I'm being driven round the bend. No privacy. No time to myself. Oh, I know it's all my fault; I wanted to live in a village. And no matter where I am, if someone approaches me, I always talk with him. I never turn down an invitation, and in Alang they are never-ending. They sincerely want me to be with them. They mean well; and as a Peace Corps Volunteer, I need to make myself available. I love it; at the same time I hate it. Still, I love it more. It's just that I really do covet some time for myself."

"How about a game of Scrabble? Jack's board arrived, and we've been playing it in the evenings, but it will be more of a challenge with three."

Jack is the consummate deliberator, determined to find the perfect word and garner the most points. Dave reads, while I write letters between plays.

"What's that whistle?" I ask.

"That's the neighborhood police patrol. They make rounds every hour during the night and blow the whistle to let other officers know all is well."

"Wow. They're probably keeping track of you. Loose Americans, you know. You guys must have a file a foot thick at the SAVAK office already."

"Yeah, and they're starting one on you now," Jack snorts as he ponders his next word.

One game leads to another, another, and another. Exhausted, at 4am we give up and turn in for the night.

FRIDAY, NOVEMBER 20, 1964 We wake up late, play another game, and have lunch before I head back to Alang.

"Can't you stay another night and go back tomorrow morning?"

"No, I have to get back to the village. Besides, I'll see you Wednesday so we can catch the bus to Tehran early Thursday morning. I'm looking forward to getting away to the big city. Shaban Ali wanted to come with me. I told him I had business at the Peace Corps office, that we were having a Peace Corps conference. For my own sanity I need to get away for a few days. So I suggested that another time we will go to Tehran together."

It's a long wait at the station before one of the derelict buses lurches off for the villages to the west, allowing plenty of time for beggars to make their customary rounds. "Today is Friday, the holy day, the best day to give alms to the poor," they beseech. They even give change after they ascertain their due. The "onion lady" particularly fascinates me. Wizened and frail, she says nothing. She grasps the stem of a large brown onion and looks at me sorrowfully as she holds out her other hand for my compassion.

I wend my way down the pathway to Alang. The sounds of children playing soccer with a worn-out ball emerge from the schoolyard. Men are out for their *gardesh* (walk), enjoying the pleasant warmth of the setting sun before the evening chill sets in.

Friends greet me. "Where were you? We missed you at the wedding dinner. Be sure to come tonight."

"I went to Gorgan to see Mister Jack and Mister Dave. Sorry I wasn't here last night. I'll be there this evening."

TODAY TEA IS AT THE HOUSE of the teachers Ismael Mirsalehi and Yavar Khanpoor. Their wives and children greet me courteously. They have heard a lot about me from their husbands and fathers. The families share with the woman teacher in Alang three second-story rooms of a building on the other side of the village from where I live, each family to a room. A small, open area serves as their communal kitchen. They share duties of cooking and cleaning up. The women, enduring life in a village, enjoy each other's company and support.

Mrs. Housaini, who teaches the girls, wants to take my class, but she must return to her home because her child is an infant and not well. Her husband is in the army. I have met him in the village a number of times. She asks if I will teach her and Mr. Mirsalehi and Mr. Khanpoor English at least three nights a week.

"Our families have dinner together every evening and you can join us. We will take time to speak English." Ismael and Yavar agree this will allow them to advance with the language too. They are enthusiastic.

"Will you show us how to do the Twist?" Yavar asks.

"Yes, will you do it?" everybody insists.

"Oh, no, I can't do it."

"Please." Yavar puts a record on a small phonograph. It is Persian music. "Come on, do the Twist." They start clapping their hands and rocking their heads and shoulders to the sound of the music. "Come on, do the Twist."

Bashfully, I get up and twist to the tinny sounds issuing from the little box on the floor. The children love the excitement, and join in the fun. Yavar, too, gets up and mimics the movements. Everyone laughs and claps as the record stops.

"In Hawaii I'm called Mister Twister," I awkwardly admit. "Get a stick and put on another record. I'll show you how to do the Limbo."

"What's the Limbo?"

"Just wait. I'll show you."

Yavar runs out and comes back with a stick.

"No, that's not long enough. It needs to be about this long," I say, gesturing. He returns with another stick.

"OK, Yavar and Ismael, hold the stick up about this high." I indicate a height of about three feet. "Now put on the record."

I slink under the stick and they cheer and clap. "Lower," I tell them.

They hold the stick about six inches lower and I easily pass under it.

"Lower!" everyone calls out.

Again I shimmy under it, my back and head almost scraping the floor. They love it and shout, "Lower."

"No. I can't go lower!"

Now the children delight in trying it.

"Show me some Persian dances," I urge them.

They start the record again. Yavar and the children begin to dance. With reservation, Ismael joins them. We all clap our hands and laugh. We are having so much fun I hate to go to the wedding celebration.

As Ismael, Yavar, and I walk the dimly lit streets to the bridegroom's house, I reflect on what a different experience that was—not like the Alang I have come to know. Women—Mrs. Housaini and the men's wives—were in the room with us, not just briefly slipping in covered by their *chadors* and waiting on us. They weren't even wearing *chadors*. This will be fun, spending a few evenings a week with them.

SATURDAY, NOVEMBER 21, 1964 Don Croll, the regional Peace Corps supervisor, arrives with my airfreight, a locker of 250 books, and a tool chest. The warmer clothes are appreciated, as snow already caps the tops of the mountains behind Alang. I snigger derisively as I hold up the precious rolls of toilet paper inside. He grins and perceives I've already adapted.

He seems to approve of my living in a village, but is concerned that my kitchen has not been completed and that I have the stove and tanks of gas in the same room where I sleep.

"Also, be sure you turn off the Aladdin heater before you go to bed, and don't turn it on in the middle of the night and then fall off to sleep. I don't want you suffocating from lack of oxygen in this little room. A volunteer in another country died from asphyxiation from a heater like this."

SUNDAY, NOVEMBER 22, 1964 *Gosh, it was cold,* I say to myself as I wake up. *And these broken windows don't make it any warmer, with the wind blowing right through.* I've been in this place four weeks, and no attempt has been made to fix the windows, let alone get my kitchen done.

My landlord's wife is washing dishes in the courtyard when I grab the *aftabeh* to head for the *mostarah*. We exchange greetings. I decide this is the time to remind her about getting the windows fixed. Her voice turns loud and shrill. I can't decipher what she says as she is speaking Gilaki interspersed with a generous mixture of Alangi. Her tone and gestures imply she is making excuses and wants to put off fixing the windows even longer.

In exasperation I say, "If they're not fixed by tomorrow, I'm going to Kordkuy to get them fixed." I turn and don't look back as she jabbers on.

MONDAY, NOVEMBER 23, 1964 My broken windows are replaced first thing in the morning. *"Wow. That little tantrum yesterday had an effect.*

The recent cold makes me thankful my airfreight arrived and I now have the warm army jacket my Uncle Hugh gave me. However, I conclude it was a bad choice—too much association with the US Army and not the image I want to convey as a Peace Corps Volunteer.

"Tom, so you *are* part of the United States Army," my friends say when they see me in it.

"No, this is my uncle's old jacket," I respond, wishing I had shopped around for a more appropriate winter coat before I left Hawaii.

TUESDAY, NOVEMBER 24, 1964 *An evening to myself,* I enthusiastically contemplate as I finish washing dishes. My fantasy is short-lived, however. I hear a knock on the door. It is Gholam Husayn from downstairs. His wife does my laundry. I am pleased to see him, to have the opportunity to talk with a real *kargar* (laborer), to find out about his life and his aspirations. In fact, I am honored he feels comfortable to visit me on his own.

My Farsi still requires intense listening, thinking, and translating, and his Farsi is peppered with abundant portions of Gilaki and Dehati (village dialect). Over tea and cookies, slowly we converse. I learn about the importance he places on the education of his three little boys, Musa, Isa, and Ruholla, and his dreams for their future.

When he leaves, I tell him, "Come back often. My Farsi will become better, and it will be easier to talk." He smiles. I know he will.

The next morning, as I shave on the balcony, I see the boys playing in the basin their mother uses for laundry. I grab my camera, run down the stairs, call the boys' names, and snap their picture. *Perfect.*

"No," their mother scolds. "They are dirty and they are wearing old clothes. It is not good. You should take their picture when they are nicely dressed."

"I am sorry. This is the way I want to remember them—playing in the tub."

Isa, Ruholla, and Musa

ENCOUNTERS AND CIRCUMSTANCES

THURSDAY, NOVEMBER 26, 1964 Jack, Dave, and I board the big comfortable TBT bus in Gorgan at 8am bound for Tehran. "There's Alang, down this road in the grove of trees," I point out to Jack and Dave as we pass. At Sari we stop for lunch—two choices, kebab and rice or *khoresht* (stew) and rice. Everyone ingests the food as if the bus is taking off in minutes. We do the same and await our chance to use the *mostarah*, disgusting as it is.

Two hours on, at Amol, the bus turns south towards the mountains. The road is paved but is no more than a narrow two-lane path full of potholes that, at first, ascends beside a river. The lush green forests and fields of the Caspian littoral give way to wild and barren slopes that reveal the force of ancient seismic upheavals and recent landslides that in places divert the course of the river. Villages nestle dramatically beneath overhanging cliffs. Minuscule green terraces cling to the canyon walls and evince man's struggle to survive in this harsh environment. A cascade of water falls between towering clefts and forms a thin silver sliver that tumbles hundreds of feet and disappears behind a village at its base. The manifest greatness of nature overwhelms us.

The driver hugs the middle of the road, lays on the horn as we approach blind corners, and quickly swerves out of the way, horn still tooting, when another vehicle sails past. In some spots boulders nearly block passage. We peer over the edge of the precipice and soberly ponder the rusting and forgotten carcasses of buses and cars far below on the valley floor.

As we climb higher and higher, snow blankets the peaks and valleys surrounding us. The sleek blue-and-chrome bus strains to gain altitude on the treacherous snow-packed road. At dusk we momentarily stop at a wayside stand.

"Jack and Dave, I have to touch the snow." They grin and probably think, *This silly Hawaiian.*

When I open the door, the blast of cold hits me. I jump down, grab a handful of snow, drop it, and look up. There, in hushed majesty, looms Mt. Damavand, the rays of the setting sun reflecting off its snow-draped summit, a perfect and symmetrical cone over 18,500 feet high.

Mt. Damavand

The lights of Tehran sparkle below us as we descend into the city and encounter anew the insanity of its traffic. The supposed eight-hour trip takes twelve hours. What a way to spend Thanksgiving *and* my 24th birthday!

Jack knows an inexpensive hotel—a regular Peace Corps hangout not far from the Peace Corps office. He urges, "Let's go for a drink. It's Thanksgiving and Tom's birthday. We ought to celebrate."

Though I find bars depressing, I'm not going to be a party pooper tonight. Jack gives explicit instructions to Dave and me on how to act and what to do in the bar. "We can only afford one drink each—one each day we're here. That's all our budget will allow. When the bar girl comes to our table, let me do the talking. I'll tell her she can join us, but we aren't buying any drinks for her. There's nothing in them anyway, and you're paying for the most expensive drink in the house."

We order martinis. When the girl brings the drinks, Jack plays hard-nosed and tells her, "You can join us, but we're not buying any drinks for you."

I'm mortified by his bluntness. The girl sits at the small round table between Jack and me. He and Dave start up a conversation with her. I remain silent, uncomfortable she doesn't have a drink too. A leg touches mine. Abruptly and instinctively, I retract. Then the leg finds mine again. This time I hold steadfast. The hair on my back begins to tingle. I am aroused. Nevertheless, I'm too embarrassed to talk with her. She gets up. As she slinks away, she invitingly rubs her hand across my back. I flush, but try to act as if nothing fazes me.

Dave says with a smile, "She likes you."

"Yeah, she sure does, but she thinks *I'm* a hard ass," Jack retorts.

"I wonder why she thinks you're that? Humph," I say smiling.

FRIDAY, NOVEMBER 27, 1964 The Peace Corps office bustles with volunteers in Tehran for the holiday. I talk to Peace Corps officials about the poultry scheme they are promoting. This would entail introducing healthy American chickens. Not a bad idea, since chicken is a staple of the Iranian diet, and those that reach the pot are invariably scrawny.

"An expert will come out for about three days to set it up. First you need to find a farmer who wants to do it. That will involve locating a room or building a hut where we can install heaters to keep the chicks warm."

"I'll look into it and see if I can find a farmer in Alang or one of the other villages who's interested."

"Keep us informed. How do you like living in a village? We hear your Farsi is pretty fluent already."

"Oh, I like it in the village. I'm always busy, and now I'm more comfortable with the language." I don't mention there are days I'm going crazy from never having any time to myself.

After the meeting, I see many of the guys from my training group. I tell them I am considering setting up one of the chicken projects in my village.

"Be careful of that. The Peace Corps suckered me into it. I found a farmer who agreed to do it. We built a brooder, the chicks were brought in from Tehran, and all was going fine. But the farmer let the kerosene spill all over the heater and everything went up in smoke. We had roasted chicks long before their time. Besides that, the farmer was upset with me. He lost his building. It's lucky the whole village wasn't set on fire. I'm warning you. I've heard other guys have had troubles with this venture as well."

Someone suggests, "Let's go to the café at the American Embassy for lunch. They have great hamburgers there, just like being at home, and the beers are real American beer, not Iranian *abe jou.*"

We're already salivating. We jump in taxis and head to the Embassy on Takht-e Jamshid. Seeing the American flag gives me goose bumps but, inside the building, I feel strangely out of place—like being in a foreign country. *What's happened to me? I've been in Iran two months and I already feel out of place in America. Everyone is speaking English!* It's surreal to overhear and understand a casual conversation even in the restroom.

The other guys seem right at home, but I'm uneasy. We almost take over the entire café. The reunion is a rowdy, boisterous celebration that carries on the entire afternoon. Embassy employees and visitors glare disapprovingly in our direction, but nothing stops us.

"Let's meet here for lunch tomorrow," someone proposes as we are ushered out at closing time. Everybody approves.

SATURDAY, NOVEMBER 28, 1964 I can't bear another day at the Embassy. I roam the streets of Tehran on my own and spend hours in bookshops. There are so many books on Iranian history and art I want, but I don't have enough money. I buy one, Roman Ghirshman's *Persia: From the Origins to Alexander the Great*—450 pages, with magnificent photos and maps. It's all I can afford—twenty-five US dollars—one third of my monthly living allowance. There are three more books in the series, so I'll have to save to get them and all the other books I want.

It's snowing as I step out with my treasure—cold, but it's fun to see the tracks of footsteps in the fresh powder on the sidewalk. Large wet flakes cling to my eyelashes. My blond hair is stippled with a sprinkling of shining crystals. What a change from the hot, dust-covered city we experienced two months ago!

The youthful owner of an antique shop I visited those first days in Iran remembers me. He knows English, but I greet him in Farsi, *"Salaam allekum, hale shoma khoobeh?"*

He smiles. "You have learned Farsi well already."

*"Merci."** We continue in Farsi. "I'm living in a village in the north, near Gorgan. I like it very much, but I'm glad to be in Tehran for a few days."

"In a village!" He finds it inconceivable. "Isn't it difficult living in a village? Are you all alone?"

"Yes, but the villagers are very welcoming. They are my friends now."

I show him the book on Persian art I bought. He is impressed that I am so interested in his culture and art.

Among the unusual things in the shop, I find an old wooden textile stamp with carved floral designs. It will be perfect to print Christmas cards on the aerogrammes I'm going to send back home, I decide. *"Chand misheh"* (How much is this)?

"For you, fifteen tomans."

I have already priced stamps in other shops. They were at least forty tomans, and weren't as high quality as this one. *That's only two dollars. How can I bargain for that?* I give him the fifteen tomans. He wraps the stamp and I put it in my coat pocket.

"Come back whenever you are in Tehran."

"I will. I love to look at what you have in your shop."

It's now dark. I've had a wonderful day enjoying a world still mysteriously exotic to me. As I tread to the hotel, I look back often to see my tracks in the snow. There is something fascinatingly imaginative about fresh snow. Here, in a land far from all I know, I draw my presence upon a clean white slate. Someone adds to the drawing, or more snow falls, and tomorrow's sunshine will erase it entirely.

A taxi pulls up. An attractive woman gets out and the taxi takes off. She's well-dressed, not wearing a *chador*.

---

* Iranians commonly use the French *merci* for thank you.

"Hello," she greets me.

"Salaam," I respond.

"Mekhaid" (Do you want)? she asks, pointing to herself.

I'm startled and flustered. *"Na, nemekham"* (No, I don't want).

"Chera? Kheili khoobeh" (Why? It is very good).

"Baleh, vali khoob neest" (Yes, but it's not good).

As I hasten away I recall what I said to her, agreeing it is good, but not good. *That's a strange one,* she probably thinks.

Wow, she took me unawares. I wonder how much she charges? I wonder if you can bargain? I wonder what the going rates are? But where would we have gone? We couldn't go to the hotel. Jack and Dave might be there. At least she didn't flash me, as other PCVs have experienced. They have told me about walking down the street when suddenly a woman opens her *chador* to show everything. It's too cold this time of year for them to go around like that, I figure.

Jack and Dave laugh rakishly when I tell them about my encounter. "Why didn't you bring her here?" Jack asks, his eyes gleaming lecherously.

"I didn't think you'd approve, what with that two-year vow of celibacy you took." He gives me a dirty look.

"Gee, Tom, you have them all after you," Dave remarks.

"Yeah, and he doesn't do anything about it," Jack sneers with disdain.

SUNDAY, NOVEMBER 29, 1964 With all those tantalizing temptations and near-encounters, I resolve I need to go to Mass. When I see the *"chadoris"* in the front, I smile, calling to mind Nick and my first Mass in Iran.

I spend the day prowling the streets of Tehran and exploring antique shops with incredible things. I will have to save my money to get any of them. Persian miniatures in one shop particularly capture my attention.

"How much is this?"

"Eighty tomans."

That's about $10.50. It can't be authentic at that price. But, it's nice. I wonder how much I could get him down?

I say, "Too much."

"How much will you pay?"

"I don't want it." Applying the artistry I learned from Shaban Ali, I turn away.

"For you, I will give a special price, sixty tomans."

Wow, that was easy. I tell him, "No, it's still too much."

"How much do you want to give me?"

"I don't want it. I don't have much money."

"Tell me how much you want to give me."

Reluctantly I say, "Thirty tomans."

"No, too little. But you can have it for fifty tomans."

"No, I can't afford that." I turn to leave the shop.

He calls after me. "Give me forty tomans and it's yours." I oblige.

TUESDAY, DECEMBER 1, 1964 My heart quickens as I proceed down the path to the village. *Funny, I've missed this place—but when I'm here I can't wait to get away to have some time to myself.*

I throw my bag in my room and rush down to see my friends.

"Salaam allekum," I'm greeted warmly by the villagers, especially by my sidekicks at the Sherkat-e Sargardon, where the spirit of jest reigns supreme.

"Did you have a good time in Tehran? What was the weather like? What did you do?" The questions are relentless and, as always, become more personal. *"Koja rafti* (Where did you go)? Bazaar *rafti* (Did you go to the bazaar)? Shemiran *rafti* (Did you go to Shemiran)? Toopkhaneh *rafti"* (Did you go to Toopkhaneh)?

"Toopkhaneh?"

"Baleh, Toopkhaneh. *Rafti?"*

I'm puzzled and have forgotten there is a large square in Tehran called Meydan-e Toopkhaneh. *Toop means ball and khaneh means house,* I think to myself. They catch me breaking the word apart, so I understand it. *Ball house.* I turn red.

They all laugh. Reza makes a suggestive gesture. *"Baleh, rafti?"*

Embarrassed, I feel myself turning redder. *"Na,"* I say raising my eyebrows and head slightly and clicking my tongue in the typical Iranian negative manner.

They laugh harder. *"Dorugh megi. Hatman rafti* (You lie. Certainly you went). *Hatman* Shahr-e Nou *rafti."* And they all laugh more.

I know about Shahr-e Nou, the red-light district in Tehran. However, from that day on Toopkhaneh has a special coded meaning in Alang. They no longer ask if I went to Shahr-e Nou, just Toopkhaneh.

They pry deeper into every fantasized detail of my activities and my life. "Did you do it *ba lebas ya bi lebas"* (with or without clothes)?

That's a weird question, I think. Then it dawns on me they want to know if I did it with or without a condom.

Next, "Are you circumcised?" They have asked this many times before, but they are never satisfied with my affirmative answer. They have heard and are certain American men are uncut. In Iran, circumcision is an important celebration in a man's life, performed when a boy is six or seven, that signifies passage to manhood.

Still embarrassed, I describe my escapades with the bar girl and the street lady. They don't buy every bit of my stories, convinced I am cleansing them for their consumption, but I hear them agree the women in Tehran are brazen and come on to foreign men. I calculate they are envious.

"You need to take an Iranian wife. We'll help you find one, a very *khoshgel* (pretty) one."

I've heard this before, and they've done nothing about it. *Fat chance,* I think, *here in the village.*

"But, of course, you would have to become a Muslim and be circumcised."

The fun goes on and on at my expense. I wish I didn't blush so easily; it just incriminates me more and more. Yet I appreciate the acceptance the teasing implies.

To escape even deeper prying I invite the guys to my house for tea. They are captivated by the pictures in my new book on Persian art.

"How much did it cost?" Iranians like to assess the value of everything and determine if you got a bargain.

"One hundred and ninety tomans."

"One hundred and ninety tomans!" everyone exclaims. They are shocked any book would cost that much and I would pay it.

"That's what it would cost in America. It's a superb book, and I want to learn about the art and history of Iran. There are more books I want to buy, but I have to save my money before I can get them."

Shaban Ali clearly approves of my saving to buy books on Persian art and history. Nonetheless, all recognize the sincerity of my interest in learning about their culture.

"How much did you pay for this miniature?"

"He wanted eighty tomans, but I bargained and got him down to forty."

"Way too much. But it must be old. Look at the paper." They debate the merits of my purchase and whether I paid too much. "No, maybe he got it for a good price. He's an artist; he knows."

"And this textile stamp, how much did you pay for it?"

"Fifteen tomans."

"Fifteen tomans! What did he want at first? Did you bargain?"

"He wanted fifteen tomans. I paid him that. He is my friend. I was in his shop when I first came to Iran. Stamps not as finely carved were forty tomans in other shops."

"What are you going to do with it? It's only a piece of wood with some carving on it."

"I'm going to use it to print Christmas cards on the aerogramme letters I send home. Besides, I want to have things from Iran I can take back to America. I will enjoy them all my life. They will bring back wonderful memories of Iran."

THURSDAY, DECEMBER 3, 1964 Someone invites me to lunch. I decline without success. I think of the three little fishes my landlord's son Ghorbon brought me yesterday. I had not eaten them because Yavar and Ismael begged me to come to their house for dinner. I hope they will still be good this evening. However, after class, when I open the cupboard to make tea, their unpleasant odor is overpowering. Immediately I shove them into my blue plastic garbage container and push the cover on tightly. Again Yavar and Ismael insist I come to dinner.

Once home, I brush my teeth on the porch, turn out the solitary light hanging in the center of my room, and crawl into bed before the generator across the street silences. Immediately I perceive a strange and eerie radiance permeating my room. I look around and discover my garbage can resplendently aglow. Mystified, I hesitantly approach it and realize the fish have turned luminescent. Guardedly I place the container on the porch outside my door. *This is disconcerting. Now the light is out here. I hope no one sees it, especially my landlord.*

When I open my door to make my usual early morning trek to the essential facilities I find my garbage can toppled and the fish gone. *Obviously a cat spotted the glowing light and took care of it. I wonder if the cat glowed too for the rest of the night,* I contemplate as I gather the stray papers strewn about.

FRIDAY, DECEMBER 4, 1964 "Tom, a *pahlavon* is coming to Alang today," my pals tell me excitedly.

"A *pahlavon*? What is that?"

"A *pahlavon*." They show me their muscles. I get the idea—a strongman.

"Yes, it will be awesome! We want you to be the official photographer. Can you do it?"

"Of course. I'd be happy to."

Under the warming late-autumn sun, the men of Alang pay their few rials and file into a large courtyard. "No, Tom," they insist, "you don't pay. You are the official photographer."

This happens all the time. I'm always the guest. Nobody will let me pay for anything, and I am restricted from paying for my lunch, or reciprocating their hospitality, when I'm with them in Gorgan. Today I'm not sure if somebody paid for me or if being the "official photographer" made me exempt. However, no one will take my money.

The *pahlavon* is splendidly decked out—gray long-sleeved sweater, with a red, white, and green streamer across his bulging chest, studded leather wrist gauntlets, satiny pink pants, and tennis shoes.

The yard is prepared for the event. Benches for respected older men line the perimeter. Young men cluster behind; the children are in front. Beyond, women peer over the crumbling walls. A tree in a nearby yard offers grandstand viewing for fifteen gatecrashers. Two jeeps from Alang are on hand. The *pahlavon* struts his stuff and then lies on the ground at the end of a long, thick plank. One of the jeeps is driven along the length of the board, climbs the *pahlavon's* back and rests there. The crowd gasps and cheers. Next, he gets under a jeep and, with the sheer force of his legs, lifts the back end of the vehicle in the air. Following each feat of strength, he displays his powerful muscles, and the crowd duly acknowledges his prodigious might. I'm fascinated to witness a real wandering entertainer who goes from village to village to perform and earn his living—just like the Old West in America.

Pahlavon

He ends his repertoire with an extraordinary performance in which he braces himself between two reversing jeeps. I grit my teeth as he deftly holds the straining vehicles apart. Their wheels spin. Dirt flies, nearly obscuring the performance. They stop. He emerges from between them, bows, flaunts his strength, and the crowd wildly hails him.

MONDAY, DECEMBER 7, 1964 "Tom, you are carrying too much money with you," Shaban Ali tells me. "It might be dangerous if people see how much money you have."

"But it's the check I get from the Peace Corps each month. I don't cash it until I need more money. Then I have a lot until I spend it."

"*Baleh*, but it is too much, and it's not necessary to spend it all each month. Save it for when you go on a trip in Iran, or when you have enough you can buy a rug to take back to America. When we go to Gorgan we will open an account at the Bank-e Sadrat. Each month, you can put your money in the bank. They will give you a book that shows how much you have. Wherever you go in Iran, you can go to a Bank-e Sadrat and withdraw money and the new total will be written in your book. The book has your picture in it so only you can use it."

"Do they have Bank-e Sadrat everywhere in Iran?"

"Yes, everywhere. There is even one in Kordkuy."

"Wow, that's excellent. Thank you for telling me."

That evening I think, *Shaban Ali is like a big brother, constantly looking out for me. Sometimes he makes me so irritated because he won't let me do things myself—but I know he means well. This may be the same as my brother and me. We fought so much when we were growing up—I was the big brother and Alan felt I was always bossing him around. Maybe that's the way it is between brothers. Friends are different. We're more like equals; if we weren't, we wouldn't be friends, I suppose. Even so, my brother is more important to me than any of my friends. Shaban Ali is like that—my friend, but really my brother.*

TUESDAY, DECEMBER 8, 1964 A letter from the Peace Corps informs us that, because the intention of the Peace Corps is to have volunteers integrate with Iranians and into their culture, henceforth the café at the American Embassy will be off limits to Peace Corps Volunteers.

I smile. We obviously had too rowdy a time there on our Thanksgiving break. The snooty embassy people can't stand raucous, backwoods guys taking over the place. Oh, well, that doesn't bother me. I'd rather explore the city anyway.

WEDNESDAY, DECEMBER 9, 1964 Mr. Vahdati unexpectedly shows up in Alang to see how I am doing. He takes me aside and says in English, "Don't you have a razor?"

Immediately I get the drift, and stroke my nearly week-old beard. He wants me to set an example. Instead, I'm becoming Iranian. Not that that bothers me, but Mr. Vahdati is right. I should be a role model.

Smiling sheepishly, I respond, "I understand."

THURSDAY, DECEMBER 10, 1964 "Let's go for a walk. It's such a pleasant day," I suggest to Shaban Ali when he comes to my room.

"No. I want to finish recording the Farsi books the Peace Corps gave us so we can start a library in the village council room. A hundred books is a good beginning. We'll make a bookcase and people can check out the books. It will be a fine opportunity for the young people in Alang."

"OK, then I'll go by myself."

"No. Wait until I finish and we'll go together."

"Then it will be too late. It will be getting dark. It gets dark early this time of year. I'm going now. Close my door when you leave."

I sensed he didn't want to go anyway. Being on the edge of the village, I can slip out easily and not be noticed. *Finally, time alone.*

High, soft, light clouds barely conceal the warming sun, so comfortable to someone who is used to Hawaiian weather. The snows blanketing the mountaintops sparkle in the dazzling light. The path to the highway seems short in such splendor. I meander through the dry cotton fields toward the mountains and chance upon a trail.

"Salaam allekum," an old man greets me.

"Salaam, hale shoma khoobeh?"

We converse as we amble along together. I'm unsure if he realizes I am American. He must detect my Farsi is halting. He is using a dialect, so possibly he thinks I speak only Farsi.

"Is your bicycle nearby?"

"No, I don't have a bicycle. I like to walk. It's a beautiful day."

"Where do you live?"

"In Alang."

"In Alang! That's far away," he exclaims.

"Not too far."

"Why are you walking alone? Don't you have any friends in Alang?"

"Oh, I have friends in Alang, but I like walking by myself." His questions about my walking alone and whether I have friends give me much to ponder. Undeniably, there is something wrong about being alone in Iranian culture. That's why I can never have any time to myself or go anywhere without being accompanied. People who are alone must be viewed as abnormal.

My reappearance in Alang after sundown is met with much consternation. The villagers are wild, perturbed with me and with Shaban Ali for allowing me to go off on my own.

"Where were you? Where did you go? We have been worried. Shaban Ali is very negligent to let you go by yourself. Why didn't you tell us? We would have gone with you." The questions and scolding go on and on.

"I'm sorry. I had a nice walk. I didn't mean to upset you. I was OK."

"Don't ever do this again. It is bad. Do you understand? It is bad."

I feel like a child being reprimanded. I'm uncertain if they are worried about my safety walking unattended and the shame it would bring the village if something happened to me, or if it is truly so out of the ordinary for someone to be alone that they cannot conceive of it. Or are they concerned about how Alang is perceived by others who meet me, like the old man— that the people of Alang may be thought of as uncaring and unfriendly?

SUNDAY, DECEMBER 13, 1964 It's snowing and six inches of heavy, wet snow cover the city as Barkley and I catch a taxi to the bus station in Tehran for the day's journey west and then across the mountains to Rasht, where it's overcast, damp, and cold.

Our Peace Corps conference is rejuvenating. I learn I'm the only one in our group living in a village, and am also the exception—I haven't read any of the books in my book locker. Some have nearly finished the entire locker. They have nothing else to do. My communication skills in Farsi and Gilaki are better than most, though some are using their spare time to study Farsi. Barkley regales us with stories of his visit to Alang, my arrival there, and the work he is doing in Gonbad-e Kavus. The Peace Corps now recommends that anyone wanting to live and work in a village should initiate it with the Iranian administrator with whom he was assigned to work.

FRIDAY, DECEMBER 18, 1964 It's still raining. I'm strangely restless, wanting to get back to Alang. I've been away a week and I already miss the place.

Early in the morning, Barkley and I board a local bus to begin our journey east. Clouds hang low, concealing the mountains to the south. When the Caspian is within view, it too is a dismal gray expanse of unremitting water. The ramshackle bus is cold and drafty. It stops often to pick up or let off passengers. Each time, more cold, moist air flows around us. I'm miserable.

Eventually we are directed to get off—the bus is returning to Rasht. We board another bus, equally decrepit. The rain is unrelenting. Midafternoon we reach Amol where this bus disgorges its passengers to turn around and begin its journey west. As we continue eastward on yet another bus, the rain stops.

It is dark when we near Alang. I ask the driver to let me off by the sign along the highway. He and the Iranian passengers are apprehensive about letting a foreigner off in the middle of nowhere. Barkley confirms I live there. Reluctantly the driver stops and opens the door. Even the dozing passengers are wide-eyed as I disembark. They look around for any traces of civilization. None. The dim lights of Alang are shrouded in the distant maze of barren tree branches.

"Moteshakeram," I tell the driver. *"Khodahafez."*

"See you at the next conference," I shout to Barkley. "Give my *salaam* to Jack and Dave."

I trek down the dirt road to Alang in pitch blackness. They have had some rain too, I discover as I step into mud puddles.

"Salaam allekum, hale shoma khoobeh?" Nosrat Aghayan greets me with soft, weary eyes as I round the corner and enter his tiny, dimly lit shop.

"Salaam, hale shoma khoobeh?" I politely inquire about his health too.

"Where were you?" he asks. "All of Alang has missed you."

"I was at a Peace Corps conference in Rasht. The weather is very rainy there. Alang is better."

He beams and repeats, *"Baleh,* Alang is better."

"Do you have two eggs and some potatoes? I'm making dinner."

"Sure. What else do you need?"

I see some onions, grab one, as well as a pomegranate and box of cookies. "This will do. How much is this?"

I pay him the few rials. *"Khodahafez.* See you tomorrow morning," I call out as I run off. He knows I will be back at daybreak for fresh-baked bread.

Quickly I put on a pot of rice and crack the eggs, beat them with a fork, cut up some onion, grate one of the potatoes into the mixture, throw in some of the pomegranate seeds and a little flour to thicken it, and I have an omelette much as I have seen Iranians make.

Word is out I'm home. Friends arrive as I'm eating. I serve tea and cookies, and pull out my reserve of candy. When the lights flash, I light the lantern, and we talk until late about my trip to Tehran and Rasht. I show them my two new books about Iranian art. They are enthralled at the quality of the tipped-in color plates in the book on Persian miniatures.

SATURDAY, DECEMBER 19, 1964 "Mister Tom, Mister Tom." It's Shaban Ali's voice.

He is smiling as I open the door. The first rays of the sun sneak between the horizon and the clouds above and cast our giant shadows into my room.

"Befarmayid," I invite him in.

"No. I heard you were home and I couldn't wait to see you. I'll come back. I have letters from America for you. Did you have a good trip?"

I grab my water bucket and follow him to the street to get fresh bread from Mr. Aghayan, along with water from the well.

"Salaam allekum. Ahvalet? Khoobi?" My landlord's wife greets me and asks if I am well as I step through the gateway door.

"Baleh, moteshakeram, shoma khoobi?"

"Koja boodi" (Where were you)?

"I went to Tehran and Rasht."

"Did you see your mother? *Enshahallah* (If God is willing), she is well."

"No, I didn't see my mother. She is in America, very far away, on the other side of the world. It takes more than two days by airplane from Tehran to get to her."

She has no concept of this, and can't understand that I wouldn't see my mother when I leave Alang. Likely she has never been to Tehran. Gorgan is perhaps the largest city she has ever seen.

Shaban Ali returns right after breakfast. He hands me the letters, two from Mom and one from Del. I quickly open Del's letter. She's been accepted in the Peace Corps to go to Malawi. She's excited. I'm happy she will experience this too.

"Shaban Ali, my girlfriend, Del, is going to Africa in the Peace Corps."

"To Africa? Isn't it dangerous? Aren't you worried about her?"

"She'll be OK," I assure him. "What's the news in Alang?"

He fills me in on the week's activities and the village council meetings. "Everybody missed you and wanted to know where you were. How was the conference in Rasht?"

"It was all right, but Rasht is cold and wet. Always raining. Gorgan and Alang are much better." He smiles, happy I appreciate Alang.

I show him my two new books. "Shaban Ali, I want to make a bookcase. I need three boards and some bricks. Can you help me get them?"

"Sure. Let's go now." I can tell he is curious how I am going to make a bookcase from boards and bricks.

We find a carpenter, and I select three boards and have them cut about four feet long. Then we locate some bricks and cart them to my room. I stack the boards and bricks in front of the window overlooking the street, place my new books and some I brought from America in it, and we stand back to look at our masterpiece. Shaban Ali is impressed. Later, he makes a similar bookcase in a little hut he built as an office on his property.

SUNDAY, DECEMBER 20, 1964 "Today is the birthday of Imam Mahdi."

"Who is Imam Mahdi?" I ask my associates at the Sherkat-e Sargardon.

"He is the Twelfth Imam. He never died. He was hidden by God 1100 years ago when he was five years old. He will come again at the end of time—in the mosque of Gohar Shad in Mashhad—and the whole world will live in peace for a while under Islam until the Day of Judgment. He will be there with Hazrat-e Isa" (Jesus).

"Why with Hazrat-e Isa?"

"Hazrat-e Isa was a great prophet who will reappear on the Day of Judgment—after Imam Mahdi brings peace to the world. Sometime you must go to Mashhad to see the mosque of Gohar Shad and the shrine of Imam Reza. It is very beautiful. You can pray there and then we will call you 'Mashti Tom.'"

Everyone laughs. "Mashti Tom!"

"Mashti Tom? Ya ni cheh" (What does it mean)?

"*Mashti* is what we call a pilgrim who has gone to Mashhad—like *Haji* when someone goes to Mecca."

"You mean like Hajireza's *Mashini Mashti Mamdali?*"

The gang cracks up. One of them exclaims, "*Cheh ajab* (My gosh), he knows about *Mashini Mashti Mamdali!*" They howl more.

Reza pulls the discussion back from the ridiculous to the sublime. "*Baleh*, Hazrat-e Isa was a highly respected man, but he was not God. There is only one God, not three as you Christians believe."

"No, we believe in only one God too. But there are three persons in one God—God the Father, the Son—Jesus, and the Holy Spirit."

"You are saying there are three persons. That is three Gods. Hazrat-e Isa is a prophet, not the son of God."

"But you believe Hazrat-e Maryam (Mary) was a virgin when she gave birth to Hazrat-e Isa and she was born without sin."

"*Baleh*, but Hazrat-e Isa was not the son of God."

"Then how did Hazrat-e Maryam become pregnant?"

"From the breath of the angel."

I am invariably moved by the regard Muslims have for Jesus and Mary, but I am not a theologian, and my knowledge of Farsi makes discussion of such abstract concepts very difficult. Nevertheless, learning about their beliefs and religious practices is of particular interest.

"Tom, do you believe in Heaven?"

"*Baleh*, we believe in Heaven and Hell."

"No, Tom, do *you* believe in Heaven?"

"*Baleh*, I believe in Heaven."

"What is Heaven like?"

"It's a nice place."

"Just a nice place?"

"*Baleh*, I have never been there. I don't know what it's like," I respond, causing laughter, but some bite the side of their index finger indicating displeasure over my blasphemous utterance.

"Tom, you should become a Muslim. Our Heaven is very desirable. There will be 72 houris waiting for you. Seventy-two virgins! Imagine—just for you. They will all be of indescribable beauty and sensuality, eternally young—all yours. And after you have used them all and you sleep with them again, they will still be virgins—pure—to start all over again. Imagine! Your penis will never soften. It will be hard for eternity. And you will never become tired. It will be better than anything in this world."

I look around at the guys. They are smiling as if in a state of near-ecstasy, no doubt anticipating their futures. Meanwhile, I am hoping the hardness in my pants will subside and nobody will notice. However, the guys go on and on about the beautiful maidens, sensual delights, and perpetual bliss of Heaven. I wish I could slink away, but I'm too embarrassed to get up. My problem now is, though I'm not in Heaven, I'm coping with the effects of eternity.

The more nervous I become over my circumstance, the more pronounced the pressure below my belt grows. *I hope it will go away before we leave for lunch. I'm in no condition to walk down main street like this.* Although the conversation exhausts itself, the anxiety of wanting my swelling to go away prolongs the irksome situation. I begin to pray. *Hail Mary, full of grace...*

It doesn't help. It only seems to make it worse. *Maybe she's getting even with me for calling on her in a condition like this.* I shift to *Our Father, who art in Heaven...* and, for good measure, throw in a few "Glory bes." There's no rescue from above. The more I try to rid myself of my troublesome state of affairs, the more my mind enhances the situation.

"Ya Allah," Reza says. "It's time to go to lunch." Everyone rises, I with difficulty, and put my hands in my pockets in an attempt to disguise any evidence. I make it to my room in a less-aroused state.

MONDAY, DECEMBER 21, 1964 Excitedly, my accomplices and I wait in the cold outside the Moulin Rouge. This is the night men from all around have been anticipating. I'm swept along with the mob surging through the open doors. My feet barely touch the ground.

"Sorry, Tom, we didn't get closer to the stage."

We are about a third of the way back. The lights dim and the rhythmic beat of music blares. An alluringly clad dancer slithers out—LIVE— *raqse Arabi* (Arab belly dancing). She shimmies across the stage, her hips vibrating at a rate that would cause any man-made instrument to function uncontrollably. The men go wild. She shifts gears—now deep belly and pelvic movements. Men throughout the theater begin to groan ecstatically. The performances go on and on—as do the rapturous moans all around. I'm as intrigued with the reaction of the audience as I am with the performance.

"Tom, did you like it?" my cohorts inquire afterwards. They can plainly see my approval by the look on my face, and I see theirs.

SPIRITS AND DARK TEA

.

TUESDAY, DECEMBER 22, 1964 "Mister Tom, Mister Tom," Hajireza calls enthusiastically as he opens the courtyard gateway below my room and parks his dilapidated vehicle for the night. "Mister Dave came to the bus station to give me this letter for you. Mister Dave is a very polite man."

"Moteshakeram," I thank him.

It is an invitation to Jack and Dave's Christmas Eve party. I planned to spend Christmas in Alang even though the Peace Corps is giving us a three-day holiday. Nonetheless, a party is always tempting.

THURSDAY, DECEMBER 24, 1964 Shaban Ali shows up early to wish me a Merry Christmas and help deliver the gift boxes of fruit, nuts, and candy we made for friends. They know Christmas is a special time in America, and are excited about my holiday celebration. I decline three invitations to dinner, explaining I am going to Gorgan to be with Jack and Dave. It's amazing how much more they know about us than we know about them. *Do we know anything about their holidays?*

Jack and Dave are busy getting ready for the party when I arrive.

"You have a Christmas tree, with decorations! How did you get that?"

"We got permission to cut down a tree in the forest behind Gorgan. One of our friends arranged it."

"Wow, that's really exceptional! Isn't it against the law to cut trees in the national forests?"

"Yeah, but we know people in high places," Jack chortles.

They prepared an elaborate spread of sandwiches with cold cuts, fruit, nuts, fancy desserts, and plenty of spirits. Living in a village where dark tea is the strongest drink, I am intrigued to find alcohol at an Iranian party. But this is the city, educated individuals—a different class of people.

About thirty people come; most are Iranians who are fellow teachers. Although their wives had been invited, Jack and Dave are disappointed that only eight women attend. They gather in a room separate from the men, where an air of uneasiness permeates.

Jack and Dave are very low when their guests leave at only 10pm, but I pronounce the convivial atmosphere of the party a success.

"Oh, come on. You guys are just exhausted. It was a great party, congenial conversation. People had a good time and you got them together. Sit down and have another drink. I'll clean up."

FRIDAY, DECEMBER 25, 1964 Mrs. Housaini, the woman teacher in Alang, invited me to spend the day and have dinner with her family in Gorgan. Her parents are happy to meet me, but her younger brothers, who are in high school, are spellbound to have an American in their home. In the afternoon, one of the brothers proposes we go for a walk. I'm positive he wants his classmates to see he knows an American. Ordinarily I am disgusted at being used as part of an arrogant display of social position. I'm a status symbol, I know, but this family is so gracious. Indirectly, Mrs. Housaini's brother is connected to Alang, and anything about Alang is just fine. Besides, it's good to get outside. Better yet, it's snowing. What could be more fitting? Snow on Christmas! That doesn't happen in Hawaii.

Mrs. Housaini's attractive, immaculately coiffed, and stylishly dressed sisters and cousins visit throughout the day—primarily to meet me, I'm convinced. *This is encouraging. What could be more enticing? Jack and Dave hustle mightily to get to know a few women, but they come in droves to meet me.*

Invariably, some of the first questions asked are, "How was the party? How many women came?" Clearly, Jack and Dave's party is the talk of Gorgan.

Most of the young women are comfortable talking with me, but then this is in the confines of their family home. It's not at all like the icy chill that hung over the room where the women were last night. Still, I'm perplexed as to whether I should, or how I would, take things further. The Peace Corps pointedly warned us not to get involved with women. Even though we are now enjoying each other's company, what chance do I have of getting close enough to an Iranian girl even to begin having a romance? Yet my friends in Alang keep urging me, "Stay in Iran and marry a nice Iranian girl."

My imaginative, amorous notions are dashed when I return to Jack and Dave's.

"Tom, don't go back to Alang tomorrow. There's going to be a public hanging in Gorgan on Sunday. Why don't you stay to see it? We've seen one already. It's truly something you should witness at least once while you are here," Jack tells me.

"No, I can pass on it. I couldn't handle it. By the way, what's the offense?"

"This guy was caught at Nahar Khoran with a young woman from a respectable family. She was stoned to death when they were discovered. Now he's going to be hanged. That's a sure way to send out a warning to young people to control their passions."

The hair on the back of my neck stands on end.

SATURDAY, DECEMBER 26, 1964 Hints of snow cover much of the land. As I journey down the pathway to Alang, a mysterious puff of steam emerges from the ground in the field to the right. Baffled, I wonder what it is. Farther on, another vapor ascends from a little mound, and I see a line of rising steam issuing at regular intervals from the fields. A man on his way to the highway approaches.

"*Agha, sobh bekheyr* (good morning). What is happening over there?"

"Mister Tom, that is the *qanat*. It brings water underground all the way from the mountains. The water below is warmer than the air outside, so steam rises out of the ground."

"*Cheh ajab* (My gosh). I didn't know there was a *qanat* so close to Alang."

THERE IS ACTIVITY BY MY ROOM. A door has been put on my kitchen and my landlady is plastering the walls, ceiling, and floor with daub—a mixture of clay, straw, and cow manure. I know what she did early this morning as, from my window, I've seen women doing it other days. Following behind when the cowherds drive their cattle out of the village, they scoop up the fresh, warm dung in their bare hands and put it in a large pan. Then they mix the dung, mud, and straw to a thick, sticky consistency, and with their hands, spread it on the wattle surface.

My eyes smart from the staggeringly ripe odor when I look in and greet her. She is covered with splatter from her work. I retreat to my room, hurriedly closing the door behind me. Nevertheless, the odor seems to have permeated my walls.

She instructs me to prop open the door so the mixture can dry out. Without a window for cross-ventilation, it will be months before the interior can be painted white and I can use it.

SUNDAY, DECEMBER 27, 1964   It rained most of the night—no weather for drying wet daub. It's also too muddy to bicycle to Chahardeh for the village council meeting. Instead, Shaban Ali and I walk the few kilometers.

"Should we go around the hill or over it?" Shaban Ali asks as we approach the large mound near the village.

"Let's go over it."

As we climb the hill, pottery shards are strewn in the sheep-clipped grass. "Shaban Ali, this must be an ancient site. I've seen lots of them dotting the landscape between here and Gorgan. However, when I've questioned people on the bus about them, they say they are natural formations."

"No, they are the sites of ancient villages. This one is called Deen Tepe. It has never been excavated, but there are some near Gorgan where artifacts have been found, especially at Turang Tepe."

Suddenly I see a tiny, unusual shape in the grass. When I scrape off the mud, the ceramic body of an animal is revealed. It has no legs, and the head was broken off centuries, perhaps millennia, ago, but its body is sensitively modeled. I can't believe what I've found. I've never held anything so old.

When we return to Alang, we pore through my books and find similar small ceramic animal sculptures dated as early as 2000 BC.

"Wow, Shaban Ali, 4000 years old! This is unbelievable!"

He grins.

MONDAY, DECEMBER 28, 1964 The evening is exceptionally cold and damp. Following dinner at Javad's house, a low approximately four-foot-square table is placed in the center of the room. A tray of coals is positioned under it, and blankets are spread on top and around the sides.

"Tom, put your feet under this," Javad tells me.

Little Abdullah promptly crawls under the blanket on one side of his *Amo* Tom, Rozy on the other.

"It is a *kursi*. It's nice. This is how we stay warm at night when it's very cold. You don't need an Aladdin with this."

"In America, we would say 'snug as a bug in rug.'"

Everyone laughs. "A bug in a rug is not good in Iran."

Later, in my room, I light my state-of-the-art Aladdin heater and kerosene lantern and resume a long letter to my parents.

> You asked if I felt I was wasting two years of my life for my country. Not at all, especially when I figure what a waste even six months would have been in the army. I don't think I was cut out for that at all. The whole philosophy of it doesn't agree with me, and there is so much good in the Peace Corps. However, I often feel I'm doing nothing, and wish I had some big projects going. That is when I lose sight of the fact that the Peace Corps' most important goal is getting to know people, and the only way to be effective is to be with them as much as possible. I'm always going somewhere, doing something, or have visitors. At times, I just wish for a few hours to myself. But I must admit, the people here in Alang have been so kind to me. It's the people who make Peace Corps life such a wonderful experience. Just the little unexpected things mean so much. The Peace Corps is a great opportunity for us to appreciate another people and another culture. Also, being here in this different culture makes me aware of my own for the first time. When you have lived in one culture, it is hard to see these things because then it's just there, and there is nothing upon which one can base an attitude. Being here, one can see how religion affects every action and thought in our everyday life. For the first time I see how every institution in the US is bound by the Christian tradition. Sometimes I find it hard to understand the people, but it helps me realize

how important my country and religion are to me, and how deeply ingrained our traditions are within me.

I'm fortunate to be living alone in a small village, without other PCVs, as it really gives me the opportunity to understand the Iranian people. Living in a larger city, especially Tehran, a volunteer simply becomes another American in a big city with little or no meaningful relationships with Iranians. Many of the volunteers in Tehran are so dissatisfied because they end up in a Western community and will never be able to get to know Iranians well.

IDEALIST DREAMS AND REALITY

FRIDAY, JANUARY 1, 1965 Barkley and I board the train in Gorgan bound for a community development conference in Garmsar, an all-night journey in blackness over the mountains to the forbidding Dasht-e Kavir desert. I read Tolstoy's *Anna Karenina* until sleep overtakes me, only to be woken intermittently each time we stop and vendors hawk their goods at our window. Barkley sleeps right through.

"Garmsar is next," I am awoken about 4am by the conductor.

"Barkley—Barkley, wake up. Garmsar." I shake him.

Groggily we grab our bags and stumble to the train door. Cold air bursts through a slightly open window. Traces of snow are all around.

The train screeches to a halt. We descend to the platform. The train's long, forlorn whistle calls through the darkness. Clouds of steam engulf us. The earth trembles as the train rumbles on. The steam dissipates. A lone, dim lamp lights the station platform. We look up and down the track for fellow travelers—none. We try the station door—locked.

"Barkley, what do we do? We can't stay out here in the cold the rest of the night."

"Yeah," he mumbles incoherently. Not even the frigid air can jar him thoroughly awake.

"I see some lights in the village. Maybe we can find someone who will let us in out of this cold."

But the lights are those illuminating the desolate streets. We press on. No one is awake at this hour, and to knock on a door and request to be let in seems very presumptuous.

"Barkley! Look! There's light and steam coming out of an opening up ahead. Come."

The distinctive aroma of freshly baked bread wafts gently through the street as we approach the light. We rap on the door.

"Baleh?" We hear a call from within.

"Salaam, Agha" (Hello, Mister), I call through the cracks.

The door inches open. A man in T-shirt and baggy pajamas stares wide-eyed at us. Obviously he didn't expect to find foreigners on the other side.

"Baleh? Salaam," he greets us with bewilderment.

"*Agha,* can we come in? It's cold out here."

"Befarmayid." He opens the door to the scented warmth of his bakery.

"Merci, Agha, thank you for letting us in. We arrived on the train from Gorgan, the station is not open, and there are no taxis."

"There is nothing at this time of the night, nothing." He looks at us inquisitively.

"We came to Garmsar for a conference. We are American Peace Corps Volunteers."

"You are Americans? *Bah, bah, bah.* America is good. Here, sit down. Would you like some tea? I'll make tea. Sit. Sit. Here, have some bread."

We talk for hours—till dawn—while he makes his bread. When customers arrive for the results of his nightly toil, we thank him and head for the conference site.

"*Khodahafez.* Come back again. It was a pleasure."

SATURDAY, JANUARY 2, 1965 Fellow PCVs are waking as Barkley and I check in. Most arrived in the late evening on the train from Tehran. All are excited about the two large mounds surmounted with architectural ruins that loom at the edge of town.

"Let's check them out," one of the guys suggests.

After breakfast, at least a dozen of us trek through the sand-choked byways of Garmsar. Wind-weathered walls conceal family compounds of simple one-story buildings with flat roofs. Weary camels with tasseled headdresses gaze at us in complacent boredom as they patiently stand before the worn wooden doorways to their owners' enclosures.

We crawl through underground passageways of the eroding castle mounds, climb crumbling stairways, and carefully pass along the edges of caved-in ceilings that expose the chambers below. At the summit, fragments of arches—traces of paint still visible—are etched against the bright skyline. We appear like actors populating a surreal theatrical stage—acting out a strange, half-imagined, half-known Orientalist drama—something from *The Thousand and One Nights*. The village lies far below. The desert expands endlessly to the south; to the north it is only stopped by the distant snow-covered Alborz Mountains.

Qajar castle ruin and PCVs, Garmsar

Our reverie is shattered when we return. Peace Corps officials are pissed.

"What are you guys thinking? What kind of example are you setting to your Iranian counterparts—that your work is not important? They're sitting here and you guys are out goofing off."

They're right, but the rebuke sets the conference off on the wrong foot, a much needed foot. Yes, they had invited some Iranian *dehyars*, but, disappointingly, not all of our counterparts were included. Shaban Ali was not. I felt bad, but never told him.

Sheepishly we join the sessions. At lunch and dinner, we grumble among ourselves. The next two days are just more bureaucratic jargon. The conference at Rasht was fine, but having to go to another in less than two weeks is excessive. They just need to let us do our jobs. And what are our jobs? That's the problem.

"These Peace Corps officials have their heads in the clouds, or somewhere else; they're out of touch with reality," I grouse to the guys. "The best thing we could do for America, for Iran, and for ourselves would be to get the next plane back to the USA."

TUESDAY, JANUARY 5, 1965 The *dehyars* left late yesterday or early this morning. Ramadan, the month of fasting, commences tomorrow, so they need to be home before the fast begins.

Now is our chance to vent. We take the agenda into our own hands and tell the Peace Corps what we know based on the knowledge we have gained. Over the next few days, we explain how we see our role as community development volunteers in Iran.

"We are not a repeat of USAID which often has had marginal success. We are not here to force any projects on the people. In fact, what right do we have to impose our ways on them? The Iranian programs in community development and the Literacy Corps provide effective services that already significantly aid people in rural areas. Moreover, the *dehyars* and teachers in these programs have training and access to technical expertise to bring about changes within their system. Our job is one of supporting them and of teaching life skills, not technical skills or providing technical assistance. We are here to help people—to help them realize it is they who can improve their standard of living. Our goal should be one of encouraging them not to rely on us or benefactors and protectors, but to build a consciousness that they must depend on themselves. We must help Iranians develop a sense of obligation to their communities. Iranians may not naturally be given to cooperation and mutual trust, but when we leave, hopefully we will have instilled in them genuine pride in their own self-reliance. More than anything, our role is to cultivate friendships, and to be completely forthright with ourselves toward the Iranians so they develop a trust in us. *Enshahallah,* through our example they will learn to be honest and trustworthy with each other, willing to lend a hand when others need it." We conclude, "We are here to help when they ask for it—and then, that assistance should be of the kind that motivates them to find ways to help themselves."

While we recognize the generosity and hospitality of Iranians, realistically we acknowledge the duplicity of their culture, one based on class—where certain privileges and standards apply to the wealthy, but never extend to the poor majority. Nevertheless, we are optimistic about the future, confident the Shah's White Revolution and the programs we see in community development and education will bring about meaningful change.

FRIDAY, JANUARY 8, 1965 We reach Gorgan by midday, enough time for Barkley to catch a bus to Gonbad. Dazed from lack of sleep on the long train ride, I aimlessly saunter up to see Jack and Dave. They'll be interested in the conference and how we told the Peace Corps what our job should be.

I am revived by my passion of telling the story of our minor protest.

"Spend the night here," they urge. "It's too late to go to Alang now. Take a short nap. We can go to dinner and then play a game or two of Scrabble."

"No, I really ought to get back to Alang. It's not too late," I say without much conviction.

"But today is Friday, the day of rest. You can go tomorrow morning."

They're right. It didn't take much to convince me.

SATURDAY, JANUARY 9, 1965 Midmorning, waiting for a local bus heading west, I resume reading *Anna Karenina*. People from Alang board, and are curious about where I have been for a week. A man notices the picture of my family I use as a bookmark and asks about my parents and brother. I hand it to him and it is passed around and talked about with consuming interest. An old lady takes the picture, gently kisses it, and hands it to me.

ALANG IS QUIET during Ramadan. People sleep late, few are on the streets, and there are no weddings. No adults eat, drink, or smoke from sunup to sundown. Women rise at 4am to prepare a meal that is completed before 7am. Then everyone returns to bed. The fast is broken at 5:30pm.

Dad, Tom, Mom and Alan, Honolulu Airport, September 22, 1964

MONDAY, JANUARY 11, 1965 A letter to my brother, addressed to his work-place:

Dear Alan,

The lights have already blinked, so I will be writing most of this by lantern light. I just came back from the teachers' house where I give English lessons. Tonight my lesson was interrupted by an hour-long news broadcast. That is the reason I'm writing you now, so in case you are getting any of this news back there you know I'm OK and you can tell Mom and Dad not to worry. I'm not writing them because I don't know how the situation between Iran and Egypt is being played up in the papers and on the radio back there, and I wouldn't want Mom and Dad to be concerned if they didn't know about it already.

Anyway, for at least a week the people here have been very worked up over the situation between Egypt and Iran. They have openly told me war would be the best thing, they can lose nothing, and only gain by it. This attitude is widespread throughout the country, as when I was at the conference in Garmsar last week the *dehyars*, which were from all over Iran, were very upset about it and sent a message to the Shah that they wanted to go to war and that war was the best option. They asked to be granted radio time, but I don't think they were granted it—at least I didn't hear that they were. Yesterday an Egyptian spy was caught in Iran, so it brought it to a new head again, and then tonight the radio broadcast. Of course it was in Farsi, so I had a hard time understanding it, but I got the gist. After it was over, I asked one of the teachers what they said, and all she said in English was the people of Iran and Egypt want to go to war and that the people here were very uncomfortable. I was able to get a little more out of the broadcast, about the US giving millions of dollars to Egypt in aid over the past years and Russia also giving assistance to Egypt. It stems from Nasser wanting to take some of the Iranian states in the oil-rich Persian Gulf. He has also sent troops into Yemen and, from what I infer, the Iraq-Iranian border is full of United Arab Republic (Nasser's) troops.* Anyway, in the event something breaks out here I'm perfectly safe in Alang and the surrounding community, and I will stay in Alang until I am given orders to leave by the US Government and the US Army in Gorgan evacuates me. It is their job to get us out of the area if the need arises. If anything does happen, the people in Alang would take extra special care of me and I really feel safer here than I ever did walking the streets at night in Hawaii. I will not be leaving Alang except to go to Gorgan for supplies until the end of March, when I plan to take a vacation.

If news sounds bad in the States you can show this letter to Mom and Dad so they know everything is OK. I will let you use your judgment, but keep the letter while I'm here so if something should ever occur you can show it to them then.

Aloha, Tom

---

* Numerous incidents strained Iranian/Egyptian relations from the late 1950s onward. Iran viewed Nasser's involvement in the Arabian peninsula as imperialist and expansionist, and his attempts to build Arab unity with him at the helm as a threat, chiefly because he challenged Iran's claims to Bahrain and other Gulf islands. Nasser renamed the Persian Gulf the Arabian Gulf, and referred to the Iranian province of Khuzistan as Arabistan. Nasser viewed the Shah as a pawn of Western imperialism, and Western bases in Iran, as well as Iran's support of Western-endorsed pacts, rankled him. Meanwhile Nasser's Gulf actions and his military shopping in Moscow fueled Iran's long-time fears of Soviet expansion and its perceptions of a Soviet desire for access to Iran's warm, oil-rich ports. In December 1964, the Arab League tried to stop the flow of Iranian oil to Israel (Iran supplied 80 percent of Israel's oil), and, in an attempt to isolate Iran from the rest of the Muslim world, declared trade with Israel and any recognition of that state constituted a denial of the Arab cause. For an expanded discussion of Iranian/Egyptian relations 1952–1971, see Shahram Chubin and Sepher Zabih, *The Foreign Relations of Iran: A Developing State in a Zone of Great-Power Conflict*, (Berkeley: University of California Press, 1974), 140–69.

WEDNESDAY, JANUARY 20, 1965 "Mister Tom, Mister Tom. *Beah, beah.*" Villagers eagerly call me to come and help them. It's not clear, but it has to do with chickens and eggs. We run off to their place, and I discover they have purchased a chicken incubator and are setting it up. I remember the Peace Corps gave us information on incubators when they were promoting the poultry projects, so I run back to my room and return ready to pitch in. They had it pretty well figured out themselves, but my presence and perceived expertise lend an air of confidence to their endeavor. *Now, this is exactly the kind of assistance we were agitating for at Garmsar,* I think with satisfaction. *It's fortuitous the Peace Corps gave us this; it proves our point. Iranians can initiate these sorts of projects on their own. The idea is theirs, not ours. Then they take possession. This is the way it should be.*

FRIDAY, JANUARY 22, 1965 "Prime Minister Hassan-Ali Mansur was shot in Tehran," Jack and Dave greet me gravely. "He's still alive, in a hospital, but it doesn't sound promising. He just got out of his car and was entering the Majles to give his first State-of–the-Union address. He took three bullets at close range. It's good you're here in case we have to be evacuated."

"Oh, my gosh, I hope not. This is dreadful. The poor people in the villages believe Mansur is there to help them."

I came to Gorgan to be with Jack and Dave on Saturday evening and Sunday, the anniversary of the martyrdom of Imam Ali. The Peace Corps had advised us to get our food supplies and not go outside while Iranians are mourning the death of their revered Imam. Barkley arrives from Gonbad, and two volunteers come from Shahi. We vigilantly listen to news of the Prime Minister's condition on the radio, reflect on how it echoes America fourteen months earlier when Kennedy was killed, grumble about the Peace Corps and our jobs, and read or play Scrabble until the wee hours of the morning.

WEDNESDAY, JANUARY 27, 1965 "The Prime Minister has died," Shaban Ali tells me.

"I'm sorry. He was trying to help the poor people of Iran."

"The Shah has appointed Amir-Abbas Hoveida as Prime Minister."

THURSDAY, JANUARY 28, 1965 "Tom! Did you hear the news! *Time* magazine has been banned in Iran," Jack excitedly exclaims as he answers the door when I arrive for my now weekly visit to Gorgan. His eyes glisten with delight. This is exactly the kind of excitement he relishes hearing about and conveying to others.

"*Time*'s been pulled from all the bookstands across the country. I sure wish I could get a copy," he continues. "It seems that *Time* called the Shah 'a properly possessive Arab husband.'* What an insult! An Arab! He's furious, and insists that *Time* and the US State Department issue apologies. It all stems from *Time*'s reporting on the Shah's adverse reaction to a derogatory photo-montage of him in Cologne's *Stadt-Anzeiger*. That wasn't enough to make him livid, now this. *Time* should know better than to call a proud Persian an Arab, especially the Shah. Americans just don't understand that all Muslims are not Arabs."

SATURDAY, JANUARY 30, 1965 "Mrs. Housaini has been transferred to a school in Gorgan," Yavar and Ismael inform me.

"I'm sorry to hear that. Who will teach the girls in Alang?"

"We will have them in the same class with the boys."

"Excellent. It's important the girls acquire an education too. Being in Gorgan will be much easier for the Housainis. Her family will be able to take care of little Reza while she teaches."

"We want you to come to our house tonight and every night for dinner and speak English with us."

"Oh, I would love to. I enjoy being with you and your families very much, but I have other work to do certain evenings. I am happy to come two or three times a week."

It's true I like being with them, but I feel I ought to be available to everybody in Alang and not make it appear I have chosen to be with select friends. "I'm sorry. I can't come tonight." I see they are disappointed.

I make a pot of soup, have dinner, and intend to read *Anna Karenina*. Very rarely do I have an evening to myself. However, Shaban Ali drops

---

* "West Germany: The Shah Was Not Amused," *Time* 85 no. 4 (January 22, 1965), 26.

by. It's always easy conversing with him. He learns English and I learn Farsi—so different from the evenings when my room is full of visitors and they begin to talk together and I have little idea of what is being said, or tune out in exhaustion.

"Shaban Ali, the *dehyars* in community development are so crucial for the villages. There ought to be a similar program where women *dehyars* work in the villages to teach women about healthful food, sanitation, taking care of children—even being a midwife who could assist in delivery. The government could set up training schools for women as they do for *dehyars* and the Literacy Corps. Every village should have a woman *dehyar*."

"I agree. There are women who do this, but there are not enough—a few in each province—and there are thousands of villages. They cannot get out to each village. One worked in Alang a number of years ago. We could try to get another of these ladies to give lessons to the women in Alang."

"Yes, that would help Alang. But the program must be bigger, like the Literacy Corps and what you are doing in community development. The Shah should establish a national program that would be useful to the thousands of villages all over Iran."

MONDAY, FEBRUARY 1, 1965 I'm inwardly excited to send my report to the Peace Corps this month, the perfect chance to reiterate our message from the Garmsar conference that the Peace Corps needs to supply community development volunteers with sufficient technical information to be of assistance when called upon. I write about helping set up the incubator, but how, otherwise, things are the usual—village council meetings and my English classes. I am still bristling I never received any guidance regarding water supply systems and raising sheep and cotton I asked for shortly after I arrived in Alang. I am tempted, but refrain from writing, "With the kind of technical backup the Peace Corps gives us, our only real goal can be friendship and understanding. It would make the people and me feel a lot better if I could get support from the Peace Corps when it's requested."

TUESDAY, FEBRUARY 2, 1965 The discordant and prolonged grating creak of the gateway doors opening below my room typically announces each day—if no one has woken me earlier. I then wait for the building to shudder as the doors hit the walls at their sides. But today this is broken by frenzied exclamations. I recognize the voice of Hajireza, the bus driver, above all others. A crowd quickly gathers below my room. I scramble into clothes, stumble out onto my balcony, and look down. Hajireza is distressed, and everyone is gesturing and shouting. The cacophony is so intense I barely catch a word, but as I look at the bus I comprehend. From above I see the right front tire is flat. He probably doesn't have a spare. I descend the narrow stairs at the far end of the balcony to join the group. Then I ascertain the severity of the situation. All *four* tires are flat. Slashed!

In my wavering Farsi, I empathize with Hajireza and tell the crowd, "Last night before the lights went out, when I was writing a letter in my room, I heard a 'pisssh' sound even above the noise of the generator across the street. But I wasn't concerned. When I finished the letter, I walked in front of the bus on my way to the *mostarah*. I didn't observe anything or anyone. It was dark and I didn't look around."

I feel bad for Hajireza, and am troubled this could happen in the idyllic village of Alang. Who would do such a thing? Who could harbor such hatred of another person in this peaceful little village?

WEDNESDAY, FEBRUARY 3, 1965 Today is Eid-e Fitr, the first of the month of Shawwal. Morning prayers followed by a breakfast of specially-made sweets and day-long celebrations mark the end of the dawn-to-sunset fast during the month of Ramadan. My friends wear fine new clothes, and I join them as we go from house to house to visit, drink tea, and eat sweets and fruit. The women are especially pleased I like *halva*, a delicious, chewy patty made from ground rice and walnuts.

"Here, take some home." Mulla's mother hands me several wrapped patties as I depart. My *moteshakeram* and smile relay my appreciation.

At lunchtime, my landlady sends up a big bowl of soup with her son Ghorbon. He is fifteen, a tall, lanky young man with an ample Iranian nose who helps his father tend their farm. He affectionately calls me *Aghaye* Oshkhor (Mr. Soupeater), as his mother often sends him up with a large, hearty bowl of soup. Other days I might be *Aghaye* Dooshgeeri (Mr.

Showertaker), depending if I've just come back from taking a shower at the bathhouse in Kordkuy.

THURSDAY, FEBRUARY 4, 1965 Late in the afternoon there is a knock on my door. It is Barkley.

"What a surprise! You came all the way from Gonbad?"

"*Baleh*, thought I would check on you. Dr. Drake told me you weren't feeling too well when he stopped by about a week ago." Dr. Drake is the Peace Corps doctor who makes occasional field visits to volunteers.

"*Baleh*, I caught a cold. He gave me some medicine. I've been taking it and it makes me very groggy. Even had a slight temperature for a few days, but I've recovered now. I'm tired all the time. Also have the runs a lot. There is hardly a week that goes by without a severe case of 'Tehran Trots.' I hate to get on buses because of the thought of having to go. Almost every time the bus starts out I double up in pain and have to hold it for hours. Dr. Drake doesn't think I have dysentery. He thinks it's the way I'm dealing with culture shock, taking it out on myself rather than on others."

"Dr. Drake really liked your little place out here in Alang."

"*Baleh*, Alang is special. I like it too. Nevertheless, I get frustrated by the lack of privacy and constantly having to cope with Farsi. By the end of the day I can't stand it any longer. I get so tired, but I keep going. I'm glad you came so I can speak English a bit. I haven't had a chance to read any more of *Anna Karenina*. I don't even get to read the USIS bulletins about current events. I barely know what's going on in the world.

"We had a little excitement here in Alang two nights ago. The tires were slashed on the bus right below my room. I might have heard it. I was writing my report to the Peace Corps and I heard some 'pisssh' sounds. I went downstairs to the *mostarah* shortly after."

"You went down shortly after you heard the sounds?"

"*Baleh*. I didn't think anything of it."

"They could have used the knife on you!"

"I never thought of that. When I went down I didn't realize anything was amiss. The next morning I was just distraught my friend's tires were slashed."

SATURDAY, FEBRUARY 6, 1965 "Mister Tom! You have company—Mister Jack and Mister Dave." It is the exuberant voice of Hajireza, the bus driver. He gave them the exalted seat right behind him on his bus as he made one of several daily trips west from Gorgan. Today he made the diversion into the village as he delivered Jack and Dave right to my doorstep. His curious passengers wait patiently in the bus, engine running, as Hajireza assures the guys are delivered safely to their destination.

"*Merci*, Hajireza, for bringing Jack and Dave right to Alang."

"*Ghorbanet*" (You're welcome).* His golden grin reveals his joy in having had this special opportunity. No doubt he is thrilled to have his passengers see that his home village is so important, even Americans come here.

"Wow, your place is neat—so Peace Corpsish—with these hand-plastered mud and cow manure walls. You can even see the bits of straw in it. And the bricks and boards bookcase," Jack and Dave exclaim.

"*Mahi, mahi, mahi*" (Fish, fish, fish), I hear in the distance.

"Someone has fish for sale. Let's go down and I'll buy some fish for dinner. Then I'll show you around the village."

Jack and Dave are taken with the rustic quality of Alang and its gracious people. It is their first time in an Iranian village. "This is the Peace Corps at its most elemental," they tell me.

The guys at the Sherkat-e Sargardon greet Jack and Dave reservedly—after all, they're teachers—but show their informality with me, joking as usual. Jack particularly enjoys their stories of my misunderstanding of Farsi words and Iranian *taroof*. It's clear I'm a source of entertainment in Alang.

"Would you like tea? I'll make some tea," Reza asks.

"*Baleh, moteshakeram*," Jack and Dave respond.

Reza had expected their polite and requisite refusal at first, but he was prepared to insist. He smiles and hands someone a kettle and tells him to get water from the well.

There is no teahouse in Alang, so Reza's tailor shop is the de facto local watering place. Hot coals are always available for the samovar, as Reza uses them for his heavy old pressing iron.

---

* The word *ghorban* suggests a kind of reverence on the part of the speaker. A literal meaning is "You, for whom I sacrifice myself."

The sound of the electrical generator disturbs the stillness of the village as darkness descends. We say *khodahafez* to the "Do Nothing" guys and stop at *Aghaye* Aghayan's tiny shop for groceries—potatoes, onions, some spinach, and a flat round bread freshly baked by Mulla's sister.

I clean and filet the little fishes for frying, wash and cook the spinach, and slice and fry the potatoes and onions. Jack and Dave are introduced to the traditional Iranian way of eating—on the floor, sitting cross-legged around a cloth.

"Wow! This is delicious. The second best meal we've had since we've been in Gorgan. We had steak one night when we were invited to the home of the US Army officers in Gorgan."

"Steak! You guys were having steak and you didn't tell them you knew a poor, starving Peace Corps Volunteer in a village near Gorgan they should invite too? What kind of friends are you?"

"Sort of like the friend we have who wouldn't share the treasure he found on the streets of Tehran," Jack retorts.

"Oh, but I was thinking of you. I was doing that to protect your virtue. I didn't want you contracting some exotic social disease because I led you into temptation. What would you tell Dr. Drake?"

"Oh, you're so altruistic," he sneers. "We were thinking of you too. We didn't want you sampling the pleasures of the big city and becoming more depressed living in a village. It was all for your benefit."

"Oh, thanks. Now who's altruistic?"

"This bread is terrific. We like the *sangak* we get in Gorgan but this is a really robust, chewy bread," Dave interjects, changing the subject.

"I'll get a fresh one for breakfast tomorrow morning. Eat up now. We'll have oatmeal and hot cocoa too, if you'd like it, before you catch a bus to Gorgan. I'll make some tea now, and there's oranges and cookies."

Mulla delivers two bedrolls and blankets and stays for tea. More guys arrive to meet Jack and Dave. My little room with its bulky furniture becomes crowded. When the lights blink, everyone rushes home.

"Is this the way it is every night? You have a roomful of visitors?"

"Yes, if I'm home. That's why I never have any time to myself. I can only read on buses or at your house. All kidding aside, you guys are a real lifesaver. There are times I just have to get away from the Farsi and converse in English for a while."

"We wish you'd come to Gorgan more often. It's a break for us too."

"My friends sure enjoyed meeting you and hearing your stories of New York and San Francisco."

"Iranians always are eager to meet somebody new," Dave comments thoughtfully.

"I sometimes wonder if it has to do with living in an isolated place—a desert or island mentality—where you long for contact with the broader world. It's like being in Hawaii and our aloha spirit. This isolation may be what contributes to the Iranians' incredible hospitality. Invariably they are grateful to meet someone from another place and receive news from afar."

SUNDAY, FEBRUARY 7, 1965 Bad news. I breathe heavily as we listen to the radio at Yavar and Ismael's house before dinner. I only make out some of the Farsi, but I sense the magnitude of the broadcast.

"Tell me what happened," I ask as Ismael turns off the radio.

"The Viet Cong attacked an American base, Camp Holloway, in South Vietnam."

"And Americans were killed?" I ask for his confirmation of what I heard.

"Yes, at least eight."

"That's what I understood. And many soldiers were injured."

"Yes, more than a hundred."

I take a deep breath, thinking about my brother and if he will have to go to Vietnam.

"Ten aircraft were destroyed and fifteen more are damaged. President Johnson ordered an attack on North Vietnam, and US fighter-bombers have been bombing across the 17th Parallel. Soviet Premier Kosygin is in Hanoi right now."

"Oh, my gosh. What will this lead to?" Yavar and Ismael observe the impact this news has on me.

"Stop talking about it," Ismael's wife demands. "Dinner is ready." She and Yavar's wife try to lighten the mood as we eat, but they easily see my anxiety. I, too, note their uneasiness that this conflict could escalate into a world engagement that might have an impact on the lives of their young families as well. I look at the children. Vida and Farsheed are silent, as if they comprehend the enormity of our concern.

When the lights blink, I bid goodnight and, dispirited, plod home, seeming to carry my whole being in my hands. *It's strange, I have all these friends here, but I feel so alone and remote. Why is the world like it is? Why can't we just get along with each other? What's the use of the Peace Corps? Why do we even bother?*

TUESDAY, FEBRUARY 9, 1965 Thin, high clouds filter the warming sun as Shaban Ali and I go for a morning walk to the cemetery and the quiet fields beyond. Women are planting gardens, men are readying plots of land, and the refreshing chartreuse color of sprouting wheat already blankets the fields. It has been a short winter, but the sun still glistens brightly off the snow-packed mountains behind the village.

"This is where Alang used to be," Shaban Ali tells me as we wander through a farmer's plowed tract. "They found the big ceramic pot here, the one we showed you in the barn with the American bull when you first came to Alang. They've also uncovered some gold coins."

We pick up fragments of glazed ceramics and discover some hexagonal bricks the farmer has cast in the hedgerows at the side. "The farmer hates these bricks. They dull his plowshares."

"Shaban Ali, these pieces of ceramics are very old. How old do you think they are?"

"They are over 750 years old. Ancient Alang was destroyed in the invasions of Genghis Khan that swept through this part of Iran. He and his men leveled whole cities all across northern Iran."

"Genghis Khan! That was in the early 13th century!"

"*Baleh*, likely the entire village was destroyed and most of the people were slaughtered. Subsequently, Alang sprang up on the other side of the tomb of Ibrahim, where we live now."

My mind immediately flashes on Vietnam and the possibility of a world hostility that could change all we presently know. Troubled, I say, "Alang has had a very tragic history—beginning here, and now being over there."

I try to purge the awful thoughts from my mind. "I would like to follow the farmer when he plows his field. Look at this ceramic shard. It appears to have calligraphy on it."

"Sometimes he finds larger pieces. I will tell him to save them for you."

"Wow! I would like them. This is exciting. Alang is that old?"

We peel off our sweaters as we continue searching for shards. The sun is becoming hot. The air is unsettlingly still.

MULLA COMES BY as I review what we're going to cover in class today. He sits quietly, looking at some of my books.

"Mulla, what's happening?"

A blast of nearly hurricane-force wind rattles the very bones of the house. The sound of tin roofs desperately straining to remain in place is deafening. We stare out the window, expecting to see sheets of metal flying through the air. Then, in an instant, all is calm—deadeningly calm.

"Mulla, what was that?"

"Wow! That was a strong wind. It blew off the Caspian Sea and the Soviet desert."

"Does that happen often?"

"Sometimes, but that was very bad."

Mulla and I meet Shaban Ali as we head for class. He, too, was shocked by the strong gust of wind. It becomes part of our lesson for the day. I learn unexpected winds often roar furiously across the deserts. We progress to other subjects, but an hour later, another gale-force gust bursts upon us. Now it returns from the mountains like a raging lion not satisfied by its previous angry rampage. We crouch, eyes raised, anticipating the metal roof parting and revealing the sky above. Again, quickly, an uncanny calm descends upon the village. It is broken by short, intermittent blasts throughout the remainder of the afternoon.

RUMBLINGS AND FIBBERY

WEDNESDAY, FEBRUARY 10, 1965 "*Salaam*," Jack and Dave greet me. "Do you want to go to the cinema tonight? There's an Indian film in town Iranians are talking about—*Sangom*. Apparently it's a real tearjerker. Silly Iranians, they're so emotional," Jack scoffs. "They cry over the least little thing. Let's go. I'll bet we won't cry. American guys don't get so carried away like that."

At dinner Dave says, "You seem very somber today, Tom. Is something bothering you?"

"Well . . . I went to see Mr. Vahdati. I feel so unsettled about something he said. We were talking in Farsi about Alang, and he said something I couldn't believe, so I had him say it in English."

"What did he say?"

"He asked me if I was ready to leave Alang in a few months. It just took the wind out of me—like someone punched me in the gut. I don't know why I feel this way, but I do." I bite the side of my upper lip. "I have come to love Alang and its people. They're my friends—they're like my family. I'm not sure I want to leave. I feel terrible, all confused."

"Did he tell you anything else?"

"Well, after Don Croll and Dr. Drake saw you guys a couple weeks ago, they stopped to see Mr. Vahdati. Don told him they were going to transfer me to another part of the country. Mr. Vahdati said it like I already knew. I don't know what to say. It's very hard to imagine I'll be leaving Alang and you guys. It won't be the same any more." I look down at my plate and twist my mouth.

"Oh, they probably won't do it; you can always tell them you don't want to go to the new place," Jack tries to cheer me up. "Besides you're essential to making our Scrabble games more stimulating."

"Thanks," I respond, halfway smiling, "but I'm disturbed about not achieving any big projects during the two years I'm here. Shaban Ali is fully capable of accomplishing the development proposals in the villages without me. I often think I'm wasting my time here. Nevertheless, it takes time to figure things out. I've been in Alang short of four months now, and I'm just beginning to learn about the village and the people. But I also think I should be using my education in a more constructive way while I'm here—doing what I actually know how to do. The problem is in Alang I don't seem to know what it is I'm supposed to do. Still, I love Alang. It's my home now. The people have adopted me, and I've adopted them. It's so difficult to imagine not being there."

"Oh, come on, let's go to the movie. It will do you good, get your mind on to something else."

"Yeah, it sounds just like what I need to see—a real sad movie," I retort with sarcasm.

Sangom is spectacular, with dramatic cinematography of the sweeping grandeur of India and the tourist destinations of Europe. In particular, it offers sensitive insights into human relationships in another culture. At the end of the long film, as everybody rushes to exit, three tough Americans remain seated, trying to stifle sniffles and not let each other see they are wiping their eyes.

We walk home in silence. Finally I say, "It's been a while since I've seen a movie in Farsi. I understand so much more now. It's almost like seeing a movie in English."

THURSDAY, FEBRUARY 11, 1965 Barkley arrives from Gonbad. We both detect Jack and Dave are in a less-than-positive mood today.

"Everyone back home thinks Peace Corps Volunteers have it so tough, that we live under such grim conditions," Jack complains.

"Yeah, and that we're all doing these great things—building bridges, schools, bathhouses, and teaching in schools that don't have teachers,"

Dave chimes in. "What's so important about English anyway? Most of our students will never use it."

"You're right. No one in America has a clue about any other place in the world and what the Peace Corps is all about," I concur, swept along with their rancor. "They think we have it so rough, and we're working wonders. I'm always busy and never have any time for myself, but at the end of each day, does it really make any difference? What's the point?"

"The Peace Corps is still the best program America has to help the world understand America, to give people in other parts of the world the opportunities they need and want, and to build the friendships so vital to world peace. Even if one of your students goes on to do something for Iran, you will have made a substantial contribution, and chances are there will be many who will become leaders in their communities and in Iran. Don't ever underestimate your potential," Barkley reminds us.

"Yes, I believe in the Peace Corps, but so many Americans think our life is so difficult. Look at me out in Alang. My life has never been so undemanding. I never had so much money back in the States. You guys in cities may be different because you have ways of spending the money we get each month—restaurants, the cinema, taxis, and other things. In Alang, we have none of those things—not even a teahouse. I'm lucky if I can spend one-third of my monthly allowance. Shaban Ali, my *dehyar*, makes about the same amount I do, but he has a wife and three children to feed. It's just not fair."

"Yeah, absolutely we could use more money each month. Living here in Gorgan is expensive, but look at this place. It's as nice as any house in America. In fact, it's better than the places I rented when I was going to university," Jack continues. "We should take a picture and send it to *Time* or some other national magazine and write an article telling what the Peace Corps is really like."

"Wait a minute," Barkley cautions. "Don't do anything like that. Don't destroy the integrity of the Peace Corps. America and the world need the Peace Corps."

"Yeah," I agree, "the Peace Corps definitely provides the most hope for changing the world. C'mon you guys, we can't spoil all the good it does."

FRIDAY, FEBRUARY 12, 1965 It's sort of getting to be old hat to see other Peace Corps Volunteers. And frankly, it's a real downer. All they do is complain. I'm better off staying in Alang. But this is a short reunion in Shahi. Most of us head off with a stiff leg as soon as we get our gamma globulin shot in the butt.

On the way home I stop at another volunteer's house to pick up my bicycle. He had gotten a motor scooter, so the Peace Corps gave me his. It is loaded on top of an old bus going east. By late afternoon, we reach the signpost for Alang. The bike is unloaded and I gingerly place my numb rear on the seat and head to Alang. It's embarrassing to have the fanciest, shiniest new bicycle in the village, with lights, bell, and kickstand. This confirms my Americanness and our wealth and loud showiness. I'm trying to fit into the village—to be one of them—and this sets me apart.

I'm stopped by a group of self-assured, well-dressed young men out for a stroll, "Wow, you got a classy bicycle! Was it made in America?" Immediately, as always, a group of children surrounds to eavesdrop, but they are also truly captivated by the beauty of my new bicycle.

"No, it was made in Iran," I happily respond.

"But, it's so nice."

"Yes—and it was made in Iran."

"Why didn't you get an American bicycle?"

"Iran makes very good bicycles. Why should I get an American bicycle?"

"But you have an American watch and American clothes and shoes. Your camera is from America. Everything from America is of the highest quality."

"This bicycle from Iran is first-rate. I like it."

"Yes, but America is rich. We know from American movies. You should have an American bicycle."

Discussions of this nature are endless. For Iranians, everything about America is better. Daily I grapple to build their national pride—a sense of their collective- and self-worth. I am happy the children are hearing my defense of their country.

"Not everybody in America is rich. My family is not rich. Everyone in my family works. We have always worked very hard to live. Even my mother works. She works as a babysitter."

"We don't believe you. You went to university. Anyone who goes to university is rich. You had a car, too."

"I worked every summer and while I was taking classes so I could pay for my tuition and buy books and supplies. I lived at home because I could not afford to live in the university dormitory. My brother and I bought an old car. I took him to work on my way to the university."

"Oh, we know you lie. You are a rich American. All Americans are rich. You have a camera. No one in Iran has a camera unless he is rich."

"It is only a Kodak Pony camera. My family got the camera by saving Green Stamps." I attempt to describe the concept of savings stamps, but realize there is nothing in their culture that comes near to explaining this.

"You claim you go to Tehran or to conferences when you leave Alang for a few days, but you go to America to see your parents and brother. When are they coming to visit you?"

"My parents cannot afford to travel to Iran to see me, and I can't go to see them. It's too far, and it costs too much."

"You must have done something very bad in America and you had to escape. That's why you came to live in a village in Iran. No rich American would ever live in a village like this unless he was running away."

The children look at me wide-eyed while the young men grin, relishing my discomfort. This frustrating line of reasoning often comes from a few of the sons of the richest men in Alang or the smart young men on the streets in Gorgan and Kordkuy. They know they won't serve their military duty; their father will pay someone off. They will go to university, never have to work, and may have a fancy car as well.

"No, I'm here as a Peace Corps Volunteer. I'm here to help you in any way I can. President Kennedy started the Peace Corps to provide assistance to countries around the world and so people in other countries would learn about real Americans, not just the ones you see at the cinema. And he wanted Americans to learn about the people in other countries. He wanted us to become friends and, when we return home, to tell about the people we met in these countries."

"If you're here to help us, help me get into a university in America. I want to go to America. America is good. Everything in America is good."

"If you want to study in America, you need to apply to an American university. That's for you to do. I can help you fill out the forms, but I can't tell the university to accept you. Of course, you'll have to know English well."

"See, you're not really here to help us. You are here as a spy, an American spy. You are part of the CIA. We know all about the CIA and the terrible things they do. They got rid of our great Prime Minister Mossadegh," another sly young man intervenes.

"I'm not a spy. Leave the CIA out of this. I don't like the CIA. I would never be part of it. The Peace Corps has nothing to do with the CIA."

"That's what you say. That's what you are directed to say because you are part of the CIA."

"No, I'm not. I told you, I don't like the CIA."

Smiling at my uneasiness, they continue, "That's what you say. You write a report each month. You say you send it to the Peace Corps but it goes directly to the CIA. America is very clever. The Peace Corps is just a slick cover-up. America sends the Peace Corps all over the world to be spies. It sounds convincing—peace and friendship—but you're really here to be a spy."

"I told you I'm not a spy. Why would the Peace Corps put me in a village like Alang if I were a spy? What makes Alang so important to America? If I were a spy, certainly they wouldn't have me here in Alang."

"Oh, you're just here to learn the language more quickly so you can do your work elsewhere in Iran. America is clever."

"Veleshkon" (Stop it). Shaban Ali and Mulla approach and come to my defense. They tell the children to scatter and give disapproving glances to my tormentors.

Shaban Ali smiles. "Wow, you got your bicycle. Super." I discern his disappointment, as it will be that much longer before he is able to get a motor scooter.

"Beah, bring your new bicycle. Mulla, come with Tom to my house for tea. You're welcome too," he politely invites the village know-it-alls, confident they will refuse his offer of *taroof* and he will not pursue it.

"I'm sorry the Peace Corps didn't give me a motor scooter. I wish you could have gotten one too," I tell Shaban Ali.

"It's OK. Your bicycle is all right. I'll speak to your landlord about finding a place for it."

MONDAY, FEBRUARY 15, 1965 "*Salaam*, Tom. Stop."

My heart sinks when Ghasem hails me as I try to zoom undetected through Kordkuy on my bicycle. I have learned to travel fast and take the back streets to avoid being caught. Today is a bad day.

"Tom, you are my friend. How are you?" Instantly others, many others, gather around. Ghasem is in his glory, basking in the attention his association with an American brings him. I counter his English in Farsi. He continues in English, I in Farsi.

"Tom, come to my house. We are friends. You are my good friend."

"Sorry, I can't today. I have errands to do and I have a meeting in Alang," I respond in Farsi. It is a half lie, one I have used on Ghasem many times before.

He is persistent. "My friend, you must come to my house. We are the best of friends," he tells me in Farsi so the curious bystanders will envy his close relationship with the foreigner.

Mercifully, I extract myself from him and the gawking onlookers, and escape to the *hammam* and post office.

WEDNESDAY, FEBRUARY 17, 1965 The weather valiantly struggles toward spring. Days of warm sunshine attempt to dry the soggy, rutted streets of Alang, but cold, gray, cloud-draped skies and rain seem to win the battle. Notwithstanding, Shaban Ali and I find a few clear days to work in the garden. Tofigh Rahemi has given me a portion of his garden to raise some vegetables of my own.

"Shaban Ali, do they ever put manure on this soil?"

"No, I don't think so."

"We need to get some manure or fertilizer and work it into the dirt before we plant the seeds. It would have been best if manure had been put on in the fall so it could have soaked in during the winter rainy season. Where can we get some manure?"

I get a vague answer like, "It will happen."

FRIDAY, FEBRUARY 19, 1965 To the astonishment of my guests, I make popcorn. I shake the pan over the burner of my gas stove. Their eyes broaden as they hear the kernels popping. I hold the cover down as the last kernels spring to life, melt some trusty Shahpasand shortening (almost like butter), pour it over the popped corn, and salt it.

They are fascinated by the delicious treat from America and want a few kernels to plant. I explain, "You won't get any corn if you only have a few plants. You must have many plants near each other so they can cross-pollinate and produce babies. I will grow a large area of corn so we can all have some for next year."

They appear skeptical about my explanation. No doubt they think I'm being selfish with my supply and don't want to share it with them.

SATURDAY, FEBRUARY 20, 1965 *"Cheh ajab"* (Unbelievable), Shaban Ali exclaims as he stares in disbelief at the picture of a walnut with a tiny brass hinge on it in my *Print* magazine.*

"Oh, *baleh*. That's the way we raise them in America. It's too much work to take them out of the shells, so we grow them with hinges on them," I respond, struggling to keep a straight face.

He looks at me quizzically and detects my restrained but subversive smile. With wide eyes he, too, grins, and I burst out in laughter. I explain it is an ad for a paper company, and they do clever things to catch your attention. "Good, isn't it?"

My friends now often catch me in preposterous exaggerations about the wonders of American inventions and customs. This only encourages me to fabricate a more outlandish one the next time and they devise ludicrous ways of tricking me in return.

SUNDAY, FEBRUARY 21, 1965 "Yavar, look what you left at my house again," I say with playful rebuke. I hand him his rosary—more commonly called worry beads. "You forever leave it at my place. Obviously you don't worry. You want me to do your worrying for you. That's why you leave it."

---

* *Print* is a bimonthly graphic design magazine.

He looks at me sheepishly and grins. "Tom, I don't want you to worry. I leave it with you so you can do my praying for me."

"Yavar, in America if someone leaves something at our house three times, we keep it," I say, smiling mischievously.

"Here. It is yours."

"No, Yavar. I am joking."

"No, it is yours. *Befarmayid.*"

"But it is your rosary. You need it to pray. I was just joking. It's not true. We don't do that in America."

"No, Tom, I want you to have it."

The *taroof* stalemate drags on, passing the rosary back and forth. Finally, with a touch of guilt, I accept.

TUESDAY, FEBRUARY 23, 1965 After days of waiting for the weather to clear Shaban Ali says, "It's dry enough for us to work in the garden today. Let's plant the seeds you bought."

"But we've never gotten any manure. I'm not going to plant anything until we fertilize." I stand there obstinately. "Where can we get manure?" We locate some, work it into the soil, and plant potatoes just as I had learned from my father when I was a kid on the farm (two eyes to each cut segment of potato you put in the ground), radishes, parsley, eggplant, tomatoes, and sweet corn. In another area, far from the sweet corn, I plant a patch of popcorn from the precious cob I brought from America.

WEDNESDAY, FEBRUARY 24, 1965 Like every day, Yavar and Ismael enjoy tea, cookies, and candy at my house.

"Your tea is so flavorful. What kind of tea is it?" Yavar asks.

"It is Twinings Earl Grey tea from England. I got it in Gorgan."

"It has such a distinct aroma."

I appreciate having them over. We are becoming fast friends.

"Come, it's time to go to our house for dinner," Ismael says.

"I'm sorry. I can't make it tonight."

They look at me very disappointedly. "Why? Do you have other plans?"

"Yes."

"Are you invited to someone else's house?"

"No." There is no use lying. Everybody in Alang knows what I am doing all the time. They would find out. "I want to stay home this evening."

Hurt and displeasure register in their faces. "Oh, please. You have to come tonight. We won't see you for a few days, as tomorrow you're going to Bandarshah with the Boy Scouts."

"Yes, but tonight I can't make it. I'm sorry." I don't remind them I have been at their house every evening this week. "I really enjoy being with you and your families, but I feel guilty about giving the impression I have chosen certain people above others in the village. I must be available to be a friend to everyone in Alang. I can't come to your house every night."

"Please, you must be with us tonight. You won't be here for several days."

"Yes, but I can't come tonight." I don't tell them the suggestion of a restricted friendship and their insistence on my being with them every evening is causing me stress. In fact, today I have had a slight case of the "Tehran Trots" thinking about how I am going to broach this with them.

"I'm sorry I can't come. Say *salaam* to your wife and children. I'll be happy to come next week."

As soon as I hear them pass through the gateway door, I run down to the *mostarah*, grabbing the *aftabeh* on my way. I get there just in time.

INCONGRUITIES

THURSDAY, FEBRUARY 25, 1965 The compact, shiny two-tone blue bus filled with boys and their teachers picks its way across the plain on a painfully narrow dirt byway elevated above the bleak surrounding fields. *It's bizarre we would take this route from Kordkuy to Bandarshah and not go on the main road. Maybe the driver doesn't have a license,* I muse.

Suddenly the bus twists and groans, the rear lunges to the side. Silence momentarily overcomes the noisy boys. The teachers call out to Allah and Mohammad, and the boys parrot the invocation. We hang precariously over the ditch on the right. The driver sweats to bring the bus back up on

Boy Scout outing

the grade, but we slide even farther down. The teachers persuade the driver to let us off before he makes another effort to alleviate our perplexing problem. Eventually, with lots of opinions and pushing, the bus settles back up on the berm and we press on.

We are on a three-day Boy Scout outing to Bandarshah and Ashouradeh. Two of the teachers in Alang and several from Kordkuy are the Scout leaders, and they wanted me to join them for the holiday weekend. Dutifully I wrote to the Peace Corps for authorization to go, but received an answer not granting permission. *Hmm,* I thought, *this seems like a prime opportunity to interact with the youth of Alang and Kordkuy. What better way is there of reaching parents than through their children?* Some of these boys will be the future leaders of their communities and Iran. This is the best way of building long-term bridges of friendship and peace. The Peace Corps just doesn't see things the way I do. I decided to go anyway. Besides, this is a holiday weekend. I would have gone to Gorgan to spend the long weekend relaxing with Jack and Dave. That would have been a lot less stressful than having to operate in a foreign language with a group of rowdy boys.

Bandarshah is a dreary, treeless frontier town. Buildings on the main street are crumbling remnants of a recently hoped-for glory, now patched together like a youthful but battered and forgotten soldier, covered in casts and bandages.

"He's taking pictures to show how poor Iran is," I overhear one of the Boy Scout leaders warily say to another. I'm troubled my casual recording of the decaying town would be interpreted in this manner, and resolve to be more judicious with my use of the camera.

The Boy Scout headquarters in Bandarshah is cold and drafty, but we keep warm with activity. A portable phonograph and records afford glorious entertainment. Reluctantly I am coerced to do the Twist—to Persian music, of course. It's a hit, and the Scouts and their leaders join the fun.

FRIDAY, FEBRUARY 26, 1965 We joyfully follow the train track from the town to the sea for our excursion to Ashouradeh and the sturgeon and caviar processing plant at the end of the long, narrow peninsula that stretches eastward at the southeastern tip of the Caspian.

"Why do the pier and track end here? They end on dry land, nowhere near the sea," I inquire as I gesture to the saline wasteland.

"The sea used to be much higher. Not too many years ago this area used to be in water. The sea is constantly evaporating, and the rivers that drain into it have been dammed and diverted for irrigation. The water becomes saltier and saltier," one of the teachers explains.

"Wow. Without a doubt, this shows the impact of human beings on the environment," I respond. "What will happen to the fish and other marine life in the sea if the water continues to recede and becomes even saltier? This could be horrendous." Optimistically, I determine that discussion of concern for the environment in the presence of the Scouts could have a positive outcome.

"*Baleh*, but Iran shares only a minor portion of the Caspian coastline with the Soviet Union. They control most of it, and we don't get along with them, so there is little we can do."

At a recently constructed dock, we are met by the manager of the sturgeon processing plant and pile into his boat for the short trip to Ashouradeh.

"Do you have your SAVAK pass with you," he asks, "in case you are stopped by the police? We are very close to Soviet fishing claims when we are on the island. In fact, until 1952 the whole peninsula was controlled by the Soviet Union."

"*Baleh*, I always have it with me."

He is a jovial, friendly man who is happy to meet an American and enjoys talking to me. It's probably rare for a foreign visitor to speak Farsi. He leads the boys in popular Persian folk songs as we head across the water, towing a large skiff to the island after delivering a load of sturgeon.

"*Baroon, barooneh zeminah tar misheh…*" I begin the haunting Persian folk song about a young Persian girl planting rice in the rain that we learned in Peace Corps training in Utah. Our host's eyes light up, and he promptly carries the melody along and gets the Scouts to join in. They are thrilled I know this song that so typifies their northern Iranian culture.

Ashouradeh is a stark contrast to the squalor of Bandarshah. Everything is neat and clean—evidence that, with care and determination, change can occur. An excellent lesson for the boys.

As we tour the facility, we are told about how the fish are caught and brought in, the competition with the Soviet Union over fishing rights, the cleaning of the fish, the extraction of the caviar, and that the prized white caviar is reserved for the Shah. Then we are taken into the freezer. Giant white logs of fish are stacked to the ceiling all around us. The largest fish can weigh anywhere from 1,000 to 2,000 pounds.

As excited as we are to see the enormous frozen fish, we welcome retreating to the warmth outside. After lunch we board the boat for the journey back.

"Come anytime," our host tells me as he shakes my hand.

"*Moteshakeram*, thank you for a great time. I would love to come back and it would be a pleasure to see you again. *Khodahafez*."

On our hike back to Bandarshah, the boys persuade me to do the Twist one more time. It is impossible to do it on the stones in the bed of the track, so I do it on the rails. They are impressed. "Here, here." They hold out money for me as they do for dancers at wedding celebrations. I feel foolish and get some of them to join me in the fun.

SUNDAY, FEBRUARY 28, 1965 Special mail today—my first letter from Del since she arrived in Africa. She's enthusiastic about the Peace Corps and being in Mzuzu, the provincial capital of northern Malawi, where she teaches five French classes at the government secondary school. There are seven PCVs in Mzuzu. She lives in a modern brick house—a duplex—with a patio and all the conveniences of home, including a refrigerator. But she says she is learning to cook on a wood stove "so I can train my cook. I also have a gardener. We have dances every Saturday night, and I'm involved with a number of student clubs."

A cook! A gardener! A refrigerator! A modern brick house with a patio! Poor girl, she is learning to cook on a wood stove! I'm incredulous. *Dances every Saturday night! I'll be lucky if I ever get to a dance these whole two years! And two servants! One is not enough!* I look around at the manure-encrusted walls of my little room and think how wonderful a refrigerator would be. I don't even have electricity but for a few hours each day. And my friends are concerned that she's gone to darkest Africa!

Mom's letters are consistently full of inane questions and comments. "Are you eating well? Buffalo meat! It sounds terrible! Are you sure it's OK? Is it tough? Is it gamey? Do you have enough toilet paper? Can you buy it there? Should we send you some more?" Then in two weeks—it takes that long to get a response—"You're not using the toilet paper you packed in your airfreight! What are you using? Old newspapers? Should we send you the old Sears-Roebuck catalogues? Your underwear must look frightful! I can't imagine cow manure on your walls! Does it stink? Are you warm enough? Should we send you some warm clothes? Do you have enough money? Are the people poor? How can you live without electricity all the time? You have to get your water from the village well? Don't you even have running water? And you use an outhouse? That's worse than being on the farm!" Two weeks later there will be more. As much as we try to explain, Peace Corps Volunteers acknowledge it is hard for parents in America to envision another place in the world.

Her letter today asks, "Do you know Sal Johnman? We heard all about him on *The Dinah Shore Show* and the outstanding work he is doing. He's a Peace Corps Volunteer in Iran who's building a bridge at Pol-e Bihajat. For thousands of years the people have wanted a bridge but have never gotten one. Now Sal is doing it. Have you met him?" Somehow any association with Sal would make me important.

I answer, "The Dinah Shore program must have been very interesting. Yes, I know Sal Johnman. We know him all too well, and Peace Corps Tehran does too. Iranian officials have requested his dismissal from several projects. Whenever we have a conference, he does more to make our group unsatisfied than you can imagine. Barkley and he really get into it because Barkley always has to fight back and bolster our spirits. Following a conference, Barkley is completely exhausted. Incidentally, the bridge at Pol-e Bihajat was never built. There is absolutely no demand for a bridge, as this is in the desert and there is water only about two weeks every year. One year the water takes one route and the next year another path. If the bridge were built, it might be on dry land forever."

Unfailingly, our Iran Peace Corps Volunteer newsletter is filled with helpful tips about living in Iran. This month there is a perceptive rejoinder to a volunteer's recommendation on how to deal with toilet paper in the Iranian plumbing system. "Burn it before you wash it down," the writer had advised. Now another volunteer comments, "That's a brilliant idea." But painfully advocates, "Stand up before you light the paper on fire."

MONDAY, MARCH 1, 1965 "Stop laughing! We'll get beat up and have to run for our lives. You're laughing at the wrong times," Nosrat Seyed Alangi and Sohrab Jahangery, both teachers in Alang, admonish me as we watch the film *Aroos Farangi* (Foreign Bride) at the cinema in Kordkuy.

We bicycled to Kordkuy to see the film with the other teachers who went on the Boy Scout outing over the weekend. The movie is a satire on the peculiarity of European and American customs. To emphasize the strangeness of foreign traditions, Iranian customs likewise are exaggerated. The ridiculous mistakes and misunderstandings of the foreign bride elicit outrageous laughter from the Iranians. I find this funny but the exaggeration of Iranian customs is even more humorous and, it's true, I am laughing by myself. It's hard to stifle my amusement at the antics of the taxi-driver bridegroom and his family and their reaction to his foreign bride.

We escape the cinema without incident. Obviously the teachers were embarrassed by my laughter at the Iranians. Nowhere in Iran have I felt threatened or in danger, except while in a vehicle barreling crazily down the highways—not even in Kordkuy. But I have learned in my travels that Kordkuy has a reputation as the toughest town in Iran. When I say I am from Alang, near Kordkuy, Iranians' eyes widen and they say, "Kordkuy! *Texas-e Iran*" (Texas of Iran).

Seyed Alangi and I bid goodnight to Jahangery and the teachers from Kordkuy. Our voices are drowned in a strong wind that howls through town. It's from the west, so it blows us home as we navigate the rutted, rock-strewn highway by the light of my bicycle lamp and Seyed Alangi's flashlight. We stop and pull into the ditch when a lone transport truck passes us. We dismount and push our bicycles down the path to Alang, bracing ourselves against the wind. Now the strong crosswind nearly blows us over.

All night I await the sudden removal of my tin roof as I hear the metal stretching and screeching, and feel the building shudder despite its determination to remain stalwart against the dreadful fury.

TUESDAY, MARCH 2, 1965 Dawn arrives calm and bright. The early sun wakes me as it peeks in the transom windows above my double doors, fleetingly emphasizing the unevenness of the daub-covered wall across from my bed. I turn over to grab a few more winks.

"Mister Tom, Mister Tom." It's Shaban Ali.

My eyes must look like a rooster's ass, I surmise as I greet him.

"How was the movie?"

"It was very funny. You should see it. Come in."

"I can't stay long, but I must go over our schedule for today. We have a council meeting in Ghalayesh this afternoon. We can check how the new school is coming along."

"Good. It will be great to see our friend the Literacy Corpsman. I wonder how he's doing?"

Progress towards completion of the school in Ghalayesh is slower than in Ghalandarayesh, but the Literacy Corpsman and the villagers are looking forward to the beginning of construction when the rains subside. The entire village is now a bleak and muddy quagmire, but then, I wade through deep mud in the streets of Alang too.

ALTHOUGH I CANCELLED CLASSES TODAY, dinner is at Ismael and Yavar's. The children are excited to see me—it has been a week. Yavar's five-year-old son Farsheed asks his father for some paper and pens. He sits and draws pictures for me—some of birds, another of a village bus with its driver, passengers, and a policeman directing traffic.

"Who is this?" I ask about a colorful drawing.

"That's me!"

"I thought so. You have dark hair."

"Here, this is for you."

"Oh, Farsheed, thank you. I will always keep it to remember you."

He smiles and hands me the drawings of the bus and birds too.

His little sister Fereshteh and Ismael's two-year old son Davood compete for my attention. Both are a delight, she, a bit more reserved than the mischievous Davood. Vida, Ismael's four-year old daughter, is shy. She helps her mother prepare dinner between intervals of sitting with her father and listening to our relaxed conversation. I'm fond of these families and regret I ever disappoint them by not coming. However, this could too easily slip into a nightly engagement that would restrict my friendships with others.

Ismael turns on the radio to catch the evening news. The easiness of my tranquil evening within the gentle protection of Iranian families is shattered. We somberly look at each other as we listen. News is bleak. The US has commenced air attacks on major sites in North Vietnam— the objective: to destroy North Vietnam's air defenses and industrial infrastructure. I cover my mouth with my hand as I listen intently to the Farsi, straining to comprehend every word.

"Now, for sure, we are at war," I mumble.

Ismael switches off the radio before his wife enters with the cloth for the floor and the dishes and silverware. We sit there silently until she leaves.

"It's not good, is it?"

"*Baleh.*" Ismael and Yavar say quietly. We look at the children playing.

Vida, Davood (l.); Farsheed, Fereshteh (r.)

NEW MOTIVATIONS AND VIETNAMS

THURSDAY, MARCH 4, 1965 I need to be in Gorgan this weekend. Can't miss this opportunity. I heard Kathy was coming. This definitely brightens the scenery. She trained in the same Peace Corps group as Jack and Dave, and was teaching in Tehran. She is being reassigned to Gorgan to teach English in the girls' school, and will be living with an Iranian doctor and his wife, who is a midwife.

We entertain her with dinner at the Hotel Miami and a game of Scrabble, but decide it's prudent to get her home at a reasonable hour. We definitely don't want the police patrol to turn in a report on us her first night in Gorgan.

FRIDAY, MARCH 5, 1965 Late in the morning we get Kathy and go to lunch, then return to Jack and Dave's to play more Scrabble.

"Wow, it's nearly four o'clock. I should get a bus back to Alang."

"Oooh," Jack responds, "what's the point in going now? You can go tomorrow morning."

"Yeah," Dave chimes in. "We can play some more Scrabble. You might as well stay another night."

"No, I need to get back."

"For what? What are you going to do?" Jack retorts. "What's there in Alang? Besides, Kathy's just arrived and it's imperative we give her a proper welcome before she starts work here in Gorgan."

"Well, you're right. I could go back tomorrow morning. You guys really know how to twist my arm."

"It's not hard," Jack smiles slyly.

SATURDAY, MARCH 6, 1965 *"Salaam allekum,"* my cronies greet me when I drop in at the Sherkat-e Sargardon for a dose of verbal and intellectual scintillation. "Well, how was it? How is she?"

I ignore their questions, pretending I don't understand, but my blush at their insinuation betrays my comprehension.

"Tell us. Was it good?"

I had told them a Peace Corps girl was coming to Gorgan, so they knew my weekend diversion to Jack and Dave's was heightened by motivations other than seeing the guys.

"You didn't come back last night. It must have been very good." Reza's dark eyes glisten wickedly.

Everyone chortles.

I feel myself getting redder. "We *all* had a good time," I counter, trying to alleviate my discomfort by emphasizing the all. "We talked and played Scrabble."

"Scrabble? What's scrabble?"

"It's a game where you make words."

Reza looks up the word in his Persian/English dictionary. He guffaws and tells the guys something in Farsi. They laugh boisterously. Scrabble could have a very suggestive meaning in Farsi. I blush more.

"So, how was it? *Rafti*" (Did you go)?

"Na." There is no point in pretending I don't know what they are alluding to.

"You lie. Certainly you went. That's why you didn't come back."

Oh, my gosh. Just because I stayed in Gorgan an extra night I incriminated myself even more, I think.

"No, I told you, we talked and played Scrabble."

They hoot more, presuming they caught me in a trap.

"What's her name, the Peace Corps girl?" Reza asks.

"Kathy, Miss Kathy."

"Miss Kosi!"

There is uproarious laughter. I understand why and, with effort, suppress a grin. Persians have a hard time pronouncing the English "th" sound, but I know the use of the word *kosi* (a woman's private parts) is intentional.

It's an unfortunate name, I conclude, blushing and perspiring.

There are more lurid questions and insinuations. All the while, I struggle to uphold my innocence and Kathy's honor, but it ends in praise of America. "America is great," one of my tormentors rejoins. "Look at how their government provides for its men, sending a Peace Corps girl to Gorgan just for the Peace Corps guys."

"*Baleh*, but it's a shame they didn't do it earlier," one of the more thoughtful asserts.

MONDAY, MARCH 8, 1965 A somber mood pervades the Sherkat-e Sargardon this morning as I approach.

"*Salaam, Tom, hale shoma chetoreh?*" Reza lucklessly attempts to tune his transistor radio. My friends make out bits of the news broadcast between the static. I am lost to the crackling noise.

The guys look at me mournfully.

"Tom, America has sent ground troops into Vietnam," Reza solemnly tells me in English. "3,500 men."

I breathe deeply. No one says anything. We just listen. I sit there quietly, thinking. *My life has been a roller coaster of emotions ever since I got here.*

Reza turns off the radio.

"Will you have to go home now? Will you have to go to Vietnam?" one of the guys asks.

"No, I won't have to go while I am here, but when I go home I may be sent to Vietnam."

"Oh, by then the war will be over. America will have won," another reassuringly offers.

Everything is strained. Forlornly I say, "*Khodahafez,*" and wander off to my room.

THURSDAY, MARCH 11, 1965 The Pahlavidezh Turkoman bazaar captivates Jack, Dave, Kathy and me. Bright red rugs and fabrics cover the earth and the drab mud-brick walls lining the street. In one area, timid sheep and sprightly goats await their purchase. An occasional camel blinks its bored eyes at us and continues chewing. Tall and stately men with prominent

Central Asian cheekbones appear even taller in their long, dark coats and high astrakhan hats. Women wearing colorfully embroidered headdresses and paisley or floral shawls shyly stare at us. Kathy's exceptional height is the subject of wordless interest. The Turkoman are polite and reserved—salesmen who are not pushy.

Turkoman Bazaar, Pahlavidezh

Jack and Dave are tired and go home upon our return, but Kathy and I have not had enough, so we prowl the bazaar in Gorgan. I already know the best places—where the rugs are, the copperware, the woodworking and the jewelry sections, the fresh vegetables, and the colorful and aromatic spices. We have fun exploring together, but her presence walking beside me—not a respectable ten paces behind—and the fact that she's not wearing a headscarf or a *chador*, generates unwarranted attention. Young men on the streets make offensive comments and sounds. *What a difference when a young woman is present,* I think to myself. When I walk the streets alone, everybody is polite and cordial. We ignore the molesters as if we never heard them. Frequently older men reprimand them. Inwardly we feel vindicated.

FRIDAY, MARCH 12, 1965 My appearance in Alang after two nights in Gorgan prompts more churlish smiles and innuendos from the young men in the village. They relish imagining my activities and making me uneasy with their prying and scurrilous questions. They're eager to know, "Does she only do it with Peace Corps men or will she do it with Iranian men as well?" They are decidedly envious of my newfound opportunity and any denial is hopeless.

The driving rain while I was in Gorgan made the streets of Alang a nearly knee-deep mire of mud. "Yuk!" I exclaim as I open the door of my room. I almost gag and my eyes sting from the stench of cow manure. The west wall and curtains at the window are drenched halfway up, and the felt rugs on the floor are soaked. Fortunately the bricks and planks of my bookcase spared my precious library from damage. Shaban Ali and I drag the sopping rugs out and hang them over the balcony. For days, until everything dries, it seems like I have chosen to live in a cow barn. *Wow, this is the Peace Corps at its most primordial. I didn't join to live in luxury,* I tell myself, *but this is worse than living on the farm. At least there only the animals lived in the stink.*

MONDAY, MARCH 15, 1965 Shouting on the street outside my room awakens me. I part the curtains and peer down. Something has happened. Quickly I put on my clothes, run downstairs, and find my landlady at the gateway door. She is sobbing and calling out as she pushes her daughters back. Cautiously I look around her and see the bleeding gash on her husband's face as villagers try to restrain him, his son Ghorbon, and my friends Javad and Reza Abtahi. I attempt to step through the doorway, but Mulla shoves me back.

"What happened?"

"It's a fight," Mulla answers.

"Stop it," I yell above the din. A few look toward me, but the shouting and melee persist.

Someone shouts, "Mister Tom is here. Stop it!"

Gradually the villagers quell the ruckus and usher my landlord through the gateway to have his face cleaned and bandaged. I turn away as I see the blood. I hear the outcry of the Abtahi brothers as they are dragged away to their compound around the corner.

Young Ghorbon paces agitatedly. "Your friends did this," he shrieks at me, clutching a club.

Mulla follows me upstairs.

"What happened?" My eyes are wide and frightened.

"They're fighting over a piece of land. The old road to Alang divides their fields, but every year each has moved his fence a little farther out onto the road. Well, this year they moved them too far, and the fight started. It's very bad. A few years ago, ten people were killed in a nearby village over a similar dispute."

My heart sinks. *And I'm right in the middle of this,* I think.

"Stay out of it," he tells me. "Don't go out if they are fighting, and don't talk to them."

All day long I am on edge. I see my landlord stride out of the courtyard with an axe over his shoulder. Anxiously I wait to hear more shouting, but quiet prevails—fortunately.

Can there ever be peace in this world? If people who know each other can't get along, how can we expect nations to get along? Even in a peaceful little village like Alang terrible things occur. I am distressed. *No wonder we have Vietnams.*

TUESDAY, MARCH 16, 1965   Shouting again wakes me. I run down to the gateway door. *Haji* Torfeh is nearby. Apprehensively I step over the threshold and go to her. She entreats the villagers to stop. Between her pleadings she informs me both sides gathered guns during the night. However, *Haji* is relentless in her pursuit of peace. "For the sake of Allah and our prophet Mohammad stop this," she begs. An uneasy calmness descends upon the angry crowd. Slowly it disperses.

Such power she has, I say to myself. *Who says women have no authority in this country? Everyone respects her in Alang. If anyone can stop this quarrel, it is she.*

BECOMING MASHTI

THURSDAY, MARCH 18, 1965 "Mister Tom, Mister Tom."

I ignore the calls from the street at 11 o'clock at night as I pack to go to Mashhad for Nou Ruz (New Year) with Shaban Ali.

"Mister Tom, Mister Tom. Come down!"

Reluctantly I pull the curtains aside, open the window, and look into the blackness below. *"Baleh?"*

"Mister Tom, your friends have come. Americans. They are your friends. They have come by jeep. Come down and see them."

"No, I'm busy and I need to get to bed." I suspect this is another hoax to get me out and talk for a while. It happens all the time. *"Shab bekheyr."*

"No, Mister Tom, you must come."

I resign myself to the insistence, close the window, and go down.

We head for the area of the new well in the center of town. He's right—there *is* a jeep there, and a group of villagers has gathered around. Hesitantly I approach and say, "Hello?"

"Hello." I'm greeted in the darkness by a distinctly British accent. "We're on our way from England to Australia, and got lost on the road to Gorgan. We thought this might be the way. We gathered from the people that an American lives here. What are you doing here? Where are we?"

"You are in a little village called Alang. Gorgan is about thirty kilometers farther on down the main highway." I motion. "I'm shocked you turned off on the little road to Alang."

"The main road was so bad. So we turned off at a big sign, assuming this was the way. Your name is Tom?"

"Yes."

"Hello, I'm Geoff. This is Peter. That's William and Anne." I shake each of their hands as I reach into the dark interior of their vehicle. "This is a surprise to find someone who knows English in such an out-of-the-way area of Iran. What are you doing here?"

"I'm an American Peace Corps Volunteer. I've been living here about five months now."

"Invite them to your house for tea," the villagers urge me. "Tell them they can spend the night in Alang. They should sleep here tonight."

"Would you like to come up to my house for tea? The villagers want you to stay here in Alang."

"No, we must be getting on to Gorgan. It's already very late."

"Yes, it will be almost midnight before you get there. It will be very hard to find a place at that time. You might as well stay in the village."

By now, Mulla appears, having been awoken. He says, "Tell them I will open my courtyard gate. They can put their jeep inside. I will bring them up to your room."

"One of the villagers has offered his home. He says you can put your jeep in his courtyard. It will be safe there."

They look at each other in the darkness.

"The villagers want you to stay. It will be better than traveling over these roads in the dark. The road is poor, especially this time of year."

The young men of the village accompany me to my house. Mulla brings the guests and I finally see their features by the dim light of my kerosene lantern. My little room is crowded. Two hours quickly pass as we share stories and I serve as translator.

FRIDAY, MARCH 19, 1965 Alang is abuzz with excitement. It is momentous to have foreigners spend the night in the village. There is a constant coming and going of people at Mulla's house. All want to meet the visitors.

"This place is like Victoria Station," Geoff says with a smile.

"I wouldn't know. I've never been to England. But this is the way it is here. Persians are very gracious. They love meeting people and are always eager to extend their hospitality.

"Shaban Ali and I missed the morning bus from Alang to Gorgan. Could you give us a lift out to the highway so we can catch a passing bus?"

"Sure—in fact, would you like a ride to Gorgan? It may be a little crowded, but if you don't mind you can pile in with us."

"That'd be super. Thank you."

As they let us off in Gorgan I tell them, "Have a safe trip. Drive carefully."

"Have a good trip too. Thank you for the Persian hospitality in Alang."

"You're welcome."

"Goodbye, thank you," Shaban Ali proudly tells them in English.

We go to the station to catch a bus to Mashhad; however, the next bus doesn't depart until dusk.

"Shaban Ali, I don't want to take an all-night bus ride to Mashhad. We would get there in the middle of the night, and it will be hard to find a hotel room. I came all the way from America and I want to see what Iran is like. I may never get to Mashhad again. Let's stay in Gorgan tonight and take the 6am bus tomorrow."

He looks at me. "There's nothing to see. It's only desert."

"But the desert is beautiful." I see he is disappointed. "We can stay at the Hotel Chahar Fasl and go early tomorrow morning. It will be better."

Reluctantly he agrees.

"*Salaam*, Mister Tom," the owner of the hotel greets me. He smiles and is delighted we are staying there.

"*Bah, bah, bah,*" he tells Shaban Ali, "Mister Tom has learned Farsi very well. He speaks like an Iranian now. He has become Iranian."

I am pleased. It is the highest compliment.

SATURDAY, MARCH 20, 1965 "Who is the person next to you? Where is he from?" the man near Shaban Ali asks. He and his wife and an older woman board the bus with us in Gorgan.

"This is Mister Tom, Mr. Tom Kehlobeh. He is an American."

I hold out my hand to greet him, "*Salaam, hale shoma khoobeh?*"

"*Salaam*, Behrangi, *Aghaye* Mustafa Behrangi," he introduces himself and asks Shaban Ali, "He knows Farsi? How does he know Farsi?"

"*Baleh*, he knows Farsi. He lives in Alang. He is an American Peace

Corps Volunteer. We work together in community development."

The women peer from behind their *chadors* and smile.

"And, what do you do, *Aghaye* Behrangi?" I inquire.

"I am a forester in Gorgan. I have heard of the American Peace Corps. There are two Peace Corps teachers in Gorgan, aren't there?"

"There are three here now. A Peace Corp woman came two weeks ago to teach in the girls' school."

All day long the bus wends its way through the desert, sending up a trail of dust behind. The desert's vastness is transcendent. Faraway mountains, barely visible in the haze, hover over slices of lakes at their feet. *Can this really be only a mirage?* I remain absorbed in my thoughts. The sensuous physical beauty of the earth transfixes me. It contains all the supple grace of a primordial sleeping woman—a temptress lying there to seduce me.

The bus is absurdly overcrowded, more like a village bus than one of the sleek behemoths that traverses routes between major cities. I look around; most passengers sit in a daze, their eyes closed and their heads bobbing to the rhythm of the bus as it jostles over the worn, rock-strewn roadway. They ignore the incredible beauty I perceive.

The driver repeatedly stops to pick up more passengers. A wail of complaint arises as the newcomers crawl over those already sitting in the aisle to stake out a claim somewhere behind. The driver admonishes the grumblers, "These are fellow pilgrims on the way to Iran's most holy city. Have mercy on them." We all know more passengers mean more money in his pocket. The Nou Ruz holiday is a great opportunity to capitalize on the annual pilgrimage. I complain the least, not because of my Farsi, but because I've learned to expect the worst.

It is dark when we arrive in Mashhad—7pm. It was a long, hard journey.

"Stay here in the bus station. *Aghaye* Behrangi and I will look for a hotel," Shaban Ali tells me. The women remain behind too—to the side, but near. My role is to be their protector, but it must not be obvious.

Later—much later—the men return, harried. "No hotel rooms are available anywhere. But we found two rooms in someone's house. It's the best we can do. The city is full of pilgrims."

Shaban Ali and *Aghaye* Behrangi dicker for a horse and buggy cab. "It will be cheaper and we can all fit in one." Shaban Ali apologizes for the mode of transportation. Little does he realize my enthusiasm, especially since the horse is fitted with elaborate woven trappings.

We head down the street and turn a corner. My heart skips a beat. Ahead, in radiant golden splendor, is the shrine of Imam Reza, its domes and minarets bathed in spectacular, shimmering light. We all gasp. I shiver with excitement. My eyes water from the sheer astonishment of experiencing something so extraordinary—so otherworldly—like living in the *Arabian Nights*. Shaban Ali smiles. He is aware of my entrancement, and thrilled to be the first who experiences this moment with me. I keep staring until we turn into a side street, then several others, and stop in front of a nondescript courtyard door. It looks like the others, except for the number on the plaque above. Shaban Ali knocks and a man opens the door.

"Befarmayid." He takes Shaban Ali and me to our room and Mr. Behrangi and the women to another.

"I'm sorry it isn't better, that there are no beds," Shaban Ali apologizes as we put down our bags.

"This is fine. I don't mind sleeping on the floor."

"Let's go. I want to take you to the shrine."

"Shouldn't we eat first? It's past 9 o'clock." I have been hungry for hours.

"No, let's go to the shrine first and then we'll eat. I can't wait for you to see it. It won't take long."

I make a mental note of the distances and number of turns among the alleyways as we head out to the main street. There it is again—the shrine. I shiver anew at the unqualified splendor of the vision. My knees nearly buckle as we stand beneath the towering and majestic entrance *iwan*, its gold and blue tiles bathed in magnificent light.

Thousands of pilgrims mill about the first courtyard. I'm overwhelmed by the magnitude of humanity and the brilliance of the tiles covering every surface. We make our way to a second courtyard—more people; then another and another, each as crowded and splendid as the one before. At last we near the portal to Imam Reza's tomb. Thousands of shoes are all about. Shaban Ali and I remove ours as well. We wait and follow closely behind hundreds of pilgrims entering the holy precinct. We advance only as the ones inside exit, their faces stained with tears. Inside, it is no longer the radiant splendor that astounds me; it is witnessing the intensity of grief and mourning that stirs me. For some inexplicable reason, here I cannot look around. A feeling of respect overcomes me. I look down in submission. I regret I don't understand the full significance of Imam Reza.*

"Tom, let's get out of here. It's New Year's Eve. It is too crowded tonight. We will come back the day after tomorrow, when there aren't so many people. It will be easier to see then."

Quietly we exit, collect our shoes, and proceed to the entrance. All the while I stare in awe at the brilliance of the tiles covering the walls, minarets, and domes. Never in my life have I seen anything so resplendent and powerfully moving. As we stop to admire the splendor, we notice a guard looking at me.

"Let's go," Shaban Ali urges me. We turn to leave. I feel a tug at my coat sleeve. It is the guard. Shaban Ali is unaware I've stopped.

"Where are you from?" the guard demands.

"Amrika."

"Come with me. You're not supposed to be here."

I start to go with the guard and don't call for Shaban Ali. I don't want to get him in trouble too. But Shaban Ali perceives I am not with him. He looks and sees me going off with the guard. He hurries to us.

"He is my friend," Shaban Ali tells the guard. I look at him, unsure if my eyes convey the sadness I feel for him.

The guard brusquely glances at Shaban Ali, "It makes no difference. You should know better. You come too."

As we jostle our way through the crowds, the guard meets an officer, "I found this American inside the shrine, over there, near the entrance. We're on our way to the office."

---

* The shrine commemorates the martyrdom in 817 CE of Shi'a Islam's eighth Imam, Reza. The famous Abbasid caliph Harun al-Rashid died in Mashhad in 809 CE, and his son, al-Ma'mun, built a tomb for his father and another for his son-in-law, the pious Reza, whose support al-Ma'mun failed to receive but needed to quell a series of revolts. When the Imam's charismatic presence at the royal court posed a threat to al-Ma'mun's rule, Reza died after eating poisoned grapes sent by al-Ma'mun. The tomb was built to disguise any implication in the crime. Shi'a Muslims, however, held al-Ma'mun directly responsible for Imam Reza's death, and over the centuries, local Sunni rulers or marauding Turkoman and Mongol forces repeatedly destroyed the tomb. In the early 17th century, when the Safavids established Shi'a Islam as the state creed, the Holy Shrine was rebuilt, and Mashhad became Iran's pre-eminent pilgrimage site.

"Get him out quickly. He hasn't seen anything yet. It's New Year's Eve. We're too busy tonight and it's too much paperwork to go through."

We are ushered out. My heart is pounding, and I suspect Shaban Ali's is too. Safely away, I look at him and say, "Shaban Ali, I don't have any identification with me. I left my passport and residence permit in our room."

His first expression is one of shock, and then he grins. He looks at his watch. "We were in there almost an hour." We both start laughing.

"Let's go eat."

It is 11:30pm when we return to our room. "Tom, you stay here. I want to go to the shrine to pray."

SUNDAY, MARCH 21, 1965 "Happy New Year, Tom," Shaban Ali wakes me.

"Happy New Year to you too," I say groggily.

We halfway smile at each other. No doubt, we are both thinking about the same thing—our close encounter last night.

"Let's get some breakfast," he tells me.

We head through the alleys and down the street toward the shrine. Pilgrims are eating at little tables in a crowded shop. Shaban Ali and I go to the counter to order.

He notices the startled look on my face. "Oh, this is *kalle pache*. It is very special. It is made on very important days, like New Year's, but every day is special when you are on a pilgrimage, so you can always get it in Mashhad."

Surely he sees my eyes popping. I say nothing.

"It's very good." It's evident he realizes he has to convince me.

I look at the large tray with a hole in the center on the counter. Nearly twenty sheep's heads, meticulously arranged so they look out at customers, encircle the perimeter of the tray. Some have grand curling horns. On others, the horns are very small. Here and there, a tongue hangs out the side of a mouth. The cook spoons a greasy broth from the pot beneath the central hole over the staring heads. I want to die.

"Two," Shaban Ali says.

The cook takes a bowl, sets it on the counter, grabs a head, and holds it over the bowl. He takes his fist and with a swift blow to the head I hear "ka-chuk." The contents fly into the bowl—eyes, brains, tongue, everything!

I do my best to refrain from grabbing another bowl and filling it too.

The cook then spoons some of the greasy broth into the bowl. He places the bowl and a spoon on a beat-up metal tray, slaps some *sangak* on the side, throws on some greens, and hands it to me. *"Befarmayid."*

"Moteshakeram," I reply with trepidation.

"Ka-chuk." Shaban Ali gets his next. We go to a table. I look in the bowl. "There are eyes floating in there," I tell Shaban Ali.

"Baleh, they are luscious." He spoons one from his bowl into a folded piece of *sangak*, pops on a sprig of greens, and places it in his mouth. "Oh, this is delicious," he says with obvious relish. "Try it."

I tear off a bit of *sangak*, timidly dip it into my bowl, and put it in my mouth. *Well, I've been baptized. I guess I'm becoming Iranian*, I tell myself. *This is my breakfast. I better eat it.*

"Good, isn't it?" Shaban Ali smiles as he savors the delicacy.

"Baleh," I agree halfheartedly. I work at my bowl—even try one of the eyes. I swallow it whole. The other waits, staring at me till the end.

"Did you like it?" Shaban Ali asks.

"It was OK," I answer cautiously. I don't want to appear too enthusiastic for fear he will want to have it tomorrow again.

"Tom, I would like to go to the shrine to pray. Do you want to go back to our room and wait for me?"

"No. You go to the shrine. I would like to look around Mashhad."

"You won't get lost?"

"No, I know the way back to our room. But I could meet you at the entrance to the shrine when you finish your prayers."

"Are you sure you won't get lost?" he asks again anxiously.

"No, I'll be fine."

"Kheili khoob. After lunch we'll go to the tomb of Khajeh Rabi. It is very beautiful. You will like it."

IT'S FUN SEARCHING through the little shops of Mashhad, mainly those that have old things. When I meet Shaban Ali and the Behrangis, we browse through more shops—sparkling gold jewelry, turquoise, perfumes, silver objects, new carpets, colorful scarves, commercial-looking velvet tapestries, and pilgrimage souvenirs. I am bored, but wait patiently while they look and bargain. They grow impatient when I stop in a junk shop, and discourage me from asking about prices. I take note of where the shop is so I can return when Shaban Ali is at prayer.

Shaban Ali is correct. The tomb of Khajeh Rabi* is unforgettable. Sitting majestically on a dry plain outside the city, it is shrouded by a grove of leafless poplars. Their linearity is echoed in the wooden scaffolding that sheaths the grand dome, which is under repair. Tiles sparkle in the brilliant sunlight. Persian families spend New Year's Day picnicking among the long, spiny shadows of the barren trees.

"Shaban Ali, let's investigate the village over there." It is farther on, not on our way back to the city. "It looks interesting. I would like to see it."

"Why do you want to go there? It's just a village."

"Yes, but the architecture is so different from Alang. Everything is made of mud bricks. The roofs are flat or have little domes, not like in the Caspian area. It would be fun to walk through a village like this."

Though he is tired from our journey to Khajeh Rabi, grudgingly he consents. Within the picturesque beauty of the humble village, everything is presented with integrity, in its most fundamental form—light playing off the adobe walls, shadows accenting arched recesses, and the monochrome uniformity of the earthy color. There is honesty here, I determine, a respect for ancient traditions.

Shaban Ali fails to be impressed, and I am cognizant of the vast chasm that exists between Iranians and me. They would rather peruse shops with tacky modern curios or walk in the faux-swanky neighborhoods of larger cities, as we did the evening we spent in Gorgan. There, ostentatious monstrosities that grandiloquently imitate and exaggerate the most banal features of contemporary Western architecture compete with each other for attention. *The epitome of bad taste,* I ordain. *Or am I being arrogant—a product of my design education?* Nonetheless, I wish Iranians would develop a respect for themselves and for their history and traditions. If only they

---

* The tomb honors a follower of the Prophet Mohammad, Rabi'a ibn Khothaym, who led 4,000 men to help Ali, the son-in-law of the Prophet. While in Khorasan, Imam Reza often came here to pray. The structure dates from the early 17th century, but has undergone numerous restorations.

would cultivate a native way of articulating and expressing their culture, and not be so enamored of the West.

Can I really be effective as a Peace Corps Volunteer when I look at things so differently? I want them to make advances in education, health, and sanitation, but I also want them to retain their own wonderful heritage—to respect what they have and not blatantly accept something American or European. I may never find a way to convey this, yet I hope, somehow, they will come to appreciate the importance of being Iranian.

Shaban Ali and I walk silently. I am thinking my thoughts and, he is thinking his. We have a long way to go to understand each other.

MONDAY, MARCH 22, 1965 I head for the area near the shrine with the shops I took note of yesterday.

"*Salaam*, Mister Tom."

I look up. "*Salaam, Aghaye* Muslemi Aghili. *Hale shoma chetoreh? Bah, bah, bah.* What a surprise to see you in Mashhad. Are you on a pilgrimage?"

"*Baleh. Hale shoma khoob hast?*"

"*Baleh, kheili khoobam. Moteshakeram.*"

"Did *you* come to Mashhad on a pilgrimage too? Are you alone?"

"No, I came with Shaban Ali Rahemi. He is at the shrine now. Praying."

"This is my wife." We nod and greet each other reservedly. Then Mr. Muslemi Aghili's countenance turns serious. "We arrived in Mashhad this morning. We are tired from the long bus ride from Kordkuy. We can't find a hotel room anywhere. What hotel are you at?"

"We are not at a hotel. There were no rooms available when we got here either. So Shaban Ali found a room in someone's house. Mr. Behrangi and his wife and mother from Gorgan are at the house too."

"Do you know anyplace we might stay?"

"The owner of our house has no more rooms available; but come with me. I'll help you."

I take the Muslemi Aghilis through the alleys near where we are staying, and knock on a door. A man appears. "Excuse me. Do you have a room for my friends? They came very far—from Kordkuy—on a pilgrimage. They are tired and can't find a hotel. Do you have a room for them?"

"No, I'm sorry. Our extra rooms are filled."

I knock at the next door. Same story. We continue down the alley without any luck. Finally a man says, *"Baleh, befarmayid."*

The Muslemi Aghilis go to see the room while I wait in the courtyard. They return smiling. "It's excellent. Thank you for helping us."

"You're welcome. Why don't you rest now? Shaban Ali will be thrilled you are in Mashhad too. I have met many people I know here. It seems everyone is in Mashhad for the holidays."

"Everyone knows you, Mister Tom," he says with a smile.

TODAY IS MY MOTHER'S BIRTHDAY, and I'm determined to buy her a piece of turquoise. Mashhad is known for its turquoise, mined in nearby Nishapur. I resume my mission to find the shops I couldn't linger in before. I couldn't buy anything when I was with Shaban Ali and the Behrangis, as they insisted I get the prized and flawless pale blue stones that look like cheap plastic. I like the less-expensive, varicolored turquoise that has other metals mixed in. "That is inferior," they told me whenever I selected a piece that had beautiful abstract designs swirling through the stone.

I find a choice pendant, and succumb to the lure of a set of cufflinks for myself. They are rather inexpensive compared to the prices the Behrangis paid for the fine blue stones. But I am most proud of my ability to bargain.

Dawdling along the streets, looking in shops, I'm half-aware my feet are sore. Momentarily I sit down and remove my shoes to stretch my toes. *Oh, my gosh! I've worn holes in both shoes! And I didn't bring another pair.* I shrug, put my shoes back on, and continue. A small embroidery hanging in the window of a run-down furniture and hardware store catches my eye.

"Salaam allekum," I greet the shop owner as I enter.

"Salaam," he says, but ventures nothing more.

I gesture to the embroidery and ask in Farsi, "How much is this?"

His face lights up a bit. "Three hundred rials."

That's $4.00, I think to myself. "Too much," I tell him.

"How much do you want to pay?"

"It's in poor condition. It has holes and some of the embroidery is worn away." I try to convince him it's not worth much. "I'll give you 150 rials."

"No, too little. But, for you, you can have it for 200 rials."

Wow, that was easy, I say to myself.

"No, still too much. Look, it is damaged, not good. I'll give you 150 rials for it, and that's the highest I will go."

"OK, give me 175 rials and you can have it."

Wow, that's just $2.30. And it was so easy to get him down. I'll hold out for the 150 rials. Shaban Ali and my friends say I don't bargain well, so I better stick to my guns.

I reiterate, "One hundred fifty rials."

We haggle over the last 25 rials for nearly half an hour, but he won't budge, and I'm stubborn too. I indicate I'm going. Surely he'll run after me, I speculate.

"Khodahafez," I tell him.

"Khodahafez," he responds.

I leave. He doesn't call me. I'm disappointed. *I should have given him the 175 rials. But I'm a man of principle. I have to learn to bargain the Iranian way.*

I meet Shaban Ali at the shrine. *"Aghaye* Muslemi Aghili and his wife from Kordkuy are here in Mashhad," I tell him. "They couldn't find a hotel room, so I helped them find a place in a home near where we are."

Shaban Ali laughs. "You found them a place to stay! An American finds a place for Iranians in Mashhad!"

"Baleh. I knocked on doors and asked if they had a room for my friends who were on a pilgrimage. We went to about eight houses before we found a room. They like it very much. We must see them."

Shaban Ali shakes his head, "Tom, you have become Iranian—more Iranian than Iranians."

We laugh. "But Shaban Ali, I have made a hole in each of my shoes. Too much walking." We laugh some more.

At lunch I show him the turquoise I purchased. He despairs and concludes the jeweler fleeced me. "Tom, you have to be careful. Iranians are very clever. They see money when they see Americans. He sold you very poor quality turquoise. You paid too much."

"But this is the kind of turquoise I like and I bargained for it. I got him down to almost half of what he wanted."

"It's still too much."

We see the Muslemi Aghilis and they recount our escapade finding a room. They, too, marvel at my ability to negotiate in Iran. "Tom has become an Iranian already," they agree.

Shaban Ali grins. I'm certain he feels he is part of this transformation.

That night I sleep fitfully, thinking of the embroidery I passed up because I was too miserly to pay another 25 rials. *That's only 30 cents.*

TUESDAY, MARCH 23, 1965 "Tom, I want to go to the shrine to pray and then shop for my family. How much money do you have? I'm running out. Can I borrow some from you? I'll pay you back in Alang."

"Sure. How much do you need?" I wonder if, overnight, he has calculated this to be an effective means of curtailing my callous spending. "While you're at the shrine and shopping, I will explore Mashhad a bit more." He doesn't argue. *Seems like I've worn him out in two days,* I muse. "Don't forget, this afternoon we are going to the city park with *Aghaye* (Mr.) and *Khanoome* (Mrs.) Muslemi Aghili," I remind him.

"*Baleh.* I'll meet you back here before lunch."

I find more junk shops in another section of Mashhad. They are filled with marvelous and unfamiliar objects, but the old lacquer pen boxes particularly appeal to me. Most have flowers; however, one has a battle scene.

"How much is this?"

"Three hundred rials. That is Shah Ismael Safavid in battle. He was the founder of the Safavid dynasty over 450 years ago. Shah Ismael is very famous. He established Shi'a Islam in Iran."

"How old is this?"

"It's at least a hundred years old. It's from the Qajar dynasty. These kinds of pen boxes were very popular then."

I am fascinated, even if one end of the cover is missing. It seems to be made from multiple layers of paper. Russian Cyrillic print is visible where some paper layers are missing on the bottom of the box.

"It is a little expensive for me. Would you take less?"

"I could let you have it for 250 rials."

"I don't have much money left. I am here with my Iranian friend. He is on a pilgrimage. Would you take 125 rials?"

"No, for you, my best price is 200 rials."

We settle on 175 rials. I don't want this to be a repeat of the embroidery that lost me sleep.

Apprehensively I show Shaban Ali the pen box at our room. I am excited by it—by its connection to Shah Ismael and Iranian history—but I'm afraid he will think I'm a spendthrift.

"How much did you pay for it?"

"One hundred and seventy-five rials."

"Tom, you paid way too much. I'm sorry. I should have been with you. Iranians think Americans have too much money. They know you will pay anything."

"But he wanted 300 rials at first. I bargained. I told him I would give him 125 rials."

"That was still too much. Look. It's broken."

"But it's antique. It's very old. It shows Shah Ismael Safavid."

On our walk, he tells the Muslemi Aghilis about my bad purchase. They agree the shopkeepers of Mashhad prey on foreigners. But the pen box is my treasure, and I want to learn more about Shah Ismael.

"Tom, my wife likes your ring very much. Would you let us take it to a jeweler to have a mold made?" *Aghaye* Muslemi Aghili asks me. "I would like to have a ring like it made for her."

"Sure. This is my high school class ring. Many of my classmates got one with a stone under the crest. I couldn't afford one with the stone."

"Excellent! I will have the jeweler make it with a turquoise stone."

We go to a jewelry shop where a mold is made. They settle on a price.

I whisper to *Aghaye* Muslemi Aghili, "I'm amazed—it costs $5.00 less than I paid for mine seven years ago, and you're getting one with a clear blue turquoise stone!" He smiles with satisfaction.

"Tom, it's so much fun being with you. I want to learn English from you. Can I attend your classes? I will come from Kordkuy on my motor scooter every day."

"I would be happy to have you as a student."

Shaban Ali adds, "That's fantastic! We can learn English together."

At dinner Shaban Ali tells me, "I want to go to the shrine to pray one more time before we leave. Tomorrow morning we have to be at the bus station very early. You can stay in our room."

"I'll just wander the streets. I like looking in the shops and seeing the city. The golden domes of the shrine are so beautiful in the gleaming lights. I want to see it one more time."

"But don't go into any shops. The Mashhad shopkeepers are too clever."

"*Baleh.* I promise. Besides, I don't have much money left."

Mashhad is magical at night with the domes and minarets of the shrine glistening, and the clear bare bulbs glowing in the shops. I'm enthralled. The streets are filled with pilgrims out for their evening promenade, looking in shop windows. Often I stop to gaze at the sparkling gold and silver contents within. In one, a globe-shaped silver candy dish arrests me. It is trimmed with a band of turquoise and has a bird finial on the top. It's so simple and elegant compared to the razzle-dazzle of everything else.

The shop owner comes to the door and greets me. *"Salaam,"* I respond. "Where was the round container made?"

"Here in Mashhad. Nice, isn't it?"

"Baleh. Chand misheh" (How much is it)?

"Fifty tomans."

"It's very pretty, but I don't have much money. I've already spent it all. I'm leaving Mashhad tomorrow. *Moteshakeram. Khodahafez.*"

I don't go far. I check my wallet—sixty-seven tomans and five rials, exactly. I should be able to bargain for it and get it for less. I'll still have money to buy some fruit and candy and get back to Alang.

I return to the shop to admire the candy dish in the window. The shop owner grins.

"Could I see it, please?"

He reaches to grasp the bowl among the glittering display, and knocks over another piece.

"I'm sorry," I say.

"No problem." He rearranges the toppled piece. He opens the candy dish. His face drops. "Expensive," I hear him mutter under his breath. "I told you it was fifty tomans, so you can have it for fifty. It should be ninety tomans. We paid sixty for it."

My heart sinks. What a predicament! *Now what do I do?* I had intended to bargain. *Now I can't do that, for sure.* I look at him.

"I told you fifty tomans, so it's yours for fifty."

"OK, I'll give you sixty. I know that's what you paid for it. I'm sorry I don't have more money. I'll have only 75 rials for the trip back to Gorgan. It will be enough for my breakfast, lunch, and the bus to the village."

I return to our room without looking in any more shops. I put the candy dish inside my bag so Shaban Ali won't see it. *But how am I going to conceal it from him? He'll find out I'm down to my last rials when we order meals. Then he'll suspect I bought something. He'll howl when he hears I paid more for it than the shopkeeper originally quoted. He'll think I'm so stupid.* I sit there in a mental quandary.

"*Salaam*, Tom," Shaban Ali greets me when he returns from the shrine. "You're very quiet. Tired?"

"*Baleh.*" Hesitantly I venture, "Shaban Ali, I bought something. I have only enough money to get back to Alang. I hope you didn't spend all yours."

He looks at me with a knowing grin. "At least we have our bus tickets and have paid for this room. So now what did you buy?"

Warily I dig it out of my bag. His face lights up.

"Tom, *bah, bah, bah*. It's beautiful, very beautiful. How much did you pay for it?"

"Sixty tomans." I wait for the ridicule.

He inspects it carefully. "Tom, this is a very good buy. Did you bargain? What did he start out at?"

"Fifty tomans," I say sheepishly. "But he made a mistake," I quickly interject. "It was in the store window when I asked about it. I left because I thought I didn't have enough money. Then I went back and when he got it out of the window he said he made a mistake and it should have been ninety tomans and he paid sixty for it."

"Tom, it is exquisite. Certainly worth sixty tomans. This is what you should be buying, not the broken old pen box and inferior turquoise. I want the Behrangis to see it. They will agree."

He runs off to their room. They return and admire the shining treasure radiantly sitting on the floor.*

THURSDAY, MARCH 25, 1965   Shaban Ali and I make the obligatory, if belated, Nou Ruz rounds of visitations. Everyone says, "Tom, we missed you. Next year you have to stay in Alang."

Aghaye Tofigh Rahemi and Ezetollah are happy to see me and to learn I went to Mashhad and the shrine of Imam Reza.

"Now you are *Mashti* Tom," Tofigh tells me. His eyes begin to water. Shaban Ali relates our escapade in the shrine on New Year's Eve. The Rahemis are pleased I was able to experience the magnitude of the pilgrimage and see the shrine. For them, and everybody in Alang, it is important I witness and come to know Islam.

"Jafar Rahemi, son of *Haji* Sabsi, is home on leave from military duty. He wants to meet you," Shaban Ali tells me as we near their house.

"Salaam allekum," I am greeted warmly and pulled into their home. Jafar is a strikingly handsome man, a fact of which he is confidently aware. His good looks are matched by his gregarious charm.

"We must go to the cinema in Gorgan—Shaban Ali, Mulla, Reza—we can go in my father's jeep. Plus we can check out the *ab o hava*." There is a spark in his eye.

I grin. This means weather, but he's using it to refer to the finer elements of Gorgan that young men admire. He discerns my knowing look and remarks, "Tom *zerange* (Tom is clever)! He knows Farsi well." His eyes glisten.

"I hear there is a Peace Corps girl in Gorgan. You must introduce me to her. I want to meet her."

"Baleh."

But Jafar's outgoing manner is somewhat disconcerting. This is a real man of the world, I deduce, very sure of himself.

---

* I sent the candy dish to my parents. My mother wrote, "I polished the dish and rubbed all the silver off." She was inconsolable.

TOO MUCH THINKING

FRIDAY, MARCH 26, 1965 Alang celebrates the Nou Ruz holiday for another week. I am disappointed Reza and Javad Abtahi can't come to my room to observe this revered Persian tradition properly; but the fight with my landlord has curtailed their visits.

There are endless invitations to lunch and dinner, no village council meetings, the teachers are away, and my classes are cancelled. I have more time to think, especially at night. I lie there awake. It's not good—thinking. *What is the value of my being here? What is my purpose?* I had such high expectations when I joined the Peace Corps. *I've been in Iran six months now, and what have I accomplished?* I can see only minimal instances where I might have been a benefit—where I've provided some technical assistance. Community development is so difficult to achieve and evaluate. *What can I accomplish in the remaining time I'm here? What about those three big projects the Peace Corps demands?* It's not easy to accept I may never see any tangible results from my time here. I wish I could find a way to use my education and abilities to benefit Iran. I love Iran. First and foremost, I love Alang and its people, and they love me. That's the problem—now really close friendships have developed. This is what makes it so hard. They received me warmly. They have accepted me as their brother and their son. They would hate to see me leave, and I would hate to disappoint them by taking a job somewhere else. But I'd like to use my talents to serve Iran.

For days and nights these agonizing thoughts—one moment pushing one way, the next pulling me back—race through my mind and draw my spirits down. Then Mom sends a letter from Aunt Catherine. Her stepson,

Dicky, George's half-brother, died of a heart attack. I am devastated. He was six years older than me, and had a family.

The same day I receive a letter from Kathleen, a teenage sweetheart. She followed me to Hawaii, but by then I found Hawaii's exotic dark-eyed beauties too enticing. She returned to Minnesota, but never forgot me. She says she is waiting for me. *How do I deal with this?* She's still a friend, "but just a friend"—I told her when she left Hawaii.

SATURDAY, APRIL 3, 1965 "Stay in Alang ten years instead of just two," my friends plead. "Become an Alangi. Marry a nice Iranian girl and live here." The villagers already realize my presence is temporary, and Shaban Ali is being teased that he will be lost when I depart.

He helps me move into my newly painted kitchen. It is minuscule, but I manage to fit in both cabinets, my little table for the stove with the gas tanks underneath, and a chair. There are about 18 inches between the edge of the table and the wall. Compact, but manageable.

The holidays over, Shaban Ali schedules village council meetings. Yavar's and Ismael's families return. Classes resume. *Aghaye* Muslemi Aghili comes from Kordkuy for my English class. My students are happy he's joined us. There is less time to think.

SUNDAY, APRIL 4, 1965 House cleaning! I hang the rugs over the balcony and beat the dirt out of them. My work creates a sensation in Alang—the neighbors watch as clouds of dust rise and drift over the roof. I relocate my desk and the Peace Corps book locker and marvel at how much room I now have.

I go to bed exhausted, but wake up startled. Randy and my friends in Hawaii were speaking fluent Farsi. *How can this be? I slaved so hard to learn Farsi, and they speak it so well without even trying. It's not fair.*

Then I realize it was a dream. I've been dreaming in Farsi! In fact, this seems to have been occurring for a while now. My dreams are no longer in English, and I don't even think in English most of the time. I plan my days in Farsi.

I lie there awhile, pondering the transformation.

MONDAY, APRIL 5, 1965   Before class, a friend stops by my room. He often comes, and if I'm preparing the day's lesson, he sits quietly waiting for me, looking at my books. He says something in Farsi. I don't understand and, as I frequently do when I'm busy, ignore it. He takes my Farsi/English dictionary.

"Su . . . sui . . . suiceed. Suiceed, that's what I am going to do."

I reel around in my chair. What am I hearing? I look at the word he is pointing to in the dictionary.

"Suicide," I say.

"*Baleh.* That's it. Suicide. I want to do that."

Oh, my God, help me. How do I deal with this? is my reaction.

"*Chera*" (Why)? is all I can muster.

"Nobody likes me. I am useless. Everyone would be better off if I weren't around."

"No, you have many friends. I am your friend. We are friends. In fact, you are one of the best friends I have ever had. *Man doost et doram*" (I am your friend).

"*Baleh*, you are my friend, and maybe a few others. But when you leave Alang, I want to leave too."

"You are one of the most-loved young persons in Alang. I know it. Besides you have a wonderful wife and little boy. They need you. You must see your little boy grow up and help him become a great man. Please think about this. You are loved and needed by many. You are important to your family and to all of Alang. Please stay alive for me, for your wife and son, and for Alang. We all need you. *Hatman* (Certainly) we need you." I put my arm around his shoulder. "Come. Let's go for a walk before I go to class."

At night, before I go to sleep, I ask God, *Did I do OK? You know I'm not used to this.* And, I thank Him for any help He gave.

WEDNESDAY, APRIL 7, 1965   "Tom, I have very bad news." Shaban Ali's face is tense and troubled.

"What's the matter? What happened?"

"*Aghaye* Muslemi Aghili's little boy drowned in the well while he was in our class yesterday. His son was only six years old."

I put my loosely clasped hands to my mouth and close my eyes, endeavoring to suppress my sorrow. I sigh heavily.

"Oooh, I'm so sorry. If he hadn't come to my class, his little boy might be alive . . . I'm so sorry. If I hadn't met him in Mashhad, he would not have come to my class. This is so unbearable. I feel awful. I shouldn't have come to Iran."

"Tom, it's not your fault. It isn't because you came to Iran or that you saw him in Mashhad," Shaban Ali tries to console me.

Later, we all look at and reflect on the empty chair in the classroom.

Aghaye Muslemi Aghili attended three classes. He never comes again.

FRIDAY, APRIL 9, 1965 I had to get away—if only for a few hours—to be with Jack and Dave. There has been too much stress to deal with—deaths and talk of suicide.

I wait at the station for a return bus to Alang, staring deeply into silent space, only casually aware of the subdued Friday afternoon inertia around me. The mournful song of an empty can bounding down the *jub* (gutter) amplifies my pensive musings. I look, and see lettuce leaves—a hundred empty green rafts tumbling in the rapids. The cadence is etched in my glazed eyes. *The current of life flows ever onward,* I tell myself. I board the bus.

SATURDAY, APRIL 10, 1965 Carrying a terrible sense of guilt, I bicycle to Kordkuy, fearful that I will see *Aghaye* Muslemi Aghili and won't be able to express my sympathy adequately.

However, other trepidations accompany my every trip to Kordkuy— anxiety over encountering Ghasem and other overbearing young men who demand my friendship. I recognize their jealousy that I have chosen to live in a village, specifically nearby Alang, that my friends are Alangis, and that I have overlooked them and the relative benefits of their larger town.

Regardless, there are many in Kordkuy I am happy to see—among them the teachers, the soldiers at the army station, the postman, and the policeman. Today the police officer gleefully calls me to a halt. Daily he stands in the middle of the central crossroads directing traffic that either disregards him or competently zips through town on its own.

"Salaam allekum, hale shoma khoobeh?" I greet him.

He grabs my handlebars as I dismount and with a smile replies, "How are you doing, Tom? Are you enjoying Iran?"

"Baleh. I like Iran very much." His eyes register his satisfaction with my response. "I went to Mashhad for Nou Ruz. It was wonderful. The shrine of Imam Reza is very beautiful."

"Tom, now you are a *Mashti*," he says with a smile.

"Baleh." By now a crowd of onlookers has gathered—eavesdroppers, gawkers. Meanwhile, traffic, including speeding transport trucks and buses, flies past us as we stand in the middle of the intersection.

Soon Ghasem spots me and joins us. "Tom, my friend, how are you?" He steers the conversation to English, leaving everyone else out. "Come to my house. I am your good friend." His arrogance in front of his countrymen infuriates me.

I look around, irritated with Ghasem and self-conscious that I am the center of attention. I blurt out *"Meimun kojast"* (Where is the monkey)? as I look at the mob surrounding me. Immediately the policeman takes his baton and beats back the crowd. They disperse, some narrowly missing the vehicles speeding past. I regret what I said. It was a deliberate play of words, an inappropriate use of their language, not lost on the policeman: *meimun*, means monkey, whereas *mehman* means guest.

In the solitude of the bathhouse, I mull over what transpired. *Tom, you have to accept you are an anomaly here and people are going to gather to stare and listen to you talk. . . . But there are times I absolutely can't stand it any longer.*

AT ISMAEL AND YAVAR'S there is the routine tuning of the radio to get the evening news. Suddenly my limited understanding of the broadcast causes my hair to stand on end.

"Ismael, Yavar, what's happened?"

"A soldier tried to kill the Shah. He shot his way into the Marble Palace, armed with a machine gun. The soldier and two guards were killed. The Shah regrets the senseless killing, but attributes his survival to his belief in God and the importance of his mission for our country."

I shiver and remember how I heard the news of President Kennedy's assassination. But now I am a foreigner living in another country. *What if the Shah had been killed? What would happen to Iran without him? Would we be evacuated?* Although I have deep concern for the well-being of the Shah and Iran, the thought of being separated from Iran before my two years are completed preoccupies me.

SUNDAY, APRIL 11, 1965 The morning is warm—a true herald of spring. Maybe hoeing the garden will get my mind on something else.

Except for the potatoes, the garden is a disappointment. The ground is nearly white. Someone sprinkled commercial fertilizer on the plot, and seeds are sprouting only around the edge where they missed. *So much for insisting we fertilize.* The manure would have been sufficient. They don't realize more is not better. Next year they should have an abundant yield.

WEDNESDAY, APRIL 14, 1965 Excitement in Alang! The day all my cohorts have been waiting for. The young men are well-shaven and finely groomed. With horn tooting, the anticipated carriage rolls in—Hajireza's rattletrap bus. His face is ablaze with his golden grin. All run to welcome the very special guest. Women clutch together at the side, peering intently from behind their *chadors*.

There is almost an audible gasp as Miss Kathy descends. She has two escorts—Mister Jack and Mister Dave.

"She is so tall," one of my buddies whispers.

"Which one is her husband?" another interjects.

"Neither. She's not married."

"Well, then, which one is her brother?"

"Neither."

A look of consternation crosses their faces. Her visit may not have been a wise idea. I introduce Kathy to those who ardently want to meet her. Aside from the quiet little discussions that erupt all around, my friends are on their best behavior.

"Let's go to my room for tea," I suggest. "Then we can go for a walk around the village. I want you to see it." Acknowledging that it's best we be properly chaperoned, I invite some of my closest friends to tea as well.

Reza is disappointed he has to stay behind because of the fight with my landlord. "We'll come to your shop in a little while," I assure him.

"Yes, you can't miss the Sherkat-e Sargardon," he says in English, with a big smile on his face.

"What's the Sherkat-e Sargardon?" Kathy asks innocently.

"It's the 'Do Nothing Company'—the local hangout. Actually, it's Reza's tailor shop. Reza and I, however, are the only two who have titles in the company. He's the *rais* (president) and I'm the *moallem* (teacher). They inducted me the day after I got here. I guess they had already figured out what the Peace Corps is all about."

Reza laughs and Kathy, Jack, and Dave smile.

Kathy, too, likes my humble abode. She, however, has been in villages in Mazandaran, as she goes on midwife calls with *Khanoome* Pirqeybi, her landlady. Often she aids in delivery under the most difficult conditions. The entourage of attentive young men expands as we usher Miss Kathy through the village. Reza and the "Do Nothing" guys expectantly await the official delegation. He has the samovar filled with water and hot coals. Soon tea is ready. He even has little tea cookies today. Finished, he closes his shop and joins our tour.

"We'll go past the school to the Imamzadeh," I suggest. "Then we can continue to the highway to catch a bus for Gorgan."

Many accompany us to the highway to give us a grand send-off. Silence descends upon the village bus when Kathy and her three male escorts board. There are sideways glances and hushed whispers as places are found for the four of us near the front.

THURSDAY, APRIL 15, 1965 Alone, I board the TBT bus bound for Tehran. I will be there for Good Friday and Easter Sunday. On Saturday I want to evaluate my work in community development with Peace Corps officials. No one except Mr. Vahdati has ever mentioned a transfer. Peace Corps silence and the resulting indecision are driving me mad.

I look toward Alang as we pass. It is barely visible among the budding trees. My eyes water; I have never alluded to an impending move to anyone in Alang. I'm not sure I could deal with leaving, and I don't want anybody to think America or I renege on a promise. They expect me to stay for two years. Nevertheless, I feel I should be contributing more to Iran.

Everything's been kept to myself. If Dr. Drake is right, this may be what is contributing to my stomach problems. In fact, the moment the bus departs Gorgan, pain swells in my insides. I silently hold it until our first stop—hours later—but there is no relief. I endure all the way to Tehran.

Despite my discomfort, the joyous sight of the earth rebounding from the dismal drabness of winter is refreshing. Flooded rice paddies mirror the radiant sky. Farmers, bent in attentive submission to their husbandry, contrast with the sprightly vigor of their sprouting seedlings.

Farther along, we turn south, following the valley of the Haraz. The river's winter, silver rush is now a turbulent, brown surge of raging torrents released by the melting snows in the mountains above. Villages, seemingly asleep on my previous journey to Tehran, are awakening to the twinkling eyes of spring. The now-familiar steep-sided walls of the mountains loom up. Rocks hang menacingly over the bus in contorted checkerboard formations. We climb, twisting higher and higher. The bus stops abruptly. A shepherd prods his flock against the mountain wall to let us pass while his shaggy dog keeps a vigilant eye on his charges.

We stop briefly at the pass. Mt. Damavand, cloaked in snow, shimmers gloriously in the waning sunlight. Flowers emerge among the rocks at the side of the road on the downward approach to Tehran. Darkness descends, and the advancing lights of the sprawling city glisten in the clear, crisp air.

FRIDAY, APRIL 16, 1965   The city is transformed—no longer the sand-encrusted modern edge-of-the-desert encampment of when we arrived or the frozen metropolis of the recent winter. The sparkling sun is a welcome contrast to the cloud-shrouded, rain-soaked skies along the Caspian.

The treasures of the Musée Iran Bastan, Iran's archeological museum, are staggering. Long-spouted ceramic vessels from as early as the 10th century BC, small ceramic animal sculptures similar to the one Shaban Ali and I found on the tepe near Chahardeh, Luristan bronzes, and gold-winged lion rhytons from the Achaemenian period have me spellbound. But the polished monumental sculptures from Persepolis, with their rich, dark-brown color, are transfixing. They further inflame a desire to visit the ancient site near Shiraz—to see firsthand Iran's majestic past.

"The museum is closing," a guard notifies me as he shuts the windows.

I look at my watch. *Hmmm. I've been here three-and-a-half hours and haven't seen enough. I'll definitely come back.*

At a tiny local eatery, I have lunch of *khoresht-e sabzi* (green vegetable stew) and rice before heading for the bookstores. There are too many choices. I discover Sykes' two-volume *History of Persia*. It contains an illustration of Shah Ismael in the battle of Chaldiran. *Wow, it's almost the same illustration as on the lacquer pen box I bought in Mashhad. And it says it's a copy of a picture in Chehel Sotun in Isfahan. I have to get these books. I need to know more about Shah Ismael and Persian history.*

SATURDAY, APRIL 17, 1965 "I love it in Alang," I tell the Peace Corps associate director. "The people are wonderful and they have accepted me as their son and brother. I'm always busy. In fact, I never have any time for myself. I'm achieving a lot in terms of friendships, of Iranians getting to know an American, but that may be all. I'm concerned I'm not making any contribution to Iran. I may never accomplish those three big projects we're required to bring about in the two years we are here. I have so much to offer using my education in art and talent, but that's impossible in Alang. My Iranian co-worker is completely competent doing the work on his own. We spend a lot of time discussing community development efforts before we go to village council meetings, but my job is pretty much just talking. And friendships."

"Tom, there's a position opening up at Pahlavi University in Shiraz that you might be perfectly suited for. We don't have adequate information about it, but it would involve working with student organizations. Perhaps you could use your art background there."

"Wow, Shiraz! At the university!"

"Yes, Pahlavi University is a special endeavor of the Shah. It even bears his name. It's a brand new university, less than three years old. Money is not an object. He wants to make it the best. It is on an impressive site overlooking the city."

My heart is palpitating. *This is so exciting. I couldn't have foreseen anything better. Shiraz, of all places,* I think to myself.

"Mention it to the director when you talk to him. Tell him I suggested you might be ideal for it."

"Thank you so much. This would be terrific. I would really like to use my art background in some way while I'm here."

My next appointment, with a rep from the region that includes Shiraz, is not encouraging. In fact, my interview with him goes so poorly, I choose not to refer to the university position in my subsequent meeting with the director. I simply outline my work in Alang and state my wish to contribute to Iran in a more substantial way that uses my education and abilities.

"Tom, I told you to discuss the job at Pahlavi University with the director when you met with him. You didn't!" the associate director bluntly reprimands me when I see her in the office. "I had lunch with him and he told me you didn't ask him about it. Why didn't you?"

"The regional rep from Shiraz discouraged the idea, so I thought I better not bring it up."

"Well, the director said he kept thinking of the position at Pahlavi while he was talking to you, but decided not to broach the subject until he looked into it more. With your background, you might be ideal for this position."

"I can't wait to hear from you. I hope it will work out."

Many PCVs are in Tehran for the weekend, and Peace Corps headquarters is the place to connect. While we galvanize with each other, discussions culminate in grumbling and a search for a "watering hole." That's all we seem to do now when we get together. It always makes me feel worse. My interests are elsewhere—experiencing Tehran and the cultural attractions of the city. Besides, I don't want to let on I'm seriously evaluating my effectiveness and there's a possibility I might be transferred to Shiraz. After all, it was I who first went to live in a village—and on my own initiative. Either way—that I may be dissatisfied or if I'm not selected for the position in Shiraz—I don't want to "make shame," as we say in Hawaii.

"Hi, Tom. How are things in the village?"

"Hey, Mike. It's good to see you. I'm doing fine, thanks. You came in from Langarud for the weekend too?"

"Actually, I get into Tehran a lot now. I've been transferred to Karaj to assist in the training of Sepah-e Danesh."

"Wow! You like it?"

"Yes, it's so much better. The job is more structured and I'm working with young people. The Sepah-e Danesh is such a worthwhile program."

"Yes, it's a brilliant idea. There are Sepah-e Danesh men in two of the villages I work in. They're top-notch. They couldn't be better. Totally dedicated young guys. I'm so proud of them."

After chatting awhile, Mike asks, "What are you doing this afternoon?"

"I plan to see the crown jewels. Do you want to go with me? I spent three-and-a-half hours in the Musée Iran Bastan yesterday. It was spectacular. Only left because they were closing. I visit the museums each time I'm in Tehran. I can't get enough of Persian history."

"I've seen the crown jewels. You'll love them. Why don't we meet tomorrow morning to send off those packages we talked about?"

"Fine. See you then."

I nearly soar out of the Peace Corps office, anticipating Shiraz. It's 4:00 when I reach the Bank-e Markazi Iran (Central Bank of Iran), where the crown jewels are held in an underground vault. I ascertain that I have an hour to see them. It should only take a few minutes to see some crowns and the famous jewel-encrusted throne. I've never been very fascinated by jewelry anyway.

As I walk through the door of the vault, I am stunned cold at the immensity of the collection and the display—a huge, dark room with millions of jewels sparkling in sleek, spectacularly lit glass cases. This is incredible—a treasure greater than all of Fort Knox!

A guard informs me, "Only one piece has been appraised—this little emerald snuffbox over here. Five million dollars!"

"It's so little (2.5" × 1.5" × 1"). There are so many other, bigger things."

He grins. He knows I'm impressed.

The Pahlavi Crown, made for the 1924 coronation of Reza Shah, is magnificent, but the Kiani Crown from the reign of Fath Ali Shah Qajar, who ruled from 1798 to 1834, takes my breath away. Even with its thousands of jewels, it possesses a restrained and simple splendor.

The famous Darya-e Nur (Sea of Light) diamond is big (1.5" × 1"), but it looks like a piece of glass to me.

The Takht-e Naderi throne, constructed during the reign of Fath Ali Shah, is sumptuous beyond imagination. I resolve that I must read about Fath Ali and the Qajars in my new books. The sand castles at Garmsar and the pen box I bought are from the Qajar period.

Most dazzling of all is a nearly two-foot globe on a stand, its seas composed of emeralds and the land of rubies. But Iran, England, and Southeast Asia are made of diamonds. It contains over 51,000 precious gems that weigh a total of 18,200 carats. Naser al-Din Shah Qajar, who reigned from 1848 to 1896, ordered fabrication of the globe to consolidate many of the innumerable loose stones into objects less subject to dissipation. Even so, there are cases with container upon container of unset stones.

"I'm sorry, we are closing," the guard tells me apologetically. "Come back another time. You're always welcome."

"Oh, I will. This is truly unbelievable! *Khodahafez.*"

My eyes momentarily sting from the bright, crisp light on the street outside, having spent an hour gazing at the shimmering gems in the semidarkness of the bank vault. But they adjust well to looking at more rugs in the many shops along the street. It's strange—at first I couldn't stand the gaudy designs and colors of Persian carpets, but they're beginning to grow on me. I just might go home with a rug.

SUNDAY, APRIL 18, 1965 Mass on Easter Sunday in a Muslim country seems decidedly out of context. It has been at least four months since I've been to Mass. All the ceremony seems perfunctory compared to the passionate fervor of the faithful I so recently witnessed at the shrine of Imam Reza in Mashhad.

As arranged, Mike and I go to the central post office to mail our packages. The interior is vast and crowded. "I wonder which line we get in to mail a package, Mike?"

"Can I help you?" Startled by the perfect English, we turn around to find a young Iranian offering his assistance. When we indicate what we need, he says, "Follow me. We have to get them wrapped in cloth and sewn up."

"How is it you know English so well?" I ask as he sews up a package.

"I was in the States for two years, studying architecture in Florida. I married an American girl there. She will be coming to Iran this summer. What about you guys? Why are you in Iran?"

"We're American Peace Corps Volunteers. I'm stationed in a village near Gorgan, and Mike is in Karaj. He's training the Sepah-e Danesh. I do community development work in five villages."

"You're living in a village! That must be very difficult. Not even I could do that."

"Oh, I love the village and the people. They are so generous. Persian hospitality, you know. The villagers are my best friends."

He smiles.

"Can you help me fill out this form?" a lady asks Mike and me in Farsi. "I don't know English."

"Mike, this form is in French and German. Do you know either of those languages?"

"I can read German. Here, let me help you," he tells the lady.

"Give me your package; I'll sew it up for you while you fill out the form for me," she offers.

Now a man and woman approach me. "Could you please write this address in English on these envelopes? Our son is in America and we don't know how to write English."

"Sure, but I don't have a pen."

"Here is a pen. You will need it to address your packages too."

Mike and I, and the young architect, smile at each other. *This is Iran,* I conclude. *Six strangers meet and come together to help each other.*

Nearly an hour passes before we have our packages mailed. "It was a pleasure to meet you guys," the architect tells us. "I'll give you my address. Look me up whenever you're in Tehran."

"This is what makes Iran so wonderful," Mike says to me as we leave.

"Yes, it's unquestionably the people. Mike, I want to see the Golestan Palace before I return to Alang."

"I've already seen it. I have to do some shopping. Let me know when you'll be this way again. It's always good to see you."

"Same here. Come visit us in Mazandaran sometime." Yet I feel funny inviting him when I might be leaving.

Golestan Palace, with its gardens, pools, fountains, colorful tile work, and extravagant mirrored halls, is mind-boggling. I've never been in a royal palace, and feel very out of place. With its French furniture, chandeliers, and drapes, it seems so phony. Everything is too ornate—even the rugs— definitely not to my taste. I think, *I'm glad the walls of my little hovel in Alang are made of daub. I guess, at the core, I'm truly a peasant.*

THE LONG BUS RIDE HOME is agonizing. I keep thinking of Shiraz. *But that means leaving Alang and all my friends. Stop thinking about it! It's driving you crazy. Read! It will take your mind off of it.*

But it doesn't. My stomach is revolting again. I sit there holding it. I close my eyes—praying the bus will make a stop. I keep hanging on.

"Are you not feeling well?" the man across the aisle asks. His wife looks around him at me with a look of concern.

"I'm OK, thank you." My face flinches as pain shoots through my intestines. *They can tell, I'm sure.* Valiantly I struggle to sustain the conversation he initiates. It's not easy to concentrate on two things— holding it and talking without letting it show on your face. Beads of perspiration surface on my forehead and upper lip. I wipe them away.

"Are you really OK?" his wife interjects.

"*Baleh*, I'm fine." I lie with obvious difficulty.

Mercifully, we reach the summit of the pass for our pit stop. Cautiously I rise and try to get to the door before anyone else. Of course, I'm not successful. Moving causes the pain to intensify. Carefully I step down out of the bus and heedfully join the line for the privy. Waiting is not easy. Although patches of snow are all about, and Mt. Damavand frigidly watches nearby, I perspire even more. I begin to shake, not from the cold, but from trying to remain composed under the adversity of excruciating pain. *It's strange how pain increases, the closer you get to relief,* I deduce.

Finally it's my turn. Awkwardly I inch forward, enter, and, trembling, rip down my pants and squat. Comfort is momentary; the pain returns. I explode again. I know it's not over. *I can't wait here in this position forever.*

Other people are waiting too. The bus will be leaving. I clean myself in the well-established Persian manner, pull up my pants, exit, and wash my hands with soap. Then I join the line again. There's no point in being reckless, I decide. I progress to the front of the line, and another attempt at total relief.

After the bus departs, my intestines continue their revolt. I hold on. Sari—another stop, this one for dinner. Painfully I join the line for the more indispensable amenities. Food is not what I desire. After finding some satisfaction, I rejoin the line.

"Oh, my gosh, that's the bus," I mutter as I squat there. The driver is sounding the horn. Quickly I prepare myself for another exit, wash my hands, and board the bus. *It's four hours more to Alang. I just need to hold out that long. Only four hours,* I say to myself. I will myself to sit as still as I can as the bus bounces over the rutted roadway. The man across the aisle and his wife are aware of my discomfort.

Three hours on, we stop at Behshahr. "My wife says you should stay with us tonight. We are getting off here. You cannot go on to Gorgan. Please come to our house. We will get a doctor for you."

"Thank you, but I need to get to Alang. It is only an hour more. Right after Kordkuy. Then I will be OK."

"No, you are welcome at our house," the woman tells me. "You cannot go on alone. Please."

"No. Thank you. I just need to get home. Please don't worry about me."

Reluctantly they leave me behind as they disembark in Behshahr. They say something to the driver as they descend the stairs, look back at me, and call out, *"Khodahafez."*

"Khodahafez. Moteshakeram," I reply.

At Kordkuy I rise, take my bag, and carefully move up the aisle toward the driver. "Please let me off at Alang. It is the first signpost past Kordkuy."

"It is late—very dark. I can't let you off there."

"Please. I'm not feeling well. My home is there. I need to get home. I cannot make it to Gorgan."

He looks at me warily. "Your home?" Undoubtedly he thinks, *Weird American.*

"There's the sign. Let me off here. Please." But he continues to barrel along. I grab the door pulls and shake them.

Alarmed, he slows down. Many awaken. "Why are we stopping here?" I hear some mutter.

"The American is getting off," somebody responds. "He says his home is here."

Now the passengers are awake and chattering in disbelief. They peer into the darkness. There are no lights anywhere.

"Moteshakeram. Kheili mamnunam (I'm very grateful). *Khodahafez,"* I call back as I step down onto the road.

I see the dim lights of the bus disappear into the night as I gingerly begin down the pathway to Alang. I walk slowly. Though speed is imperative, my condition demands the most deliberate movements. Suddenly intense pain sears through my intestines. I stop. *Do I unload here? I have no toilet paper or water to clean myself.* I stand there until the pain subsides, only slightly. I stiffly push on, praying I will reach home before I explode. *Thank God my house is on this side of Alang.*

At the schoolyard, I turn toward the village. It is shrouded in darkness. The pain worsens as I approach my home. I barely amble on. At last, the gateway door! I push against it. It's locked! I shudder, then, begin to pound on the door. Bang, bang, bang.

"Ghorbon, Ghorbon, *beah,* Tom *ast. Beah, beah."*

Bang, bang, bang, I pound more. Eventually, I hear the familiar shuffle of broken-down shoes approaching, then the gratifying sound of the board that fastens the doorway being slid aside.

"Befarmayid," Ghorbon mumbles.

"Behbakhsheed (Excuse me). *Moteshakeram."*

Cautiously I crawl through the doorway and set down my bag. Ghorbon closes the door and fastens the wooden latch. I inch toward the *aftabeh* and fill it with water. With difficulty, I ascend the three steps to the *mostarah.* Fortunately, I know this place—exactly how many steps the hole is from the door. In pitch-blackness, I guardedly guide my feet till I feel the edge of the hole, orient myself, lower my pants, and squat. "I made it," I murmur, almost prayerfully.

I pick up my bag where I dropped it near the back of Hajireza's parked bus. Gholam Husayn, whose wife does my laundry, is snoring as I quietly ascend the stairs near the family's tiny room. *Home.* I grab my flashlight and descend the stairs for another bout in the pungent little cubicle. I make several more trips downstairs before comfortably settling in for the night.

ONCE THERE WAS A BOY

MONDAY, APRIL 19, 1965 I awaken to the sounds of the gateway being opened and Hajireza singing a familiar Persian tune. I feel a little weak—but I'm home. That's all I needed.

I go to the edge of the balcony and call down, "Hajireza, *salaam. Hale shoma khoobeh?*"

"Mister Tom, *salaam. Shoma khoobi? Bah, bah, bah.* You returned! How was Tehran?"

"It was very nice, but it's better to be back in Alang. What's the news?"

"*Heechi* (Nothing). No news—same old thing. I'm glad you're back. I must be getting on to Gorgan," he calls to me as he climbs in the bus. "*Khodahafez.*"

I wash up in the usual inch of water in a basin within the confines of my kitchen, put on clean clothes, grab my water bucket, and head to *Aghaye* Aghayan's for fresh bread.

"Mister Tom! *Salaam.* You returned," he greets me with a hearty smile.

"*Baleh. Salaam.* I got back very late. How are you and the family?"

"We're fine. Thank you. What do you need? A loaf of bread, I'm sure. Anything else?"

"Not right now. The bread will be enough."

He hands it to me. I hold it to my nose and deeply inhale its rich and discernible aroma as I give him the few rials. "I'll see you. *Khodahafez,*" I tell him as I head for the well.

After breakfast, I run off to see Shaban Ali, but meet some of my pals from the Sherkat-e Sargardon on the street. They welcome me with smiles and outstretched hands. "Well, how was it? Tehran," they want to know, eyes glistening. "Toopkhaneh *rafti?*"

I know what they mean—our special code. They invariably imagine I go to Tehran for only one reason.

I raise my head and eyebrows and click my tongue in the Persian negative manner. *"Na raftam"* (I didn't go).

"Dorugh megi. Hatman rafti" (You lie. Certainly you went), they allege, confident of my presumed deception. "And what about the Peace Corps girl that came out here to Alang? What was her name? Miss Kosi?"

"Her name is Miss Kathy," I state emphatically.

"Baleh, Miss Kosi," they repeat with palpable delight.

Exasperated, I free myself from their prying innuendos and continue to Shaban Ali's house.

"Shaban Ali—*salaam,*" I call out as I slip through the gateway door.

"Salaam, Aghaye Mister Tom. How are you?" he asks me in English, smiling broadly as he comes to the doorway of his room. *"Beah.* Have some tea. I didn't expect you back already. When did you return?"

"Last night. It was very late. I was sick and I wanted to get back to Alang. So I had the bus driver drop me off by the road. He didn't want to stop. It was nearly 11pm. I think he and everyone on the bus thought I was crazy, getting off in the middle of nowhere."

"That wasn't smart—your getting off the bus in the dark and walking down the road alone. Are you OK now? What was the matter?"

"Baleh. I'm fine now. I'm back in Alang. I'm always better here. I had an upset stomach. How are you and the family? What's the news in Alang?"

"We're all well. No news in Alang. We missed you."

"Do we have any village council meetings this week?"

"Yes, we have one here today, and tomorrow we go to Bala Jaddeh and Ghalandarayesh. I know you like to go there, so I didn't schedule it until you would be back."

"Good."

We go over the meetings' agendas and my trip to Tehran. I don't tell him about a possible transfer to Shiraz. "Let's go to the garden. The weather is perfect."

"*Baleh*. Spring has arrived," Shaban Ali responds.

At the garden, I exclaim in shock, "My gosh . . . what happened? Even the cauliflower and cabbage around the edge where there wasn't too much fertilizer are gone. But most of the radishes made it."

"The snails did this. We should have put some poison out before you went to Tehran."

"It looks like our work was pretty useless," I say with a disgusted smile.

TUESDAY, APRIL 20, 1965 "We all missed you," Ismael and Yavar tell me. "The children keep asking when Mister is coming. Can you come to our house for dinner tonight?"

"I'm sorry. I can't tonight and not the next few nights. Mr. Kucheek is getting married, and I'm invited to dinner." They look at each other, but say nothing.

Mr. Kucheek is one of the main "employees" of the Sherkat-e Sargardon. His father is wealthy. He doesn't have to work. Mr. Kucheek—Mr. Little— is his nickname because of his stature.

The dinner party is the predictable, dismal male diversion—everybody sitting around the room, nearly silent, me valiantly trying to keep conversation going. This and the next couple of evenings are unusually reserved. I retire to my room exhausted.

FRIDAY, APRIL 23, 1965 "No! I don't like her! I don't want her! No! Don't make me do it! No! No! No! Help! Help! No!" Mr. Kucheek screams, tears running down his face, as several friends drag him back to his compound. He kicks and struggles to get away again. The bride and her family have arrived at his house.

Oh, my gosh, this is mortifying. Poor girl. Poor Mr. Kucheek, I say to myself as I watch in near shock. I don't believe what I am seeing. *Is this what arranged marriages are all about? How cruel. How awful. Thank God for our American way, even if one out of four ends in divorce.*

Reza and Shaban Ali whisk me away. Likely they observed my displeasure, and are distressed to have me witness this. We walk silently for a while.

"Mr. Kucheek told his father he didn't want to marry the girl," Reza tells me. "But his father insisted. He said, 'She is a respectable girl,' and he went ahead and arranged the marriage. Mr. Kucheek was against it from the beginning. His father said it was time he got married. Mr. Kucheek is almost 25, you know. Most guys in Alang get married at 15 or even younger."

I say nothing.

Shaban Ali interjects, "That's why Mr. Kucheek's best friends, Ahmad and Parviz, went to Tehran. They didn't want to be here. They didn't want to be part of it. They claimed they weren't well and were going to a doctor in Tehran. It was a pretense."

Still speechless, I think, *How could parents do something like that?*

"Tom, put it out of your mind," Reza says. "Forget it. I'm sorry you saw this."

"*Baleh*. Go up to your room and get a good night's rest. Things will work out," Shaban Ali attempts to console me. "*Shab bekheyr.*"

"*Shab bekheyr,*" I repeat with a troubled sigh.

SATURDAY, APRIL 24, 1965 "Once there was a boy who was in love with a girl..."

Reza begins a story in my advanced English class. "They were very much in love. They wanted to marry each other. The girl was very beautiful, and her father was very rich. But the boy was poor. He was only a tailor, and he worked very hard in his shop each day."

I realize the story is autobiographical, and wonder if Ismael and Yavar perceive that as well. One time when I was at Reza's house, as his wife dutifully served us lunch, he said in English, "I did not want to marry my wife, but my father arranged the marriage." I was embarrassed he said this while she was in the room, even if it was in English.

He continues his story, "One day the boy and girl decided to run away and get married. However, they were caught and forced to return to the village. The boy's father arranged his marriage to another girl. He is very sad. He does not love his wife. He still wants the other girl. Now she too is not happy, married to another man."

SATURDAY, MAY 1, 1965 Shaban Ali and I spade up a portion of his courtyard for a garden, build a fence of interlaced sticks to keep the chickens and animals out, and plant nearly forty tomato seedlings. This is promising. This was a wasteland. His family can use the vegetables and it may encourage others to make a garden near their houses as well.

"Shaban Ali, is Mr. Kucheek OK? I haven't seen him since his wedding."

"Tom, he has not spoken to his wife and they have been married a whole week now. He is very depressed."

"But he was always so jovial."

"Yes . . . you are very lucky to be an American. You can select your own wife. Here, a father chooses the wife for his son. Sometimes the marriage is determined when the boy and girl are very little. Maybe it is because the fathers are friends or it will profit their businesses. Often the boy and girl do not love each other. But they are married. They have children, many children, but there is no love. It is not good. Many of the marriages you have been to have already ended."

"Already ended!"

"Yes, the girl went back to her parents and refuses to return to her husband."

"Shaban Ali, I thought in countries where marriages are arranged there was very little problem—not like in America and Europe, where young people select their own partner and then discover their choice was not right and they get a divorce."

"No, in America you marry someone because you love her and then you share a life together. Here in Iran there is no sharing. The man has his work and he has his fun separate from his wife. He goes to the cinema or travels with his friends. The woman is left at home. She must cook and take care of the children. They live separate lives. It is better when you love somebody—when you do things together. It may be different in Tehran, but in the villages that is the way it is."

I don't ask the obvious question. I don't want to risk the answer if it is negative. After all, we traveled to Mashhad together, without his wife. They have three children, and another is on the way. However, inwardly, I feel that here there is the respect of a loving husband and wife.

Nevertheless, I contemplate how I was told everything was good when I first arrived in Alang. Everyone was praiseworthy. The rich men cared for the poor, and were interested in improving the daily life of the people in the villages. Nothing was wrong. Arranged marriages were better because fathers understood the needs of their children and looked out for their well-being by selecting a proper mate, not like in America where young people fall in love but divorce is rampant. They only gave me the bright side. Now that I've been here six months, I'm finding out there are problems. The rich take advantage of the poor by charging exorbitant interest rates. The poor struggle more and more while the rich get richer. The rich man pays off someone so his son won't have to go in the military. There are fights. People get hurt.

We work silently for a long time.

ASHURA

SUNDAY, MAY 2, 1965 "Tom, come to the mosque tonight," Shaban Ali tells me on our return from Kordkuy. "Today is the beginning of Muharram, the month of mourning. The villagers want you to see what we do during Muharram, and they have asked you to dinner."

"Thank you, I would like to be with you, but the Peace Corps says we should not go to the mosque during Muharram because it would not be good if even one person is uncomfortable I am there. I would not like to offend anybody in Alang. It's best I don't go."

"No, we all want you to come. Please come."

"No, Shaban Ali, it is better I stay home."

I think about his request. It's so difficult because most of the villagers would be very happy if I came, but the letter from the Peace Corps was very emphatic: "Don't go! Especially do not photograph the processions. There have been instances where foreigners have been attacked and beaten because they were viewing or photographing these religious practices."

THURSDAY, MAY 6, 1965 Daily I am invited to the mosque for dinner and, with difficulty, decline. I wish the Peace Corps had never sent that letter. It makes it so hard to figure out what's best to do.

Each evening, someone delivers dinner to my room. One day when I tell Shaban Ali about all the food that has been sent to me he comments, "Oh, and chicken too! Only the *mullahs* get chicken."

Preparation for Ashura, the 10th day of Muharram, has heightened. Today, in the square outside my room, a group of wandering minstrels performs a "mystery play" that narrates the tragedy of the martyrdom of Imam Husayn in AH 61 (AD 680) at Karbala in present-day Iraq. Although I am curious, I can't comprehend the story, and I'm very uneasy about watching it because of the letter from the Peace Corps. I don't know what is acceptable for me to observe and what is not.

SATURDAY, MAY 8, 1965 "Please come to the mosque with me for dinner," Tofigh Rahemi tells me when I see him on the street. Briefly I debate how to answer him, but the letter from the Peace Corps flashes into my mind.

"Oh, *Aghaye* Rahemi, I would like to, but the Peace Corps says we should be very careful and not upset anyone by going to the mosque during Muharram. I'm sorry. It's best I don't come."

He looks disappointed. "Then go to my house for dinner. My son Ahmad will have dinner with you." He instructs a little boy to run to his house, "Tell them Mister Tom is coming to dinner tonight."

Distraught, I resolve if I am asked again I will go, no matter what the Peace Corps instructed.

SUNDAY, MAY 9, 1965 Several men from the village council and Shaban Ali invite me to watch the preparations for the mourning processions that start at the mosque and lead to the cemetery and Imamzadeh. "We want you to come. Everybody wants you to come."

"I will. Thank you for asking me."

A feeling of acceptance overcomes me when I enter the courtyard of the mosque. Tofigh Rahemi's look of extreme gratification that I have come is evident. People are aware of my entry, but their concentration is completely directed to the ritual. All are dressed in black. Old men beat their chests in devotion to Husayn, while young men, in perfect unison, sling chains against their backs and march to the beating of drums and the chanting of *Ya Husayn, Ya Husayn.* Most have shirts with an opening in the back so the chains sear the flesh. Some backs are already black and blue. I, along with the older men, follow as the marchers circle the courtyard and proceed to the Imamzadeh. Never have I seen anything so powerfully moving—so mysteriously inspiring.

MONDAY, MAY 10, 1965 Since the Peace Corps recommended we not go out for the next two days, I plan to go to Gorgan to be with Jack and Dave during Ashura. When I mention it to Shaban Ali, he registers disappointment that I won't stay in Alang to witness this time of sorrow.

"Everyone in Alang wants you to be here. Tomorrow and the next day are very special days. People come to the Imamzadeh Ibrahim in Alang. They carry banners and chant as they strike themselves in ritual flagellation. You must see this. Alang is the only village nearby that has the tomb of a holy man, so people come from all around. It is like a pilgrimage."

"Shaban Ali, are you sure it's OK I see this? What if someone from another village objects?"

"It's fine. No one will have a problem. Besides, you can remain in your room and watch the processions from your window. We want you to stay."

"OK. I would like to. I hope nobody will be displeased that I see this."

BEFORE DUSK, I hear the familiar clanking sounds of Hajireza's bus and the big gateway doors creaking open below me. Then the motor silences and begins its well-deserved nightly slumber.

"Tom, Mister Tom, a letter from Mister Jack and Mister Dave!" Hajireza excitedly runs up to my room. *"Salaam,* Tom, *hale shoma chetoreh?"*

"Alhamdulillah (Praise to God). *Hale shoma khoobeh?"* We talk awhile.

The letter reads:

How are you? We have been concerned about you. We haven't seen you in a long time. Why don't you visit us any more? It has been a month since you've been here. Come to Gorgan for the two days of mourning. We have several days of food on hand. Incidentally, we have moved. It is a much nicer place closer to the bus station to Alang and it is cheaper than the old place. See you tomorrow.

At dinner in the mosque, I sit next to Tofigh Rahemi, across from the *mullahs.* They are always so gentle and respectful, questioning me about Christianity, and telling me about Islam and, now, Ashura. It is 10:30 before I return to my room after marching with the village men in procession.

TUESDAY, MAY 11, 1965—ASHURA Pilgrims bearing large embroidered calligraphic banners and flags process through the village. A chanter leads, and bare-footed men shout *"Ya Husayn, Ya Husayn"* as they rhythmically march and flog themselves with chains. The emotional energy released is overpowering. I watch in amazement from the protection of my little room overlooking the road to the Imamzadeh.

This has all the pageantry and high drama of a Cecil B. DeMille production—like watching *The Ten Commandments* for real. I wish I had a tape recorder to record this. *Hmmm, I wonder if I could get a picture by hiding my camera inside my shirt and having the lens poke out between the buttons? I could walk up to the window, click the shutter through my shirt, and turn away. It might be worth a try—as long as I don't get caught.*

I go to the seclusion and security of my windowless kitchen to fabricate my ingenious and surreptitious scheme. Nervously I step out onto my porch and then enter my room. I lock the door and pull the drapes on the balcony side in case somebody comes up. I can't take a chance of being caught. I'm starting to shake from nervous anticipation. How will I ever get a good picture? *Sit quietly for a while and calm down,* I admonish myself. *Wait for the best opportunity when the banners, flags, and marchers are all in a perfect location.*

From the rear of my room I see it coming—large black banners and a blue flag leading the chain-wielding marchers. Apprehensively I step to the window, click the camera, and dodge away. The moment was perfect. *If only I didn't shake.*

The crowd surges on. I advance the camera and wait for my next opportunity. The next group is marchers from Alang. *I must be extremely careful, as they'll be aware of my presence.* I get the camera ready and walk toward the window, the camera concealed beneath my folded arms. *I'll step away briefly at the right moment and then quickly turn around and click the shutter beneath my shirt.*

"Mister Tom. *Aks begeer"* (Take a picture), someone calls.

Momentarily I freeze. There's no way they could have seen my camera.

I shout back, *"Na, khoob neest"* (No, it's not good).

"Na. Khoobeh. Begeer" (No. Good. Take it).

"Are you sure?" I question. "No one will object? What if one person doesn't want me to take a picture?"

"No one. We all want you to take a picture."

"*Kheili khoob*, let me get my camera." I couldn't very well pull it out of my shirt in front of the window. Besides, they know I keep my camera in the cabinet in my kitchen. I duck down on the floor of my room, extract the camera from my shirt, wait a moment—almost long enough to have gone to the kitchen—walk to the window, and plainly hold the camera in full view for all to see.

"*Aks begeer*," they shout. I take a picture, then another and another.

Ashura, Alang

"Come down and take some pictures here."

The procession is moving fast. There is no time to put on shoes. I slip into my rubber slippers and head for the street. Weaving in and out between the rows of chain-slinging marchers—taking pictures—I feel the sting of chains nicking me as I dodge between them. The procession ends on the other side of the village. Mourners gather around me. The looks on their faces tell me they are honored I came, was with them, and took their pictures.

Returning to the village center, Tofigh Rahemi sees me. There are tears in his eyes as he remarks, "Mister Tom didn't even wear shoes out of respect to Imam Husayn and us."

Processions and flagellations go on throughout the day. I go to the garden to weed, pull up the radishes, clean them, and send them to the mosque. Alang is hosting a nearby village for dinner.

The intense emotion of witnessing Ashura and working under the hot sun leaves me exhausted. I go to bed early, but wake up repeatedly throughout the night to the chanting of *Ya Husayn, Ya Husayn.* At 4:30am, as the first vestiges of dawn appear in the east, the chanting and marching through the village persist. As the sky brightens, I watch in bewilderment from my window. *How do human beings have the stamina to keep going like this?*

CAUGHT RED-HANDED

THURSDAY, MAY 13, 1965 In a dirt alley at the west end of Gorgan, a long continuous wall, interrupted only by the cadence of the unvaried metal doors, conceals the uniformity of the houses on the right. An empty field implies similar homes will be planted on the left. I press the little button beside a door and hear the raspy buzzer beyond. Footsteps approach. The door opens.

"Well, it's been a long time," Jack greets me. "*Befarmayid*. You've lost weight." The door slams behind us, echoing throughout the neighborhood.

"Yes, it's been a while. How have you guys been? Wow, this place is nice. I was surprised when your letter said you moved. What prompted that?"

"We heard about this new area of Gorgan. We liked this place, so that was it," Dave chimes in. "Why didn't you come for Ashura? We thought you would be here. We had plenty of food on hand and we could have played a lot of Scrabble."

"Everybody wanted me to stay in Alang for the observances. It was incredible. I'm glad I was there, but I wish the Peace Corps hadn't sent that letter warning us not to go out. It made it very hard for me to decide what to do. I marched right with the men and even took pictures of them. They wanted me to be with them. It was pretty intense. They went all night long. I don't know how they do it. Alang is very important because of the Imamzadeh Ibrahim. Men came from miles around in pilgrimage processions, carrying banners and beating themselves. It is something I'll never forget."

"You've been OK?" Dave asks.

"*Baleh*. However, I was pretty sick for a couple days. Had a bad temperature. Shaban Ali and I had gone to a village council meeting in one of the nearby villages, and when we got back I started getting the chills. I even got out my winter coat and sat there with the windows closed and my teeth chattering. Everyone else was in shirtsleeves. The villagers were really concerned. They kept checking on me, and brought me soups to eat. I got out my Peace Corps medical kit and took some terramycin. By night the next day, my temperature was gone. The following day I was still weak, but I taught my classes."

"Good thing it wasn't anything more." Jack announces, "Kathy had anthrax."

"ANTHRAX!"

"Yep, anthrax. The Peace Corps was preparing to send her body back to the States."

"Fortunately she got it here," Dave interjects. "The Iranian doctors recognized it right away and knew how to treat it. They wouldn't allow her to be sent to Tehran or release her to the American doctors."

"Yeah, in the States it's always fatal. There are about six cases in the US each year," Jack asserts. "The persons die before the doctors figure out what it is and how to take care of it."

"Is she OK now?"

"Yeah, just fine. The doctors think she contracted it in Alang, the day we were out there. That's why we were worried about you when we hadn't seen you in such a long time. We thought you might be dead. But the bus driver from Alang assured us you were well."

"Let's walk up to Kathy's and then go out to eat," Dave suggests. "We can come back here and play Scrabble or pinochle. We've got a lot of catching up to do."

"Perfect. I want to hear how things are going for all of you."

"What about you? Did the Peace Corps say anything about shifting you to another site when you were in Tehran?"

"Well, there is a possibility I'll be reassigned to Shiraz."

"Shiraz! Wow! The best! The center of culture. What will you be doing?"

"I would be working at Pahlavi University."

"Pahlavi University!"

"*Baleh*, with student groups and probably teaching art. I would really like that. It would be rewarding to do something I know how to do. My job in Alang is too nebulous, and I can't use my talents and abilities. But I'm distressed about leaving Alang and my friends. They've been so good to me. That's the reason I haven't been in to see you. I feel obligated to spend as much time as possible with them in case I get transferred. I may not. I haven't heard from the Peace Corps since I was in Tehran. You know how long it always takes to hear from them."

Back at Jack and Dave's, I hear the familiar whistle. Smiling, my eyes light up.

"I see SAVAK has followed you here too. You couldn't escape them."

"Yeah, they're filling out a form right now that Kathy and you are here with us. I can just imagine what it says," Jack retorts as he deliberates on a word. Our Scrabble games extend far into the night.

"It's about time I got home," Kathy reminds us.

"What time is it? Oh, my gosh, it's nearly 11:30. Word will be all over Gorgan tomorrow we had this wild party till the wee hours of the night."

Kathy's eyes sparkle as she suppresses an embarrassed grin. We all escort her up the street to her home.

"Let's have another game. I'm still wide awake," Jack proposes when we return.

"OK. Tomorrow is Friday. We don't have to get up early."

FRIDAY, MAY 14, 1965 "It's great to spend a relaxed day with you guys, but I should be getting back to Alang."

"Why? You could go tomorrow morning. In fact, you might want to see Mr. Vahdati. You haven't seen him in a while, have you?" Dave prods.

"Yeah, why go now? Let's all have dinner together, and we can have a few more games. Then you can go tomorrow. We haven't been together for a long time," Jack joins in. "In fact, if you go to Shiraz, this will come to an end. We won't see you any more."

"Well . . . yeah, you're right. It's really not necessary I get back to Alang tonight. You guys sure know how to tempt me."

We all read between plays while someone concocts the perfect word. Again, it gets late.

"I'll walk Kathy home tonight. There's no point in all of us going," I volunteer. There are no arguments.

SATURDAY, MAY 15, 1965 "So, how was it?"

"What?"

"You and Miss Kosi. You were with Miss Kosi last night. It was very late—about 11 o'clock. How was it?" the young men of Alang razz me.

I blush. *Oh, my gosh. How do they know? News has already traveled to the village.* Defensively I reply, "I was just walking her home."

They all grin. "Sure! That's what *you* say. And what else? Was it good? We *saw* you." They are thrilled they caught me red-handed.

"I just walked her home. That's all. We were at Jack and Dave's— playing Scrabble."

"You call it Scrabble, huh?" they laugh scurrilously.

I blush some more and start to perspire, not just from the heat of the sun, but from being put on the spot. I strive to uphold Kathy's honor, and all of ours as well. *Wow, we can't do anything without all of Iran knowing and thinking we're loose Americans.*

"What were *you* doing in Gorgan at that time of the night?" I challenge, smiling, trying to deflect their prying questions and innuendos and turn the accusations on them.

The verbal duel escalates. No one admits to anything.

SUNDAY, MAY 16, 1965 Though I know I'm heading for more linguistic combat, the magnetic attraction of the daily joust at the Sherkat-e Sargardon is irresistible.

"Tom, America is a very strange country. You have the highest standard of living in the world but your women are so thin," Reza gibes. "You don't take care of them well. You don't feed them enough. You starve them. What's the matter with America?"

"But being fat isn't good."

"No, Tom, women must be substantial. If not people will think you are not a good provider. They will think you are a poor man and can't afford to feed your wife. Besides, women who are fat are more desirable and better in bed. There is more there for you."

The gang laughs. I attempt to repress a smile, but turn red. They laugh even more.

"Tom, you must take a nice plump Persian woman—one so ample she is almost breathless when rising. Her breasts should be full and round, her hips sloping, and her buttocks so well padded as to nearly hinder her passage through a door. She would be better for you. She would make you happy and everyone will know you are a very successful man."

Though I'm not convinced a large amount of excess flesh is what I yearn for, I respond, "Well, you must help me find one—but not one too fat. Come on, you guys, here in Alang, you need to arrange this," I call their bluff.

There is wild hooting. "But you must become a Muslim and..."

"I know," I interrupt, "I must be circumcised. Well, I'm halfway ready. I just need to become a Muslim."

"*Baleh*, but we'd have to check you out first. We have no proof. It's only what *you* say."

ALL THE WAY HOME

SATURDAY, MAY 22, 1965 "Tom, Mr. Croll came to see you yesterday. He gave me this letter," Shaban Ali tells me. "He didn't have time to go to Gorgan. He needed to get back to Tehran."

I surmise it is what I've been waiting for. It's a short, hand-written message: "Tom, Come to Tehran this week. Don."

"Shaban Ali, he wants me to come to Tehran." I turn away with a lump in my throat, unable to say anything more.

DINNER AT JAVAD ABTAHI'S with my friends begins as our accustomed easygoing, laid-back gathering, but someone says, "There's only a year left. Tom will be going home. Alang will never be the same."

The statement puts a damper on the evening. I despair. There is no way I can tell them it might be much sooner.

"Tom, stay in Alang," Javad says. "Don't go back to America. We are just like brothers. Marry an Iranian girl. Become a teacher in Alang."

"*Baleh, dokhtare Turkomani begeer*" (Yes, get a Turkoman girl), Reza urges, eyes glinting. "They are very pretty." The guys start to snap their fingers and sing the popular Persian folk song about wanting a Turkoman girl. It lightens the mood a bit, but the thought of my departure in a little more than a year is becoming difficult for the village to accept.

SUNDAY, MAY 23, 1965 With a heavy heart, I trudge to the highway with my suit and enough clothes for a week. It's even hard walking down the pathway to Jack and Dave's. Everything I'm familiar with is coming to an end.

"My gosh, you're back already!" Dave greets me at the gate.

"*Baleh*. Don Croll came to Alang on Friday and left a message for me to come to Tehran."

Dave smiles, "This is it. You'll be going to Shiraz. This is what you've been waiting for."

"*Baleh*, but now I don't know if I want to go. I mean, I *want* to; I want to do more for Iran, and I could do that at the university, but I don't want to leave Alang. I feel like a traitor to the villagers. They're already lamenting that I'll be gone in a year. It's awful."

"Let's get Kathy. We can have dinner at the hotel and go to the cinema. That will get your mind off of it."

The film does little to quell my thoughts of deserting my friends in Alang—and Jack, Dave, and Kathy too. *It's your own fault. This is how you are. You always start something; then in the end, you don't want to do it. Just like joining the Peace Corps; the last night you didn't want to leave your friends. Then it was your idea to live in a village, but in the end you wanted to stay in Gorgan. Then you were the one who wanted to get transferred somewhere else. You kept badgering the Peace Corps to find you a better job. Now they have found one and you don't want to go.*

MONDAY, MAY 24, 1965　*Traitor,* I tell myself as the bus passes Alang. I look out the window, but I can't see. My eyes are too wet. I furtively wipe my nose and keep staring so the other passengers won't notice. It is a long time before I open *The Brothers Karamazov.*

The coolness of spring, savored during my previous trip to Tehran, has given way to summer heat. I take a taxi to our usual hotel, deposit my suitcase, and run to the Peace Corps office to see Don Croll.

"He's already left for the day," the director informs me. "Come back tomorrow. We're working out a schedule for you at Pahlavi. He'll go over it with you, and we'll be sending you to Shiraz to check it out."

TUESDAY, MAY 25, 1965—8:00AM　I'm swept into the central post office in Tehran with the hordes of Iranians who push their way in as the doors open. I find someone who can tell me where I go to get something out of customs. I show the clerk the notice I received in Kordkuy. He looks at it meticulously as ashes drop from his cigarette. Then he looks at me and carefully scrutinizes the paper again. He hands the paper back and shrugs.

"But I need to get this out of customs," I tell him in Farsi.

He shrugs again, and points to another window. More waiting.

"*Salaam,*" I greet the clerk when I get to the window. "I need to get this package from customs."

"*Baleh,*" he grunts. He too looks at me like it's already been a long day. I hand him the paper. He stamps it and hands it back to me. "Go over there—that line."

Gradually I work my way to the front of the third line and hand the paper to another clerk. I watch him go off and talk to someone else. They both disappear. He reappears without the paper. He ignores me.

"*Agha,* what about my package?"

"Wait." There is no explanation.

I'm beginning to perspire, convinced I will never see my portfolio that I had my parents send, and I don't have the paper any more. And though it is early morning, the stifling heat of Tehran's summer, the crush of humanity, and the oppressive cigarette smoke contribute to my uneasiness.

Nearly a half-hour later, the other man returns with a package that might be mine. It is covered in oil. I almost die. *My portfolio will be ruined,* I lament to myself and break out in more perspiration. *I'll never get the job in Shiraz, and my career is ruined.* I was going to use the portfolio to apply to grad schools.

They converse awhile. Another man joins them. Together they look at the paper and the box and discuss something. The man who brought the box goes off. The other two men seem to be trying to figure something out. The man returns with someone else. Now, all four engage in conversation. This goes on and on. They motion for me. I cautiously say, *"Baleh?"*

"It says here it is books and educational materials."

"*Baleh.* That's what it is."

"But it is valued at $13.00."

"That is the value my parents put on it. It is from my mother and father."

"We need to open it."

"Fine, *befarmayid.*" They cut open the box. I hope they are not cutting into the artwork. I can hardly stand this. The torment is excruciating.

At last they pull out the portfolio. When the plastic wrapping is pulled away it is in perfect condition. *Alhamdulillah,* I whisper to myself.

They take a passing glance at the photographs of my work and the university yearbooks I designed. However, the portfolio of my textile designs puzzles them.

"Are you going to sell these textiles in Iran?" they ask.

"No, these are examples of the textile design work I can do. I am going to Pahlavi University to teach. This is all educational material."

"Educational material?" they look at me askance.

"Baleh," I insist.

Another clerk comes by and joins in the inspection while they try to determine my real motives in having textile samples sent to Iran. One of them gets multiple copies of a form, systematically inserts carbon paper between each page, and fills it out. I wait with a presumed air of patience, but I'm fraying at all ends.

Finished, the man carries the form to another clerk. I watch as they confer. Each page of the form is stamped and signed. He returns. He reassembles the portfolio into its box and says, "Come with me."

We reach another office, another official. "What's in here?" he asks.

"Clothing samples," the clerk replies.

"Educational materials," I assert. "I am going to Pahlavi University for a teaching job. I am an American Peace Corps Volunteer."

"Open it," he tells the clerk. "I need to see it." The clerk complies. "Hmm, educational materials, huh?" He looks at me.

"Baleh, educational materials," I persist.

They step to the side and speak in muffled tones while I try to remain calm and patient.

"You will have to pay duty on the importation of these clothing samples." The official signs the form and hands the clerk the paper. "Follow him."

I put up no argument. Anything to get out of here.

A bureaucrat at a desk carefully reads the form and looks at me. "That will be eight tomans duty."

I hand him the eight tomans (about one dollar). He stamps the form, signs it, and gives it to the clerk. We return to the officious functionary. He scrutinizes the form to confirm I paid the customs fees. The clerk hands me my portfolio.

"Clothing samples, huh?" the official retorts in English as I depart.

"No. Educational materials. *Khodahafez.*" I turn away.

IT'S ALREADY 10 O'CLOCK. I must get to the Peace Corps office to see Don Croll. I hail a cab. One with several passengers slows momentarily. I call out the address on Takht-e Jamshid. The driver raises his eyebrows and speeds on. Another slows. This one shakes his head, signifying "Where do you want to go?" I tell him. He motions for me to get in.

"How much?" He states a price. "Too much." I counter his offer. He smiles wryly and heads on.

Another stops. "Where?"

"Takht-e Jamshid." I give him the number. "How much?" It is a lot less. *"Kheili khoob."* I get in. He delivers several other passengers and picks up more along the way.

"Where are you from?" he asks me in Farsi.

"Amrika."

"Amrika! Besyar khoobeh (Very good). *Amrika kheili khoobeh"* (America is very good).

"Baleh. Iran *ham khoobeh"* (Iran is also good). I continue in Farsi, sincerely wanting him and the passengers to know I love Iran.

"What are you doing in Iran?"

"I'm an American Peace Corps Volunteer. President Kennedy started the Peace Corps."

"Oooh, Kennedy was good. Very good. I am sorry."

"Thank you. *Baleh*, Kennedy was good."

"You know Farsi very well. How did you learn?"

"I live in a village near Gorgan."

"In a village! Isn't that very difficult?"

"No, I like it in the village. The people are my friends."

I hand him the fare as we stop in front of the Peace Corps office.

"*Khodahafez*. Thank you."

"It was a pleasure to talk to you," he says. "Enjoy Iran. *Khodahafez*."

Don Croll describes the job in Shiraz. "They want an advisor for student publications and someone to lead them in developing student organizations. Your expertise working on the yearbooks and with student groups in Hawaii is perfect for this position. Exactly what they want."

"Is there any chance I could also teach some art courses?"

"Show them your portfolio and mention you would like to teach art as well. They may be open to that too. Take the bus to Shiraz tomorrow. It's a long ride, at least 15 hours. I'll contact the people at Pahlavi and tell them you'll be there on Thursday. After lunch, I'll give you the schedule and the names of whom you'll be seeing."

I leave the Peace Corps office hardly able to fathom what is happening to me. This is better than anything I could ever imagine. Now I'll be doing something worthwhile here in Iran.

I explore the shops on Khiaban-e Ferdowsi, but somehow nothing seems as important as the prospects of going to Shiraz to work at the university.

"HEY, YOU'RE BACK. Glad to see you," the uniformed man at the hotel greets me. None of us has ever established what his job is. He's just there. A secret SAVAK agent, I've always figured. I'm politely friendly, but that's it. I don't want to get to know him too well.

"*Shab bekheyr,*" I bid him goodnight and head to my room. It's a large, cavernous space with numerous beds and little else. A German has staked out a cot on the opposite side of the room. We greet each other. He knows little English and I, no German. There is a knock on the door. I go to open it. It is the man with the uniform from downstairs.

"I was wondering if we could talk awhile."

"*Baleh, befarmayid.*" I offer him the single chair. I sit on the bed.

"Are you enjoying Iran?" he begins.

"*Baleh*, I like Iran very much." My answers are guarded. He tells me about other Peace Corps Volunteers and asks if I know them. I don't.

"I would like you to come to my apartment. Many American friends have been there. Here, I can show you pictures."

I look at the pictures but don't recognize any of the guys.

"Why don't we go for a walk and we can stop by my apartment for a while? It's not far from here. I'll make tea and we can have cookies, and spend a little time talking."

"I'm pretty tired and tomorrow I have a long bus ride ahead of me. I could come another time I'm in Tehran."

"Oh? Where are you going? Back to Gorgan?"

"Baleh," I lie. I don't want him knowing too much about me in case he's some secret agent. He already knows I'm from Gorgan.

"Have you ever been on the roof of the hotel? The view of Tehran at night is very beautiful from there. You should see it."

"No, I've never been there."

"Let's go now. I would like you to see it."

Apprehensively I agree to go. It's a way of getting him out of this room. And once I've seen it, I can excuse myself.

We head up the dimly lit stairway. At the top, a window opens to the roof. I look out and see the lights of the city all around. It does look spectacular. It's dark, and I'm not able to see where I might be stepping if I crawl through the window. With the obligatory Persian politeness I suggest he go first. *"Befarmayid."*

"Na, befarmayid," he insists.

Reluctantly, I go first, raising my leg to get through. Immediately I freeze and retract. The guy pressed unnecessarily close to me as I climbed through the window. In fact, I think I heard his heart pounding. Or was it mine, thundering in my ears? At any rate, *I don't like this.*

I pull back and say, "I can't see where I'm going. You go first." I step aside and urge him to go.

He starts through the window and gets on the other side. Instantly I bolt for the stairs, taking two steps at a time. My hand is shaking, and I fumble with the key in the door. I get it open before I see him following. I slam the door shut and lock it, then sit on the bed to calm down. My mouth is dry and I shake like a leaf, fearing there will be a knock on the door any second. It never occurs.

The creep. How disgusting!

WEDNESDAY, MAY 26, 1965 The bus departs south Tehran at 5am. It takes a long time to maneuver the streets of this crowded part of the city, even at this hour. Yet we sail along at the usual aggressive breakneck speed, horn tooting, as smaller vehicles and pedestrians scramble out of the way. The young man across the aisle observes my painful alarm and considerable relief as the bus squeezes past narrow misses. He no doubt sees my white knuckles as I clutch the arm of the seat.

"Where you from?" he ventures in halting English.

"*Amrika*," I respond in Farsi, signaling I know the language. "Where are you going? Isfahan or Shiraz?"

"Shiraz. My name is Rahmin."

"I'm going to Shiraz too." I extend my hand. "My name is Tom. I am an American Peace Corps Volunteer." He had never heard of the Peace Corps. I explain it was President Kennedy's vision to send young Americans to other parts of the world to help in any way they can. "Why are you going to Shiraz?" I ask.

"I want to become a taxi driver. Some friends said they would help me."

Our conversation takes my mind off the insane maneuvering out of the city, but it is interrupted often by sudden stops and close calls. With the teeming city left behind, the vast, epic sweep of desert engulfs us. The glaring brightness of the cloudless sky and the unending near-white sand confirm the scorching heat outside. Scattered along the route, weathered villages evince the boundless human effort to survive amid the wind-worn desolateness of this absolute wasteland. Dust devils dance in the distance and vast lakes reflect the barren scarps of far-off mountains, then disappear into nothingness. There is no water anywhere—only a mirage.

Somewhere along the route to Isfahan, we stop for a short break. A man on crutches struggles to disembark. Everyone but Rahmin ignores him. *This is an exceptional young person,* I think. He is right there to lend a hand. His regard for the other passenger is sincere.

Our arrival in Isfahan is spellbinding. The sparkling blue-tile domes of the mosques glistening in the noonday sun and the grand scale of the Meydan-e Shah with its fountains and flower gardens help me realize why European travelers of the 17th century called Isfahan "half the world."

"Our stop here will be one-and-a-half hours," the driver tells us.

"Would you like to see Chehel Sotun?" Rahmin asks me at lunch. "It's not far from here."

"*Baleh.* We have at least an hour before the bus leaves."

Chehel Sotun, the Palace of Forty Columns, sits within the cooling splendor of shaded gardens. A large pool echoes the twenty columns of its *talar* (porch), imbuing the palace with its exotic name. Here Safavid rulers received their foreign envoys. Enormous wall paintings depict the glory of Persian victories and the submission of vanquished monarchs. The large 19th century painting of Shah Ismael attacking the Ottoman Janissaries in the famous 1514 battle of Chaldiran in northwestern Iran is the scene that inspired the painting on the little pen box I bought in Mashhad.*

The road from Isfahan to Shiraz is more of the same bleak, searing desert, distant mountains, and the occasional shepherd and his flock seemingly lost in space. Though they are far away, I feel a closeness—an affinity between them and me. It is a kinetic, haptic space—one intimate, magnetic, and dynamically charged. In these limitless desert wastes of sparse material wealth, life and man's relationship to his surroundings take on a deep and significant meaning. Here, where I am not bombarded by a confounding array of visual clutter, I am beginning to perceive new and meaningful spatial sensations.

Before dark, as the bus sails past, I momentarily glimpse some carved reliefs beside the road.

"It is Naqsh-e Rajab," Rahmin tells me. "They are from the Sassanian dynasty, more than 1700 years ago."

I saw carvings so old—and not in a museum—even if it was only for a split second! I marvel to myself. Observing my excitement, Rahmin smiles.

The bus turns to the left around an outcropping and my eyes pop. I rise out of my seat to get a better look—Persepolis—the near-legendary capital of Darius the Great! The city was founded around 515 BC, only to be destroyed by Alexander the Great in 330 BC. I strain to see all I can

---

* Although Ismael appears victorious, the battle was a resounding defeat for the Persian army; it established the modern border of Turkey and Iran, and marked a change in warfare from cavalry archers used by Shah Ismael to artillery employed by the Ottomans.

before, at the base of the immense double stairway to the platform above, we sharply turn to the right, heading off across the plain to Shiraz.

Rahmin grins. He and the other passengers witness my enthusiasm, obviously with a bit of amusement. "Would you like to see it? My friends and I will take you there on Friday."

"Oh, I would like that very much."

Fifty kilometers on, we descend from the arid Zagros Mountains to a lush green plain. There sprawls Shiraz, a city of cypresses, roses, and poets. The bus passes beneath the graceful arch of the Koran Gate. I sense the blessings bestowed upon me by the Holy Book above.*

THURSDAY, MAY 27, 1965 The taxi ascends the rocky hills overlooking the city. Although the university is under construction, it exhibits a unity of design that reveals a Persian Islamic aesthetic. "How wonderful to build a new university with an architecture based on Iranian traditions and culture," I tell my first interviewers, two Iranians.

They exhibit pleasure that I recognize and appreciate what is being done at Pahlavi. After the requisite cup of tea—in a Western teacup with a saucer—they brief me, in impeccable English, on the courses of study at the university.

"Pahlavi is a liberal arts university with schools of agriculture, medicine, and engineering. His Majesty the Shah is determined to make Pahlavi University the best in Iran. We are working closely with the University of Pennsylvania to set the highest standards for our students. The Peace Corps tells us you have worked with student groups, and you were editor of the University of Hawaii yearbooks. We are looking for somebody like you to be an advisor for student publications and also to student organizations, especially in drama and music."

"Yes, I was art editor of the university yearbooks for two years." I present the books from my portfolio. "It was an innovative direction in yearbook publication because we approached each as a 'pictorial essay' that tried

---

* Originally built in the 10ᵗʰ century within the city walls, the gateway has sustained repeated earthquake damage. Karim Khan Zand (r. 1750–1779) ordered that a Koran be placed in the gatehouse of his capital city so all travelers would be blessed as they entered or left.

to capture the essence of life on campus. Of course, my senior year at the university was a momentous one, with the assassination of President Kennedy and Civil Rights Week on our campus. The Rev. Martin Luther King, Jr. and other civil rights leaders came to Hawaii for this event. The book is meant to capture the enormity and emotion of this year in history."

I show them more of my design work, and the portfolio of textile designs. They are impressed.

"Maybe you could do workshops for our students. We are always looking for ways of getting them involved and providing learning opportunities outside the classroom."

"Do you have an art department here at the university?"

"No, not now. We might develop one in the future."

Of course I'm disappointed. We discuss their visions of my role at the university before they take me to meet an American with USAID who is one of the foreign consultants to the university.

"Hello, Tom," he greets me casually. "Thank you for coming to Shiraz to meet with us. The Peace Corps recommends you highly. We want a person with your background to lead our student organizations." He tells me more about Pahlavi University and the job. "What have you got here?"

"It's a portfolio of my work. The Peace Corps suggested I show it to you, as they thought I might also be able to teach art courses at the university."

He bristles a bit. "Oh, we don't have an art department here yet. But I'd like to see what you've done." He looks at the yearbooks and my work briefly. "I can see you would have one horrible time here; this university is nowhere near ready for anything like this. Your work has achieved far too much sophistication for this school. Regardless, we need a coordinator for our student organizations. We will be in contact with the Peace Corps and they will let you know."

"Thank you for the opportunity to meet with you. Pahlavi is a very inspiring place."

"Tom, my wife and I are having a party tonight. There will be lots of Americans there, including the Peace Corps Volunteers stationed in Shiraz. I'd like to have you come. Here's the address. Give it to any taxi driver. He'll find it with no problem."

"Thank you for asking me. I'd like to come."

"We'll see you this evening."

Well, that was curious, I think to myself as I stroll across campus. So very cordial—even inviting me to a party—but telling me I'd have a "horrible time" here.

"Hello," a young man greets me in unbroken English. "Are you a new professor here?"

"No, I'm an American Peace Corps Volunteer, and I may be coming to Shiraz to work at the university. Are you a student at Pahlavi?"

"Yes. I'm studying engineering. What will you be doing here?"

"I will be an advisor for student organizations. I've been involved with student groups in the States. What year are you in your studies?"

"I'm a junior."

"How's the university?"

"Fine. I like engineering. I'm glad the classes are in English. It is good preparation for going to America."

"'Going to America?'" I say, disappointed by his objective.

"Yes, that's what I want to do. I intend to go to the States for a graduate degree when I finish here."

"Do you like Pahlavi?" I probe to find out more about the school.

"Well, it's sort of like a high school. They want us to be involved in all sorts of student activities. I like that, but it often takes too much time away from our studies. Then we have to work extra hard to catch up with what we're supposed to learn."

Revealing, I say to myself. I tell him, "Learning to work with others in student groups is beneficial to your education too."

"Yes, but I can't wait to get to the States. Everything will be good there. Everything is good in America."

"Well, study hard. *Enshahallah,* you will be able to go to America. Then you can come back to Iran and do great things for your country."

"Oh, if I go to America I will marry an American woman and stay there. Things are better in America."

Is this the kind of people I will be working with? I reflect, disheartened.

"Well, all the best to you," I say as we part. *"Khodahafez."*

"Goodbye. I hope to see you on campus once you get the job."

Wow, that's a bummer. What's the point of coming to Shiraz to work with student organizations? Being a student activities coordinator is likely a job as vague as community development in the villages. I was hoping I might be teaching art courses at the university. I know I could do it. In fact, my education in textile design could have a constructive impact on the design industry in Iran. But obviously that's not possible. And if the students are like the one I met, I wouldn't be preparing them to help Iran; I would be aiding in their plans to leave the country—permanently!

The party, too, is a psychological wake-up call—mostly Americans and other foreigners, with just a few Iranian wives of foreign expats. No one is speaking Farsi. I feel like a fish out of water. I've been in the village too long. I've become too Iranian.

"Tom! What are you doing in Shiraz?" I turn to see a guy from the US Army I had met in Gorgan when I first arrived in Iran.

"Hey, Bob! You're in Shiraz now? I thought you were still in Gorgan."

"I was transferred to Shiraz over six months ago. In fact, I'll be returning to the States next week. What about you? Are you still in Gorgan? What brings you to Shiraz?"

"I've been living in a village west of Gorgan ever since I first met you. The Peace Corps sent me here to check out a job at Pahlavi University."

"Pahlavi! That would be super. Shiraz is so much better than Gorgan. Gorgan is a backwater. Here there are lots of Americans and Europeans. There are parties all the time. Hey, you need your drink refreshed. Don't be shy. There's always plenty of booze here. Let me introduce you to some of the Peace Corps Volunteers who are stationed in Shiraz. We all know each other. Constant parties, you know."

Most of the volunteers are teachers from other groups. One of them tells me, "You'll like it here. With the US Army and the people from USAID, there are oodles of parties."

"Do you like your work here?" I ask innocently. "Do you get a chance to meet many Iranians?"

"Oh, yes, at work. That's pretty much it. We don't mix socially."

"So, how's your Farsi?"

"We hardly use it. We always speak English. We only use Farsi in the bazaar."

I leave the party disillusioned, troubled. *Is this what I want?* The job seems ambiguous—no more structured than the work I do in Alang. Worse, here the American community is one big clique, with very little connection to Iranians.

FRIDAY, MAY 28, 1965 "Takht-e Jamshid (Persepolis) is straight ahead," Rahmin and two of his friends tell me as we descend the desiccated mountains surrounding Shiraz. A long, arrow-straight road leads east across a broad plain toward distant barren foothills. At the end of the road, a few lonely columns and rectangular shapes disclose man's imposition on the landscape.

The excitement I felt two days before as we quickly passed in the bus returns. It is almost uncontrollable; truly remarkable that now, as we climb the wide, gently inclined stairs to the terrace above, I am walking in the footsteps of men who were here nearly 2500 years ago—Darius, Xerxes, and Alexander the Great. At the top of the stairs I am humbled as we stand at the threshold of the Gatehouse of Xerxes I. Enormous guardian animals—winged bulls with human heads—frame the entrance. I feel insignificant, powerless amid such majesty. Clearly they were meant to command respect, to glorify the invincible might of one of the world's most powerful empires. Everywhere we go, the scale and grandeur of the site and the precision of the carvings astonish me. I cannot take in enough. There is too much to see. I could come back often if I take the job at Pahlavi University.

In Shiraz, Rahmin and I visit the late 18th century Masjid-e Vakil. I marvel at the coolness of the prayer hall, where young men—students—quietly assemble and peruse their books. The colorful and ornate floral tile panels form a welcome complement to the stately uniformity of the columns within.

In late afternoon, families leisurely savor the gardens surrounding the tomb of the celebrated 14th century poet, Hafez, whose lyrical poems of love and the beloved are imbued with Sufi mystical meaning. Children run with playful abandon along the pathways, and the scent of roses permeates the air.

Flowers and elegant paths also surround the poet Saadi's tomb. Stately cypresses soften the starkness of this modernist building with its turquoise dome crowning a porch supported by narrow, unornamented columns.

Shiraz, the city of poets and roses, is one of Iran's most beautiful cities. *How wonderful it would be to work in such a place,* I muse, *the very cultural center of Iran. This is very tempting.*

SATURDAY, MAY 29, 1965—5AM "Rahmin, thank you for coming to see me off and for taking me to Takht-e Jamshid yesterday. It was nice to meet your friends, and seeing the ancient capital of Iran was very special."

"Tom, I am happy to have met you. I hope you get the job at Pahlavi University. When you come to Shiraz, we'll go to Takht-e Jamshid again. By then, I will be a taxi driver so we can go to many other places too. There is a lot of history around Shiraz. I know you like history."

"*Baleh*, I will let you know if I get the job. *Khodahafez.*" We shake hands, and I board the bus for the long fifteen-hour trip back to Tehran.

We wave as the bus pulls out of the station. *What a neat guy,* I think as Rahmin recedes in the distance. He never once said, "We are friends," or "Let's be friends," as most other Persians say immediately upon meeting. It always makes me cringe, as it seems so insincere. We became friends without saying it. It's just something we knew. Interesting, it didn't seem that necessary to him. Each time when others say it, I agree I am their friend; I couldn't say otherwise. But it's an empty expression. True friendships are natural, unencumbered, not demanded—almost sacred. Rahmin wasn't even trying to learn English from me. He respected my Farsi. Never once did he ask, "What's this in English?" or "What's that in English?" These persistent questions become so irritating. Sometimes I regret I even know English. And he's a gentleman—the way he helped the man on crutches on the bus. He's always concerned about others.

I keep thinking of him as the bus heads east and we pass Persepolis and Naqsh-e Rajab. Abruptly, the bus slows and stops. The driver lays on the horn. Everyone sits up, straining to peer out the window ahead. The road is filled with goats and sheep scurrying in all directions. Young boys with willowy sticks and their mongrel dogs scramble to herd the animals to the side. This is the Qashqai, a nomadic tribe, on their migration to higher summer pastures. Women with dozens of brightly colored spangled skirts draped over the flanks of donkeys clutch their babies and return our glass-separated gaze. Dark hair and vivid, kaleidoscopic scarves and shawls frame their confident faces. Others, their skirts billowing, hasten to maneuver the flock to the side. Drably dressed men, heads topped by beige felt caps with tall, upturned rims, nonchalantly calm their heavily laden camels. Slowly, with much noise and complaints from the driver, we weave our way through the maze of animals and press on across the infinite desert.

My reading of *The Brothers Karamazov* is broken by my fascination with the desert and thoughts of the future. Never in my life have I had time to think about what is important to me and what I want to do—not just now, but what I want to do when I leave Iran. I have always acted impulsively. There was never time—or I never took time. The fifteen-hour bus ride affords lots of time to weigh options.

The coolness of morning transcends to midday, and the bus persists in its pursuit of the withering heat and the desert. I am fortunate to have gone to Shiraz to see the situation at Pahlavi. The job is nebulous at best—not much different from what I'm doing now in Alang. Most dreadful of all, I'll be immersed in American culture within a foreign country. I will have come halfway around the world to spend most of my free time with other Americans.

Not for me! I decide. *I came to Iran to be with Iranians.* Perhaps I'm sort of a snob, but these foreigners who can't fit in with local culture and enjoy it bother me. Maybe I can be the exception . . . I can avoid the parties, the drinking, and get to know Iranians. But is this what I really want? Most of all, I have come to love the people of Alang. They have become my family, and they have adopted me. I could not turn my back on them. They would never forgive me. What would they think of me? What would they tell the people in the other villages I work in? My leaving might be interpreted as a bad reflection on Alang and their hospitality. How would they feel about an American who drops in out of nowhere, wins their trust and love, and then cops out on them—as if I didn't even care? The fact is I do care. I care a lot. The truth is I miss Alang. I'm going back. It is my home.

Calmness overcomes me. Again I have determined my future.

With inner resolution, I open *The Brothers Karamazov*. I am struck by a passage in Dostoevsky's novel that is graphically familiar—an old beggar woman is given an onion. This is uncanny. Here she is—the "onion lady" in Gorgan. What does this mean?

We arrive in Tehran before dark. *No way am I going back to that hotel— ever!* I vow. *Not with that repugnant creep there.*

I find a hotel near the Meydan-e Toopkhaneh and get a taxi to Peace Corps headquarters. Likely the staff will be gone, but I'll drop off a note. That way I can get a bus to Gorgan early in the morning.

No one is there. I sit on the steps in front, open my drawing book to a blank page, and begin writing. "Thanks for providing the opportunity for me to go to Shiraz to see about the job at Pahlavi University. I have decided to stay in Alang. The people have become my friends and I cannot leave them." I did not know how prophetic that sentence was, but it was written from the heart. "Thank you, Tom." I tear the page from my book, fold it, and slip it into the mailbox.

SUNDAY, MAY 30, 1965 "Hello, what your name?" the young man next to me on the bus asks in English.

"Hello, my name is Tom. What is your name?" He thinks awhile. "My name is Tom," I respond again. I wait a few seconds, then say, "What is your name?"

He smiles. I wait. There is thoughtful silence.

"Esme shoma chi'eh" (What is your name)? I ask in Farsi.

"Abbas. My name Abbas," he says hesitantly. He offers his hand. We shake. I begin where I left off in *The Brothers Karamazov*.

"What is your country?"

I look up and say, "America, *Amrika*. Are you from Tehran?"

"Amrika, Amrika," he echoes blankly.

"Baleh, Amrika. Shoma maleh koja hastid" (Where are you from)? I ask,

doing my best to force this annoying exchange into Farsi. There is no immediate reply.

"I live Tehran." He smiles. I smile back and resume reading.

"You read?"

"Yes, I *am* reading." (I wanted to say, "Yes, I am *trying* to read.")

"What you read?"

"*The Brothers Karamazov.*" I show him the cover. "It is a Russian novel," I tell him in Farsi.

There is no reaction. I open the book again.

"How do you say *'Tu kheili khooshgeli'* in English?"

He is using the familiar pronoun. He probably wants to use this on a girl, I suspect.

"You are very pretty."

I see him repeating it many times to himself. I return to *The Brothers*.

"How do you say *'Man doost et doram'* in English?" Again it is the familiar.

"I love you."

The limited conversation drags on—he refusing to speak Farsi except to ask how you say something in English. I am irked, but remain civil.

Thankfully, he disembarks in Babol. He's unmistakably going to the Caspian seaside for a holiday. He'll doubtless use his newly learned phrases on some unsuspecting damsels. I should have given him some wrong answers. That would serve him right.

In the early evening, as we approach Kordkuy, I persuade the bus driver to let me off at Alang. It doesn't take as much convincing as other times, when it was dark. His assistant quickly opens the compartment under the bus and, as the dust swirls around us, he hands me my suitcase. *"Moteshakeram, khodahafez,"* I call out as he jumps back on the bus.

I stand there momentarily, watching the rising cloud inch toward Gorgan. I cross the road and venture down the pathway to Alang. I feel a lump in my throat and my eyes moisten slightly. *Wow, I came so close to abandoning Alang. Now I am truly coming home. All the way home, unlike I have ever felt before.*

DAYS OF HIGHS AND LOWS

MONDAY, MAY 31, 1965 The joy of being home is dampened by news that chickens got into Shaban Ali's garden and ate practically all our seedlings. I manage to smile, but mumble to myself, "Oh, well, another valiant attempt to do something, only to be met by failure." We try again, plant more seeds, and cross our fingers the chickens and the summer heat will not negate our labor.

Shaban Ali and my Sherkat-e Sargardon cohorts excitedly wait to hear about my trip to Tehran. I must be honest with them. They will find out I went to Shiraz because I'm sure to slip and mention it sometime.

"Well, I also went to Shiraz. The Peace Corps sent me there about a job at Pahlavi University." Their eyes reveal disappointment. "But I'm not going. I'm going to stay in Alang. Alang is my home. You are my friends and my family. I cannot leave you." Relief registers in their faces. Resignation to the fact I am now an Alangi is complete and comforting.

THURSDAY, JUNE 10, 1965 Tehran again—this time for our two-day physical exam. Before I depart for Alang, I return to the Peace Corps office to deposit an important contribution with Dr. Drake that I was not able to unload on Tuesday or Wednesday. I had the "Tehran Trots" all the while I was in Tehran, but couldn't oblige when it was necessary.

Dr. Drake pronounces me OK. "No worms, no amoebas, no parasites, nothing. But, you're so thin. You're back down to the weight you were when you started Peace Corps training in Utah. Less than two months ago you were 160 lbs. Now you're down to 132. What happened?"

"I don't know," I shrug. "I knew I was losing weight. I have lots of room in my pants now. I couldn't even button the top button when I was here at Easter, and when I would bend over I could hear threads popping."

"Well, try not to lose any more. Be sure to eat well. But be careful what you eat in Tehran this time of the year. This is the last time I call volunteers in for physicals in the summer. Too many of you got sick."

I thank him, as if my good health were his doing, even if I was miserable while I was here. I leave the office optimistic I will be in good shape once I get back to Alang. Even though Peace Corps friends want me to stay for the weekend, I head for the bus station. I can't wait to get out of Tehran. It's hot and filthy; the stench of urine permeates the air. Besides, I can't miss one of the most noteworthy days I'm likely to witness while I'm in Iran.

SUNDAY, JUNE 13, 1965 Shaban Ali and I stand with the village men and children in the little square in front of the new school in Ghalandarayesh. Even some of the little girls, modestly concealed in their white summer *chadors*, are here. Women huddle to the side. Arrangements of fresh flowers and forest greens ornament the square and the entrance to the school.

School, Ghalandarayesh

Certainly my pride in the Literacy Corpsman is evident. I see he is meekly proud too. The tiny school with its tiled roof shimmers in the hot summer sun. Never mind the mud-crusted walls have cracked as they dried—another coat of daub next winter will cover that. We are waiting for the arrival of the *Ostandar* (Governor) of Mazandaran. Far below, we see a cloud of dust rising behind several vehicles coming up the roadway. Yesterday we cleared rocks from the path, pushing them to the side so the governor's car would not be damaged.

Shaban Ali and I rose early again this morning to be here for this important occasion. Now excitement dissolves any fatigue. Never before has a governor set foot in the little village of Ghalandarayesh. As the awaited entourage appears, the village men fall into their assigned places in the long line of welcomers. The governor and his associates shake hands with each of us. The community draws near as the governor praises the people of Ghalandarayesh who worked so hard to build this school, and the competence of the Literacy Corpsman, who is a caring teacher for the children of the village. He stresses the vision of His Majesty the Shah of Iran, who instituted the Literacy Corps in his noble effort to bring education to the most remote areas of the country. He then dedicates the new little school. We applaud. The village council leaders and the Literacy Corpsman lead the governor into the small two-room building. Shaban Ali and I are drawn along with the special delegation. I smile my approval to my friend the teacher. Ours is a unique bond—we are both young, both corpsmen, both working in villages, both aspiring to bring a new beginning to a humble corner of the world.

Together we stroll in the shade of the trees to the headman's house and assemble in his second story room. A breeze rustles the leaves of the surrounding trees and, as it gently blows through the room, it bestows a welcome and cooling relief in contrast to the sun-parched playground in front of the school.

The governor registers surprise. "Other Peace Corps Volunteers live in the regional towns and cities of Mazandaran. You must be the only one living in a village. Isn't it difficult for you?"

"I am one of the few living in a village. I love living in Alang and working with *Aghaye* Rahemi. The work he is doing in the five villages to which he is assigned is outstanding. And, our Literacy Corpsman here in

Ghalandarayesh is commendable. I am honored to know both of them."
I look approvingly at each. "And the people of Ghalandarayesh are so
happy they now have a school and teacher in their village. The Literacy
Corps is a pivotal program for Iran."

The governor asks me if I know other Peace Corps Volunteers, including
Mr. Moore in Gonbad-e Kavus.

"Yes, Barkley Moore is my very good friend. He is doing phenomenal
work in Gonbad. He is an extraordinary person."

The governor smiles wryly, "Yes, everybody in Gonbad loves Mr. Moore."

When tea is finished, a large oilcloth is spread upon the floor. Plates and
silverware are carried in and places set around the edge of the cloth. We all
move forward and tray upon tray of food is brought in—*chelo kebab* (rice
and kebab), *khoresht* (stews), *mast* (yogurt), salads, warm bread, sodas and
doogh (a refreshing drink of water and yogurt)—the typical Persian feast.
In contrast to the squelching heat of the plain far below, the coolness of
this summer hideaway fosters an appetite. We eat heartily. The meal ends
with fresh fruit and cucumbers.

As the officials depart, Shaban Ali and I run to the schoolyard to retrieve
our bicycles and quickly follow them to nearby Bala Jaddeh, where the
governor has scheduled a meeting with the village council to review their
ideas for a water system and bathhouse with showers.

The governor expresses satisfaction with the progress being made on
both projects, and pledges the support of his office. "When you're ready,
have *Aghaye* Rahemi and the head of the development office in Gorgan,
Aghaye Vahdati, contact me. We have engineers who can help you develop
the plans. I look forward to coming back when you have running water
throughout Bala Jaddeh and a new bathhouse as well."

He tells Shaban Ali to keep the projects on track, then turns to me,
"*Aghaye* Mister Tom, it was nice to meet you. Please encourage the villagers
to make improvements in sanitation and their living conditions. Education
is a very important part of this. Thank you for coming to Iran."

"It was a pleasure to be with you as well. I will do what I can. Shaban
Ali is a fine man to work with. We will work together. *Khodahafez*." We
watch as the cars descend the mountain.

Shaban Ali and I then bid farewell to the men in Bala Jaddeh and head for Alang. Expressing my satisfaction, I say, "Shaban Ali, this has been a terrific day. I am so proud of the people in Ghalandarayesh and Bala Jaddeh. The governor was very pleased."

THE DOWNHILL JOURNEY is easy, but the stifling humid heat on the plain is oppressive. We are stopped as we reach Alang.

"Three jeeps from Alang were in a bad accident this morning," friends inform us. "Many people were hurt. Two of the jeeps stopped on the road from Gorgan and the third, with *Aghaye* Tofigh Rahemi in it, ran into them. The driver could not see because of the dust."

"Is everyone OK?" Shaban Ali and I ask. "No one was killed?"

"Everyone is alive, but *Aghaye* Rahemi has cuts on his head and legs. Others have cuts too. They had to go to the doctor in Gorgan, but nobody is in the hospital. They are all back in Alang."

"*Alhamdulillah*. Shaban Ali, we have to see how *Aghaye* Tofigh is, even if it is just to ask about him." We immediately bicycle to his gate.

"Ezetollah, are you OK?" He has numerous bandages but insists we come in. "And what about your father? We must not stay and bother you. We wanted to be sure you and your father are all right."

"My father will want to see you, Mister Tom. He will be happy you came. *Lotfan beah, befarmayid* (Please, come in). *Khooshalesh mekonid*" (It will bring him joy). He ushers us into the familiar room I called home eight months before. As Ezetollah goes to get his father, Shaban Ali and I sit there quietly, anxiously awaiting what we might see.

Slowly *Aghaye* Tofigh enters, aided by his son. His head is swathed in bandages. Shaban Ali and I rise. He motions for us to be seated. Ezetollah settles him in a chair and runs off to order tea. *Aghaye* Tofigh recounts the accident and shows us his leg.

"Fortunately you don't have any broken bones. *Alhamdulillah*," I say.

"*Baleh. Alhamdulillah*. We were all lucky. No one was hurt badly, but we are very sore. The roads are very dangerous this time of the year. There is so much dust. You must be very careful, Tom, when you get off the bus by Alang."

"Baleh," I assure him I'm careful. We tell him about the dedication of the school in Ghalandarayesh, and he is pleased I met and talked with the governor.

We finish tea and bid them, *"Khodahafez.* Please take care of yourselves. We hope you will be well soon."

"Thank you for coming."

"You're welcome."

I look at Shaban Ali as we mount our bicycles. "They were very lucky. God was watching over them."

"Baleh. It will be good when the highway is asphalt to Gorgan. Hopefully it will be completed before you leave Alang."

When the lights go out and I am by myself I reflect on the day. *Another day of real highs and lows. But God is good. Everyone is OK.*

MONDAY, JUNE 21, 1965 It has been more than a week since I visited with Tofigh Rahemi. I knock on his gateway door.

"Baleh," I hear a woman's voice on the other side.

"In Tom *ast"* (This is Tom).

"Ezetollah, Mister Tom *amadeh. Beah,"* she announces my arrival.

Shortly I hear the shuffle of slippers. The gate opens. Ezetollah smiles. *"Salaam,* Tom, *hale shoma khoobeh? Beah, intu"* (Come in).

"Hale shoma khoobeh? Behtar shodi (You are better)? You no longer have any bandages."

"Baleh, behtar shodam" (Yes, I am better).

"Alhamdulillah. Pedaret chetoreh" (How is your father)?

"He is in much pain now, but he will want to see you. Come in."

"If he is resting I will come back another time."

"No, he will want to visit with you. It will make him feel better."

I wait to see him, feeling guilty I'm disturbing him. He and Ezetollah appear at the door, his large frame leaning on his son for support. I rise and excuse myself for bothering them.

"No, we are happy to see you. You are like a son to me. You are always welcome here."

"But you are in such pain now."

"*Baleh,* my leg is very bad. The doctor says it is just bruised and I must be patient. It will be better soon."

"The scars on your head are healing well. That's good."

He had heard I went to Shiraz regarding a job at Pahlavi University. "We are thankful you decided to stay here." He smiles. "You are an Alangi. You cannot leave Alang. You are our son."

"*Baleh,* thank you. Yes, I am an Alangi. I love Alang and all of you . . . very much."

Later I excuse myself. "I hope your leg will be fine in no time. Walk on it a little bit each day, even if it hurts. The exercise is important."

"*Baleh.* That's what the doctor tells me." He looks at me with resignation. "Please come again."

"I will. *Khodahafez.*"

THURSDAY, JULY 1, 1965 A letter from the Peace Corps informs us of the death of Volunteer Francis Kirking. I think back to our time together when we unexpectedly saw each other at the Good Friday liturgy in the quaint little Catholic Church in central Tehran. Francis died attempting to save an Iranian co-worker from drowning in the Caspian, the letter explains.

He had six more months of duty in Iran, I calculate. He arrived in Iran a half-year before my group, and was looking forward to being home for Christmas. Francis was a quiet and sensitive young man from Wisconsin whom I met at the conference in Rasht. We had a particular bond, me being from Minnesota. Though I live in Hawaii, I've never lost my respect for the Midwest. Over dinner we had shared common experiences in the Peace Corps and growing up in America's heartland.

I can't get him out of my mind. Shaban Ali and my friends at the Sherkat-e Sargardon try to console me. Dispirited, I pack my bag and go to Gorgan to be with Jack, Dave, and Kathy.

It's early evening when I press the buzzer at the gate of Jack and Dave's house on the dirt lane in Gorgan. A dog barks.

"Quiet, Ziba," I hear Dave's voice over the wall. "Ziba, stay," he says as he opens the gate. "Ziba, Ziba!" he shouts as a high-spirited puppy flies out and jumps around me.

"Come in. We have a dog now. Her name is Ziba. Jack found her in the lot across the road. Ziba, *beah,*" he calls to her.

Ziba dances around at my feet, delighted to see a guest. The house reeks of the strong odor of dog. "We're still house-training her. We've had her a little over a week. She likes you. She seems to know you're American. Amazing. She doesn't like Iranians. Her hair stands on end and she growls when Iranians come. We suspect she was mistreated and abandoned. She was not in top shape when Jack brought her in."

I pet her. "Ziba is a good name for you. 'Pretty,' because you are pretty."

"You're going to stay for the Fourth of July?" Dave asks me.

"Yeah, I'm still an American," I say smiling.

"You'd hardly know. We never see you any more," Jack quips.

"We can get some hot dogs at an Armenian shop and Jack and I bought an ice cream machine. We'll make ice cream and buy some potatoes to make potato salad too," Dave chimes in. "We can have a real Fourth of July picnic."

"Wow, how American! You have an ice cream machine? Where did you find that?"

"Right here in Gorgan. We've had ice cream a lot already. It's perfect with this hot weather. And vanilla sure beats the ubiquitous Persian rose water specialty."

They too received the letter from the Peace Corps about Francis Kirking. Though they didn't know Francis, the loss of a fellow Peace Corps Volunteer takes on a personal dimension for them as well.

"Let's get Kathy," Jack suggests. "It's been a long time since we've played pinochle. We've been waiting for you to come. You've had dinner?"

"*Baleh*, I ate before I left Alang. I didn't want to catch an early bus, as they're too hot and uncomfortable this time of year."

Even at this hour of growing dusk and the expectation of cooling nightfall, the air is hot and sticky. Kathy is happy to see us and eager to spend an evening together. Since Kathy and I just learned pinochle, the guys recommend each of us partner with one of them. "It wouldn't be any fun if Dave and I play against you two because you would be beaten all the time," Jack insists.

"Fine." We agree.

It's far past midnight before we note what time it is.

"Oh, my gosh, we need to get Kathy home. What will the masses in Gorgan say about us getting her home this late? We all better take her home because the last time I walked her home alone, everybody in Alang knew about it the next day."

Kathy titters embarrassingly, her eyes twinkling.

"I'll walk her home tonight. No sense all of us going," Dave volunteers. Jack and I acquiesce.

"Tomorrow is Friday. Why don't you come around ten in the morning," Jack tells Kathy. "We can have lunch together and play pinochle all day. There's nothing else to do. Besides, it's too hot to be outside."

"I'll pick up a few things for lunch on my way over," Kathy offers.

"Thanks. Jack and I will get supplies for ice cream. It should be ready by the time you get here," Dave suggests.

SATURDAY, JULY 3, 1965 I wake up with a mild case of the "Gorgan Trots"— not too serious but I must maintain an awareness of the nearest *mostarah*. *I'm no longer used to exotic Western food,* I tell myself, not wanting to offend Jack and Dave. That ice cream yesterday was certainly very rich—too much for my village palate. Guess I've become more Iranian than I realize.

I meander to Mr. Vahdati's office, without my usual vigor. His attendant announces me and ushers me in even though Mr. Vahdati is in the middle of a meeting with men from a nearby village. He introduces me. Then he resumes the meeting. I am brought tea, and Mr. Vahdati and the village men accept another round as well.

When the men depart Mr. Vahdati asks, "How are things in Alang?"

"Just fine. But there was a bad accident involving three vehicles from Alang. Tofigh Rahemi was hurt quite badly. His leg is very sore."

"Yes, I heard about the accident. Fortunately no one was killed or anyone hurt more severely."

"Yes, they were very lucky. I came to see if I could talk to you about getting a woman *dehyar*—like an extension agent in the States—to provide training for the women in the villages. Do you have any time today?"

"I have another meeting scheduled right now which you are welcome to join. It may be worthwhile for you to see what other villages are working on. Then we could chat a few minutes before I go home for lunch."

"Fine. It's always a pleasure to meet people from other villages and hear what they're doing."

The men are fascinated to meet me, and ask Mr. Vahdati if they could get an American Peace Corps Volunteer for their village too. I remain quiet, as I still question the significance of my presence in Alang, and suppose Mr. Vahdati has similar reservations.

After the meeting Mr. Vahdati says, "Well, Tom, are you keeping busy in Alang?"

"Yes, but Shaban Ali really knows what he's doing. We spend a lot of time talking together about future projects in Alang and the other villages and what needs to be done to make them advance. Now I'm teaching only one class of English; the teachers are away for the summer. But I'm busy all the time. I like being in Alang. The people are so caring."

"I knew Alang would be the right village for you. The Rahemis are wonderful people."

"Mr. Vahdati, the Peace Corps sent me to Shiraz about a job at Pahlavi University. I haven't been into Gorgan much since I got back, and I had to go to Tehran for a few days for my physical."

"How was your physical? What did the doctor say? You've lost a lot of weight. Have you been OK?"

"Yes, the doctor is concerned I've lost weight too, but he says I'm healthy. No problems."

"That's encouraging."

"Today I'm not feeling too well. I think it was the food I ate at my Peace Corps friends' house yesterday. I'm so used to eating Persian food I get sick every time I eat American-type food. I got very sick in Tehran when I was there for my physical."

He grins. "You are becoming Iranian."

I smile. "*Baleh*. Anyway I decided not to go to Shiraz. The job was very ill-defined, and ultimately I realized I could not desert Alang. The people of Alang have become my family. I could not hurt them by going to Shiraz." I pause for a moment. "The reason I came is to see if we could get a woman *dehyar* in Alang and each of the villages. Shaban Ali and I have discussed this a lot, and he says there are Iranian women who do this work. In fact, he says one came to Alang a few years ago."

"Yes, that's right. Alang had a woman extension agent some time ago."

"Well, to me, Iranian villages would benefit greatly from a program of women *dehyars*. At least one young woman from every village could be trained to educate village women in matters such as health and sanitation and ways of improving the diet."

"Yes, that is a program to be developed more extensively. The few women who are trained cannot reach all the villages in the country. The problem is getting women who can do this *and* to whom village women will listen. In Iran, young women must be subservient to older women—especially to their mothers-in-law. It is our tradition. So it is hard to get a young woman from a village to garner the respect necessary for this kind of job within her home village. That is why we have so few women *dehyars*. Let's explore this later. Tomorrow is the Fourth of July, and you will want to celebrate. Could you come on Monday morning? In the meantime, I will give it more thought."

"OK. I'll see you then."

"And have a great Fourth of July. Be careful what you eat. No American food!" He smiles and we shake hands.

SUNDAY, JULY 4, 1965 Kathy had expanded the Fourth of July menu and proposed something special—peach ice cream since peaches are in season now. When I wake up, Jack and Dave have returned from purchasing groceries and the ingredients for the peach ice cream. I still feel rocky and wonder how much of our Fourth of July feast I will be able to consume.

"We've started the ice cream," Jack informs Kathy when she arrives.

She sees the open can of peaches on the table. She frowns. "Are you guys using canned peaches?"

"Yep. We thought it would be extra special if we used the syrup too."

"When peaches are in season? You need to use fresh peaches. Now just go out and buy some fresh peaches," she insists.

Dave unenthusiastically says, "OK, I'll go get some fresh ones. We can put them in it too."

Kathy mumbles something about *guys*.

Our picnic-style spread is fit for Americans, but I'm not up to eating a lot—the way to the bathroom is high on my priority list.

"You must have some peach ice cream," Jack pleads.

"Yes, just a little."

We all sample it about the same time and look at each other. Silence. My teeth curl—so sweet!

"You guys ruined it by putting in the canned peaches and all that concentrated syrup," Kathy scoffs.

I try a bit more and put the dish down. Ziba obligingly finishes it off.

"Today Kathy and I want to be partners against you guys," I state as we begin our pinochle game.

"No, I don't like it," Jack says. "You're both still learning. It won't be any fun for us."

"I think we know it well enough. Let's try it."

Reluctantly they agree. Soon Kathy and I are slaughtering them.

"It's only beginner's luck," Jack concedes.

MONDAY, JULY 5, 1965 My meeting with Mr. Vahdati provides no new resolution. He suggests Alang request another extension agent, but he does not foresee they will get one.

About 12:30pm I return to Jack and Dave's to get my bag.

"Have you guys had lunch?" They register a negative. "Let's go get some lunch and then I'll catch the bus back to Alang."

"You're going back to Alang today? It's too late to go now. The day will be over by the time you get there," Jack rationalizes.

"Besides, what can you do once you're there? You've seen Mr. Vahdati. Your work's done for today," Dave urges. "You might as well stay overnight. We can get Kathy and play pinochle and then go to the Moulin Rouge this evening. Somerset Maugham's *Of Human Bondage* is playing. Going to a movie will help your Farsi."

"Yeah. Then you can catch the bus tomorrow morning," Jack joins in.

I sense they had this rehearsed. I look at them skeptically.

"Here we go again, tempting me another time. And, you guys know I'm weak. Well . . . let's go see if Kathy has had lunch."

TUESDAY, JULY 6, 1965 "You're not going already?" the guys say as I grab my bag. "What can you do in Alang this morning? Why don't you go after lunch? We could play a game of Scrabble before you leave."

I look at them, shake my head, smile, and chide them, "You devils—just trying to see how far I will go."

"But it makes sense. Your class isn't until late this afternoon."

"Yeah, but I need to get back. It's always fun to be with you guys, and this was an unforgettable Fourth of July—peach ice cream and all. Thanks for the diversion."

"Don't forget about us. Come back soon."

I buy some peaches from a vendor who set his colorfully painted cart near the station and settle into a seat in the bus, but the springs poke into my under-padded bottom. I find another seat farther back. It's hardly an improvement. People fan themselves and complain about the heat. The "onion lady" appears outside the open window, holding her large brown trademark by the stem. She looks at me dolefully. I press a few small coins into her outstretched hand. She kisses her hand in supplication and moves to the next window.

Thankfully, after waiting nearly 45 minutes, the bus lumbers into motion. The breeze blowing in the windows is welcome, even if it is hot. It is late morning when I'm dropped off by the sign for Alang. I hike down the road in the sweltering heat.

PERPLEXITIES

WEDNESDAY, JULY 7, 1965 One afternoon nearly a month ago, I heard a knock on my door. *Haji* Torfeh had climbed the ladder-like stairs that lead to the balcony before my room. In her hand she held a small, faded and wrinkled photograph.

"*Aghaye* Mister, I heard you are an artist. This is the passport photo of my husband. He died of cholera on our trip to Mecca many years ago. I buried him there. I have carried this photo with me these many years. Would you do a drawing of him? Please."

I glanced at the tiny, weathered picture and thought, *I'll never be able to do this.* But I looked into *Haji's* soft and pleading eyes and said, "I'll try."

Husband of *Haji* Torfeh

Almost daily I agonized over the task put before me. However, I made a promise, and this is one from which I cannot escape. Often when she saw me at the well in the morning, she would ask if I had done the drawing. With shame, each time I answered that I had not. I just could not imagine I could do it. But today, the guilt over my procrastination and the thought that I am impeding *Haji's* tender relationship with her husband pushes me to attempt what I fear is the impossible.

With pen and ink, I set about to do the drawing. Upon completing it, I ask my friends if it looks like her husband. They confirm it does, and I make another so I will have one for myself.

Haji's eyes brighten when I give her the drawing.

"*Moteshakeram, Aghaye* Mister. . . . *Moteshakeram.*" She turns so I won't see, but I know her gentle eyes are blurred with tears.

THURSDAY, JULY 8, 1965 Something bewildering catches my eye as I shave on the balcony in the bright morning light. My landlady and her children are stuffing old clothes with straw. Ghorbon sees me and calls, "Tom, Omar! Tonight is Shab-e Omar."

"Shab-e Omar? What is Shab-e Omar?"

"*Kheili khoobeh!* Shab-e Omar is very good." Ghorbon talks to me like I have just arrived in the village—like I haven't learned Farsi. Invariably I get only the most rudimentary explanations. "Tom, *beah*, come down, *beah*."

I descend the stairs at the end of the balcony. The hot summer sun has already made this side of the building a stifling oven. The shade where they are working—making an effigy—yields soothing relief.

"Omar!" my landlady explains.

I'm still in a quandary. "Who is Omar?"

"Omar is bad. Bad!" Ghorbon tells me.

"*Baleh,* bad!" his mother reiterates. But I learn nothing more. They are excited by the well-stuffed figure they are making. She sews the shirt to the pants and gets the children to push in more straw. They concoct a head from the sleeve of an old shirt, fasten it securely, and top it with a straw hat. She begins to sing and clap her hands while the children dance around it.

I am perplexed, clueless. This is strange. Here in the village they consider it against their religion to make a human image. But then, it doesn't have a face, I conclude. But who is Omar?

"Tom, make a face on Omar," Ghorbon says. "I will get a pen." He runs to the house and returns. "Here, Tom, make a face on him. Please."

"Oh, no, I shouldn't do it," I say apprehensively.

"No. Do it," his mother commands.

"*Baleh.* You are an artist. You can do it," Ghorbon insists. "You aren't a Muslim. Do it!"

I acquiesce, not knowing how grievous the sin is that I am committing. They cheer and continue to sing and clap their hands.

Omar and children

Obviously this is special I decide as I wander off to find Shaban Ali or someone who will tell me who Omar is and why they made an effigy of him.

"Omar!" my associates at the Sherkat-e Sargardon exclaim incredulously. "You put a face on Omar! *Bah, bah, bah.* It will be a memorable night in Alang this year—Omar with a face!"

"Why? Who is Omar? Have I done something wrong?"

"No, Tom, you can do it. You can put a face on Omar. You are a Christian. It's OK for you to do it."

"Sure, I'm a Christian. I can put a face on Omar. No problem. I'm going to Hell anyway."

"Baleh," Reza says and the gang cracks up. "But it would be better if you became a Muslim."

"So who is Omar? Why do you make his effigy?"

"Tonight we will have a big party in Alang," Mulla tells me. "It's lots of fun. There will be music and dancing in the streets, and then we will burn Omar. Omar was the second caliph."

"The second caliph! Then he was good. Why are you burning him?"

"No, he was bad. He conquered Iran," Reza says.

"But then you became Muslims. That's good."

"Yes, but Ali should have become caliph," Mulla interjects. "Ali was the son-in-law and a loyal follower of the Prophet. He became the fourth caliph. He was the rightful successor of the Prophet Mohammad. His son, Husayn, married the daughter of Yezdigird, the last Sassanian king. Thus their offspring has royal Iranian blood *and* the blood of the Holy Prophet. Their successors are Muslim, plus they possess the divine right to rule. Nearly 900 years later, Shah Ismael Safavid traced his descent to that union. He restored the rightful Iranian kingdom and established Shi'a Islam as the official religion of Iran."

"Omar was a usurper," Reza adds. "He was cruel and ruthless. He seduced Fatimah, the daughter of the Holy Prophet and the wife of Ali. This caused her to miscarry and led to her death. Omar was a terrible person." *

I am beginning to comprehend the basis of the rift between Sunni and Shi'a Muslims. When I see Shaban Ali, I question him further. He discloses, "Nearby, the Turkomans are Sunni. Tonight they will be mourning the death of Omar."

I look at him in disbelief. "You mean while we are celebrating in Alang, they will be mourning?"

---

* The Sunni, in contrast to Shi'a Muslims, regard Omar as the greatest Muslim after the Prophet himself. He possessed qualities of sagaciousness that allowed Islam to advance in the critical decade of his rule; the Arabs conquered the whole territory of the Sassanian Empire, and more than two thirds of the Byzantine Empire. He was a man of humility and great simplicity, and preserved a passion for duty and justice. His concern for the poor and underprivileged is legendary.

"*Baleh.*"

"I feel very uncomfortable about this. The Turkomans are our friends. They are Muslims too."

"*Baleh,* but that's the way it is, just for this one night."

After dark, Omar is moved from our courtyard. There is frenzied jubilation in the street, and even more exuberance as the crowds of men and boys see Omar with a face. Musicians play flutes and pound drums. Men dance with reckless abandon. They make bawdy gestures and break wind with equal relish. Omar is wildly carried through the streets, thrown from group to group with undeniable euphoria. Rival groups start pulling his limbs. Someone lights a match and the straw mockery is set ablaze. Everyone cheers. The lurid dancing goes on for hours. Meanwhile, I wonder what is happening in the Turkoman villages so close by.

FRIDAY, JULY 9, 1965 "Mister Tom, let's go for a walk together," the well-dressed son of one of the wealthy men in the village proposes. He is on holiday from his studies, visiting his family for the summer. We converse in English as we stroll out of the village.

As we amble in the relative shaded coolness of the cemetery surrounding the Imamzadeh Ibrahim, a humble old man is happy to see us. He extends his hand in greeting.

"*Daste shoma kasifeh*" (Your hand is dirty). My companion pulls away.

I grab the hand of the man and wish him well.

"*Ghorbanetam*" (For you, I sacrifice myself), he says, and clasps his hands and kisses them.

My mind, however, is wracked by doubt—not that I shook the old man's hand, as I would have done it had I been alone. But I ponder how my act was intended as an affront to the disgusting arrogance of the rich man's son. *Is it appropriate that I deliberately attempted to put him down? I am his guest and I should have shown him respect. Yet the man whose hand I shook deserved my regard as well. Why do I have to be put in these situations?*

SATURDAY, JULY 10, 1965 Ismael Gilani arrives at my door. He is strikingly handsome—almost the dashing good looks of a Hawaiian beach boy. Like

Mulla, he is thoughtful and reserved. He often comes to talk privately with me while others take their afternoon nap.

"Tom, I am already 24 years old . . . and I still don't have a wife. Unfortunately, my father died when I was young. He had no brothers, so I have nobody to arrange my marriage. I have a little land—not a lot, but enough to take care of my mother and me . . . and a family . . . if I had one. But I am not rich, so it is difficult to find a woman who wants me. But . . . there is another problem . . . my skin is so dark. No one wants a man with dark skin. Only poor men—*kargars* (laborers)—who work in the fields have dark skin. No one wants to marry their daughter to a *kargar* unless they are also a *kargar*. Tom, I am not a *kargar*. I have enough land not to hire myself out to work in the fields. I have other people work in my fields. So, Tom, I may never have the wife and children I want."

I struggle to quickly come up with a compassionate response—one reinforcing and positive—in a language that still takes thought to find the right words. Here is a man of outstanding moral character who is caught between the strands of a social web with nothing to hang on to. He is not one class—the elite and restricted minority; nor is he the other—the vast majority. Those like him, suspended between, have few options. And without the necessary family support, they face enormous obstacles.

"Ismael, in Iran, can't a friend arrange a marriage?"

"*Baleh,* but when you are like me, it is hard. I am not wealthy enough to marry a rich man's daughter, and it would not be proper for me to marry into a poor man's family. The problem is nobody would want me because I am so black. Dark skin is bad in Iran."

"Ismael, you are not black. Besides, you are very handsome. In America, dark skin is considered very beautiful. People lie in the sun for hours to make their skin dark."

"But I am not in America. I am in Iran."

"I know. There are some things you can't change . . . it's the way you are born or how things are in life. But always remember, you are a very fine man inside. That is good. You will find the right woman. Ask someone to help you."

"Tom, you don't understand about Iran. Dark skin is not good."

"Ismael, I may not understand like a black person because my skin and hair are very light. It's the way I was born, and I can't change that. I may never completely comprehend what a black person feels. But I think I can understand a bit of the hurt, and I am sorry people incur any kind of hurt when they are honorable people inside. I know how Iranians feel about people with dark skin or people who are from a different group. It's not only America that has problems with attitudes about race—and I hope America will soon change because I believe, as human beings, we are all brothers—just like you and I are brothers, Ismael.

"Let me tell you a story. It's not a good story, but it's true. There was an American Negro in one of the Peace Corps groups that came to Iran. When he was assigned to a city, the Iranians wrote to the Peace Corps. 'Why did you send him to us?' So the Peace Corps sent him to work in Zahedan, near the border with Pakistan, where the people are dark-skinned. When I heard this, I felt very bad that an American who came to serve Iran would be treated like this by Iranians because his skin was black."

"Tom, I am sorry that Iranians would treat an American like that."

"Thank you, Ismael. Remember it's not the color of your skin that's important. It's what is inside you that *is* important. *Enshahallah* (If God is willing) you will find a suitable wife and have many beautiful children."

When he leaves, I contemplate how this will work out—how he can find the fulfillment in life he longs for. *If only I could help.* But, as a foreigner, an outsider, I'm like him—powerless—caught in a web that restricts options. Nevertheless, it's interesting that my friends so often come to me to share their secrets and ask for advice. *Is it because I'm outside the loop, so they feel they can divulge their most private concerns?* Little did I know I would be destined to be a "Dear Abby" when I joined the Peace Corps.

HOPE AND DISCONTENT

SUNDAY, JULY 11, 1965 The hollow tinkle of bells and faint call of voices interrupt the morning stillness. Shepherds summon their flocks for the day's journey into the rich gratuity of the mountain pastures. A rooster crows again and again, greeting the pale light of dawn. I lie in the coolness of the early morning air, listening to the soft sounds of shimmering leaves, the lilting, melodious tone of the nearby stream, and the diminishing cacophony of the night's crickets. All are a refreshing respite from the stifling, humid heat of a still night in a village on the plain. The steady breathing of Shaban Ali and our host signals they are missing nature's bounteous symphony.

Yesterday we bicycled to Ghalandarayesh for a village council meeting. I sat in the cool splendor of the headman's open belvedere, very inspired. The Literacy Corpsman was on holiday, but the boys of the village were taking notes for their fathers. Filled with emotion I thought, *Here is the future of Iran.* There is so much promise. Not a single person in Ghalandarayesh except the teacher knew how to read or write when I first came here nine months ago; now we have a school, and the children are helping their fathers.

At dusk we sat together, quietly talking and drinking tea, and watched the sun sink into the Caspian in a blaze of golden glory. A single kerosene lamp quenched the dimming light of day. Darkness descended below us, and we scanned the plain to see twinkling lights define Alang and nearby villages. The oilcloth was spread upon the floor and dinner served. Later, mats and pillows were arranged, and the lamp was extinguished. I gazed

out from the belvedere for a while, listening to the sounds of the night—
the shrieking of crickets and the gentle murmur of the stream. A big-orbed
moon kept a vigilant eye on the peaceful village. Only in my imagination
had I conceived of anything like this. I drifted off to sleep.

At 5:00am we enjoy breakfast of bread and tea, thank our host, say
khodahafez, and bicycle off. The oppressive heat of the plain rapidly
overcomes us.

MONDAY, JULY 12, 1965 Shaban Ali and I bicycle to Kordkuy to meet a
fellow *dehyar*. He takes us to two of the mountain villages he works in.
Both are already building bathhouses with showers. I am envious they are
ahead of Alang and the other villages I work in.

"Shaban Ali, Alang needs to get started on our new bathhouse."

One of the villages has two butcher shops. "Two! Alang has none. And
they are screened, so the flies can't get at the meat," I exclaim. "Not even
in the large cities have I seen this! The whole village is so neat and clean."

Our friend is pleased by my enthusiasm. On our way back to Kordkuy,
tired and hot, I suggest to Shaban Ali we stop to greet some of the soldiers
at the nearby Iranian Army station.

"Come, have an orange Fanta," they eagerly offer. They are signing up
new recruits, but they have many questions about the US Army. "Are all
young men required to go? How old are you when you go in? What is
training like? Were you in the army?"

"Yes, we have mandatory military service, like Iran. Most guys go in
when they finish high school or college, so they are usually about 18 or 22
years old. I haven't gone into the army yet. Probably I will have to when I
return to America."

"You will have to go in the army even if you were in the Peace Corps?
In Iran, if a young man has been in the Literacy Corps, he doesn't have to
join the army."

"Yes, but in America we must go anyway. However, I will be nearly 26
years old when I leave Iran, and the army normally does not take men who
are 26 or older."

"*Enshahallah* you will not have to go," one of the men tells me. "I do not want you to go to Vietnam. The war is terrible. It is not good for America."

"Yes, I don't want to go, but if I have to, I will. I hope the war will quickly end."

"We hope it will end too, and America will win."

"My brother is in the US Army," I tell them.

"Will he have to go to Vietnam? How many brothers do you have?"

"I have one brother. I hope he will not have to go to war in Vietnam."

Their concern for my brother and me is genuine, especially in light of the war in Southeast Asia and the disastrous toll on US forces.

"Come back and talk with us. Anytime. We are always happy to see you," they tell me as Shaban Ali and I depart.

TUESDAY, JULY 13, 1965 "Rinnnnnng." I turn over and grab the alarm clock. It falls on the floor, still ringing. I grope to find it and turn it off. I need to lie here and stretch. Soon I see the sky lightening. Time to get going.

"Tom, Mister Tom, *beah*," Shaban Ali calls from below.

"*Baleh*, I'll be right down." I look at my watch. *Yes, it's 5am. Just as he said. On time.*

I open the gate below my room and wheel my bicycle out. "*Salaam, sobh bekheyr,*" I greet him and our companions. We are on our way to the Turkoman bazaar at Bandarshah. It is cool at this time of day, so the eight-kilometer bicycle ride north toward the Caspian Sea is pleasant.

"Look!" Mulla exclaims, pointing. Ahead, two to three hundred camels jauntily stride across the desert. We marvel at their number, but I find it improbable that here, so close to Alang, there could be so many camels, while we see none in Alang.

The miserable, treeless streets of neglected Bandarshah are lined with the mundane wares of local farmers and traders selling everything from onions and melons to opium pipes and rugs. Stifling heat and humidity make looking unbearable. We are chased to the sea for relief from the unremitting sun, traversing the broad and bleak salt-saturated spit that leads to the welcoming water. We strip to our briefs and wade into the sea. Mud oozes between my toes. "This is disgusting," I mumble to myself. "I'm too spoiled by the sparkling white sand beaches of Hawaii." I try desperately to appear enthusiastic. We wade farther and farther in the muddy water—at least a kilometer and we're only up to our waists. I crouch down to wet my burning sun-starved body, but I can't bring myself to put my head in this abhorrent muck. I slosh to shore, wondering what I'll do once I get there. There is no place to hide from the incessant glare of the fiery sphere above. *If only the other guys will come out too.*

My wish is granted. We push our bicycles across the wasteland back to Bandarshah—and then to Alang, I hope; but I'm disappointed.

"We'll eat lunch and then go to the beach at another place. It's better there," one of the guys advocates.

What can I do? I'm with them, and I don't want to be a wet blanket.

Our second venture is worse than the first. No one desires to go into the befouled water. I am relieved, but perturbed we now have to return to Bandarshah before we head back to Alang—in the worst heat of the day!

Akbar suggests, "I know a short cut to Alang. Let's go that way."

Excellent, I think. Anything to get out of this unquenchable sun.

On our way, we pass a Turkoman village. Though there are permanent homes, yurts serve as the primary dwellings. "I have a colleague who lives here," Shaban Ali volunteers. "Let's stop and visit with him. We can get out of the sun and rest awhile." Nobody objects.

I hear a rapid "thunk, thunk, thunk" as we approach one of the yurts. Shaban Ali calls to his friend. He emerges in his baggy pajamas from behind the felt covering of the door and invites us in. *"Beah, befarmayid,* have tea with me."

It takes awhile for my eyes to adjust from the glaring unshaded light outside to the dim interior. At the side, even though men have entered, two women continue weaving a traditional Turkoman rug on a large horizontal loom. Their work is illuminated by the light suffusing through the uncovered lower portion of the yurt. Felt mats cover the exterior upper sections, but from the inside the interlaced wooden structure is plainly visible.

"It is surprisingly cool inside," I comment.

"That's because air comes in at the bottom and flows out through the hole in the top," our host explains with pride.

"Oh, it works like a chimney!"

"Yes. Although some have built permanent houses of bricks, we still like our yurts. It is our connection with the past. The border was sealed in 1921, and we could not return to our homeland to visit our families, even though they were just a few kilometers away. We are in Iran and they are in the Soviet Union. We were caught here; some of our brothers were on the other side. We never saw them again."

He directs one of his sons to bring something. The boy returns with a large sack and hands it to his father. He dumps it out in front of me.

"Money! Money everywhere!" he cackles. "Have some."

We are dazzled. I pick up a few pieces and examine them. "Russian money," I exclaim. "Rubles. Thousands of rubles!"

"Thousands? Millions!" he answers. "Take some."

My eyes grow wide. I have never seen so much money and such huge bills. "This is Russian money from before the Revolution."

"*Baleh*. It has no value." He laughs. "Here." He gives me a handful.

"Oh, no. This is yours." I hand it back to him.

"No, take some. This is what the Soviets did to us. Tricked us. It's not worth the paper it's printed on. The Soviets are very clever. They offered my grandfather all this money for his thousands of sheep and herd of camels. My grandfather had never seen so much money in his entire life so he sold them all. The Russians took everything and gave him this money. My grandfather thought he was very rich. He did not know the Tsar was gone and the money was worthless. Then the border was closed and he was stuck on this side. He was mad as hell he couldn't get across the border to use his money. He didn't know it was bogus anyway. So we have this sack of useless money. We are millionaires. Millionaires!" He throws some of the bills in the air. "Please take some. I want you to have some as a memory of the Russians. I don't want you to forget them. America must never forget the Russians."

I select three notes: one large 100-ruble bill dated 1910, with a picture of Catherine the Great on the back; an austere 1000-ruble note dated that auspicious year, 1917; and a tiny 40-ruble piece.

"Here, have more. It's only paper. Paper! They didn't even give my grandfather coins. Coins would have been valuable. He could have sold them in the bazaar. They could have been used for jewelry."

"Thunk, thunk, thunk" we hear each time the women finish knotting a row. They pound the finished knots with a comb to make the rug tight, then expertly trim the threads with large, sharp scissors. There is no drawing in front of them. The design is in their heads. The women look at me, fascinated a foreigner appreciates their labor.

Our host is equally captivated by my presence, and poses numerous questions about America, the Peace Corps, and me. "Teach Tom some Turkoman," my companions tell him. Everybody chuckles when I learn a few phrases. He serves us tea and melons and urges us to wait awhile before we return to Alang. "It's too hot now. You can go when it's cooler."

"Can I walk around the village? I have never been in a Turkoman village."

"We can all go together," he suggests.

"No, you stay here. You are tired. I will be right back. I don't like to rest in the afternoon."

My friends confirm I don't nap and, if it is all right with him, I will go for a walk. I find some boys who speak Farsi, and we while away the time conversing in the shade of a building. They are as interested in me as I am in them. I'm startled at the contrast between a Turkoman village and Persian villages. Here, there are no walls or trees—just a few houses and yurts on the flat plain. In Persian villages, houses are walled in.

I hear the voices of my friends and our host. I look at my watch. "My gosh, it's nearly four o'clock."

"Come back again," our host tells Shaban Ali. "Bring Mister. You are always welcome." He looks at me. "America is good. I am sorry American men are being killed in Vietnam."

We head toward the mountains through acres and acres of melon fields. This is one of the Turkoman's best cash crops.

"Salaam," a farmer greets us. He is an acquaintance of Mulla, and insists we share a melon with him right there in the field.

"You must take some melons with you. Take them back to Alang." He hands us each several. We strap them on the back of our bikes and thank him for his hospitality.

"Ghorban-e shoma" (For you, I sacrifice myself), he tells us as we depart and forge our way through the fields. Now Akbar is lost. We follow paths at the edges of fields heading for the mountains, trusting we will recognize something.

Finally, Shaban Ali and I see the poor little Zaboli village of Ghalayesh. As we bicycle through, men from the village council greet us and want us to stop for tea. Shaban Ali declines, saying we must get back to Alang before dark. We make headway along the path between fields of melons and rice. It is too late for my class when we reach Alang.

"Tom, where have you been? We haven't seen you for days. You're sunburned." Everyone stops me. It takes an hour to reach my room. This is not unusual. Definitely my purpose in Alang is to be a friend.

Twilight illuminates the village as I pull the drapes, contemplating the past three days. Such richness, such diversity. I have been in places where they speak four different languages and at least three dialects of Farsi. From the Turks in Ghalandarayesh to the Turkomans in Bandarshah to the Zabolis in Ghalayesh to the Persians here in Alang, each has unique customs and wears distinctive clothes. I have been in cool, lush forest villages near where leopards prowl at night, and those of the hot, barren desert where camels roam. All are within six kilometers of Alang. And, I am here in Alang. My Alang. Nothing could be better.

WEDNESDAY, JULY 14, 1965 "It looks like it's going to be a profitable yield this year," Mulla tells me. Very early we bicycled to his cotton fields to witness crop dusting; however, the plane is in a different area today.

"Where is the cotton processed?"

"There is a factory in Kordkuy. We'll go there this fall when it starts operation. They use every part of the cotton for making things, from soap to cow feed. During the winter, the women gather the dried stalks as firewood for cooking and baking bread. There is no waste."

LATE IN THE DAY I arrive at Jack and Dave's as they are leaving for dinner at another teacher's house.

"Tom, you must come along. Mr. Ahmadi will be glad we brought you."

"No, I don't want to impose upon him. I'll go see Kathy and we'll have dinner together."

"No, come with us. Mr. Ahmadi will want you to come."

Mr. Ahmadi indeed is happy I came. "Tom, it's a pleasure to see you again. It has been a while."

"Yes, he hardly comes to Gorgan any more," Jack interjects.

"I'm always busy in Alang. There is always something to do. And even during the summer, I have my English class each day."

We spend a genial evening together, and at 10:30 Jack suggests, "Let's go to Kathy's."

"Now?" I venture.

"We can just chat for a while. Besides, we ought to let her know you're here so she can plan for our pinochle game tomorrow."

Kathy is surprised to see us at this hour. She is full of news. "I had a letter from Janet today. Bob, your roommate in Logan, has terminated," she tells me. "He came back after his cancer operation in the States, but now he's decided to quit."

"Is he OK?"

"Yes, he seems to be fine, but I guess he felt he wasn't achieving that much here and should go home."

"Well, I know how he feels," Jack exclaims. "Really, what good are we here? Any of us?"

"You guys are teaching English. You're helping a whole new generation learn a foreign language," I encourage.

"Do they really need to know English? Will any of them ever use it? It's pointless. What good are we, any of us? We're wasting our time and the government's money."

"I don't know about that," Dave joins in. "The students want to learn English. It will help them in the future."

"How? How? It might get some to America where they all want to go, but what will that do for Iran?"

"They won't all be able to go to America. Some will stay here. They may become teachers too," Dave continues. "Some may get government jobs."

"It's just a waste of time and money. What is the point of the Peace

Corps, anyway?" Jack grouses. "It wouldn't be so bad if they didn't make the Peace Corps out to be something it isn't. What are *you* doing, Tom? What? You claim you're 'always busy.' Doing what? Just sitting around at the . . . the . . . the something or other . . . shooting the breeze."

"The Sherkat-e Sargardon," I volunteer lamely.

"*Baleh*, the Sherkat-e Sargardon. That's it, the 'Do Nothing Company.' We're all part of the 'Do Nothing Company'—the Peace Corps. That's what it is, the Peace Corps, the Sherkat-e Sargardon."

We all laugh painfully.

"Well, Tom," Kathy says to me, "Mark, also from your group, wanted to quit but the Peace Corps wouldn't let him terminate here. They insisted he had to go to Washington to terminate, but he wanted to travel in Europe. He was thoroughly upset and said, 'then I won't quit.' So now the Peace Corps is sending him to Ethiopia to see if he can find a position there."

"See? The Peace Corps is controlling our lives, not letting us terminate here so we can travel through Europe on the way home," Jack, our outspoken comrade, rails. "So they send him off to Africa. Even farther away! At least that gets him out of their hair, they suppose."

"Gosh, Mark is such a nice guy, very easygoing," I recall. "I would never imagine he would pack it in."

"He's a thinker. He knows when he's doing something worthwhile. I give him credit."

"That's amazing—two guys from my group calling it quits. The trouble is our jobs in community development and agriculture are so nebulous, so unstructured, we can't find much of significance to do. And the Peace Corps wants us to complete three big projects in the two years we're here. At least you guys have a job teaching English. You don't have that kind of pressure."

"Perhaps, but one of the English teachers from another group had a nervous breakdown and was sent back to the States," Kathy informs us.

"Wow, that's very depressing," I reflect.

"Yeah—we should all march into the Peace Corps office in Tehran and announce we're quitting." Jack is getting fired up. "Why don't we? All four of us! All from Gorgan. I wonder what they'd do?"

"Yeah, it might trigger a mass exodus. Wouldn't that be something?" I respond excitedly.

We laugh at the thought. "Maybe we should do it, just to make a point," Dave suggests.

"Now you guys are using your heads. Come on, Kathy, you do it too."

"Well, it would be interesting to see the reaction if everyone from Gorgan decided to leave."

"So, you'll go with us? That's great!" Jack exclaims.

"Well, I think we should sleep on it and discuss it again tomorrow," Kathy demurs. "We are meeting for pinochle tomorrow, aren't we? It certainly would be intriguing to know what the impact of four people quitting in one city would have all across the country."

We say goodnight to Kathy, determined to reform the Peace Corps, convinced it's time something is done, and that it's necessary—even our *responsibility* as Americans to undertake it.

THURSDAY, JULY 15, 1965 Jack is in high spirits. He had gotten the mail—a letter from the Peace Corps approving his vacation plans to meet his parents in Istanbul in less than a month, and indicating he would be reassigned to another city in Iran in the fall. There is no mention of our intended rebellion. I am relieved. I don't know if I could leave Alang.

Kathy is bewildered when she arrives for our pinochle session. "Such a change of attitude," she whispers to me.

"Yeah. All the Peace Corps had to do was approve Jack's vacation."

FRIDAY, JULY 16, 1965 We're up early, even though it was 12:30am when I walked Kathy home. Jack and Dave are off to Babolsar—the Caspian Riviera—and I board a bus to Gonbad-e Kavus. The oppressive summer heat of Alang and Gorgan seems cool compared to the torrid broil of Gonbad. Three other guys from our training group are at Barkley's too. It's terrific to be together for a little reunion.

Barkley looks gaunt and tired, a stark contrast to the last time I saw him.

"Barkley, are you OK? You're so thin. And you have dark circles under your eyes."

"Yes, I'm very tired. Opening the new library has been an ordeal. I'm thankful it's open, but I don't know how long it will remain."

"You don't know how long? What do you mean?"

"It's a long story."

Nothing surprising for Barkley, I tell myself. His stories are so riveting. And hearing them in his Kentucky drawl makes them even better.

"I had to get my ally the chief of police to force the governor to open it. The governor actually came to cut the ribbon, but what will happen now remains to be seen. The problem is, over a year ago the head of education received money to build a library in Gonbad, but it went nowhere. Then I came along and suggested we start a library. One of my friends promised two rooms in the best building in Gonbad. We got stacks of books donated, and I organized a team of volunteers to run the library. We were doing it without spending a single rial. Everything was progressing fine, but about two months ago, as the library was becoming a reality, the chief of education and the governor started putting roadblocks in my way. It was intense. I never knew from day to day what might ensue. One morning, the sports coach showed up at my door, all distressed, to say that, on orders of the chief of education, bulldozers were knocking down the walls of the gymnasium. You know how hard I worked to get the sports clubs organized. We ran to the chief of police and he halted it. But it's a mess. Now the sports coach is in Tehran, registering a complaint and trying to see what can be done to rebuild it. Two days before the scheduled opening of the library, the chief of education went to the governor to demand he not let the library open. Now I don't know what will happen when the chief of education returns." He looks at us gloomily.

"Barkley, I don't know how you do it. You need to be careful. Fortunately, you're living with Mr. Broumand and his family."

He looks at me quizzically. I see he has not given any thought to his personal safety.

"Well, the library is open for now. Let's go. I want you guys to see it. This afternoon, Mr. Broumand will take us to a Turkoman village. This is a *real* Turkoman village. The people still live in yurts."

The library is a reality, open, and people are enthusiastically using it.

They are impressed with the seemingly "official" American delegation that came to see what Barkley and Gonbad have done.

The Turkoman village is hardly a village—just a tiny Turkoman encampment, isolated on the vast featureless Asian steppe that extends endlessly in all directions. There are no roads. Not a tree is visible—nothing—just a few yurts covered with a patchwork of felts and animal skins, wooden carts, friendly people, and camels. Men wear their traditional long coats and tall black astrakhan hats—even in the July desert heat. Their high cheekbones are emphasized by a narrow, jaw-defining beard and slim moustache. Children wear dull red garments of customary Turkoman patterns, and woven or hand-embroidered skullcaps. We watch as a young girl milks one of the camels.

"Here, taste some camel milk," Barkley tells us.

I'm not eager, but acquiesce to a sip from the common metal bowl as it is passed around. *They can give it back to the camels,* I think as I hand the bowl on. *I hope I don't get some exotic illness from drinking this.*

Barkley finishes off what's left. "He must have a cast iron gut," I tell one of the other guys. "Nothing fazes him."

The Turkomans insist we ride a camel. One of the beasts is forced to

Turkoman Tom

sit down so I can surmount the hump. A man plops his tall hat on my head, hands me a wooden pole, and orders the camel to stand up. I hang on to whatever I can—the hat and pole and mostly nothing at the top of the hump—as the camel gyrates. *"Alhamdulillah!"* I sigh, smiling with satisfaction. I'm still on top.

"Put the pole behind your neck like the Turkomans do when they travel," Barkley shouts. "Somebody, take his picture."

Now it's Barkley's turn. He climbs atop the hump, clinging to any available tuft of hair. The camel rises to its feet in its usual ungainly manner. In the process, Barkley slides down the hump, straddling the neck. We all laugh, and I remember our PE instructor Bozo's attempt to help Barkley do pushups at training in Logan. He grabbed the back of Barkley's trunks, pulling him up and pushing him down while over 70 guys collapsed in laughter.

SATURDAY, JULY 17, 1965 It's a holiday today—celebrating the birthdays of Mohammad and Imam Sadeq.* Time by myself roving the bazaar in Gonbad is a respite from being with Americans and having to speak English. I miss not being with Persians and conversing in Farsi. Besides, the shops in each part of the country have their distinct regional provisions that reveal much about the people. The noisy metalworking areas always hold my attention.

"What is this used for?" I ask a metalsmith.

His Farsi is limited, but I determine the small copper pot is used for carrying soup into the fields.

"How much is it?

He finds it odd that I, a Westerner, want a container that laborers use to carry soup. I bargain and pay him the ten tomans ($1.25) we agree upon. He indicates he wants to do something to the pot. By now many bystanders have gathered in front of the shop. A young boy explains to me in Farsi the smith needs to silver the container so it will be safe for me to use.

---

* Both Sunni and Shi'a Muslims revere this important 8th century Islamic scholar, jurist, and teacher. Shi'a Muslims consider Imam Sadeq the sixth Imam, or leader, and spiritual successor to Mohammad.

"Oh, I don't want it silvered. I like it the way it is."

"But it is dangerous to use this way."

"That's OK. I'm not going to use it."

Everyone snickers. I suppose they are dismayed a person would buy something he is not going to use. I politely thank the shop owner and the boy and amble on with my treasure.

In another shop, a glowing red Turkoman rug catches my attention.

"How much is it?"

"Nine hundred tomans. It is part silk."

"It's exceptional," I tell the shopkeeper. He beams.

It's spectacular, but larger and more than I intend to pay for a rug. So I move on, looking and asking questions. However, the rug is unforgettable.

At Barkley's house, Mr. Broumand chuckles when he sees my soup container. I tell him about the rug.

"Let's go look at it," he says. "I'll tell you if it's good."

Mr. Broumand is very impressed. "It's magnificent, and the price is reasonable. Do you want to get it? I'll bargain for you."

"Yes, if I could get it for less."

We settle on a price of 800 tomans ($110.00). My heart is pounding. I've never bought anything so expensive.

"I will go to the Bank-e Sadrat for money tomorrow morning and pay you then," I tell the shop owner.

"Congratulations," Mr. Broumand tells me. "It's a quality rug. It's great you bought a Turkoman rug. They are the best in all of Iran. It will be a nice memento to take back to America."

MONDAY, JULY 19, 1965   A letter from Del recounts her Peace Corps experiences in Malawi. I am envious. Her engagement in constructive change is so different from mine. She has such a sense of achievement—so unlike us in Iran.

Now I understand why they told us in training the Middle East is the most difficult area. Here, few of us have any feeling of accomplishment. It's not that I dislike Iran—I love Iran and its people, but it's rare any of us feels we are being useful. There is a vast cultural chasm between Iranians and us—one largely determined by religion. Things acceptable in the US are taboo here. For women, it's even harder. Poor Kathy—she often feels trapped and disgusted. She can't walk down the street alone without men making vulgar noises and gestures, and if one of us guys is with her it's all over Gorgan immediately.

I write to the Peace Corps office in Tehran, urging they assign another female volunteer to Gorgan. "It's best for the health and well-being of women volunteers that more than one female be located together in provincial areas."

There is no response. Nothing changes.

FRIDAY, JULY 30, 1965 Friday—not a lot to do in Alang. *Maybe I should paint today,* I decide.

I boil two eggs, get some fresh bread, tomatoes, and cucumbers for a lunch, fill my canteen with water, assemble my watercolor supplies, strap everything to the back of my bicycle, and venture off.

Everybody I encounter asks, "Where are you going?"

"I don't know. I'm going to paint." Actually, I do know, but I don't want anyone to follow me.

"Can we go with you?"

"No, I need to be alone when I paint. It has to be quiet."

"We won't talk. We'll just watch."

"No, I need to be alone so I can think about what I'm doing. I won't be able to paint if others are there."

They are disappointed, even insulted that I refuse to include them. Fortunately, they don't pursue it, and I head toward Gorgan to the tomb at Roshanabad. I pull off the road into the dusty weeds each time a vehicle passes and wait for the thick brown cloud to settle before I press on. It is midmorning and already swelteringly hot when I reach the humble shrine.

Families are picnicking in the shade of scraggly trees or the building's protective roof. I forgot Roshanabad would be crowded on a Friday. I set up to work inconspicuously off to the side. I make a quick sketch on my watercolor paper, but feel like an intruder—very obvious and uncomfortable. So I pack up my work and head back the nearly fifteen kilometers to Alang. Hopefully I can find a quiet place in the fields outside the village.

Lucky to come upon a pleasant spot under a tree next to a stream, I eat lunch and begin painting. The contrast of values, colors, and shapes in the evolving painting extends beyond my earliest expectations. It's fortunate I didn't work on location; here, I'm not limited by what I see. I can paint what I feel, what's in my mind.

My return to Alang is greeted with curious questions.

"Can we see your painting? What did you paint?"

I show them my work, and they recognize Roshanabad.

SATURDAY, JULY 31, 1965 This evening we have a village council meeting in Ghalandarayesh. I can do another painting, I calculate. I pack my provisions and bicycle through Alang, stopping to sketch a street scene in the village, and head for the same cool retreat near the stream. Again the results are rewarding, and my friends are excited I've painted the thatched roof houses of Alang.

CHOLERA

SUNDAY, AUGUST 1, 1965 In midmorning, Shaban Ali and I descend the mountain with near-carefree abandon, having spent a refreshing night in Ghalandarayesh. A man stops us as we pass on the dirt road that connects Heaven with the near heat of Hell. *"Vaba oftadeh,"* he tells us.

Shaban Ali conveys a doleful and worried look. *"Vaba!"*

"Baleh. Twenty-eight people died in a village near Gorgan last night. It is very bad."

Shaban Ali looks at me, "Tom, *vaba oftadeh."*

"What is *vaba*?" I hand him the Persian/English dictionary I carry, even though I rarely use it any more.

He flips through the pages and hands me the book, pointing to a word.

"Cholera!" Even in the summer heat, a chill races down my spine.

"Baleh. It's bad. Very bad."

We talk awhile longer with the stranger who is trekking the long pathway from the road below. Shaban Ali gets the details before we part.

"Tom, this is terrible. It is coming from the east, near Zabol, and traveling rapidly across Iran. Many people are dying."

In Alang, everyone is aware of the impending calamity. I run to my room to find my World Health Organization certificate, checking to see if we have been vaccinated for cholera. Negative! More chills run down my back, and my hair stands on end.

At 2pm someone returns to Alang, reporting, "We can't go anywhere. The army has closed the roads. Soldiers are stationed every half-kilometer, and they stop all traffic! This entire area is under quarantine."

Over the sounds of the musicians and the wedding celebration in front of the bathhouse, I hear Mulla, Reza, and Shaban Ali call out to me.

"Tom, are we having class today?"

"*Baleh*. I'll be right down."

We spend most of the class talking about the cholera epidemic. Each day I discuss current events so my students gain a working vocabulary of conversational English.

"Chop, chop, chop, chop." We hear a loud sound as class is about to end. I go to the open window and look up.

"Look!" I tell the class. A pink emergency helicopter, US ARMY painted on it, thunders overhead. "It must be on its way to Gorgan with cholera vaccine." We go back to our lesson.

The "chop, chop, chop, chop" returns. I look out again and see the helicopter circling over Alang. I suddenly realize the US Army is coming to evacuate me. I check my watch.

"It's 4:30. Class is over!" I shout, and jump out the window. My students jump out behind me.

We run toward the village. Everybody else is running too, in the direction of the aircraft landing somewhere on the other side of Alang. In the excitement, the wedding celebration in front of the *hammam* is abandoned. *The poor bride in the bathhouse,* I think as we sail past. *Nobody is interested in her.*

A cloud of dust and running people easily identify the location of the landing—an open clearing on the far side of Alang. We reach there huffing and puffing. Apprehensively I press through the crowd surrounding the gangly, brightly colored bird. Thoughts swell in my mind. *I really don't want to desert my friends in Alang. Not now. I don't want to be taken away from them when they are in the most danger.*

Then I see the familiar, now-serious face of Dr. Drake.

"Tom, do you have your World Health Organization booklet with you? We need to vaccinate you."

"Right here? In front of all these people?"

"Yes, do you have it?"

"It's in my room on the other side of the village."

"Run and get it quick. We must vaccinate other volunteers today and get back to Tehran before dark. Hurry."

I run to my room, scramble up the stairs, grab my WHO booklet, and head back to the resting pink bird, forcing my way through the crowd.

Perspiring and gasping for air, I pull up my sleeve and look the other way. "Try to stand still," Dr. Drake tells me as the needle sinks into my arm. "We've already been to Gonbad and Gorgan. We're heading west in the direction the epidemic is moving. Go to Gorgan and stay with Jack and Dave until I send a telegram that it's OK to return to Alang. The guys are expecting you. Sorry we can't take you there. We're getting short on time and fuel. You'll need another vaccination in a week. I'll try to make it here for that."

As the villagers watch me being vaccinated, their helpless anxiety becomes painfully evident. Only I am vaccinated. Hundreds begin to push forward in a vain appeal for a life-saving shot for themselves as well. Mothers poignantly hold out their children as if offering them to Allah. Sensing the intensity of the moment, Dr. Drake stamps my WHO vaccination book, signs it, and promptly boards the chopper

He yells back, "Get away from the plane and tell the villagers to stand back from the swirling blades."

I plead to no avail. The surge toward the helicopter intensifies. I cannot hold them back. The deafening sound of the chopping blades above our heads drowns the pleading wails. We hit the ground as a choking and blinding dust swirls and covers us. In an instant, the chopper lifts off. It heads west.

Coughing, we brush ourselves off. I feel uncomfortable I have been singled out. I, too, want the people to be protected from this horrible scourge, yet I understand the impossibility of the Peace Corps doctor being able to vaccinate an entire village. Fortunately, they didn't evacuate me. I want to be with my friends—my adopted family—especially at this uncertain time. Still, I feel awful. If only there had been a more sensitive way to do it, away from the village.

A few older and more introspective villagers voice an indulgent interpretation of the event that unfolded. "What a great country America is. It is a country that sends a helicopter, a pilot, and a doctor to provide protection to just one of its citizens." I am only slightly placated, fearful for the welfare of the whole village.

"The Peace Corps doctor says I have to go to Gorgan to be with Jack and Dave. He wants us together in case they need to get us for any reason," I tell the villagers. I look at them and feel like a deserter.

Somberly I go to my room and pack my bag. This is so painful. I lock the door and head downstairs, say goodbye to the lady who does my laundry and to my landlord and his family, and walk to the Sherkat-e Sargardon. Shaban Ali is there too. I try to say a positive *khodahafez*, but know they detect my sadness and distress. Reza closes his shop and the gang accompanies me to the road.

Soldiers stop us. "Where are you going?"

"To Gorgan," I say.

"He needs to go to Gorgan. He is an American. The American doctor gave him orders to go to Gorgan," my friends tell them.

"It's impossible. No one can go anywhere. No one!"

"But he has a shot. The American doctor gave him a vaccination. He came by helicopter."

"Sorry, but there are no cars. No buses. Nothing. We saw the helicopter. What is the American doing in the village?"

"He is an American Peace Corps Volunteer. He lives in Alang."

"Why is he there? What does he do?"

"He teaches English," Reza replies.

"And he works with the community development office in Gorgan," Shaban Ali emphasizes. "We work together in villages near here."

While the soldiers are intrigued an American lives in a village in Iran, they reiterate that there is nothing they can do. "There are no cars. We have orders not to let anything through. There are soldiers every half-kilometer who will stop you if you try to go."

"Well, I will have to stay in Alang with you. I would rather be here anyway."

I'm uneasy all night—worried about the cholera epidemic. *What will happen in Alang and this whole area of Iran? Will they get vaccine to the people before it is too late? And I can't get to Gorgan as Dr. Drake ordered. What if they decide to evacuate us? He told me to be there.*

MONDAY, AUGUST 2, 1965 Troubled over the dilemma that I am not able to get to Gorgan as Dr. Drake ordered, I devise another plan. I'll take my bag, and bicycle to Kordkuy on the pathways between the fields so I don't run into any soldiers on the highway. There, I can see my friends at the army station and ask if they'll let me through to Gorgan.

The soldiers are surprised to see me. They saw the US Army helicopter fly over yesterday and heard I was vaccinated. They tell me, "No one can go anywhere. No cars or buses can be let through. How did you get here?"

"I came through the fields," I say, smiling.

They laugh. "Tom, you're very clever. You must go back to Alang the same way. Don't let any soldiers see you."

"I'll be careful. I am going to the *hammam* to have a shower."

"*Kheili khoob*, stop by to see us on your way home. It is better we know when you leave Kordkuy."

I go to the post office to check if I have any mail, and send a letter to Jack and Dave saying I can't get to Gorgan because of the roadblocks. I hope the letter will get to them.

SATURDAY, AUGUST 7, 1965 Still no vaccine has arrived for the people in Alang. Tomorrow will be one week since the epidemic reached this area, and Dr. Drake will be coming to Gorgan to give us our second vaccination. *I'd better get to Gorgan today. I don't want the helicopter landing in Alang a second time to vaccinate only me.*

Bus service is now available to those who have a valid certificate of vaccination. My WHO card is a key to letting me pass each roadblock on the way to Gorgan. The soldiers can't read it, but it looks official, and everyone has heard about the helicopter landing in Alang to vaccinate me.

Jack, Dave, and Ziba the puppy enthusiastically greet me. They had not received my letter.

"We were concerned about you. We went to the bus station and heard about the roadblocks. Is everybody OK in Alang?"

"So far, everyone's well. But nobody has been vaccinated. I wonder when they'll get vaccine to the villages."

SUNDAY, AUGUST 8, 1965 We patiently wait all day for the sound of a helicopter descending in the expanse of vacant lots across from Jack and Dave's. It never comes.

"Dr. Pirqeybi said he would give us the shots if Dr. Drake doesn't come. Let's go to my house and he'll give them to us," Kathy says.

"We can go there, get our shots, and then have dinner at the Hotel Miami," Jack proposes. "Then we can come back here and play pinochle."

It's early in the month, so finances are not an issue with Jack and Dave as they are at the end of each month. The allowance for volunteers in cities is woefully inadequate where there are restaurants and cinemas to go to and taxis available. We eat well. As we finish dinner, Jack and Dave request another order of meat—to go. Puzzled, I look at Kathy.

"Let's get a taxi," Jack suggests. "It's a long walk to our place and it's still hot out. Besides, the fare for each of us will be almost nothing."

Ziba eagerly greets us. She knows the routine.

"Ziba, yes, we have dinner for you. Calm down. Be good. Be a nice girl." Jack hands her the dinner they purchased at the hotel. It is devoured in one gulp. Kathy looks at me.

MONDAY, AUGUST 9, 1965 I wake up with a headache and temperature. Jack, Dave, and Kathy are fine. They attempt to convince me I shouldn't return to Alang. My temperature persists, but my objective is to be back in Alang, in my own room.

"Look, I enjoy being with you guys, but when I'm not well, I want to be in my own bed and be able to rest. We have too much fun here."

"You can rest here. We can bring you food and keep an eye on you. Also, here you're near doctors."

"No, I need to go. I'll be better once I get to Alang. Besides, I'm worried about the people there. I want to be with them."

The long bus ride west is further debilitating. I resign myself to the endless stops to check my vaccination card. Wearily I make my way down the road to Alang, go to my room, open my Peace Corps medicine kit, and determine this may be the time to take benadryl.

TUESDAY, AUGUST 10, 1965   I sleep well, undisturbed. Except for my landlord, no one knows I'm back in Alang. At 3:30, there's a knock on my door.

"Mister Tom, Mister Tom." It's Shaban Ali.

"Baleh." I go to the door.

"I heard you were back. Are you OK?"

"Baleh. I was very sick. I got back last night and went right to bed. I slept all night and all day. How is everyone in Alang? Has the vaccine come?"

"No, it has not. So far nobody has become sick in Alang, but we need to get the vaccine here. Have you eaten?"

"No, I just wanted to sleep. I had a temperature. It may have been the second cholera shot. It seems every time I go to Gorgan, I get sick. I'm always better in Alang."

"I will bring you yogurt, spinach, and rice soup. It will be good for you."

"Thank you, Shaban Ali. I'm sorry to bother you and your wife."

"It's no bother. You should have told us you were back. I would have brought you soup earlier."

Soon he's back with a cloth-covered tray. He watches as I deliberately eat. "I will be fine," I try to reassure him, but my voice is weak. "I'm sorry I make you worry."

"We just want you to get well."

Before dark, Shaban Ali comes with another tray of food. "You are feeling better," he notes approvingly.

"My temperature has gone. The soup was what I needed. Thank you."

THURSDAY, AUGUST 12, 1965   At last—vaccine! People form long lines to receive their shots at various locations throughout Alang. Shaban Ali, Reza, Mulla, Javad, and many others administer them.

"Tom, would you like to give shots too?" Shaban Ali and Reza ask.

"Oh, no, I can't do it. I can't stand to see the needle going in. I know it doesn't hurt, but I can't watch it being done. I'm sorry. It's the way I am."

SATURDAY, AUGUST 14, 1965 An air of calm and confidence descends upon the village. I bicycle to Kordkuy to take a shower and get my mail. After I return, I hear lively discussion on the street below, and run down to see what's transpiring.

"Tom, the army has sealed off Alang. Soldiers completely surround the village. We can't go anywhere. We can't go to our fields to get fresh vegetables or tend our crops. We can't open the gates of the irrigation ditches. This is serious. Alang will starve. Our crops will be destroyed."

"Why? Everybody in Alang has their shots now."

"*Baleh*, but Mohammad Abbasi's little boy was sick. They took him to the doctor in Kordkuy this morning. The doctor said he had cholera and reported it to the health officials, so now we are under strict quarantine. No one can go anywhere. This is terrible."

I, and the villagers, feel trapped—helpless. They hastily confirm the location of each sentry, and plot to slip past surreptitiously in the middle of the night to open the vital water sources to the fields and gather vegetables and melons for food.

Before sundown, friends and I go to the guard post at the edge of the village on the now-familiar path through the fields to Kordkuy.

"*Salaam,*" we greet the soldiers encamped there. "*Hale shoma khoobeh?*"

"*Salaam*. Where are you going? You cannot leave the village," we are gruffly ordered.

"Oh, we're not going anywhere. I just wanted to meet you guys."

"Who are you? What are you doing here?" Obviously they can tell I'm not Iranian.

"My name is Tom. I'm happy to meet you." I extend my hand to each. "I am an American Peace Corps Volunteer. I live in Alang."

"You live in Alang? Why? What are you doing here?"

"I work with the community development office in Gorgan, but I live in Alang. I work with the *dehyar* Shaban Ali Rahemi. I have been here ten months now, and I like it. It's a nice place." They look at me curiously.

"Do you guys have enough food and water? It's very warm out here during the day. You need to have plenty of water in this heat."

"*Baleh*, the army takes care of us, but it's very hot sitting in the sun."

"I hope you won't have to be here too long. I'm sorry. This must be very difficult for you. Too bad there are no trees nearby."

The soldiers ask more questions about me. We tell about the helicopter landing in Alang, and explain that I already have both cholera shots and a World Health Organization certificate to prove it.

As we part, the soldiers tell me, "Come back to talk to us anytime. We can have tea together."

"I will. I like talking with you too. *Khodahafez. Shab bekheyr.*"

"Tom, *tu kheili hoogheh bozi* (you are very sly). *Kheili, kheili,*" Reza laughingly tells me as we return to the village. He is using the familiar pronoun and verb tense they often use with me. At first I found this puzzling, as in training the Peace Corps insisted we would never use it in the entire two years we would be in Iran.

I look at him innocently, smiling. "*Man* (Me)? *Kheili hoogheh bozi* (Very sly)! *Manam* (I am)?"

"*Baleh.* I see through you. The soldiers like you. They want you to visit them. They don't know what to do about you. They will let you go to Kordkuy whenever you want. Very crafty!"

I grin.

SUNDAY, AUGUST 15, 1965 *Well, now to put my plan to work.* I go to Tofigh Rahemi's house to see if he needs anything from Kordkuy.

"Tom, please take this letter to mail," Tofigh tells me, "and if there's any mail for Alang, please bring it. But be careful, Tom. The soldiers may not let you go."

"I know. If they don't let me, I can't go. But yesterday I met some of the soldiers and I think they will let me go to Kordkuy. They know I have two cholera shots already."

He smiles. "Tom, you will be the messenger for Alang."

Alone, I bicycle to the soldiers' outpost on the pathway to Kordkuy.

"*Salaam, sobh bekheyr,*" I greet my new friends. "*Hale shoma chetoreh?*"

"*Salaam, Aghaye* Mister Tom. *Hale shoma khoobeh?*"

"*Alhamdulillah,* I'm fine. Did you rest well? It must be hard for you to sleep here in the tent. Fortunately, it doesn't rain this time of year. It is very wet and cold here in the winter. But in the summer we have the unrelenting heat. Stay out of the sun during the middle of the day. Stay under the tent."

"*Baleh*. Would you like some tea with us? We can make tea."

"*Moteshakeram* (thank you), not right now. I'm on my way to Kordkuy to take a shower in the *hammam* and mail some letters. I'll be back soon."

They look at each other to confirm a mutual consent. "*Befarmayid,*" one of them offers. "But come back to Alang the same way."

"*Baleh*, of course. I'll see you a little later."

"*Khodahafez,*" they all bid me.

Wow, that was easy. It pays to have friends in strategic places, I chuckle to myself.

In an hour and a half, I return by the same route. I stop to chat with the soldiers for a while; however, the heat of the day precludes having tea.

My partners in crime at the Sherkat-e Sargardon see me bicycling through Alang. Reza calls, "Tom, *beah. Beah inja.* Your plan worked?"

"*Baleh!* Here is the mail for Alang." I hold it up. They laugh.

"You are too cunning."

I smile. "Just American ingenuity." They laugh some more and I head to Tofigh Rahemi's. He is happy Alang has contact with the outside world.

"The villagers have solved the problem of irrigation and getting food by going out in the middle of the night, and you are our courier," he tells me smiling.

TUESDAY, AUGUST 17, 1965 Mohammad Abbasi's son is running around. Surely he didn't have cholera. However, the Iranian Army still surrounds Alang. I make my daily excursions to Kordkuy, and give the soldiers candy each time I pass. They look forward to my visits, not for the candy, but for the diversion of being able to talk to an American.

Vaccine for the second cholera shot arrives. It seems the emergency has passed and the people of Alang are safe.

"Tom, three people in Ghalandarayesh died of cholera. Ghalandarayesh is now under quarantine too. No one can leave the village."

"Oh, Shaban Ali, this is awful. Maybe it was advantageous Alang was put under quarantine so early. It may have protected us."

"*Baleh.* But the epidemic has spread to Tehran. Also, the hospitals in Gorgan are full of sick people, but most are well in a few days. Treatment is better now, and the government seems to have it under control."

SUNDAY, AUGUST 29, 1965   Strange sounds on the street below my room awaken me—shuffling footsteps on the packed dirt and the muffled wailing of women. I part the curtains. Men strain under a plain board coffin borne on their shoulders. They move purposefully toward the Imamzadeh and cemetery. *Should I join the mourners? I've never been asked to attend a funeral. Who has died, and of what?*

Later, when Shaban Ali comes by, he tells me, "Tom, *Aghaye* Mohammad Mahdavi died this morning."

"Oh, Shaban Ali, I am very sorry. I saw the coffin being carried to the cemetery when I woke up. It wasn't cholera, was it?"

"We don't know. He was ill less than 24 hours. We cannot be certain he died of cholera, but he and his family did not get the vaccinations when they were available in Alang. Now the army is disinfecting or burning whatever he came in contact with. Also, the Health Department has sent out an official, and he and the army have closed the bathhouse and have locked up many *mostarah* (outhouses). We have to clean up Alang."

"Shaban Ali, that is imperative. You and I know that. We've tried. It is so hard to persuade anyone things need to be done. It's taken the cholera epidemic to make this happen."

"*Baleh.* We have to clean up the *jub* (drainage ditch) that runs through the village."

"Good. Many *mostarah* empty into the *jub*. It is filthy. People assume because it is a stream that begins in the mountains, it is safe. In fact, one day I had a discussion with some men who live at the lower end of the village, and they maintained this water is safer than water from the well. They told me, 'Our wives get water from the *jub* in the middle of the night. At that time, the water is clean. It is running water, as God instructed. Praise be to Allah. The Koran commands us not to drink standing water. Instead, you should drink running water.' This could be sage advice, but the stream is very polluted. I tried to tell them this, but I was careful not to insist, just a kindly suggestion. After all, I am nothing compared to the word of the Holy Koran. They use this water for cleaning vegetables, cooking, and washing dishes. They even drink it. They were not convinced when I advised them the water from the well was much safer."

"*Baleh*, Tom, many people believe what the Koran says is always correct, and they deny germs can be transmitted in running water if outhouses empty onto the stream. The water isn't clean just because you can't see anything in it. This is a big problem in Iran. It is hard to alter old ways of thinking."

"I know. I wasn't able to change their minds at all. It's very difficult. No one listens to us. Now they are ordered to revise their ways."

"No, we won't change their minds. *We* have to clean up Alang. We have a village council meeting this afternoon. I'm going to recommend the village hire two street cleaners to keep the place clean."

"Great idea, Shaban Ali. Do you think they will go for it?"

"I talked to Tofigh Rahemi, and he supports it. We have to do it. We have no choice. The health official demands it."

"Wow, Shaban Ali. When I return from my trip, I won't recognize Alang."

TOM OF IRAN

MONDAY, AUGUST 30, 1965 Shaban Ali, Mulla, Reza, Javad, and many others see me off as I board Hajireza's bus to Gorgan. Inexplicably, I feel uneasy. It will be at least a month before I see them again—not a long time, but I now know I'll miss them. I am heading off on my four-week vacation to the Holy Land. However, I have no choice but to spend the requisite three days in Gorgan taking the regimen of pills—three pills three times a day—required to leave the quarantine area. My plan to get the pills and take them in Alang was thwarted. The Iranian government is cleverer than I.

"Aghaye Mister Tom, *salaam. Bah, bah, bah. Hale shoma khoobeh?"* I am greeted as I near the regional health office for my first round of pills.

I see the smiling face of one of the soldiers who for the first week guarded the outpost on my pathway to Kordkuy. I greet him, *"Salaam allekum. Alhamdulillah. Hale shoma khoobeh?* What are you doing here?"

"We were reassigned to the health office in Gorgan," he tells me. Word quickly gets out that I'm around, and other soldiers who manned the lonely outpost at the edge of Alang gather to see me.

"Aghaye Mister Tom, what can we do for you?"

"I came to take the pills so I can go to Tehran. I am going on a trip to Iraq, Jordan, Syria, and Lebanon."

"Beah, Tom." Against my protests one of them pulls me to the front of the long line of waiting pill-takers.

"No, I can wait my turn. I'm no different than all the others." I try to return to the end of the line, but the soldiers pull me forward. The commotion draws the attention of someone at the table.

"Tom!"

I look up. "Ismael Mirsalehi," I exclaim. "*Hale shoma khoobeh*? What a surprise to see you."

"I have been volunteering in the health office during the summer. I needed to keep busy when we're not in Alang. What brings you here?"

"I have to take the pills so I can go on my trip to the Holy Land. But first I want to visit Yavar Khanpoor and his family in Meti Kola."

"They'll be thrilled to see you. How long will you be gone?"

"A month."

"We'll miss you. School is starting in two weeks. I'm looking forward to resuming our English lessons. My family misses you. The children constantly talk about you. Can you come to our house for lunch today?"

"*Moteshakeram*. I'd love to be with all of you." My expression of sincerity in being able to see them is more important than any offer of Iranian *taroof* (politeness). He hands me the first three pills. I swallow them with the boiled water from my canteen.

"At noon, when you take the next set of pills, we'll go to my house. Vida and Davood will be delighted. My wife and parents and brother will be glad to have you as our guest."

"Very good. I can't wait to see the family again."

My friend, the soldier, leads me out. On the street, I'm pleased to see another acquaintance, a first lieutenant in the Iranian Army whom I met in Kordkuy when I first arrived. Lieutenant Tavakoli had been transferred to another city in Iran, but is on holiday in Gorgan for a few days.

"Tom, it is wonderful to see you. How have you been?" he asks me in perfect English.

"Wow, it's good to see you too. Where have you been?"

"Let's go for a walk and then we can stop somewhere for a Pepsi or watermelon. We have lots of catching up to do. Are you still in Alang?"

We talk in English, but when we meet friends, the conversation changes to Farsi. My regard for Lieutenant Tavakoli increases. He is clearly a man whose sensitivity to others is sincere. Here is a man of the highest quality.

"Tom, you speak Farsi like an Iranian now." He smiles.

"*Moteshakeram*, but I'm still learning. There is much to learn, but I think and even dream in Farsi now. I love it here in Iran. It will be very hard to go home. I have less than ten months left."

"Tom, your love of Iran is evident. That is why everybody likes you. I can see it when we walk the streets of Gorgan. Everyone knows you and wants to talk to you. You are an unusual American."

"Thank you. Yes, it will be very hard to return to America. Iran has become my home." I turn my head so he won't see the dampness at the corners of my eyes, but I suspect he knows.

As noon approaches, we go to the health office for my second series of pills. I greet my soldier friends who stand guard in front, and Lieutenant Tavakoli takes me to the beginning of the line. I explain I can wait, but there is little point in protesting.

"Mirsalehi, this is Lieutenant Tavakoli. He was stationed in Kordkuy when I first came to Iran. Ismael Mirsalehi is a teacher in Alang. I look forward to being with him and his family for lunch today. I haven't seen them all summer. He has two children, a girl and a boy."

Ismael politely invites Lieutenant Tavakoli to lunch but Tavakoli declines.

"When can I see you again, Tom?"

"What about tomorrow morning?"

"Excellent, I look forward to it. I'll see you here. *Khodahafez*."

"*Khodahafez*."

I down the pills, and as we head for his house, Ismael says, "I'm not working this afternoon. Why don't you spend the rest of the day with us? We will come back for you to take the next set of pills. Tom, I have arranged you only have to take the pills for two days instead of three."

"Really?" My eyes register surprise.

"Don't worry. It's OK. Two days is enough. Besides, the pills plug you up." He smiles. I smile too.

"Mister," Vida and Davood squeal as they see me step through the courtyard gate. They fly into my arms and hug me. *Khanoome* (Mrs.) Mirsalehi smiles warmly and greets me. Ismael's parents and brother Taghi are equally welcoming—beaming with joy.

"I wish you had told me Tom was coming. I would have prepared something nicer," I hear *Khanoome* Mirsalehi reprimand her husband.

"It's OK," I interject. "Everything you make is so delicious. I just enjoy being with all of you."

She looks embarrassed that I understood.

Lunch in the easy company of family is special. Ismael's parents ask questions about how I find Iran and exhibit quiet elation over my answers. Taghi, who is in high school, is happy to practice English. He is reserved and somewhat shy, not a pushy young man. Time passes quickly.

"Ismael, the container with the dirt in it in the *mostarah* appears to be Chinese," I comment as I return from the outhouse across the courtyard.

"*Baleh*, it may be Chinese. It has been in the family for years. I don't know when we got it. We used to plant narcissus in it. Now it sits in the corner of the *mostarah*. It may have come to Iran on a caravan from China."

My mind lingers over faraway places and people connected in time. *Who brought this? How did it get here? When did it come to Iran?*

As the heat of the day shifts to an imperceptibly cooler early evening, Ismael and I wander up the street for the third round of pills.

"*Aghaye* Tom, *salaam,*" I am greeted as we near the pill-taking station. "It's great to see you. How have you been? Are you going somewhere?"

It is a police officer. I tell him about my upcoming trip.

"*Hatman* (For sure) you will have to visit Karbala in Iraq and the Dome of the Rock in Jerusalem."

"*Baleh*, I certainly will."

"*Beah*, Tom, come take your pills." The officer pulls me to the front of the line. My protests would be useless. Ismael would have taken me to the front anyway, so there is no point in refusing the officer's courteous insistence.

I down the pills and the three of us converse outside. "Tom, come to Gorgan more often. If you ever need any help, let me know."

I assure him I will. Ismael and I stroll the streets of Gorgan, meeting more friends along the way. Tired, we return to the Mirsalehi home for dinner. As we sit watching Vida and Davood play, Ismael observes my eyelids drooping. "Tom, *chashmeh shoma mesle koone merg khoorus memoneh.*"

"*Baleh,*" I agree smiling disconcertedly. "I'm very tired. It has been a long day. I must be going. I'll see you at the health office in the morning."

The children are disappointed. "Don't fret," I tell them. "I'm going on a trip now, very far away, but I will be back soon. Then we can have fun together again. I have missed you all summer." They each give me a big hug and kiss.

WEDNESDAY, SEPTEMBER 1, 1965 *This is no way to start a trip,* I reflect, strangely unsettled about departing. I'm hoarse from talking for two days straight, and there are blisters all over my feet. I'm in a state of near exhaustion.

Lieutenant Tavakoli is waiting at the TBT bus station to see me off before 7am.

"Tom, have a safe trip. Be very careful traveling in the Arab countries. They are not like Iran. Being with you has been terrific. I appreciate hearing about your impressions of Iran."

"The pleasure was mine. I learned so much more about Iran's history and gained new perceptions of your country. *Moteshakeram. Enshahallah,* we will meet again. *Khodahafez."* We shake hands as I board the bus.

"*Salaam,* Tom," Captain Parhami, also an Iranian Army officer, greets me. We shake hands and I sit beside him. We met when he was in charge of the first group of soldiers who held Alang under quarantine. My overtaxed throat gets no reprieve; however, it is a small price to pay for getting to know Iranians.

"Tom, in three months the army is sending me to America for a ten-day tour of duty."

I sense his excitement over the prospect of going to America. "Only ten days! I hope you will get to see some of America too. It's a big country. I have seen very little of it."

Between the frequent stops at army-held checkpoints, each about six kilometers apart, he asks me questions about America and what to see. As we near Alang he notices my glances toward the village that I call home.

"Tom, I'm concerned about you living in a village like Alang. You should find a home in Kordkuy. It would be much better than being in Alang. There is electricity all the time, a cinema, teahouses, and places to eat. And they have a bathhouse with showers."

"Oh, I would never do that. I like Alang. Besides . . . there is something about Kordkuy I don't like."

"Well, I admit Kordkuy is not the most desirable place, but it has more to offer than a village has. Why don't you like Kordkuy?"

I avoid telling him the truth. "I don't know why I don't like it. Something irritates me about the place."

At that moment, the sleek TBT bus comes to a halt in central Kordkuy. My heart sinks as I see a passenger get on. He shakes my hand and takes the empty seat behind me. It is Ghasem. *Damn, that seat would be empty!*

Quickly I bury my head in my book. It is to no avail. The pest, and the main reason I dislike Kordkuy, immediately taps me on the shoulder. Instinctively I feel I must be polite, but my responses are sparing of words and repeatedly I return to the book. My nemesis is persistent. Each time I turn around briefly to answer him. It's as if he knows I keep trying to avoid him and he deliberately goads me.

I engage Captain Parhami in conversation, but the annoying pest interrupts us.

"Tom, you are my friend. Let's talk," he insists in excellent English. "Are you going to Tehran? You can stay with me. I will show you all the popular spots of the city. You will like it."

"I'm going to Babol," I say with relief.

"But you will be coming to Tehran. I will give you my address. You must stay with me. I know all the best places in Tehran."

Any journey with Ghasem would be too long, but with the interminable checkpoints I become exasperated that the usual hour and a half trip between Gorgan and Behshahr now drags out to three and a half. Each time we stop, our vaccination cards are reviewed to confirm we have the necessary shots and have taken the requisite pills.

"We are near Behshahr. This is the second last stop," Captain Parhami informs me as soldiers enter the bus and review our papers. "There will be no more checkpoints. We will be out of the quarantine area."

"Let me see your medical papers," one of the soldiers tells the bus driver.

"I am the bus driver."

"*Agha*, I need to see your papers," the soldier demands.

The driver produces something.

"Where is the certificate that you have taken the necessary pills?"

"*Sarbaz* (Soldier), I am the bus driver," he says with reserved authority.

"*Agha*, I must see the certificate that you have taken the pills for three days. Let me see it. No certificate, the bus stays here."

"But, *Sarbaz*, I am the driver!"

"*Agha*, your papers!"

The bus driver stands to confront the soldier, but other soldiers swiftly come to the support of their comrade. They usher the driver off the bus. Tempers flare. Pandemonium erupts. Men quickly rise and join the argument. Both the bus driver and the soldiers receive the blame. The bus remains stationary. We wait and wait under the sweltering sun. An occasional, *"Ya Allah,"* breaks the frustrated silence.

Ghasem persists in talking to me. I try to concentrate on my book between his interruptions.

Much later, another driver arrives from outside the quarantine area. A chorus of *Alhamdulillah* rises as the bus starts up. As we pull away, I glance at our first driver sitting beside the road with soldiers surrounding him. "It's essential to have your papers in order," I mumble guiltily, even if mine are spurious—only two days of pills instead of the requisite three.

In Babol, I say *khodahafez* to Captain Parhami and wish him a pleasant trip to America. "I hope to see you when you return. I want to hear all about it." I muster the requisite *khodahafez* to Ghasem.

He calls out, "Goodbye, I'll see you in Tehran. We are very good friends."

The driver of the worn-out bus that passes the village of Meti Kola is incredulous an American wants to go to this tiny village and not the fancy casinos on the beach at Babolsar.

"I am going to the Khanpoors'. They live in Meti Kola."

"I know the Khanpoors. They are your friends? *Bah, bah, bah.*" He drives along, picking up and letting off passengers at nearby villages.

"*Aghaye* Mister, this is Meti Kola, right there among the trees. There's a boy. He will take you to the Khanpoors'."

"Pesar" (Son), he calls out, "Do you know where the Khanpoors live?"

"Baleh," the boy replies.

"*Lotfan* (Please), take Mister to *Aghaye* Khanpoor's house. *Mefahmi*" (Do you understand)?

"*Baleh,*" the boy shyly responds.

"*Khodahafez, moteshakeram,*" I thank the driver and wave goodbye.

"What is your name?" I ask my little escort.

"Amir," he answers with reservation.

"How old are you?"

"Six years old."

"Do you know Farsheed Khanpoor? You're about the same age."

"*Baleh.*"

His answers are hampered by his respectful apprehension. We reach a courtyard gate and Amir calls, "*Aghaye* Khanpoor, *Amrika-i amad*" (an American came).

I hear joyful squeals of "Mister *amad!*" I look through the gateway and see Yavar, his wife, and Farsheed and Fereshteh flying toward me. Yavar's smiling parents quickly follow. Farsheed and Fereshteh shower me with hugs and kisses and hang on to me as we walk to the house. I'm as excited to see them as they are to see me.

"*Kheili khoosh amadid*" (We are very happy you came), *Khanoome* Khanpoor welcomes me.

"We were waiting for you all summer," Yavar enjoins.

"I'm sorry I couldn't come sooner, but Alang was under quarantine because of the cholera epidemic. It was very difficult to leave the village and to get out of the quarantine area."

"How long can you stay? We must go to the seaside together."

"I'm going to Tehran tomorrow."

"Tomorrow!" he and his wife exclaim. "Tomorrow! You have to spend several days with us."

"I need to get to Tehran to obtain my visas to travel in the Arab world. Some of my holiday has already been taken up waiting in Gorgan to take the necessary pills. But I was determined to see you here in Meti Kola."

"There is no point in your going to Tehran on Thursday. The embassies will be closed on Friday. You won't be able to get your visas then. You can go to Tehran on Saturday. It will be fun to go to the beach together."

"Hmmm . . . well, you're right. I won't be able to get any visas on Friday. However, I'd better go to Tehran on Friday afternoon so I can get to the embassies early Saturday morning."

We catch up on all our news; we haven't seen each other since school ended. The children buzz around me, vying for my attention.

Yavar suggests, "Let's go for a walk. I want to show you Meti Kola."

I am transfixed by the picturesque cleanliness of the little village. Whitewashed one-story houses, many with thatched roofs, glisten in the sunlight. Meticulously groomed meandering walls conceal spacious courtyards containing fruit trees and trimmed lawns—not at all like the stark enclosures surrounded by weathered brick walls in Alang. A precise line separates the upper white-painted section of the walls from the dung-colored lower portion. Everything is neat and clean.

As we stroll and shadows begin their lengthening stretch, we near the schoolyard where the young men of Meti Kola are playing volleyball. The game stops when we approach. All gather around. The boys have already heard there is an American in the village.

"Tom, this is *Aghaye* Sayeed Houman, the Sepah-e Danesh (Literacy Corps) teacher in Meti Kola."

"Pleased to meet you. How long have you been in Meti Kola?"

"Almost a year. I have heard about you from *Aghaye* Khanpoor. It is a pleasure to meet you."

"Likewise. Don't let us interrupt your game. Please continue."

"No, join us. We'll start another game."

The workout is vigorous, although my skills at volleyball nowhere match those of Iranians.

"Come to our house for dinner, *Aghaye* Houman. I want you to get to know Mister Tom," Yavar extends an invitation as we finish playing.

"Oh, thank you. I should not come when you have a guest."

"*Taroof nakon* (Don't *taroof*). Please. You are most welcome."

"Thank you. I will go home and clean up."

"I look forward to getting to know you," I interject as we part.

The evening and dinner with the Khanpoors is the typical casual gathering we knew in Alang. I enjoy the antics of Farsheed and Fereshteh until they each collapse in a corner of the room, exhausted. Yavar's humor and easygoing nature make getting to know Sayeed enjoyable. Soon we are joking about the things young men in Iran habitually talk about.

FRIDAY, SEPTEMBER 3, 1965 Yesterday the Khanpoors and I came to Babol to visit friends. We played bingo, roamed the streets, and went to an Indian movie in the evening. I reflect on how unusual it is for an entire family and their friends to go to the cinema together. You wouldn't see that in Gorgan. Obviously the Caspian Riviera is far less conservative.

The Khanpoors, their friends, and I go to the sea at Babolsar. Although the beach is not the glistening white sand of Hawaii, the waves almost compare to the perfect bodysurfing waves in Kailua.

"Tom, come back. Don't go out so far," they call to me with consternation. Unlike me, none of them can swim, so they bob near the water's edge, the women wearing bathing suits, but also wrapped in their soaked *chadors*.

All at once, I'm in the perfect spot for a launch. I kick and stroke hard with my feet and arms, and sail smoothly to shore atop the wave. Momentarily I disappear in the roiling water. I stand up, smiling with exhilaration, but as I wipe my face, I observe their look of fear. I turn and head out for another wave.

"Tom, stay here. Don't go out so far."

I don't heed their advice. The excitement of riding waves causes me to lose track of time.

I panic as I come to shore. My bus leaves Babol at 4:00. Quickly I change and bid *khodahafez* to everyone. It's 3:25 before I grab a taxi to Babolsar. Then I have to get a car to Babol and a taxi to the bus station. Only with a bit of luck will I make it. But luck is with me. The taxi driver picks up others, all of whom want to go to Babol. So he rushes me to the bus station. In four-and-a-half hours, I am in Tehran.

THURSDAY, SEPTEMBER 9, 1965 Finally, some visas in hand, I depart for Tabriz and the Turkish border. My goal of reaching the Holy Land through Iraq was thwarted, as Iraq closed the border because of the cholera epidemic in Iran. The only way of getting there is to go through

Turkey and cross the border into Syria. It took ten days of my month-long vacation to take the necessary pills, travel to Tehran, and obtain visas. And I still have to get several visas while I'm traveling! If anything, being in the Peace Corps is teaching me flexibility and patience.

There are few cities or towns between Tehran and Tabriz and almost no villages—just rocks, sand, and low, rugged hills sharply outlined in the desert sun. Unremitting monotony—and a vast and inconsiderate sun-scorched sky. Except for witnessing two bus accidents along the way, the journey is uneventful. The accidents are a reminder that I feel perfectly safe in Iran and with Iranians, but the roads are always an inescapable danger. However, being here and experiencing Iran is worth all the risks.

I would give up everything to have been here.

As we approach Tabriz, the empty landscape slides into a promise of hope. Nestled in a valley surrounded by deep red-and-yellow mountains, Tabriz retains a quaint, small-town atmosphere.

At the hotel I meet Errol, who had trained with me in Utah. "Tom, you must see the bazaar. It is one of the oldest covered bazaars in the Middle East and was a major stop on the Silk Route. Let's go now. We'll be having dinner with a USIS official and his wife who live in Tabriz."

FRIDAY, SEPTEMBER 10, 1965 Two PCVs stationed in Khoy, 150 kilometers northwest of Tabriz, are happy to see fellow Americans, and take Errol and me to an old Armenian church dating to the 4th century. Its narrow slit windows and thick walls are testimony to its turbulent past as a place of refuge and fortification. Inside, the wall paintings exhibit the work of vandals intent on destroying the graven image.

Khoy's vaulted bazaar, with its dimly lit stalls of spices, meats, fresh fruit and vegetables, household wares, and every marketable item imaginable, begins with a black-and-white stone gateway. Two lions carved in low relief protect the upper reaches of the arch. This is all that remains of the city's former defensive walls.

Farther on, in Shahpur we see Dave, another PCV. He regales me with his tales in Iranian Azerbaijan—especially of his hike to Rezaiyeh at night.

"One day, at four o'clock, I got this crazy idea to walk to Rezaiyeh to see

Errol. That's about a hundred and ten kilometers! Well, I was making good time, as the heat of the day had passed. Cars would stop, and I was asked where I was going and if I wanted a ride. They probably thought I was nuts turning down a ride and walking to Rezaiyeh alone. All was going well as I trudged along in the dark. Suddenly, I could hear the howl of wolves in the distance. No cars had come along in hours. About two in the morning the howls kept getting louder, and they seemed like they were circling me. I kept going. There was nothing else I could do—no place to find shelter. The sounds got louder and louder and came from all sides.

"I felt I would soon become a tasty morsel for my unseen terrors. The dim running lights of a vehicle appeared behind me. *'Alhamdulillah,'* I thought, 'but I have to make sure the car stops.' So I stood in the middle of the road waving my arms, hoping they would see me before they ran into me. But the alternative of having my bones picked clean by wolves was even less acceptable. Fortunately the driver did see me. 'What are you doing out here at this time of the night?' he asked in bewilderment. 'I'm on my way to Rezaiyeh,' I told him. 'Can you give me a ride? The wolves are circling me.' He took me to Rezaiyeh, but I'm sure he thought I was one loony American."

"Gee, Dave, how to make Americans look good," I retort. "No wonder we all have to work so hard to improve America's image."

By chance, in Shahpur we meet the Acting US Consul from Tabriz. He is on his way to Rezaiyeh. "Do you guys want a ride?"

Errol and I quickly accept. "I'm certainly not going to walk," I interject. The Consul looks at me quizzically. He had not heard Dave's story.

We pile in the jeep and, as we crest a pass, I catch my first glimpse of Lake Rezaiyeh with the limitless, distant mountain ridges on the other side. My heart leaps.

"It's like being in a 19th century grand landscape painting—the kind British artists did in India," I exclaim. Errol and the Acting Consul smile at my enthusiasm.

"The lake is so saline, no fish or plants can live in it," the Consul explains. "There's no outlet for the water."

A bit farther on, we slow. The Consul pulls off on a dirt track below a cliff. "Look closely. High up on the mountain is a Sassanian rock carving of Ardashir I and Crown Prince Shahpur receiving homage after their victory over the Armenians."

"Wow, there's so much history all over this area."

"Yes, I detect your interest in history, Tom."

"Yeah, and I couldn't have come to a better place than Iran."

He drops us off at Errol's house in Rezaiyeh. "Why don't you guys come to the hotel this evening? Dinner will be on me. Tom looks like he's well overdue for a good meal."

Errol accepts—no *taroof*. I'm taken aback by the brazen American manners.

The Consul greets us in the lobby. "Let's go to the bar and have some drinks before dinner."

The lights are low, musicians play on a small stage, and a generously proportioned woman with a bouffant hairdo, a tight sleeveless dress, and lavish makeup croons a popular Persian song. I am startled to think I am in Iran. Although *abe jou* (Iranian beer) is available at the Hotel Miami, Hell would freeze over before this would occur in Gorgan. I try not to show my uneasiness. *Maybe I have become too Iranian! Am I just a country hick living out in a village in Mazandaran?* Peace Corps Volunteers in Azerbaijan have a social life very different from mine. They seem to be in constant contact with each other, and with American officials in the area.

Back at Errol's house, I think about the last two days and my interaction with Americans. Maybe I *have* become "Tom of Iran." I'm still a young American in Iran, but I'm no longer totally at ease among Americans. In fact, I feel more comfortable with Iranians. I like my Iranian self. "Tom of Iran" is free and untroubled, not like the Tom who in America has to be responsible, accountable for everything—everything in the past and everything in the future—the "American Tom" who has to be concerned about what other Americans think of him. I'm not convinced I like my American self. My Iranian identity is easier, more fun. I can be a *nafahm* (simple-minded), someone who doesn't understand, as they often call me in Alang. I can laugh at myself. I can breathe deeply the free and peaceful Iranian air. *Will I ever be able to leave this?*

I think of Alang—*my Alang*. My eyes begin to well.

LESSONS FOR THE UNWISE

MONDAY, SEPTEMBER 13, 1965 *"Befarmayid,"* a young Iranian offers me a pastry as the bus lumbers between Khoy and the Iranian/Turkish border.

"Nemekham (I don't care for any). *Moteshakeram."* I raise my head slightly, blink, and click my tongue in the Persian manner of refusal.

"Na, befarmayid. Taroof nakonid (Don't *taroof*). *Man taroof nemekonam* (I am not making *taroof*). *Lotfan begeer"* (Please take one).

"Kheili moteshakeram," I refuse again.

"Na, hatman begeer (No, definitely take one). *Lotfan"* (Please).

"Moteshakeram." I take one of the cream-filled pastries, knowing it would be impolite not to accept. He's interested in how I know Farsi. He's going to school in Germany, and is disappointed I'm only going as far as Erzurum.

Except for the border guard stations, the division between the two countries is barren and desolate. We pass uneventfully through both stations, and, my passport stamped, I realize I am in Turkey.

As the bus speeds westward across the plain, suddenly my entire body shudders uncontrollably. There, to the north, basking in the sunlight and towering above a broad, flat plain are the majestic twin cones of Mt. Ararat! *This is "chicken skin."* No one needs to tell me what mountain this is. Words are useless here. The mountain speaks of its authority and spirituality with singular power. I am humbled to be human in its presence.

I begin to perspire, and my stomach suggests it's in revolt. I sit awhile, hoping the sensation will pass. Fortunately, there's a toilet on this bus. But I wait too long, and it's occupied. I wipe the sweat from my face, cover my mouth with my handkerchief, and carefully maneuver to the back to be next in line. *If only that person would hurry. I don't know if I can hold out much longer.*

At last the woman emerges. The confined space and odors of the little cubicle make me retch, but nothing comes. Now I'm perspiring profusely. I take down my pants, squat, and balance over the hole, hanging on to anything for support as the bus rocks from side to side. Relief is momentary. I stay there as long as I can withstand the smell and the awkward position I'm in.

Soaked with sweat, I exit the little room, but remain at the back of the bus. Without a doubt, it was that pastry. I should have known better than to take the one with the cream filling.

Eventually I return to my seat. I'm weak, still perspiring, and miserable—and it's five hours to Erzurum.

In midafternoon, the bus driver drops me off in front of a modest hotel in the central part of Erzurum. I wave to him and my Iranian acquaintance who offered me the pastry.

My room is adequate. The toilet is down the hall—it's all they have.

TUESDAY, SEPTEMBER 14, 1965 Somewhat improved, I'm aware I cannot continue on, and must be attentive to the location of toilets. *I probably should eat—but only the bare essentials. I need to regain some of my strength.* Fortunately, the Turkish word for tea is the same in Farsi—*chai*—and I am able to point to bread when the waiter approaches me at the restaurant.

Later, as I sit at a table pondering how I am going to order lunch, the waiter comes and gently grabs my shirt. He leads me to the kitchen and opens pots. Everything looks too rich. I cup my hand and pretend I am spooning to my mouth with the other. Then I rub my stomach and make a pained look. His face lights up. He opens another pot. It is soup. I nod my head that it is perfect and point to some bread nearby. Immediately he brings me the soup and bread. When I finish I hold out some money and he takes his due.

Slowly I amble about Erzurum, explore the old citadel and some Seljuk tombs. Within the quiet courtyard of a 13th century *madreseh* (theological school), a Turkish family smiles and nods to me. I reciprocate the silent greeting and turn to study the building.

Then their teenage son says in English, "Hello, what is your name?"

I respond, "Hello. My name is Tom. What is your name?"

He gives a thoughtful look. After a few moments he answers, "Yes." His parents and grandparents beam with pride.

"What is your name?" I repeat.

"Yes."

His family stands tall and smiles approvingly.

I smile and say, "Thank you."

"Thank you," he repeats.

As they leave we bid each other a polite goodbye.

I recall seeing large slices of watermelon in the refrigerated case of the restaurant where I had lunch. Watermelon would be so much more refreshing than drinking horrible halazone water, and all I have to do is point to it. I don't need to know the language.

The waiter smiles and greets me as I proceed to the case and point to a huge slice of watermelon. He grins. I sit down at my usual table.

As I relish the watermelon, I see the Turkish family across the room. They smile broadly. I too smile and acknowledge them. When I finish, I signal I want to pay my bill. The waiter points to the family and indicates

Turkish family

they paid it. I look at them. They beam with considerable satisfaction. I go to express my appreciation. All I learn is that they are from Istanbul.

"I come from America—America," I repeat. "From Hawaii." I am not sure they understand. I point to my camera and to them to show I would like their picture. Together we go outside. The women stand to the side, but the men and children cluster together and I snap their picture, the waiter looking out the window behind them.

"I WANT TO GO TO SYRIA . . . Syria," I explain at the bus station. I point to Syria on a map.

"Syria, no."

I look at the map and see Gaziantep is near the Syrian border, north of Aleppo. "Bus to Gaziantep?"

"Gaziantep, *evet* (yes). Syria, no."

"How much?" I rub my fingers together to signify money.

The man writes the price down and asks me a question. Suddenly I catch on. He's asking when I want to go. "Tomorrow."

He grins. I smile, wondering how I am going to make myself understood. He writes 4:00 on a piece of paper. I think he means 4am.

Oh, my gosh. I don't want to leave in the middle of the night. I wonder if they have another bus. I write 8:00 on the paper.

"*Hayır*, no."

Then I clue in. He may be telling me the bus is departing at 4:00 today. That's unacceptable. I don't want to travel at night. I want to see Turkey. So I say, "Erzurum," and gesture with my clasped hands to my head while closing my eyes to show I want to sleep in Erzurum. I roll my hands to (hopefully) indicate tomorrow, and say, "Gaziantep."

He chuckles toothlessly. *"Yarin."*

I hope that means tomorrow, I apprehensively say to myself.

"What time?"

He doesn't understand. I hold out my wrist with its watch, and circle the watch with my finger.

He smiles and writes 7:00 on the paper.

I hand him the money and repeat my motions of sleeping in Erzurum and going to Gaziantep tomorrow. He smiles again, gives me a ticket, and I feel marginally certain we understand each other.

WEDNESDAY, SEPTEMBER 15, 1965   We arrive in Gaziantep about 4pm. I deposit my suitcase in a nearby hotel and go out to see the city, which stretches on and about a series of hills. I chance upon a parade of folk dancers dressed in characteristic costumes from the various regions of Turkey. Excitedly I follow them, taking pictures as they march through the streets. Close to dark, the parade ends.

Oh, my gosh. I don't know where I am. I forgot to keep track of where I was going when I started following the parade. I break out in a sweat, run back to the nearest cross streets, but can't remember which way the parade came. I turn left. Nothing appears familiar. I turn around and run back to the intersection. I panic; it will soon be dark, and then I'll never find the hotel. I can't ask anyone where the hotel is. I don't know the name of the hotel. And nobody in Turkey seems to know English.

Think, Tom. Think. What can you do?

My heart pounds overtime. *I could ask somebody where the bus station is to Erzurum, but the problem is to find someone who speaks English. I really need to figure this out more quickly. Maybe if I go to the top of that hill, I can look over the city and pinpoint the hotel and the bus station.*

I run up the hill. The city sprawls in all directions. *Now what? Tom, you crazy fool. Why didn't you write down the name of the hotel? Look around. See if you can see anything that might be familiar.* But I can't. Breathing heavily, I try one direction. I hurry down to the area, aimlessly darting around. I halfway recognize a building, but almost everything is beginning to look the same. In desperate fright, I run down the street. Some buildings look vaguely familiar. I keep running frantically.

Suddenly I identify the bus station, and then the hotel. I nearly collapse. My whole body is shaking. *Tom, you idiot! Have you learned anything from this?*

THURSDAY, SEPTEMBER 16, 1965   "Aleppo?" I ask at the bus station.

No response.

"Halep?" I had seen the Turkish name for Aleppo on a map. "Syria, I want to go to Syria—Halep."

"Halep, no. Antakya. Antakya, Halep," he shouts to make me understand.

He's probably telling me I can go to Aleppo from Antakya. Antakya—that's Antioch of the Bible. *Well, I'll go there and see if I can get to Aleppo.*

I am entranced by Antioch and its history. At the edge of town, I find the Church of St. Peter, built into a cave. This is where St. Peter preached to the first Christians on his way to Rome. *I'm here,* I say to myself, *where St. Peter actually walked!*

As twilight fades, I stand on a bridge overlooking the River Orontes and picture what it would have been like to be here at the time of St. Peter. It's extraordinary that I—just me—could be where Christianity had its beginnings, and where so much history has taken place.

FRIDAY, SEPTEMBER 17, 1965 Eager to see more of Antioch, and afraid I'll miss something, I wander through the market, where vendors are setting up their stands of fruit and vegetables and butchers are putting out freshly slaughtered carcasses. It had rained during the night, and the trees and streets sparkle magically in the sunlight. Again I head for the Church of St. Peter. Nearby an aqueduct spans a gorge. I scramble across and follow the remains of a massive fortification wall that snakes up the mountain. At the top, fragments of walls define the 10th century citadel overlooking the city. Far below, Antioch appears like a giant mosaic. Alone, I explore the ramparts and the remnants of buildings with their arched vaults and narrow windows. The late summer sun signals its refusal to diminish its midday performance, and my reverie is broken. I must get off this mountain before it gets any hotter.

The archaeological museum is a feast of another kind. The Roman mosaics are spellbinding. *How fortunate I am to be able to see this, to be here, to see the world.* I'm ushered out when the doors close. Again I linger on the bridge over the Orontes. Tonight tears of disbelief and gratitude mingle with the water that flows below—water meeting water. *How can I be so lucky?*

FOR MY HEALTH

SATURDAY, SEPTEMBER 18, 1965 Crossing into Syria adds another country to my passport. Aleppo is one of the oldest continuously inhabited cites in the world. Here, the contrasts between Christians and Muslims, the new and the old—sleek Chevrolets vying with small overloaded carts pulled by donkeys or oxen—provide a rich cultural amalgamation that makes Aleppo special.

The citadel dominates the city. A monumental stone bridge leads from an outer gate across a deep moat to the fort's enormous entrance tower. Its imposing formidability truly intimidates.

A funeral punctuates my visit to the Maronite Cathedral of St. Elias. The coffin is transported in a golden chariot-like confection mounted on the back of a pickup truck. Mournful cherubic angels surmount and surround the concoction. What a way to go! Somber black American hearses are so boring.

I pass the beautifully patterned and varied domes of a modern underground bathhouse on my journey to the *souq*, where Muslims and Christians of all sects and ethnicities meet, shop, and trust each other. The sparkling, mysterious interior is both intimidating and friendly. Tired but obedient and painfully overloaded donkeys negotiate narrow aisles crowded with buyers who haggle with vendors for spices, silks, ceramics, soaps, household goods and groceries, or for objects made of precious metals. I walk for hours, absorbing the endless cornucopia of sights, sounds, and smells, and resisting the coaxing of shopkeepers to have a glass of tea. I can't torture myself by looking at things I may want. I'm at the beginning of my trip and I don't know how much money I may need. I only brought $250 with me, and I spent part of that traveling through Turkey.

SUNDAY, SEPTEMBER 19, 1965 *Oh, my gosh! I don't believe it!* I exclaim and shiver in the heat as the bus approaches Palmyra, an oasis far out in the Syrian desert. It was a whole day's journey—first from Aleppo to Homs, then on a local bus eastward to the ruins of this ancient Roman city. The driver drops me off at a government guesthouse. I'm the only visitor.

My mind staggers in its attempt to take in the enormity of this ruin. I was struck by Persepolis for the clarity of its aged carvings, but here, the sheer scale of the city, with its grand colonnaded thoroughfare and crumbling ancient temples, is breathtaking. Though I'm alone, life really could not be much better. *I'm so fortunate to experience what I have in this life. I only wish Del or Lily could be with me.* I stroll wistfully among sand-covered fragments of architectural friezes. The desert encroaches. It claims everything. All of life is fleeting.

MONDAY, SEPTEMBER 20, 1965 All day I meander among the ruins, not wanting to miss any part of it. Last evening, before the sun set, was a prelude. Today is my day to explore and dream.

Thoughtfully I observe and touch the intricate carving of a fallen Corinthian capital, envision the man who set his chisel to the stone and the team that placed it high upon a column. I marvel at a sinuous frieze of grapevines, and stare in awe at the sight of the striking Temple of Ba'al and the Roman theater. The enigmatic, blocky tomb towers at the base of the mountains outside the deserted city extend for over a kilometer. I follow them, not wanting to miss a single one. The midday heat does not discourage me as I climb the mountain to the 16th century Arab castle that overlooks the abandoned city. Nothing can quell my excitement. Little can surpass Palmyra.

TUESDAY, SEPTEMBER 21, 1965 I roam about the lazy little town in the Beqaa Valley of Lebanon, determined to wait until tomorrow to visit Baalbek's famous Roman temples. Here there is no grand bazaar as there was in Aleppo, or open market like Antioch, only tired shops and their keepers waiting for the day to end. Suddenly I stare breathlessly into the window of a dusty antique shop. A wooden panel with a worn painting of the Resurrection of Christ has me transfixed. I wonder how much it is? *Tom, don't kid yourself. Certainly it's far too expensive for you to consider with the frugally budgeted money you brought on this trip.* But, gosh, it's beautiful! I could just go in and ask the guy what he wants for it. *Don't be ridiculous. It's out of the question. You don't have enough money. Forget it.*

Anxiously I walk down the street—thinking. It wouldn't hurt to go back and ask about it. I might be surprised.

I stop, turn around, and start back to the shop. Then I stop again. *No, you can't. Don't even court temptation. You're torturing yourself. Be sensible.* But I rationalize that it can't hurt. I can find out. Nothing lost. I'll be strong once he tells me how much it is. At least I'll know I can't afford it. That will be the end. No more temptation. No more thinking about it. So I return, stare at the painting for a while, and enter the shop.

"Hello."

"Hello," the shopkeeper replies, barely looking up from the Arabic newspaper he is reading.

"Excuse me. How much is the painting in the window?"

He looks at me, sizing me up—thin, wearing a dark polo shirt, jeans, and grubby tennis shoes. "Expensive." He goes back to his newspaper.

"Yes? How much is it?"

"Eighty dollars US." He smiles disdainfully, confident he pegged this young American traveler correctly.

"Thank you." I leave the shop and stare at the painting.

Eighty dollars. If I bargain, I might get it for half. That wouldn't be too bad. I'd just have to scrimp on what I spend for the rest of my trip.

Inside I ask, "Could I see the painting, please?"

The man rises, seems irritated I am bothering him, but he reaches into the window to retrieve the painting. He sets it on the counter and returns to his paper. I carefully examine it. A lot of paint is missing, but the head of Christ and that of the angel and the soldiers are plainly visible. The faces of the Marys at the tomb are missing. It is very primitive, but extremely beautiful. The wood is weathered. There are two holes with the remains of wooden pegs in each corner, obviously how the painting was attached to a larger structure. The back shows evidence of the wood being hand-cut. There is an Arabic word on the reverse.

"Can you tell me about the painting?"

"It came from an old church near the Syrian border."

"How old is it?"

"I don't know. It's old."

"Would you take $40 for it?"

"No, it is $80. I won't take less. If you don't buy it, someone else will." He peers at me above his newspaper.

"But, sir, there is a lot of paint missing. It's in poor condition."

"That's why it's only $80."

I grudgingly offer, "What about $50?"

"No." He doesn't even look up from his newspaper.

I am exasperated by his intransigence and the fact he ignores me. *Well, maybe if I leave his shop, he'll call after me.*

Unhurriedly I walk down the street, expecting him to call me back. I walk and walk, more slowly with each step so he'll have plenty of opportunity to summon me. Nothing. *Damn. My little plan didn't work. Well, I can't pay $80 for that painting. So that's it. Get it out of your mind.*

Unfortunately, I can't get it out of my mind. I sleep fitfully, thinking of the painting.

WEDNESDAY, SEPTEMBER 22, 1965 Staggering . . . unbelievable . . . beyond imagination! The six surviving columns of Baalbek's Temple of Jupiter loom into the sky—their enormity further emphasized by the huge platform they stand upon. I thought Persepolis was great, and Palmyra too, but this is amazing! How incredible that I'm able to experience this. A few years ago I was a farm boy in Minnesota, with no prospect of seeing the world. I have been to Hawaii—and now here, seeing things I dreamed about as a kid! Pensively I contemplate the awe Rome aimed to instill in the peoples of its far-flung provinces. Such power! Even in the 20th century, I feel insignificant as I stand among these humbling buildings.

By midafternoon, I can hold out no longer. The painting is on my mind. I check how much of my trip money I have remaining, and calculate what I've spent since I left Iran. If I got the painting, I could *probably* make it back to Iran, but I couldn't fly to Tehran from Tel Aviv. That means not going into Israel, because if I do, I won't be allowed to reenter the Arab countries to take a bus across Jordan and Iraq.

This is ridiculous. I don't need the painting. Maybe the shopkeeper has given it a second thought, and will lower his price today . . . *but if he doesn't, do I buy the painting anyway?* It's a lot of money. Not buying the painting may cause me more sleepless nights. *I can't afford to ruin my health. I need to buy it for health reasons.* I will casually stroll by the shop. I'm sure when I pass, the owner will call me in. Then I will be at an advantage, and I can bargain.

I progress down the street, deliberately slowing as I near the shop. It's critical the shopkeeper see me. I stop momentarily in front to gaze at the painting, satisfied I've been seen. Then I continue on. I must give him a chance to realize he can't miss this sale. Certainly he'll beckon me.

But he doesn't. I'm chagrined. Again my plan didn't work. Now, it's I who has to take the initiative once more. With wounded pride, I turn around and return to the shop.

"Sir, could I see the painting."

Silently I say, *It's so beautiful.* My hands are trembling. My heart is racing. The shopkeeper just stands there looking at me with that confident look. *He's so maddening.*

Finally, I say, "Sir, I will give you $70 for the painting."

"I told you it was $80. It is $80. If you want it you must pay $80."

Darn, he makes me angry. But I can't show it, I fume.

"But it's not in good condition."

"If it were in good condition, it would be much more. It is $80."

"How about $75?"

"Eighty dollars."

Resigned, I give him the eighty dollars. My ego is severely deflated. But I'll sleep tonight. My health is worth it.

PALESTINIANS

FRIDAY, SEPTEMBER 24, 1965 Beirut is a sprawling, modern city with high-rise buildings, wide avenues, and beautiful beaches, but its Western appearance is disconcerting. I feel out-of-place here.

I heard about the flashing neon signs. *Delilah. Tammy. Candy. Beth.* They go on and on—endlessly—promoting their merchandise, even in broad daylight. I linger, admittedly enjoying the sights and being solicited. It is just part of the city, not discreetly tucked away as it is in Tehran!

SUNDAY, SEPTEMBER 26, 1965 Damascus, in contrast to Beirut, is a city more to my liking, a lazy, easygoing place. I am back in the Middle East—there are few cars, minarets and the domes of mosques are never out of sight, and people methodically go about their business. Torn awnings provide protection from the heat and glare of the punishing sun. Vendors push their wooden carts, mounted on spindly bicycle wheels, down the cobbled streets to peddle meager goods—sprigs of fresh dates, watermelons, or packages of tea or candy. Horses and donkeys convey larger loads.

I find a hotel near the bus station. Four other guys share the room.

"Hello." They greet me and introduce themselves.

"Hi, I'm Tom." We shake hands.

"Where are you from, Tom?"

"America."

"Oh, America. America." They look at each other.

"Yes, America, from Hawaii, in the middle of the Pacific Ocean."

"Yes, we know where it is. Why are you here?"

"I'm a Peace Corps Volunteer in Iran and I'm on holiday. I just came from Lebanon. I've been traveling for two weeks. The day after tomorrow I go to Jordan."

"We're from Jordan. Amman. We're studying for our exams at the university. What is a Peace Corps Volunteer?"

"It is a program begun by President Kennedy. Americans go to other countries to help in any way they can. I am in Iran for two years."

"Help? What do you do?"

"I do community development work in five villages in the northern part of Iran. I also teach English in one of the villages."

"Do you like Iran?"

"Yes, I like Iran very much. I like the people."

"Do you like the Shah?" They glance at each other. "We don't like the Shah. He sells oil to Israel. Are your friends Muslims?"

"Yes, of course they are Muslims."

"Do they like the Shah?"

"Yes, he's doing much for the poor people of Iran."

"If your friends are good Muslims they should not like the Shah. He's bad. He helps Israel. Good Muslims don't help Israel."

Wow, I think to myself, *I've gotten myself into a pickle. These guys don't like Israel or anybody who associates with Israel.* I remain silent.

"We are Palestinians. We hate Israel. We also hate England and America because they support Israel."

"Oh," I gulp. I have never liked discussing politics, and I feel threatened by their overt statements of hostility to Israel and America.

"The Shah is bad—a pawn of America. He does what America wants. So he sells oil to Israel."

I don't reply.

"What about you, Tom, do you like Israel?"

"I don't know. I've never been there." My answer is lame, but I don't know what else to say.

"Are you going to Israel?"

"No." I think, *How fortunate I can honestly say I'm not going. That painting I bought of the Resurrection of Christ is already saving me.*

"Good, Tom. It's best you don't spend your money there. It only helps the Israelis. Our families used to live in Palestine. Now it is Israel. Our homes were there. Our farms were there. We were forced to flee when the Israelis took our land. Now we're refugees living in Jordan. We have nothing. We lost everything—our homes and our land. Someday we will get it back. We will go to war with Israel and we will get back what was taken from us. We would have fought Israel already, but we know America will aid Israel. That's why we hate America. It's because of America we have not gone to war. But the day will come. We will not stop until every Jew is killed or pushed into the sea. If we have to wait a hundred years, we will do it. We will kill every Jew."

"But war is bad. Many Palestinians will be killed too."

"We will win. We will never give up. We will get our land back. And, Tom, what about you? America is in Vietnam. America should not be there. America is the enemy."

"No, America is in Vietnam to save the country from becoming communist."

"But that is not what the people want. They don't want America deciding what's best for them. They want to live their lives and not have Americans killing them. This is what America will do if we attack Israel. Someday we Palestinians will become strong—stronger than America and Israel combined. Then we will go to war, and we *will* win."

"I'm sorry. I'm disrupting your studies. I appreciate talking with you, but I want to get out and see Damascus."

"We enjoy talking to you too. You're a good American. But we don't like America. America is bad. Johnson is bad."

I am alarmed by the magnitude of their animosity, but what a priceless opportunity to hear about issues I have never given any thought to.

This is the trouble with Americans—we are so isolated and narrow in our thinking. We have no perspective on the whole world.

MONDAY, SEPTEMBER 27, 1965 The grand scale of the Great Mosque, with its 8th century mosaics and restful prayer hall, is impressive. It is one of the oldest and largest mosques in the world. It began as the Temple of Jupiter during the Roman period, and became the Church of St. John the Baptist in the 4th century. Within the prayer hall, I am puzzled by a large domed structure sandwiched between two massive columns. It is the shrine of St. John the Baptist, supposedly where his head lies. Muslims kiss the metal grill that surrounds the shrine. I am in a quandary.

Back at the hotel, I offer, "Hey, guys, have some fruit."

"Tom, thank you. Let's have some now. How did you like the mosque?"

"It's remarkable. But I have a question. Muslims kiss the shrine of St. John the Baptist. Why do they revere the shrine of such a prominent Christian?"

"It is the shrine of the Prophet Yahya. He is St. John the Baptist. For us, he is an important prophet, like the Prophets Mohammad and Jesus. The Great Mosque is not only significant because of the tomb of Yahya; it's where Jesus will descend from Heaven at the time of Judgment."

I register amazement. We spend much of the afternoon discussing religion.

"Hey, I'm taking up your time. I'm going out to see more of the city."

TUESDAY, SEPTEMBER 28, 1965 "Passport," the soldier, with a gun slung over his shoulder, stands before me and demands. "I need to see your passport."

"It's in Damascus," I respond cautiously.

"No passport, no go on the bus. Get off the bus."

"My passport is at the Iraq Embassy in Damascus. I am getting a visa."

"No passport, no go Damascus. Get out."

I'm sure he sees the fear in my eyes, but I refuse to get off the bus.

"Where are you from?" he asks.

"America."

"I must see your passport or you cannot go to Damascus. Do you understand?"

"But my passport is in Damascus."

A man near me whispers, "Don't get off, but in Syria you always need to carry your passport." He pleads with the soldier as others shout in Arabic.

Irritated, the soldier relents. I am not certain if it is the pleadings, or my obstinacy. I shiver and my heart pounds as the bus rolls on. *My gosh, I could have been forced to languish out here in the desert.*

Soldiers had stopped us at a checkpoint outside of Saidnaya on our return to Damascus. There had been no stops on the journey to Saidnaya, a small town about thirty kilometers out of the city. I had gone there to see the chapel of the Icon of the Bleeding Heart, where oil drips from the wood of a painting of the Holy Virgin and Child. Both Christians and Muslims come here to be healed by the holy oil.

THURSDAY, SEPTEMBER 30, 1965 Dialogue with my new friends over the Israeli-Palestinian debacle preoccupies me and has delayed my departure for Jarash. "Hey, I need to get going. The morning has passed. I'll never get to Jarash and Amman."

As the bus trundles to the Syrian/Jordanian border, I think about my Palestinian friends. I'm sad to have left them, that I'll never see them again, and I wonder what will happen to them. I'm distressed, but also admire their resolve. Their hatred of America and Israel bothers me, but they look at things precisely the way they are. America must start to look at the world in a different way. *Why do we think we have to be the policeman of the world? What right do we have to decide how other peoples' problems should be solved?*

"You can't stop here now. It's almost dark and there's no place to stay in Jarash," the bus driver tells me. "There are no hotels. You must go to Amman."

"No, I want to get off here." I surmise he does not suspect the kinds of hotels I frequent—definitely not the standard tourist places.

"I'm telling you, there are no hotels in Jarash. You must go to Amman. There are lots of hotels in Amman." Others join in, trying to convince me not to get off.

Frustrated by my stubbornness, the driver reluctantly opens the door. "There is no hotel here," he calls out as he takes off. "And there will be no other buses tonight."

The little town of Jarash is deserted and quiet as I walk up the main street. *Maybe the bus driver was right.* I find a teahouse. Three guys at one of the tables greet me.

"Hey, Mister, join us. Where are you from?"

Their greeting bolsters my lagging confidence. "From America. I just got off the bus from Damascus. I'm looking for a hotel."

They smile. "There are no hotels in Jarash."

My heart sinks. *Now what do I do?* The bus driver was right.

Turning for the door I say, "Then I must get a bus to Amman."

"Sit down. Have tea with us. There are no more buses to Amman today."

"But I need to find someplace to stay."

"Sit down. Relax. You can stay with us," one of them offers.

Relieved, I sit down with them. I order an egg and some bread.

The way to their place is through narrow, dark alleys lit by an occasional bare bulb hanging from a pole or scant illumination emanating from open windows. Their room is large, almost devoid of furniture. One bulb suffices to light the entire interior.

"We're sorry, Tom, we have no beds. You will have to sleep on the floor."

"That's OK."

They, too, are Palestinian refugees. I listen to their stories of displacement and their hatred of Israel, Britain, and America. I feel grateful to them for taking me in, but also terribly vulnerable being a lone and hated American in a strange place. They probably sense my uneasiness and assure me, "Tom, you are different. You are a good American. We like you. We just hate America. It is Johnson. Johnson is bad."

Hours pass; we all grow weary. They turn out the light. Presently there is snoring around me. I lie there, thinking about the problems unleashed upon the Palestinians when, during World War I, Britain recommended the establishment of a national home for the Jewish people in Palestine, and then the United Nations created Israel in 1948. And, regretfully, the United States was complicit in this. My mind spins. *How can this be corrected now?*

EYES OPENED

FRIDAY, OCTOBER 1, 1965 Like Palmyra, the spectacular ancient Roman ruins of Jarash seem to stretch immeasurably in all directions; however, here, though the hills are brown from the late summer heat, there is no drifting sand to encroach upon the boundless rows of columns.

Midmorning I catch a bus to Amman and inquire about transportation to Jerusalem. There's a minibus at one o'clock. While I wait, I think of how a Coke or Pepsi would hit the spot. I wander down an alley near the station, find a cooler outside a small shop, and point to a Pepsi. The shop owner opens it and I inquire how much I owe him. He writes down the price. I am appalled. It is many times more than I paid for a Pepsi in Syria and Lebanon. I conclude he is overcharging me because I'm a tourist. I set down the Pepsi and walk away without a sip. The shop owner starts screaming at me. I am disgusted he would take advantage of me, but I am also shamed by his shouting. Hurriedly I head for the bus station.

In Jerusalem, I find a hotel at 25¢ a night—right in my price range. Never mind that the toilet is down the hall and there are twelve beds in the room.

I throw my bag under a bed near a window, look out to the west, and see a wall. *My God, this is the wall that separates Jordanian and Israeli Jerusalem! I'll never be able to go on the other side, yet it is only a few feet away.* The reality of experiencing the divided city shakes me.

I look at my watch—almost three o'clock. It's Friday. The Stations of the Cross on the Via Dolorosa will begin shortly. I must get there. Jerusalem, and being here for the Stations on a Friday, will be the highlight of my trip to the Holy Land. I can't miss it.

I tremble as we begin the Stations—following the path Jesus took in agony as he carried the cross to Golgotha. My faith is invincible. First it was Antioch, where St. Peter preached to the early Christians, then Damascus, where St. Paul was lowered over the city wall—and now Jerusalem, where Christ actually walked.

Pilgrims vie, practically fight, with each other to carry the cross—even for a short distance. Somehow I can't bring myself to do it. It seems so unwarranted to liken myself to Jesus. Competition for the opportunity to bear the cross heightens as the procession nears the Church of the Holy Sepulcher. This is Golgotha—Calvary! Where Jesus died for us. I am overwhelmed to be here, but disheartened by the human spectacle.

We process into the holy church for the final stations. Women with dozens of rosaries dripping from their hands rush to the rock with the hole where the cross rested, and plunge the rosaries into it satisfied their purchases will be specially blessed by their act of devotion. I cringe with disgust. *This is like the crass commercialism of Waikiki. Such disrespect.*

Saddened and shaken, I leave the church, unsure of the intensity of my faith. Distressed, I stroll back along the Via Dolorosa and stop at the Church of the Scourging at the Pillar. Silently and alone I pray, moved beyond comprehension that I am in this holy spot.

"Welcome," a priest tells me in front of another church. "Please come in. Do you want to see the pillar where Jesus was scourged?"

"I just saw the pillar in a church up the street."

"Oh, they say it is the pillar. But we have the real pillar. Please come in. I will show it to you."

Apprehensively I listen to the priest's story as he shows me the pillar. I am rattled that there are two pillars. I wonder if there are even more. I turn to depart, and the priest signals he wants a tip. I hand him a few coins and thank him. I'm not sure why I thanked him. The encounter infuriates me.

I pass other churches, but don't go in, afraid I will find more pillars, more holes in the rocks, or more sepulchers. Cramped shops containing religious trinkets and probable antiques abound, filled with tourists buying rosaries, bottles of holy water, or little statues. In one I find an old terra cotta lamp—perhaps from the time of Christ. I inspect it carefully.

"How much is this?"

"Get out!" the shop owner yells. "You were here this morning. Get out!"

The customers look at me. I am horrified and embarrassed. "No, it wasn't me. I only arrived in Jerusalem a couple of hours ago."

"You lie!" he growls. "You were here this morning. Get out of my shop!"

Humiliated, even shaking, I leave. Confused, I wander about the old city. Shop owners try to attract me into their shops, but their solicitations irritate me. I have no desire to look. My aimless perambulations continue until the shadows turn to darkness.

Dinner is simple and forced—uncomfortable. I would prefer not to eat or be around anyone. I speak to no one. Disturbed, I walk, trying to figure out what I think, why I am here, why I even wanted to come. I trudge through the dimly lit byways of the old city and chance upon a gateway, the Lion's Gate, in the walls. From there I gaze across an area of darkness toward scattered lights in the distance. Below, in a valley, the lighted mosaic façade of a church seems inviting. A bridge crosses the valley to a road that leads to the church. Arriving, I discover it is the Basilica of the Agony in the Garden. The gates to the church and the garden are locked.

I sit on a rock near the roadside. Overcome by emotion, I burst into tears—nearly uncontrollable crying. I'm confused, disappointed, disgusted with myself, repulsed I have come this far in life without having my faith tested, discouraged that the realities of the Holy City are not what I had always envisioned. My faith has been that of a child, I chastise myself. I was so inspired by Antioch and Damascus—their simplicity, so honest, but Jerusalem is like Waikiki—empty, self-serving, selling itself. Where is the place I know from the Bible and the holy cards the nuns gave us in catechism classes? It's gone, ugly, a sham. Everyone is out to make a buck—the priest in the church, all the shopkeepers. And the tourists eat it up—buying scads of rosaries, holy water, cheap statues and holy pictures—getting them blessed at all the holy sites, convinced they will be saved because they came to Jerusalem—because they trod in the footsteps of Jesus. And the man in the shop who screamed at me—it was so demeaning in front of all those people. What was his problem? *But, Tom, you were awful too—the ugly American—when you didn't pay for the Pepsi you ordered in Amman because you thought the vendor was overcharging you. Never mind that you didn't drink it. The shopkeeper opened it. What you did was terrible. No wonder Palestinians hate Americans. You are to blame too.* Tears stream down my face as I sit there in the semi-darkness.

"What is the matter? Can we help you?" Two passing young men stop in front of me.

I am startled, embarrassed, somewhat frightened to be found in this isolated spot. I had not seen anybody approaching. "I'm OK. I just need to be alone. Please go away."

"Did something happen to you? Why are you here? You should not be here alone. It's dangerous here in the dark."

"Please, go away. Please. I'm OK. Nothing happened to me. Go, please. Leave me alone. I want to be alone."

"No. Come with us to the city. It is not safe to be here by yourself."

"Thank you. I need to be by myself. Alone. Please go."

They walk off. Their expression of concern only slightly allays my overarching grief. Nonetheless, inwardly I blame myself, my behavior in Amman, my naiveté, my blind faith. *Tom, it is time you grew up. The world is not like you imagined it, how you want it, and it's never going to be that way.* That thought and, added to that, my newly realized plight of the Palestinians plunge me into more sorrow. I begin a letter to Father Dever to convey my disappointment in the Holy Land.

The process of writing serves as a catharsis that quells my emotions. I put my pen and notebook away and return to my hotel near the wall that separates this divided city. Still dispirited, I turn in for the night.

Without warning, the lights go on. Several men cross the room and gather around my bed. *What are they going to do to me?* I grab the sheet as if it's going to be torn off me imminently and I'm going to be led to some unknown fate. I look with fear at the three figures looming over me, their faces dark and unrecognizable against the bright fluorescent tube that streaks behind their heads.

"Are you OK?" one asks.

"Yes," I answer cautiously.

"Are you sure?"

"Yes." My eyes are wide with fright. I lie there stiffly clutching the sheet.

"OK. Goodnight." They depart, turning out the light.

My heart races. I begin to shake. *What was that all about?* Maybe those were the two guys who saw me in front of the church at the Garden of Gethsemane. Maybe they watched me as I sat there crying and writing the letter to Father Dever, then followed me through the old city and saw me enter the hotel. They must have spoken to the hotel owner and they decided to check on me.

SATURDAY, OCTOBER 2, 1965 It was a horrible night. My mind repeatedly replayed the rueful events of the day. Plus, all night long I could feel sand falling on me. The bed, floor, and I are covered with fine grains of plaster. It had fallen from the ceiling during the night. *Oh, well—that's what you get for 25¢ a day. It's all you can afford. Who knows how much money you'll need to get back to Iran?*

In solitude, remote from everything, I again exit the city by the Lion's Gate and look across the dry Valley of the Kidron to the Mount of Olives. I cross the bridge to the Basilica of the Agony in the Garden. Inside I kneel, make the sign of the cross, and say a few prayers, then look around. A priest latches on to me to ensure I see the actual rock Jesus prayed upon while his disciples fell asleep nearby. Reluctantly I hand him the few coins he pointedly expects.

Another priest finds me as I approach the Tomb of the Virgin. He explains, "This rock is the real one where Jesus prayed." I politely listen. He too exacts recompense for his valuable information.

Farther up the hill, the beautiful onion domes of the Russian Orthodox Church of Mary Magdalene enchant me. However, I learn a rock in the orchard nearby is irrefutably the rock on which Christ spent his last troubled night on earth. I part with another tip.

Ascending the Mount of Olives, a young man approaches me.

"Hello. Do you want to see the footprint of Jesus in a rock?"

"No, thank you." By now I want to hear no more stories about Jesus and see no more rocks Jesus touched or stood upon.

"Why? You are Christian, aren't you?"

"Yes, but I don't want to see Christ's footprint."

"Why? It is very good. It is where Jesus ascended into Heaven. I will show you."

"I don't want to see it." I turn away.

"Wait, you must see it. I will show you."

"No, I don't want to see it. Leave me alone. Goodbye."

"Mister, you will like it. You don't have to pay me."

"I don't want to see it. Thank you. Goodbye."

"Goodbye." His voice registers disappointment, even disgust.

The scrawny olive trees provide little relief from the midday sun that burns the Mount. Ahead, a low wall surrounds a small modern building, and an openwork cross surmounts a metal gateway door. The hinges signal my arrival with a grating screech. Inside, however, all is quiet. I am alone in the little Franciscan chapel. All is serene and uplifting. Simplicity abounds. An altar with a crucifix and six candleholders stands before a magnificent window with a chalice and host and fantastic radiating rays of metalwork etched against the sky. But most sensational is the view beyond. There, across the Kidron Valley, is the city of Jerusalem with the Dome of the Rock majestically set apart.

At last, I have found peace—the peace my faith had always given me. I kneel and pray, thankful for being here.

SUNDAY, OCTOBER 3, 1965 Bethlehem truly is the little town I envisioned. Only a few houses nestle among the dry hillsides. Manger Square and the Church of the Nativity are plain to the point of being austere. Seeing the star on the floor in the crypt that indicates the spot where Jesus was born buoys my faith. I climb the church tower. Even the dark bronze bells silhouetted against the brightly lit village below stir me. Indeed, this is the little town of Bethlehem—calm and peaceful.

My skepticism and indignation return as I confront Jerusalem. But a familiar object grabs my attention as I stand gazing in the window of a shop—a lone jar of Skippy Peanut Butter. I don't believe it—*Skippy Peanut Butter*. Imprudently I step inside.

"How much is the jar of peanut butter?"

My eyes bulge as I consider how much it is. *Ten dollars!* That's at least ten times what it would be in Hawaii.

I walk out, but stare at the jar through the window. I reenter the shop and say, "That's way too much. Would you take less?"

"This isn't America. It had to be shipped here. Shipping is expensive."

"Would you take $5.00?"

"No. It cost me a lot."

"I'll give you $7.00 for it."

"No." We settle on $8.00. I realize I've indulged my wanton deprivation.

Tom, you are so stupid. Totally ridiculous. Paying $8.00 for a jar of peanut butter! Back home you rarely ate it. You don't even know if you'll have enough money to get back to Iran—you may have to hitchhike—and you spend $8.00 on a jar of peanut butter! What's the matter with you? You paid eight times more for that little jar of peanut butter than you are paying for your hotel room for four nights. Does that make any sense? You're absolutely out of your mind!

But it's Skippy, I rationalize. It will be a treat, if a very expensive one.

MONDAY, OCTOBER 4, 1965 My last day in Jerusalem and I need to see the Dome of the Rock. Everyone in Alang insisted I see it. And I'll hike back up the Mount of Olives to the peaceful little Franciscan chapel.

The Dome of the Rock is serene and resplendent. It stands alone in the center of a grand esplanade that dominates the city. Its golden dome surmounts a tile-encrusted octagon and sparkles radiantly in the sunlight. It is a spot Jews, Christians, and Muslims revere.* Its singular presence, strikingly isolated in an otherwise crowded city, speaks of timelessness— of eternity. Its authority, its power and grandeur humble me.

Reflectively, I view the Dome and the city from the little chapel on the Mount of Olives. I have found the few spiritual places in the city.

---

* The Dome of the Rock was built in the late 7th century, and is the earliest remaining Islamic building. Its location on the most sacred spot of the ancient world symbolizes Islam's absorption of the traditions of Christians and Jews, and proclaims Islam as the continuation and concluding statement of the two preceding religions. Here, on Mount Moriah, according to Jewish tradition, Abraham came to sacrifice his son Isaac—or, as Muslims believe, Ishmael, son of Hagar, the handmaiden of Sarah, and a forefather of Mohammad. Here Solomon built the First Temple of Jerusalem and, after its destruction four centuries later, Herod built the Second Temple. For Muslims, the sacred rock beneath the dome is the spot where Mohammad miraculously ascended to Heaven, accompanied by the Angel Gabriel in the famous Night Journey.

CLOSE CALLS

WEDNESDAY, OCTOBER 6, 1965 At 4:00 in the afternoon, I catch a shared taxi from Amman to Baghdad. I had wanted to go during the day, but they tell me, "The desert is too hot in the day. It's too dangerous. The car could overheat and we all would die. That is why we go at night. It's a long way to Baghdad. There are few towns along the route."

It is dark, but very warm when we stop at the crossing between Jordan and Iraq. Visa clearance is a quick formality. I hate the monotony of traveling at night, not being able to see, worrying if the driver is falling asleep, and, being squashed among other limp, inert passengers, not able to sleep myself.

I start to get cold. I wish I had my sweater. Too bad it's in the suitcase, and that's at the bottom of the trunk. I can't ask the driver to stop and take everything out in the middle of the desert. *Endure, Tom!*

I peer at my watch in the dark—it seems to be only 11pm. It will be hours before dawn and it gets warm again. It gets colder and colder as we press eastward in the darkness. And I have to pee. *Just hold it, Tom. Surely the driver will eventually have to go too, and he'll stop.* But we travel on and on.

Hours later, we do make a pit stop. I debate if I should have the driver unload the trunk to get to my suitcase. I decide it is expecting too much. Having peed should be enough to make me feel better.

Midmorning we reach Baghdad. I'm tired and sore from sitting for more than 16 hours and having the guy next to me slouching on top of me as he slept. I find a cheap hotel, rest for a few hours, then go out to see the city and get my bus ticket back to Iran.

FRIDAY, OCTOBER 8, 1965 "Hello. Can I sit next to you?" a man in his forties inquires.

I had noticed him as we waited to board the bus. His suitcase was identical to mine, but new and not beat-up.

"Sure, welcome."

"Where are you from?"

"America. Hawaii."

He was born in Iran, is a Christian, lives in Iraq, and is going back to visit family. When we stop for lunch he says, "My wife made me a big lunch. Would you join me?"

"Oh, thank you. I can buy my lunch. It is very kind of you to offer."

"No, I would like to share my lunch with you. Please join me."

His invitation is sincere and I accept.

"Your wife is an excellent cook. You are a lucky man," I tell him as we partake of his wife's loving labors.

"Thank you. You are Christian and I'm pleased to share with you. I wouldn't offer to any of them." He looks around at our fellow Muslim travelers.

My heart sinks and I almost choke. Inwardly I groan. *This man is abhorrent. Not very Christian, and definitely not Muslim, the kind of Muslims I know.* Being polite, I only mutter. "All the Muslims I know are very kind and generous people." Our conversation thereafter is stilted and uncomfortable.

Our passports are stamped at the Iraqi border station. We claim our bags after they are unloaded in the Iranian customs checkroom. A Pakistani family on their way home from a pilgrimage to Mecca is ahead. They are taken aside, ordered to open their suitcases and show everything they have with them. Iranian officials begin tearing apart at least seven quilts they are bringing back from the Holy Cities. Every bit of stuffing is pulled out and dumped in one large heap on the floor. I agonize over their plight and become nervous about what will be done to me when it's my turn. *How will I explain the painting?*

My turn comes. I show my American passport and am waved through. No one asks to see the contents of my bags. I am thankfully incredulous. *Why is it I can go through without any checking while others, Muslims, are given such a hard time? Is it because I have an American passport?* My suitcase is loaded on an Iranian bus along with those of the other passengers—some with their baggage significantly reduced. *Well, I'm back in Iran,* I tell myself with a sense of joyful deliverance. *I made it! I'm home.*

Sweltering in the bus under the hot sun, we wait for all the passengers to clear immigration. The seat next to me remains empty. My acquaintance, who was so kind only because I was Christian, has not returned. I hear noises—someone rummaging around on top of the bus. The driver's assistant boards, the doors are closed, and we start off. I look back, see the Christian man standing beside the road, but MY SUITCASE IS BESIDE HIM! Undeniably it is mine. It is all beaten up. I run to the front of the bus shouting in Farsi, "My suitcase is back there! Stop! Stop!"

"No, that's the man's suitcase. He was denied entry into Iran."

"No, no! That's my suitcase! Stop. Stop." I grab the doors, rattle them, trying to get them open. "Stop! Let me out! That's my suitcase!"

The driver does stop, certain he has to placate this crazy American or who knows what he'll do. He opens the doors. I jump out and run back to the man, grab the suitcase and quickly head for the bus. My former friend shouts, "Don't take my suitcase!"

"No, it's *my* suitcase." I stop, show him the nametag, and run to the bus. Breathing heavily and perspiring, I drag the case to my seat. The assistant offers to put it on the top of the bus. "No!" I protest, and hang on to it as if it is the most precious possession I have. He climbs to the top of the bus to search for the other bag as we wait, and I calm down.

Wow! That was a close call. I almost lost the painting, after sacrificing so much to get it. And, the jar of peanut butter! Good thing I looked back.

AS THE DAY'S LIGHT DIMINISHES, we stop in Kermanshah for dinner. I pull my bags off the bus. There is no way I am going to let them out of my sight. I order rice and *khoresht-e sabzi* (green vegetable stew). It's so nice to be back in Iran, having "soul food" again.

In darkness we wend eastward in the traditional Iranian way—without headlights—first to Hamadan, then northeast to Qazvin, and on to Tehran. The passengers around me are sleeping; the driver and his assistant, talking. Soon I note their chatter has ceased. The assistant is slouching in his seat—asleep too. It's nearing midnight. The driver's head nods. I'm wide awake, watching him and the dark, lonely road ahead. I say a few prayers. I'm not going all the way to Tehran, I decide. I hope he can make it to Qazvin without falling asleep. It will still be a couple more hours to Tehran. I don't want to be on this bus any longer than necessary.

Seeing the driver's head nodding more, I go to him and say, "Please let me off in Qazvin, near a hotel."

"But your ticket is to Tehran."

"*Baleh*, but I want to get off in Qazvin."

"Everything will be closed in Qazvin. No hotels will be open."

"That's OK. I want to get off in Qazvin."

Now he's undoubtedly convinced this American is crazy. However, my request has the advantage of waking him up and giving him something to think about. His assistant has also awoken.

As we pull into Qazvin, I move to the front of the bus with both my bags. "Hotel," he gestures with his hand and opens the door.

"*Moteshakeram. Khodahafez.*"

"*Khodahafez. Shab bekheyr.* Hotel," he reiterates pointing to the building.

"*Baleh. Moteshakeram.*"

I stand under a solitary streetlight and read the unlit hotel sign to confirm that the Farsi says hotel. The door is locked and there are no lights inside. *OK, Tom, now what do you do? It's cold out here on the street.*

I start pounding on the door. No one comes. I pound more. I keep pounding. Finally a man arrives, unlocks the door, and says, *"Baleh?"*

"Do you have a room?"

He raises his head and clicks his tongue in the customary Persian negative manner, but motions for me to come. We ascend a dark stairway, venture down even darker hallways, and end up on a balcony overhanging the street. He points to a bed.

"Chand misheh" (How much is it)?

"Seh toman" (Three tomans).

That's less than 50¢, and this isn't a time to bargain.

"Khoob. Moteshakeram. Behbakhsheed," I thank him and apologize for

bothering him. I take off my shoes and crawl into bed with my clothes on. It's cold out here, but at least it's a bed.

SUNDAY, OCTOBER 10, 1965 In Qazvin, I decided to go to Tabriz so I could take a bus to Ardebil, see the shrine, and go on to Astara, the border town between Iran and the Soviet Union. There, I can take a bus along the Caspian Coast to Alang. It may be my only chance to see the Caspian in decent weather. The rainy season is coming, and by the time it ends, I will be heading back to the States.

I have an aisle seat on the right side of the bus to Ardebil. A turbaned village man sits beside me, dozing. We climb along the narrow mountain roads, inching our way east. Suddenly horns blare. Everyone cranes his neck to see what's happening. Our bus and another are playing "chicken" on a tight hairpin turn. A seemingly bottomless ravine drops off on our side as we ascend, and the cliff of the mountain constricts the other side. Neither driver gives way. Each tries to maneuver past the other at the apex of the turn, horns blasting, expletives flying. Passengers call on Allah as they half stand to get a better view of this insanity. I tensely hang on to the seat in front of me. Abruptly our bus lunges to the right, nearly plunging over the cliff. Everyone jumps up and to the left as a chorus of *Bismillah-e Rahman-e Raheem* (In the name of Allah, the Merciful, the Compassionate) echoes throughout. The turbaned man next to me lands squarely on my lap. The two vehicles scrape past each other. Another chorus of *Bismillah-e Rahman-e Raheem* resounds through the bus.

In Ardebil I am told, "There is no bus to Astara. The Caspian area is under quarantine because of the cholera epidemic. No buses can go there."

Oh, my gosh—the cholera epidemic is still here. I hope everybody in Alang is OK, I think to myself. "But I need to go to Gorgan. I want to go along the Caspian Sea."

"Sorry, it is impossible now. You must go to Tabriz and then get a bus to Tehran. You can go to Gorgan from Tehran."

"Back to Tabriz?"

"Baleh."

"I came from Tabriz."

He looks at me quizzically, almost mockingly. *"Baleh."*

"When is the bus to Tabriz?"

"In a half hour."

"In a half hour! I have to eat lunch and I want to see the shrine of Shaikh Safi. Is there a bus that goes later?"

"There is one that goes at 3:30 this afternoon."

The shrine of Shaikh Safi is a breathtaking Safavid structure with glimmering tilework, but I am even more thrilled to learn Shah Ismael Safavid is buried here. He is the Shah on the pen box I bought in Mashhad.

Fortunately we do not meet another bus as we maneuver the dangerous hairpin turn on the return journey to Tabriz. I look down over the edge as we pass and see the mangled carcasses of vehicles far below. *How close I came to being down there right now. Life would be over, but I sure had one hell of time while I was here.*

TRULY HOME

TUESDAY, OCTOBER 12, 1965 My heart races as I start down the road to my village. I am home. Thursday will be one year that I first ventured on this road, not knowing where it would lead—scared. Now it is home—as dear to me as any home I ever had.

I don't make it to my room, even though it's the first building as one enters the village. Friends see me, grab me, and greet me in the Persian manner, with a kiss on each cheek

"Tom, we were worried about you. We expected you back long before this. We enjoyed your postcards. Did you have a good time?"

Mulla drags me to his house, and many follow. They ply me with hundreds of questions. I barely have a chance to ask about them and Alang. When the lights blink, everyone rises and says, *"Ya Allah."* Mulla carries my suitcase to my place.

"Welcome home, Tom. We'll see you tomorrow. *Shab bekheyr.*"

I, too, bid him goodnight. I put my key in the lock. *That's strange. I must have forgotten to lock my doors when I left.* I switch on the light, taking advantage of the few minutes before the generator is silenced, and look around.

Just as I left it. Incredible! I was gone for six weeks, left my door unlocked, and everything is exactly as it was. This is Alang. This is truly home.

THURSDAY, OCTOBER 14, 1965 The day is bittersweet. Everybody is happy I'm back from my trip. While we revel in the joys of the past year, we realize we have less than a year to be together. In eight months, I will be leaving Alang and Iran.

At Mulla's, we listen to the tape recording of the day of my arrival. I'm bothered by what I said or didn't say. However, it's not what was said that day that's important. It's what took place that day and in the past year that is significant. A bond has developed that can never be broken, never shattered. It is forever. I will always be tied to Alang and its people.

Shaban Ali and I spend hours together, talking about the projects in each of the villages and what transpired as a consequence of the cholera epidemic. Certainly that, not my presence, will hasten change.

"Shaban Ali, I want to see how Tofigh and Ezetollah are doing."

"I will go with you. It has been a while since I visited them."

Shaban Ali presents us to the servant as he answers our knock on the gateway door. "Mister Tom *amad* (came). He wants to see *Aghaye* Tofigh and Ezetollah." The servant runs off to announce our presence.

We have much to share with *Aghaye* Tofigh and Ezetollah—my trip, this being the anniversary of my arrival in Alang, and what the past year has brought. Tears well in the corners of Tofigh's eyes when I tell him I went to the holy cities of Jerusalem and Damascus and saw the shrine of the two imams at Kazimain in Baghdad. They are more evident when Shaban Ali reminds him I will be departing in eight months. He and Ezetollah cannot imagine my time in Alang is winding down.

SATURDAY, OCTOBER 16, 1965   Gholam Husayn, whose wife does my laundry, comes up to talk. He is proud Musa is now in school and learning to read and write. Gholam Husayn had no education. Over the years he has learned the alphabet, and can read a bit of Farsi.

"Tom, my daughter was married during the summer. I wish you could have been at the wedding."

"I wish I could have been with you too."

I think about how young she is—only thirteen or fourteen.

FRIDAY, OCTOBER 29, 1965   "Tom, Mister Jack came with Hajireza to see you yesterday afternoon when you were at the village council meeting in Ghalandarayesh," Reza tells me when I check in at the Sherkat-e Sargardon. "He wanted to borrow money from you. Mister Jack is very funny. He doesn't know Iranian *taroof.* When we told him you weren't here and you were not returning until late, Hajireza offered to take him back to Gorgan with no charge. But I said to Jack, *'Befarmayid, chai'* (tea). Of course it was *taroof.* Mister Jack said, 'Fine, thank you.' I told him, 'But you need to go back to Gorgan with Hajireza.' Jack said, 'That's OK, I'll go after we have tea.' So I closed my shop and we went to my house for tea."

I laugh and say, *"Timafur basuteh"* (Your nose is burned). However nose in this context is the regional word for the nose of a donkey. Everyone hee-haws, except for Reza. He smiles malevolently, and I know I'm in trouble. He'll bide his time to get even with me.

SATURDAY, OCTOBER 30, 1965 "I read an article in *Reader's Digest,*" I tell my English class. "It was about a woman who says a child was born in the Middle East in 1962.* The child will grow up to unite the whole world under one religion. By the year 2000, the world will be at peace." The sentences are short and direct. I speak slowly and enunciate clearly.

Reza immediately and earnestly responds. "We believe Imam Mahdi, the Twelfth Imam, disappeared in a spring. Someday he will come as a child to unite the whole world under one religion, Islam."

"Do you understand?" I ask the class, and repeat some of my statements and ask Reza to repeat his response.

The students indicate their comprehension by their comments and agreement with Reza. "Maybe this child is the Imam Mahdi," Mulla adds.

"Maybe he is. Maybe the world will be united under one religion," I continue. "Maybe we will live in peace."

"That is what we believe," Reza states. "That is what Muslims believe. The whole world will be one religion. We will all be Muslim." He thinks a moment. "Well, maybe not exactly Muslim, but one religion. All men will live in religious harmony and goodness."

I am amazed at Reza's depth of comprehension and thinking. He, a devout Muslim, recognizes that hope for the world may lie in a belief outside Islam or any religion we know. He is a unique individual.

---

* Ruth Montgomery, "The Crystal Ball," *Reader's Digest* 87 (July 1965), 235–42.

BRAIN MALFUNCTION

FRIDAY, NOVEMBER 5, 1965 There is jubilant celebration all day long, but I fear Farsheed lies in agony. This is his circumcision. The Khanpoors wanted me to be with them in Gorgan on this momentous day in their son's life. While the guests party wildly I think about what occurred early this morning, and how Farsheed must feel. Maybe I empathize more because I, too, am miserable in my effort to suppress a cough—the onset of a cold.

By 4:30, exhausted, I go to Jack and Dave's. I dare not go to Alang because there is a wedding celebration this evening. I would be required to show up, so I would get no rest. Jack and Ziba answer the gateway door. Ziba demands my attention even before Jack and I greet each other.

"Wow, she's excited to see you! She hasn't forgotten you—and it's been months. Ziba! Calm down!"

"Where's Dave?"

"Bad news. He's back in the States. His mother is dying. She has cancer and only has a few months to live. The Peace Corps sent him home a week ago to see her before she goes."

It's like someone hit me below the belt. "Oh, gosh," is all I can muster, considering how I would feel if I received news like that.

"I don't know when he'll be back, or if he'll even be returning."

"Gosh, Jack, this is dreadful. Poor Dave."

"Oh, and I'm not going to be transferred out of Gorgan."

"Good. I would miss not having you around. Gorgan would never be the same without your caustic opinions."

"They're hardly opinions!"

"Oh, I'm sorry. They do have substance, even if they are caustic."

He grins. As usual, Jack is full of news. He seems to attract it, or, better yet, have an innate ability to scoop it out.

"Tom, guess what? Tremble, our director is gone. Fired! And you have no idea how close we all came to going back to the States. I heard we were just one signature away. One signature! I guess the evaluator who was here in the spring took a very dim report back to Washington— largely complaints about the staff and policies. You know how it is; they want us to work miracles so they can brag to Washington, but when we grumble that we lack support and aren't achieving anything, they say 'You don't realize all the good you are doing' and 'It doesn't have to be much.' Tremble was called back to Washington to answer to the report. But, he held on. He must have saved the day as we're all here, and the office in Tehran is crawling with more faces. Guess he said they needed more help. As if we need more police to keep us inmates in line. Supposedly some of the volunteers ended up writing to their congressmen about him, and that finally finished him off."

"Well, I'm glad we're still here. Everyone in Alang would have been very upset if we were forced to leave early. They're already lamenting my departure next summer. I just wish I could say I'm getting some real work done. I feel so unemployed. My monthly reports to Tehran are always the same. 'Not much happened this month, just like the previous one. The people in one of the villages are building a water system. They know much more about that than I do. Meanwhile, I am standing by.' And whenever I ask for help from the head office, I never get it. Maybe with a new director and more people there, we *will* get it, but I doubt it. Showing an interest in Iranians and being their friend is about the best we can do. Not that that isn't important, but I wish we had more of a feeling of accomplishment."

"Two new PCVs have arrived—in agriculture. They live next door to us. Jim and Noel. Boy, are they naive!"

"Oh, like us a year ago, I bet."

"You, but not me. Remember, I'm from New York."

"Oh, yes. I had put it out of my mind with all the other knowledge I've gained throughout the year. Thanks for refreshing my memory."

Jack smiles. "Let's all get together for dinner—with Kathy too."

"But let's not make it too late. I'm not doing well with this cough. I'm getting another cold."

Jim is easygoing, quick to smile and laugh; Noel, more serious—already worried about how he's going to get Iranians to carry out his ideas.

SUNDAY, NOVEMBER 7, 1965   Today is a holiday, the birthday of Imam Ali. I returned to Alang yesterday morning to take care of myself, but the obligation of attending the wedding celebration precluded getting a full night's rest. Plus the cold, damp night air definitely didn't help. My cough is unbearable. I spend the day in bed, but in the afternoon I hear footsteps on the balcony and the unfamiliar sound of English being spoken. It is Jim and Noel with two of their Peace Corps buddies from Bojnoord, far to the east.

"I couldn't wait to see your place. Everyone talks about you, Tom, and how you're living proof of how the Peace Corps should be working," Jim tells me.

"Oh, you guys, I'm doing nothing special. I'm just living here. I love the people and they love me, but I'm not achieving anything important. Some of the villages I work in have built schools, and others are working on water systems and bathhouses with showers, but all of this would happen without me. It might come a little sooner because I'm here. I'm not an engineer. I don't know how to build schoolhouses or bathhouses, or how to put in water systems. My job is to be their friend—letting them get to know an American. And I'm learning from them. My life will never be the same. I would not trade living here for anything. Not for anything."

My little room, the wattle and daub walls, even my water tank on the balcony and that I have to use an outhouse enthrall Jim. I take them around the village and introduce them—especially to my "business partners" at the Sherkat-e Sargardon. Jim and the guys from Bojnoord register delight at my acceptance into this illustrious company, more significantly with the title of *moallem*. Noel seems apprehensive, unsure of the attendant honor and the easy familiarity of the establishment's associates.

"Tom, come to Gorgan with us," Jim insists. "You can spend the night at Jack's. He suggested we bring you back."

"No, my cold is too bad. You see how I'm coughing."

"Yes, but you can get better rest there. You said you have to go to the wedding tonight, and last night you froze in the cold."

"Well, you guys may be right . . ." Jim is already finding out how easy it is to tempt me.

SUNDAY, NOVEMBER 14, 1965   Although I slept for two-and-a-half days to try to get over my cold and cough, I'm little improved. Coughing and loaded with a battery of pills and cough medicine, I head to Babol for a workshop on public health. A damp, cold fog hangs balefully over the town, and as we near our hotel by the sea at Babolsar the density of the cloud mass increases—assuredly not an environment for someone with a cold and unceasing cough. Again, any brains with which I might have been endowed at birth are not functioning. The temptation of being with the guys as we romp along the water's edge is stronger than reason. We return late at night, cold and saturated with the penetrating, vaporized fluid. The pale blue walls of the hotel room gray in the dim light of a single lamp. The bed feels like a soggy sponge. I cough through the night.

In the morning I pull on cold wet clothes that seem like I showered in them the night before. *Gosh, I thought Alang was cold and damp in the winter! Alang is paradise compared to this.*

WEDNESDAY, NOVEMBER 17, 1965   Each day the fog hangs low until late morning and rolls in again by late afternoon. Everybody glares at me as I cough. Today we go on field trips in drafty canvas-covered jeeps, sweating as we hike up mountains, and chilling as we stand around in damp villages, listening to reports of successful health campaigns.

We are about 30 kilometers from Alang as the sun begins to set. Four guys ask, "Tom, we've heard so much about your village. Can we come tonight?"

"Sure." Even though I'm feeling lousy, what else can I say?

At the highway, the five of us catch a ride on the back of a gravel truck heading east.

"I'm only going as far as Kordkuy," the driver tells us as we pile in.

"That's fine," I say. "We can walk to Alang from there."

It's pitch black as I guide the guys down the four-kilometer path through the fields to Alang. Besides the cough, I now have a temperature. But I still have to round up food, bedrolls, blankets, and pillows for the night. Fortunately I have several cans of meat—mostly pork—Don Croll brought on one of his visits. I had saved them for just such an emergency, if other PCVs should happen to drop by.

I feel too rotten to make dinner. Errol volunteers to cook. I sit in a corner, coughing, eyes glazed over. My village friends come, and my little room is filled to capacity. "Dinner is almost ready," Errol announces.

I stagger to the kitchen, gather the tablecloth, dishes, and silverware, and return to the overflowing room. Everyone pushes back as the cloth is spread on the floor and dinner is brought in. I'm too miserable to eat, and embarrassed I cannot offer a *befarmayid* to my Iranian guests; however, I don't want to take the chance that any will accept and then find out they have eaten pork. I pray none of the guys will mention the four-letter word—not that any of the Iranians would understand it *if* it were said in English. I definitely don't want anyone to know we ate pork in Alang. This is so unnerving.

Finally, mercifully, the lights blink and my friends from Alang say goodnight. Quickly we gather the dishes, pile them in the kitchen, and spread the mattresses on the floor. There is only room for three.

"Somebody can use my bed. I'll crash on the floor in the kitchen. It's better I be by myself. I don't want any of you to get whatever I have."

THURSDAY, NOVEMBER 18, 1965 Though I coughed a lot, I slept well in the foot-and-a-half space between the table legs and the wall. Errol offers to make pancakes for breakfast. With chagrin, I recount my episode making pancakes in Alang.

"They were ghastly. I made them one night; followed the recipe exactly, but they were a disaster. I threw them over the wall, assuming the neighbor's dog would find them and do away with the evidence. I went to bed hungry. The yard was clean the next morning, and I checked to see if the dog was still on all fours."

"What did you do?"

"I followed the recipe in our Peace Corps cookbook exactly! Did everything it said."

"That's odd. I've made pancakes from that recipe often and they always turned out well. What were yours like?"

"Oh, they had big holes in them and they were soaked with oil."

"Soaked with oil! How much oil did you put in the pan?"

"I filled the pan. The recipe said put oil in the pan."

Errol gives me a look that says, *Oh, you dummy,* but kindly asks, "Didn't your mother ever make pancakes?"

"Yeah, lots of times."

"And, didn't you watch her?"

"Yeah, but I never paid any attention."

"Well, Tom, the recipe says, 'Put oil in the pan.' It doesn't say, 'Fill the pan with oil.' You only need a little oil so they don't stick to the pan."

Breakfast finished, the guys head for Gorgan and the Turkoman bazaar at Pahlavidezh. I begin the long process of cleaning up my room, delivering the bedding I borrowed, and doing dishes. I find somebody's wallet. *Well, he'll be back. He can't get far without it. No point in my going out and then we miss each other on the road.* By 3pm, when I finish my chores, he hasn't appeared and I crawl into bed to get some rest.

Awakened by the grating of the gateway door below my room when the village bus pulls in, Hajireza calls, "Mister Tom, Mister Tom—a message from your friends. They want you to bring the wallet to Gorgan tomorrow."

"I'll go with you in the morning so I don't have to walk out to the road." But I think, *Great! I should run after them in my condition.*

FRIDAY, NOVEMBER 19, 1965 "The guys have gone to Gonbad to see Barkley. They'll be back in the afternoon," Jack and Dave tell me.

I'm happy to see Dave has returned. I hadn't seen him in three months.

"Hey, Tom, have you heard about the latest women's fashion rage in Tehran?" Jack inquires.

"No," I respond with a quizzical look.

"Yeah, the new Seymore *chador.*" He grins.

"Huh . . . that's a choice one, Jack."

When the guys return from Gonbad, I go to catch Hajireza's bus back to Alang. I'm told Hajireza has already left, but there's a bus going to Kordkuy.

With my cold, it's not a bright idea to wander down the road from the highway in the dark and rain. I won't be able to see the mud puddles, and I don't have my boots. I decide to return to Dave and Jack's and go to Alang in the morning.

SATURDAY, NOVEMBER 20, 1965 Staying in Gorgan overnight was not wise. Today my cough is worse. My constant hacking can be heard through the thin wattle and daub walls. Midafternoon, there's a knock on my door. It's *Haji* Torfeh.

"*Aghaye* Mister, your cough is so bad. I hear you coughing all the time."

"I'm sorry. I don't want to worry you or anyone in Alang. I'm trying to get well. The Peace Corps doctor has given me some medicine and I'm taking it."

"*Aghaye* Mister, your American medicine is not working. Here, take this." She hands me a brownish substance the size of a small pea. "Swallow it with some water and go to bed. You will sleep well—no more coughing—and when you wake up you will be much better."

"What is it, *Haji?*"

"It's opium. It will be good for you. I take it whenever I'm very sick with a cough."

"Oh, *Haji*, thank you. I can't take that." I hand it back to her.

"No, please take it. It will help you. Please. You are very sick."

I see there is no possibility of refusing. "Thank you, *Haji*."

She laboriously crawls down the stairs, looks back, and says, "Be sure to take it."

"*Baleh,*" I reply somewhat insincerely. I look at the lump in my hands as I tremble in a coughing jag. I close the door and set the tiny glob on my desk. I return to bed, but immediately sit up coughing uncontrollably. I can hardly breathe. I think about *Haji's* gift. *Haji would never give me anything that would hurt me. Never, ever.*

My whole body shakes from coughing. I stagger to my kitchen, get a glass of water, and return to my room. *Haji's* gift is gone in an instant. I sit on the bed coughing, but eventually it subsides. I lie down, waking up once or twice during the night to ascertain that I am still alive.

The next morning, I awake from the best night's sleep I've had in a long time. I'm still tired, but I slept without coughing all night.

THURSDAY, NOVEMBER 25, 1965 Although my cough has improved, going to Gorgan for Thanksgiving is not the best idea, even if Kathy is making a turkey and the Peace Corps has given us three days off. At lunchtime, Mulla comes with a tray of food.

"Tom, this is special. My wife made it just for you—for Thanksgiving."

"Oh, thank you, Mulla. This is so nice of you. Thank your wife for me."

I eagerly remove the cloth covering the steaming bowl. My eyes do a cartwheel. Fortunately Mulla doesn't see.

"It's *kalle pache*" (sheep's head), he says proudly. "We know this is an historic day of feasting in America, so my wife wanted to make something very special."

I should have gone to Gorgan, I say to myself, but tell Mulla again, "This is so nice of you." Truly I don't know what else to say. I look in the bowl and see the eyes floating—and the tongue!

"Eat. Enjoy. Then go to sleep. Rest is good for you. *Khodahafez.*"

"*Khodahafez. Moteshakeram.*"

With trepidation, I dip the bread in the broth and hesitantly spoon the contents of the bowl into my mouth, avoiding the two eyes that look up at me. *Well, Tom, this is one Thanksgiving dinner you will never forget.*

FRIDAY, NOVEMBER 26, 1965 Early, there is a knock on my door. It is Shaban Ali. He is all smiles. "Tom, we had a little boy during the night."

"Wow, congratulations. Are your wife and the baby fine?"

"*Baleh.* They are well."

"*Alhamdulillah.* What is the baby's name?"

"He is going to be Sayeed. It means happy—lucky."

"Shaban Ali, this is special. Today is my birthday too."

He glows, "Happy Birthday, Tom. You and Sayeed will always have the same birthday."

DISMISSING THE PAST

THURSDAY, DECEMBER 2, 1965 The biting cold and overcast weather of a month ago has given way to bright, warm late-autumn days. Mulla and I catch a bus to Gorgan and then one to Gonbad. Before Gonbad, we disembark and trek for nearly two hours to a remote Turkoman village in the foothills of the Alborz Mountains where Ramzan Mozandarani teaches. He is a quiet, gentle, and thoughtful young man from Alang who lives with a Turkoman family. As the waning sun rakes long shadows across the ground and up mud-coated walls, Ramzan shows us the treeless village with its flat-roofed buildings made of sun-dried bricks and yurts with their protective felts and reed mats.

Spending an evening with a Turkoman family is extraordinary. As we gather before dinner, each of us is given our individual pot of tea. Then an inordinately large tray of rice laden with chicken and kebabs is placed in the center of the oilcloth. I look around and think to myself, *They gave us silverware, but they forgot to bring the plates.* Our Turkoman host directs me to start. I look at Ramzan and Mulla and they indicate I should begin. *Well, Tom, this must be how the Turkomans do it,* and I reach into the rice with my spoon.

SATURDAY, DECEMBER 4, 1965 The remains of the ancient city of Jurjan lie scattered on the plain several kilometers west of Gonbad. We prowl the carelessly excavated mounds and pick up shards of ceramic and glass.

"Wow, Mulla, this is phenomenal. Look how beautiful these pieces are."

He smiles at my amazement. "I knew you would like it. You can keep them. This was never scientifically excavated because people have been digging here for centuries. Mostly they wanted the bricks for building their houses, but they found gold coins too. Genghis Khan came through here in the 13th century. The populace was massacred and the city left in ruin, like he did to Alang. It was horrible."

We find fragments of a small bowl and fit them together like an ancient jigsaw puzzle.

THURSDAY, DECEMBER 9, 1965 Kathy and I wander the bazaar in Gorgan. We particularly like the metalworking area, with its sights and harsh discord of sounds. I have learned to go into shops and look at what is in the back. Often old things are there—brought in by villagers—that are sold or exchanged for new pots and pans imposingly displayed in the front.

"What are these?" I ask the smith as I extract a pot from a larger one.

"Bronze. They are bronze. Old, very old." He turns away, resuming his pounding on a new vessel.

"Wow, Kathy, these are remarkable. Too bad the small one's broken, but the large one is in perfect shape. I wonder how old they are?" I turn and ask the smith, "Where did you get them?"

"A villager brought them in. His plow hit the one. He was really upset. He had to replace a plow blade."

"How much is the large one?"

He puts it on the scale. "One hundred eighty tomans."

"That is a little expensive for me. Would you take less?"

"That's the price of bronze. If that is too much, buy the smaller one."

"It is broken. It's no good."

Not convinced by my rationale, he continues his pounding.

"This guy is irritating. He's ignoring us. It's like he doesn't care if he sells it," I tell Kathy.

"*Agha*, I'll give you 150 tomans for it."

He gets up, puts the broken one on the scale. "This is 125 tomans. That is the price of bronze. If you can't get the large one, buy the small one. I will just melt them down and make something nice out of them. That is what I pay for bronze." He turns away to his work.

"Gosh, this guy is hard-nosed. He isn't going to budge on his price."

"He knows the price of bronze, and that's it. If you want it, you have to pay the 180 tomans," Kathy acknowledges unsympathetically.

"*Agha*, I want the big one. Will you take 170 tomans for it?"

"No." He resumes his work.

"*Agha*, here is the 180 tomans."

Later, Hajireza sees me struggling down the street with the hunk of bronze. He runs toward me and grabs one of the handles. "Tom, what did you buy? How much did you pay for it?"

"It's an old bronze pot. I paid 180 tomans for it."

"One hundred and eighty tomans! That is way too much. What are you going to use it for? We don't use these any more. Tom, I'm sorry, the shopkeeper swindled you. You must be more clever."

"But that is the price of bronze. I paid him the price of bronze."

"I'm sorry. Iranians are very shrewd. You paid too much."

Hajireza has the pot loaded on the top of the bus. In Alang, everyone hears of my foolhardy purchase. Arguments ensue about whether I was taken advantage of or if I have been fairly charged.

Gradually, portions of the inscription on the lip are deciphered.

"It is in Arabic," Ismael and Yavar tell me. "'*Amale Ustad Fakhr ad-Din Isfahani fe Astarabad…*' (Made by the master Fakhr ad-Din of Isfahan in Astarabad…). Astarabad was the old name for Gorgan. There is poetry on the other side. It says, 'May our end be happy.' Here it is very hard to read, but it might be a date. Tom, this is very old. It seems to say, '…in the year 737.'"

"How old is that in our calendar?" I calculate. "It's 1337! That *is* old."

"Tom, you made a wise purchase," Ismael says. "Clearly it has value."

"And the man was going to melt it down. Now I have to figure how I'm going to get it to America."

"We will build a wooden box," Mulla adds. "It will be no problem."

BABA NOEL AND THE CHRISTIAN DEVIL

SATURDAY, DECEMBER 25, 1965 Laden with pairs of shepherd's socks, fruit, nuts, candy, pencils, and little plastic toys, I catch the bus to Alang. I went to Gorgan on Thursday to be with the other PCVs; however, I can't wait to get back to prepare the Christmas stockings for the children. Shaban Ali helps me stuff the socks with goodies, and we pin them around my room. Then we rush out to tell our friends to bring their children up to my house.

Shaban Ali and my Sherkat-e Sargardon buddy Ismael Gilani arrive first, with Shaban Ali's daughters Halimeh and Maliheh, son Masood, and

Shaban Ali Rahemi, Ismael Gilani and children

his brother's children. They also bring Rozy and Abdullah, whose fathers can't come because of the fight with my landlord.

"See what *Amo* Tom has for you," Shaban Ali and Ismael tell the children. "Baba Noel came to *Amo* Tom's last night and left these for you."

Justifiably puzzled looks on the children's faces betray the strangeness of hearing about Baba Noel and receiving a shepherd's sock full of goodies.

Haji Torfeh brings little Ismael, Mulla's son. When I ask to take his picture, *Haji* holds him close to her so I have no choice but to take a picture of both of them. "Don't ever be caught taking a picture of a woman," the Peace Corps admonition flashes through my mind. But with *Haji* anything is possible.

Haji Torfeh and Ismael

SUNDAY, DECEMBER 26, 1965   Yesterday, our Christmas, was also the beginning of Ramadan, the month of fasting—no eating, drinking, or smoking from sunup to sundown. "Tom, are you going to invite us to lunch today?" my pals at the Sherkat-e Sargardon quip.

"Befarmayid," I challenge, smiling. They laugh, and the familiar "Do Nothing" daily raillery ensues. The rigors of fasting make any labor during

the month more burdensome. But, at the Sherkat-e Sargardon is any labor ever rigorous?

Near noon I rise and say, *"Ya Allah,"* indicating I'm leaving.

"Aren't you going to invite the guys to lunch, Tom?" Reza gibes, laughing and knowing he can't come because of my landlord.

"Befarmayid," I *taroof,* not wanting to be out-witted. Besides, they'll decline, and I won't say *befarmayid* a third time. However, they don't even wait for a second *befarmayid.* They rise and say, "Let's go to Tom's for lunch."

I begin to perspire. *What am I going to do now?* I'll be run out of town when news gets out that the Christian devil tempted Alang's young men and forced them to break their fast.

Six guys follow me to my room. I feel like Satan leading them to Hell— and to my doom as well. And what am I going to feed them? I only have two eggs and a little chunk of bread left over from breakfast. Clearly I can't perform a miracle. My hour has not yet come—and it never will, under these circumstances. I have a few cans of pork in my Peace Corps emergency stash. But I can't feed them pork—during Ramadan, in Alang— in addition to making them break their fast!

I put on a pot of water to make tea—purely a stalling mechanism to give me time to think and perspire more. *Maybe they're simply challenging me to see how far I'll go, and at the very end, they'll leave. They won't drink the tea, and I'll be off the hook. I will have won the challenge.*

Water hot, I prepare the tea, and load the tray with cups, sugar cubes, candy, fruit, seeds, and nuts. I check if the coast is clear before I venture out of the kitchen to my room next door. I don't want anyone to see me doing this.

Not a soul is around—in my courtyard or Mulla's. Stealthily I slip from one room to the other and set the tray down. *"Befarmayid,"* I offer each of them a cup of tea and pass the fruit and sweets. They begin to drink and eat. I perspire more. *Now what, Tom? You have to figure out something—fast!* *Pancakes!* I'll make pancakes. It's a good thing Errol showed me how. I just need a couple more eggs. No one will know I'm not getting them for myself. If I buy bread or anything else, everyone will know what evil I'm up to.

I run to *Aghaye* Aghayan's shop to get eggs. As I turn the corner, I see it's closed. *Now what?* My landlady may have a few eggs. I've bought from her before. Returning to my courtyard, sweating, I casually saunter up to my landlord's house. All is quiet.

"*Khanoome* Rahemi," I call out cautiously.

She comes to the door. *"Baleh?"*

"Do you have some eggs I could buy?"

"*Baleh*. How many?"

"Two." Prudence keeps me from buying more. She'll think they're for me.

As I climb the stairs to my room, I tell myself, *Well, Tom, you've multiplied the two eggs you had. Now see what other kind of miracle you can perform without getting caught.*

The pancakes are a success. They are not full of big holes and grease-soaked, as they were the night I feared I might have killed Mulla's dog. Again, I check to see if anybody is looking, take the dishes and silverware into my room, and then bring in the pancakes with a syrupy jam I use on my bread in the morning. I have no appetite—too hyper to eat—but I eat a pancake anyway, more out of politeness than hunger. My guests eat heartily. I make another pot of tea and offer more fruit.

When one of them signals that they should be going, I inaudibly sigh in relief. I nearly collapse in emotional exhaustion as I hear them pass through the gate below my room. Carefully I check to ensure that nobody sees me surreptitiously carrying the dirty dishes from my room to the kitchen. To destroy the evidence, I boil another pot of water and spend most of the afternoon washing dishes as silently as humanly possible. Then I anxiously wait for news to spread throughout Alang, and for my imminent forced departure.

QUANDARIES AND EASY BANTER

MONDAY, DECEMBER 27, 1965 Mondays are a ritual. I bicycle to Kordkuy, take my weekly shower, and pick up mail. Mom always writes on Sunday evening and mails it on Monday. It, too, is a near-tribal practice. I receive the letter the following Monday. Today there is a pile of Christmas letters— including one from my nearly forgotten teenage sweetheart, Kathleen. I fear to look at it, and am ashamed I never replied to her previous letter.

When I do read it, an icy chill runs down my back. She says she's trying to convince her parents to move to Hawaii. Then she adds, "P.S. I apologize for my earlier letter. But I can hope and pray you still are at least my friend and will write to me." I sigh and breathe deeply. Curiously, my eyes water; I feel almost guilty. If I *do* write, what will I say?

SATURDAY, JANUARY 1, 1966 Somewhat auspiciously, Alang begins work on its new water system. It's not their New Year's Day, but they know it's ours. Everybody, including the village elders and council members, is on hand for the excitement of the non-ceremony—digging the pit for the water reservoir near the well that gushed forth the day I arrived in Alang. I grab a spade and begin digging too. Immediately Shaban Ali snatches the spade and gives it to one of the laborers. I detect his displeasure. My symbolic act of cooperation is not met with approval.

Here is the quandary. As Peace Corps Volunteers, we must work and do what is acceptable within the norms of the host culture, not ours. I have a university degree. In their culture, anyone with education does not do physical labor—even a symbolic act of turning the first spade. In their

Digging the reservoir—Tofigh Rahemi (third man on left), Shaban Ali (right)

minds, but also in mine, I was mocking them. It was egregious—something I shouldn't have done. No wonder my friends viewed the USIA film *Years of Lightning, Day of Drums* with derision when they saw it recently in Gorgan, even though they dearly love President Kennedy. They were disconcerted about the emphasis given to the Peace Corps providing technical assistance to developing countries. "You Americans think you can go anywhere in the world and show us how to live and become civilized people," they told me. "How old is America? You are not even 200 years old. And we have had a civilization for thousands of years."

Precisely for these reasons, right from the beginning, I opted to teach English so my role as a community development volunteer became obscured. I was no longer here to show them how to live; instead, because I was a teacher, Alang garnered the envy of all the nearby villages. They all wanted an American Peace Corps Volunteer in their village too—one who would teach English and be their friend. So my role here always is one of friendship, of letting Iranians get to know the heart of an American, and me returning their love. This is the real mission of the Peace Corps.

MONDAY, JANUARY 3, 1966 "Tom, I am going to build a new house," Shaban Ali tells me, "one just for my family. Will you do the drawings? It will be a brick house. My father said I could build it in our family courtyard."

"In your family courtyard! It's so small—there is no room!"

"No, I determined where it will go and how big it will be. We need our own house. It's very crowded with four children now. We cannot live in only one little room."

"But Shaban Ali, a big brick house will be very expensive. Wouldn't it be advisable to build a simple wooden house now, and then buy some land and build a nice brick house on it? Then you can have your own courtyard and garden. You will be near your family, but not right on top of them. You want a house in Gorgan someday. It might be better to save your money to buy land and a house there. Then your children could go to high school in Gorgan."

"Tom, I need a house now . . . but perhaps you are right. I should just build a wooden house. Can you draw the plans for me?"

"Sure. Tell me how you want it—how big it will be and how many rooms it will have."

He draws me a sketch of how he visualizes the house—two rooms and a big hallway.

"Shaban Ali, why do you have this hallway? It goes nowhere. It's wasted space. You could get another room if we planned better."

"No, that is the way it should be. That's how I want it."

"OK," I say, resigned. "I'll draw it this way."

When he leaves, I get out my drawing board, T-square, and drafting paper, and draw it the way Shaban Ali wants. I also make another layout that provides three rooms in the same area. Before class, I show Shaban Ali the two drawings.

"I see what you mean about getting another room," he exclaims. "This is terrific! Then we would have separate rooms for both the girls and the boys."

Word rapidly spreads through Alang that I can draw house plans, and many want me to design their "dream homes." Yet they are still simple, basic village homes with no indoor plumbing.

SUNDAY, JANUARY 9, 1966 "We use that sentence construction in English once in a blue moon," I tell my students as I explain a difficult lesson.

"Once in a blue moon? What is 'once in a blue moon'?"

I barely know how to answer them. "Oh, it's just something we say in English. It means it rarely happens—almost never."

"But what is a 'blue moon'?"

"I don't know. It's just what we say. It's what we call an idiom. It's something we say that doesn't mean exactly that."

"Hello." We're suddenly interrupted by a disheveled man with a decidedly British accent who is standing at the classroom door.

"Hello," I say surprised. "May I help you?"

He comes forward and shakes my hand. "My name is Peter, Peter Somerville-Large. And a blue moon is when there are two full moons in one month. It doesn't happen often. That's why we say 'once in a blue moon,' because it's rare."

"Hi, Peter. My name is Tom Klobe. These are my students: Ismael, Yavar, Reza, Mulla, Shaban Ali, Sohrab, and Nosrat. And thanks for the explanation of a blue moon. How fortuitous. Just when I needed help, you came in out of the blue."

"Out of the blue?" Ismael exclaims. "What's 'out of the blue'?"

"It means that something happens unexpectedly. Peter came in 'out of the blue.' These are idioms. You have them too. In Alang we say, '*Chashmeh shoma mesle koone merg khoorus memoneh*'—'Your eyes look like a rooster's ass'—to someone who looks tired, or '*Damagh-et sukht*'—'Your nose is burned' when someone makes a fool of himself. We say 'caught with egg on your face.'"

"Caught with egg on your face," Ismael repeats. Everyone laughs.

"And, Peter, where are you from?"

"I'm from Ireland."

I go to the map. "Ireland is here, west of England. It is very green there because it rains very much. Isn't that correct, Peter?"

"Yes, Ireland is very green because of all the rain."

"Peter, please sit down. You will be part of today's lesson. It will be good for my students to hear a British accent rather than my American English. What has brought you to Alang?"

"I'm writing a travelogue about the Caspian area of Ii

"Peter, please speak slowly and distinctly. My stud
English, and they may find your accent difficult. They ai

"I am writing a book about the Caspian area of Ira
have been, people comment about you and insist I visit y
an American who lives very nearly in a 'cultural vacuum
and you have become more or less completely integrated i
Actually, they say you are rarely seen outside of your ai
Gorgan, and he told me how to get here. In fact, he too
station to make sure I got on the right bus. He informed
to let me off. I walked down the path to the village and f
boys playing volleyball. They indicated '*Amo* Tom' was
I approached the school, it was easy to find the room, as
being spoken."

"Do you understand what Peter said?" I ask the stuc
not comprehend everything, so I summarize. "Peter is a
writing a book about Iran. He is writing about the Caspian
heard about me and Alang and he wanted to visit us. Jim
him how to get here. You remember Jim, don't you?" Th
agreement. They all like Jim and his ready smile. "Do you
for Peter, about his book, or about Ireland?"

"Mister Peter, please write your name on the blackboard,"
They are fascinated by his surname and its hyphenation, a
the meanings of each part of the name. The students ask r
When class ends, Reza goes home to tell his wife he is havin
this evening. Forgetting it is Ramadan, I invite the student:
has spread throughout Alang that Tom has a visitor—a fam(
room quickly fills with inquisitive villagers.

REZA'S HUMBLE LITTLE ROOM is packed with men sitting, w
around the perimeter. Rozy is there immediately to be with
sitting on my lap, directing all my attention to her. She is aj

---

* See Peter Somerville-Large, *Caviar Coast* (London: Robert Hale, 1968). Chaj
experiences with American Peace Corps Volunteers.

strange man who speaks no Farsi. Her cousin Abdullah comes running
and the two compete for my devoted attention. Outside I hear Fakhri,
y's new little sister, crying. Reza's wife comes to the door and shyly
cates that he should take the baby. She calms in her father's arms. I
athize with Reza's wife, and how she has to deal with preparing dinner
hort notice for a houseful of men, as well as care for her children. But
nen in Iran are used to that, and they silently put up with it. However,
sister-in-law—Javad's wife—and Reza's mother are there to help.
men in Iran, and probably those throughout the world, work together
onquer the unexpected.

s we wait for dinner over tea and sweets, conversation, as usual,
ters on every aspect of my private life. "How many girlfriends do you
e? Two? Or do you have more? What are they like? Is it true one of
n is Chinese? We saw her picture in your room. If you marry her, your
dren will be half-breeds. Don't you think that's rather disgusting? The
er girl, the one in the Peace Corps in Africa, is better. She would be
ch better for you. You should marry her. And what about the Peace
ps girl in Gorgan? How convenient the Peace Corps sent her to Gorgan
you guys. Does she only do it with Peace Corps guys? Would she do
ith Iranians, too?" And again, "Are you circumcised? You must be
umcised if you stay in Iran." The prying goes on and on.

hen they turn on Peter. "You are writing about Iran? Who paid you,
how much have you received already? How much will you make on
book? What is your annual salary? Are you married? Is your wife
utiful, and is she good in bed? You don't have children! Is it because she
arren? Is it true men in Ireland remain bachelors until their forties? If
: happened in Iran, men's pricks would rust off." Both of us are relieved
en the tablecloth is handed through the door and we know the plates of
d will soon be on their way.

Dinner finished, Reza begins tuning the transistor radio. He finds Radio
ran, and we listen to a prolonged interval of commercials, then the
s of the latest gloomy statistics on American casualties in Vietnam.

Tom, why does America continue? It's obvious America isn't going
vin," Reza good-naturedly needles me. "The Vietcong are winning.

America is losing. Everyone knows the Americans stay in Vietnam because they like war. America wants to rule the world."

"We are in Vietnam because we are fighting Communism."

"Communism! The people in Vietnam don't know what Communism is. They don't care about the government. They just want to live. But America is telling them they need to be like America. It's like you here, Tom. It's a clever way of spreading capitalist ideas—the American way of life. Here in Iran, you don't fight because the Shah is under your control; so you send in Peace Corps Volunteers to spread your ideas. Very ingenious."

"Well, if you don't like it, I can leave."

"Oh, no. We don't want you to go. You are fine. But in Vietnam, you Americans should not be there."

"You want us to quit?"

"Yes. Tom, you must write to President Johnson to tell him this is necessary. We know you know him. You received a letter from him—from the White House. We saw it. You must write to him and tell him to get the United States out of Vietnam."

"You want me to write to Johnson?"

"Oh, yes. Yes."

"And ask him to take away our troops? You know, I think that's a wonderful idea."

"Now he sees the light," Reza says to the others.

"I'm thinking I'll ask the President to remove all American troops from Vietnam, and also take away aid from all over Asia. What's the point in giving money to a country like Iran? It's only wasted on corrupt government officials under the Shah. We all know that. Let these countries fight their own wars. If the Russians decide to invade Iran, there's no point in asking the Americans for help."

"No, no, Tom. Wait before you write. No one wants the Russians. The Shah is a good man, but he is too influenced by dishonest men who seek to fill their own pockets. Let's change the subject."

Momentarily we all sit quietly. I'm exhausted from single-handedly having to defend America. Though I am not sure how I feel about the Vietnam conflict, being the lone American constantly puts me on the defensive. The depressing news and the relentless harassment push me to my wit's end.

Impetuously Reza slaps me on the thigh and says, "What are you thinking, Tom?"

Startled from the sting, I await my chance to surprise him as well. This sets off a thigh-slapping, ear-tweaking, and prolonged and painful hand-clasping melee that grows increasingly rowdy. I am aghast at how my friends are carrying on in front of a guest, especially one who is writing a book. Fortuitously the blinking light saves us.

"*Ya Allah*," someone says. We all rise, thank Reza for dinner and the boisterous amusement, and say goodnight.

"PETER, WAIT HERE. I will run up to my room to get the flashlight—what do you say in Ireland, torch?—to show you where the outhouse is. It's new—one of the best in the village. My landlord was forced to build it when the cholera epidemic occurred. The old one was condemned because it emptied into the stream that ran through Alang."

I guide Peter through the ankle-deep mud, dodging the quivering mass of slumbering sheep, to a corner in the backyard where a burlap sack covers the door to the outhouse. "Here—take the light so you can see. I'll wait out here. When you're finished I'll go."

I shine the light for my unexpected guest as we climb the precarious stairs that lead to the balcony before my room. Anticipating the generator shutting down, I quickly light the Aladdin heater and the kerosene lamp on my desk and pull the curtains closed.

"Peter, I have to gather my laundry. I didn't have time to do it earlier."

In the dark, I gather my sheets, shirts and pants, pajamas, shorts, and T-shirts from the line that stretches the length of the balcony. Everything feels wet from the damp night air. Back inside, I find Peter immersed in a book from my Peace Corps locker—James Baldwin's *Notes of a Native Son*. I pull the damp clothes over the top of the Aladdin to dry them instantly. (Last winter I learned this was a practical way to iron clothes.) I make my bed, take the folded clothes to the cupboard in my kitchen, and spread Peter's mattress and blankets on the floor.

"Sorry," I say to him. "This is the best I can do. This bed is village style."

"Eh."

I take that to mean his consent. He is already engrossed in reading.

"Peter, I'm going to turn in. I'm shutting off the Aladdin so we won't suffocate. You turn out the lamp when you want. I'll see you in the morning. I put the flashlight by the door in case you need to go down during the night. Oh, I also put a roll of toilet paper there, if you need it. I've adapted to the Persian method."

"Fine," he says without looking up.

I'm not yet asleep when I hear knocking on the yard door below my room.

"Mister Tom. Mister Tom."

I ignore it. The knocking grows louder.

"Mister Tom. Mister Tom."

I can't avoid it without my landlord waking up. I pull the curtains aside, open the window, and peer into the blackness below. "*Ki-eh*"(Who)?

"Ahmad and Hassan. We saw the light in your room. We want to meet Mister Peter."

"*Baleh*, I will be right down."

Feeling like a trapped animal, I pull my pants over my pajamas and go down to open the gate. I appear at the door with my two guests, and introduce them to Peter. Hassan and Ahmad shake Peter's hand and bow politely. With my flashlight and an expression Peter detects is more saintly than sincere, I go to brew tea. I return laden with plates of fruit and cookies and, ignoring protests that are merely formal, press an orange into their hands. Then, as we drink tea, the questions begin—mostly directed to me as they know Peter doesn't speak Farsi.

"Tom, how much did that rug cost?"

"Eight hundred tomans."

"Too much."

"What about the bronze pot over there? How much was it?"

"One hundred eighty tomans. It is old. I got it for the price of bronze."

Hassan and Ahmad argue and decide it was a fair price.

"And what about this picture on the piece of wood? Who is that?"

"Hazrat-e Isa (Jesus). I got it in Lebanon."

"How much did you pay for that?"

"Eighty dollars. That is about 600 tomans."

They look at each other with alarm. "There is paint missing. And the artist was not very skillful. He did not know how to draw well. Tom, you paid way too much. You must be careful in the Arab countries. Arabs are not like Iranians. They will fleece you for all the money you have."

"But it is old, and I like it."

"Do you pray to it?"

"No, but I pray."

"How many times a day do you pray?"

"At least once a day."

"Muslims pray five times a day."

"I know. That is very good."

"Do you wash before you pray?"

"No, but I wash many times a day."

"Who is the girl beside you in that picture? Is she your girlfriend? We hear you have many girlfriends."

"*Baleh*, she is one of my girlfriends."

"She is not American."

"No, she is American. But she is Chinese."

"Chinese! Then she is not a real American. If you marry her, your children will be crossbreeds. What do you think of that?"

"That would be fine. Many people in Hawaii are of mixed races. It is the way Hawaii is."

"What about the girl in Gorgan, the one that came here one day, is she your girlfriend too?"

"She is my friend."

"She would be better for you. You should marry her."

Then they ask Peter, "You are writing a book about Iran?" I interpret for Peter and answer their questions. The conversation devolves in much the same manner as the one earlier, each question prying more into Peter's personal life, until I tell them Peter is uncomfortable answering such questions. Discussion drags on, only to be extinguished by exhaustion. After midnight, they depart. I accompany them downstairs to lock the gate.

"Is that the way it is every night?" Peter asks me.

"Just about. If I'm at home I always have company. That is why no books in my book locker are read. Most of the time, I'm invited out. It's easier that way, as I know I'll be home and by myself at ten o'clock. If I'm not too tired, I light the lantern, keep it very dim so no one will see, and write letters. Iranians with their close-knit family relationships don't understand someone might prefer solitude to being with others all the time. This complete absence of privacy was difficult for me at first. I thought I was going to go crazy, and I went to Gorgan a lot to be with the Peace Corps Volunteers there. I wasn't alone there either, but it was better than having to decipher Farsi when my brain was already fried by three in the afternoon. Gradually I got used to the lack of privacy. I decided I had to accept it. Also, my Farsi improved, and I wasn't as mentally taxed, I guess. Now my time here is ending, and I'm feeling bad about leaving my friends. I want to be with them until that day comes. I figure I'll never be able to return to Iran to see them, and they've become my family. My family in Hawaii is rather poor. Not poor in the sense that we are destitute, but we work hard to live. I wanted to travel and see the world, but I knew that would be unattainable. I even thought of joining the Navy. You know—'Join the Navy and see the world.' Then the Peace Corps came along, and it was more what I wanted to do. I'm not enamored with the military anyway, and I wouldn't make a good soldier. I may have to go into the military when I get home—even go to Vietnam. We have a deferment while we're in the Peace Corps, but when this is over I may be drafted. I'm hoping to go to graduate school, but that may not stop them from getting me." I look at him, a little surprised at how easily I've told him all this. "I'm sorry for all the prying questions, Peter. It's the way it is here. Nothing is off-limits, even to ask strangers. And the rowdy behavior after dinner was really baffling. They have never acted like that before."

"Guys in Iran are so familiar with each other—touching one another, and even holding hands when they walk in the streets. Are they homosexual?"

"Not these guys. Not at all. It's their culture. I had a hard time at first because they stood too close to me when we talked. I would back up until I hit the wall, and they would come closer. It's just their cultural space—

very different from ours. I had to get used to it. I don't know if they know how uncomfortable I was. It still bothers me a bit, but not like it did." I yawn. "Peter, I've had it. This has been an exhausting day. I need to get some sleep. You too. We may have more callers as soon as the sun rises."

MONDAY, JANUARY 10, 1966 At dawn, before the first rays of the sun stream through the transom windows, I am aware Peter is rushing swiftly to the door. Then, as he reaches the bottom of the stairs, I hear a chorus of *salaam allekum* and queries about Mister Tom.

Well, I might as well get up. I slip on my pants and head to the balcony to see Peter, toilet paper in hand, cautiously making the journey through the mud to the little hut in the corner of the courtyard. On his way, my landlord's little girl gravely hands him the *aftabeh* (ewer).

"How bad?" I ask Peter when he returns.

"I spent a considerable part of the night climbing down the ladder and crossing the yard through the sheep and the ankle-deep mud."

"Ah, the runs!" I pull the Peace Corps medical kit from its place on the shelf and delve inside. "Here, take a spoonful of this. It'll fix you. Like pouring concrete into your guts."

We set out to explore Alang, first the Sherkat-e Sargardon, where we pick up an entourage of "Do Nothing" guys. We saunter past the men digging the reservoir, the bathhouse, Reza's house where we had dinner, the mosque, and the school, to the cemetery and Imamzadeh. I explain the age of some of the tombstones, and we look out onto the field where Alang used to be—before Genghis Khan.

We stop at *Aghaye* Aghayan's to get some provisions for lunch. "I usually have eggs and bread for lunch. Is that fine with you, Peter?"

"I don't want much. No eggs for me."

"*Aghaye* Aghayan has some sugar beets I can boil. We can also get some fresh bread and yogurt. The yogurt will be good for you. How does that sound? I have my classes this afternoon. Would you like to come? Then tonight we have dinner at the teachers'. I go there a lot. In fact, they would like me to be with them every evening, but I feel I need to make myself available to everyone in the village."

"I'll pass on going to class. I would like to read some of the books in your stash. Their glossy covers should look used when you leave."

"OH, MY GOSH, THE FLIES! Peter, you didn't pull the screen on the door closed," I exclaim, totally irritated as I step into my room. "There are hundreds! Thousands! Didn't you notice them?"

"Huh?" he mutters without looking up from his book.

"Flies! Flies everywhere!" I pick up a newspaper and, to no avail, attempt to chase them out the open door. More come in. I close the screen, take the newspaper and start swatting, often hitting four or more in one swat. Reluctant to have every surface of my room covered with rotting carcasses, I gather them on the paper and toss them over the balcony. It takes the better part of an hour to rid the room of the flying, crawling creatures and their remains. Meanwhile Peter reads, looking up occasionally with an expression akin to, *God, you're obsessed with hygiene.*

Dinner at Ismael and Yavar's is the familiar casual family meal with their wives and children. Here there is no segregation of the sexes, even when strangers are present. And the women are not wrapped in their *chadors* inside the house.

"Tom, I was shocked when your friend's wife pulled out her breast and nursed the baby in front of us," Peter comments as we return to my room.

"Oh, that often happens when I'm at the home of one of my very close friends and it's only me. I surmise it has to do with whether they consider me a brother. But it's a bit surprising she did it with you there. I feel so natural here in Alang, I don't even give any thought to what's occurring around me any more. I've become 'Tom of Alang,' I guess."

TUESDAY, JANUARY 11, 1966 We set out with Shaban Ali for Deen Tepe and the village of Chahardeh. I had shown Peter the tiny bull I found on the summit, and told him about how the village is using the prehistoric mound as a reservoir for its new water system. "It's a perfect situation for a water tank; it provides the right gravitational flow down to the village. And it's cheaper to have workers hollow out the top of the mound than it is to build a water tower, as we're doing in Alang."

At the top, we observe the enthusiasm of the workers passing buckets of bricks and mortar to the summit, where the interior is being surfaced to form a waterproof tank. "Look," the foreman tells us as he kicks around in the mud and turns up something—half a skull. "Heathen skeletons! We found fifty skeletons here." As we walk, we hear the crunch of bones like dried sticks under our boots.

"As I told you, this site probably dates to four thousand years ago. They also found lots of unglazed pottery here. It's unfortunate no archeologists were called in when they discovered the skeletons and artifacts. But that would have delayed—even stopped—construction, so they lined up the skulls and pots around the edge of the pit and threw stones at them. I came the next day. Except for a few skulls, everything was smashed. I would like to have had at least one piece of the pottery as a memento of Chahardeh. I thought of taking one of the skulls, but was afraid people would think I was very eccentric to have a human skull in my room. I may be 'Tom of Iran,' but I'm not another Hamlet or St. Francis of Assisi, contemplating a skull."

"Tom of Iran" contemplating skulls

PLEASURABLE INTERLUDES

I spent the day yesterday on a bus headed for Tehran. The Peace Corps called me in with one other guy from our group to attend a sociological colloquium on the study of village life and social structure in rural Iran. We are the only ones who have been living in villages, and could be important resources. It's great to be in the big city, but I hate being away from Alang for a whole week. Now, with departure five months away, every day, every hour, and every minute count.

The day's session ends, and I head for Khiaban-e Ferdowsi to recharge my eyes and expunge my overloaded brain with a visual feast in the rug shops. In one shop I inquire about the price of an Ardebil rug. *Not bad,* I deduce. The Ardebils I saw in Tabriz and Gorgan were more expensive, and I can certainly bargain with this guy. But first I must look at other rugs, so he doesn't know which one I'm interested in. *Such a game one has to play in this country. But I've learned it well.*

As he shows me more rugs, a flashy, chauffeured automobile pulls up. Two impeccably dressed men get out. They are German. The shop owner promptly abandons me in my well-worn army jacket and jeans. Just when I want to start bargaining, these guys show up and I'm dropped like a dirty shirt. However, I'm determined to get the Ardebil. I've passed up too many before, and regretted it. So I hang around. The Germans are shown many rugs, including a striking Turkoman. I overhear the owner tell the men it is a Gomishan rug and its price. Gomishan is north of Alang, beyond Bandarshah, about halfway to the Soviet border. It's peculiar that I've never seen these types of rugs in Gorgan.

The Germans are served tea, and I am ignored. They depart without buying. I ask the shop owner more about the Gomishan. We agree on a price. Then I request to see the Ardebil again. I make a deposit on both rugs, and tell the merchant I'll be back on Thursday with the balance. I exit dazed that I bought two rugs, not one. *That will show that arrogant so-and-so he can't judge the man by his clothes and his mode of transportation.*

Feeling cocky I got such a steal on those rugs, I buy a used Bakhtiari rug in another shop. *Wow! Three rugs, just like that!* I'd better not look in any more shops. But looking won't hurt. I don't have any more money to spend.

"Hey. Tom. We're not surprised to see you here." Bill, a PCV from Hamadan, and his Iranian co-worker greet me as I leave the shop in a stupor. Both gregarious guys, they too are in Tehran for the conference.

"I just bought three rugs," I blurt out with angst and euphoria.

"Three rugs! You bought three rugs!" Bill's co-worker says with a concerned smile.

"*Baleh*, three."

"You bought them in this shop?" he asks more seriously.

"One here and two in another shop."

"How much did you pay for them? Did you bargain? You must bargain."

"I know. I bargained." I tell him what I paid and where we started out.

"I want to see the one you got here."

We go in, and the shopkeeper shows us the rug. As we leave, Bill's colleague says, "Tom, you did well. Let's go see the other two."

I take them there, and he agrees they are excellent too. "Tom, you're a real dealer. Let's go to dinner and celebrate."

SATURDAY, JANUARY 22, 1966 "Tom, you are very wise buying rugs in Iran," Hajireza tells me as he maneuvers the mud puddles on the dirt road to Alang. My treasures are securely loaded on the top of his rattletrap vehicle. "They will be very nice to take back to America," Hajireza continues. "But, Tom, don't go; stay in Alang. Become an Alangi; stay with us. Don't go to America. I am so sad you will be leaving us."

"I'm sad too, Hajireza, but I have to go back to America. I came to be with you for two years. Now I must go home. I'm sorry." Others on the old and drafty bus echo our sorrow. The prospect of my departure is becoming too vivid a reality.

At sunset I am greeted with, *"Eid Mobarak*, Tom." It is the beginning of Eid-e Fitr, the Feast of Breaking the Fast, marking the end of Ramadan. Everyone is dressed in his or her best. Tonight and tomorrow we call on each other, and extravagant displays of special foods are presented to guests. Word has spread I have three new Persian rugs, and my friends immediately assemble to see my purchases and argue over whether the shrewd vendors in Tehran took advantage of me or if I truly am a seasoned Iranian shopper.

SUNDAY, JANUARY 23, 1966 "Come to my house for the Eid, Tom," Jafar insists when he sees me. A number of our friends accompany us.

"Tom, I bought a tie, but I don't know how to tie it. Can you do it for me? You can knot it and I will put it on and pull it tight."

I struggle to make the knot on Jafar. "I can't do it on you, Jafar, I need to do it on myself." I put the tie around my neck and attempt to fix it; however, without a mirror, I find it impossible.

"Jafar, do you have a mirror? I can't do it without looking in a mirror."

"Baleh, Tom. The marriage mirror is in the next room. Go in there."

I step out with the tie hanging around my neck and walk along the porch to the next room. It is neat and clean, with a folded pile of bedding and pillows at the back. The marriage mirror is on a low stand placed so the viewer's image is well lit by the open window. I kneel before the mirror and begin to form the knot. The door opens and a girl of about fifteen appears. She goes to the back of the room as if she is looking for something. She turns, and in the mirror I see her standing close behind me—gazing at me, gently smiling—a seductive mixture of innocence and sensuality. I melt, and, as if in a dream, see only her—her beautiful clear white skin, her soft, full lips, the inviting sparkle of her lustrous dark eyes, the perfect arches of her eyebrows that dip and continue across her forehead—all framed in the casual folds of her *chador*. I notice she is fully formed, and ardently imagine her flawless shape. We are locked in the power of our image together in the mirror. My heart begins to race; my mind and body tremble with awkwardness, desire, and fear—fear I am falling into the pleasurable abyss of an enticingly forbidden realm.

Abruptly I remind myself why I'm here. Clumsily I force myself to finish the task I came to do, but my hands quiver involuntarily. I look at her and strain to suppress my heavy sighs, all the while hoping she will not be aware of what she is doing to me and of my boyish, ungallant artlessness. With the tie only half done, I realize I must get away before I explode, completely out of control. I stumble out of the room, along the porch, and into the next room trying to conceal from her and my friends the lust that the bulge below my belt makes evident.

Shaking, I finish the knot and hand the tie to Jafar. He adjusts it and I assure him it looks sharp. But nothing can get my mind off the beguiling encounter. The ache in my pants grows beyond all proportions.

Even in class, my thoughts drift to the girl and the morning's pleasurable interlude. Who is she? Where does she live? I've seen her often. First at the well, when our eyes shyly met and I turned away with my bucket of water, knowing I dare not look at a young woman in the village except for a fleeting glance. Then she's often at the homes of my friends when I'm there—Mulla's, Jafar's, and others. I have never ventured to ask about her. The risk would be too dreadful.

IN THE EVENING, while the children are playing and the women are in the adjacent room preparing dinner, I confess my morning episode to Yavar and Ismael. Both grin wickedly. Yavar asks, "Tom, *parchameh Amrika boland shod?*"

Ismael laughs embarrassingly and says with playful rebuke, "Yavar!"

I shake my head in the Persian mode of indicating I don't understand.

"*Parchameh Amrika rah bolandesh kardi?*" and he moves one of his fingers.

I turn as red as the carpet on the floor as I translate, *Did you raise the American flag?*

"*Areh,*" I warily respond in the colloquial affirmative manner. There is no point in lying. They can probably see I am aroused just telling them about it.

Both collapse in detonating laughter. "*Ofareen* (Bravo), Mister!" Yavar shouts with relish. "You are having a Persian romance. That's the way it's done in Iran."

I blush some more, regretting I even brought up the subject. "Who is the girl?" I ask, and tell them more about her.

"Oh, that is *Haji's* daughter, Shirin. She's so *sheitan*" (devilish). But they both admit she's very pretty. They are delighted over my good fortune.

The women bring in dinner, and Yavar can't wait to spill the news. "Tom is having a Persian romance."

I practically choke on my food as I hear what he divulges in front of the women and children. I feel the flush of my reddening face, and wish I had kept my mouth shut. Of course, the women want to know all about it, and hang on every intimate detail. Mercifully, I am spared any mention of the American flag.

When I say goodnight, Yavar gleefully says, "Sweet dreams," and I detect he is deliberately playing with her name.

In the dark and solitude of my room, as I hopelessly attempt to go to sleep, only one thing is on my mind—Shirin. *At least now I know her name. Shirin—truly sweet, gentle, pleasant—all the name means.* My mind races wildly, fantasizing where we might meet secretly, our passionate kisses, and how far we would go. Then, foreseeing the trouble I'm heading to, my heart nearly stops. I am plunging over an abyss—one wholly wonderful and yet infinitely terrible. But I love the excitement—the risk, the playing with fire.

I keep thinking of delicious secret rendezvous. Then I freeze with the thought of getting caught, and what her family would do to us. Or, what if we don't get caught, but she tells me she is carrying my child? Then what? My whole life would change, if we each even managed to survive. But love conquers all. Everybody in Alang likes me. They would accept it. If they didn't we could run away. But they want me to stay. I could become a Muslim. That would make everyone happy. I could teach in the village or in Kordkuy, and I could paint and put my work in a gallery in Tehran. We would manage.

Tom, you're crazy, I admonish myself. *You're an American. You have an education and plans for a career. You've already applied to graduate schools. Shirin is a village girl—young—perhaps only fifteen, maybe even younger. You're 25. She would be jail bait in America.* My raging hormones curtail any consideration of the consequences in Iran—and my mind wanders delectably to the joy of being with her—finding a hidden place.

> *. . . the place of my dreams—in the shade of the gracefully arching tree beside the murmuring stream where I paint, discreetly concealed by the cotton field around. The brooding mountains beyond keep a silent, protective, watchful eye. A cool, caressing breeze soothes me, yet I am aware that it's not the wind that has aroused the rustle of the cotton plants behind me.*
>
> *My body tingles as I hear gentle footfalls and, with anticipation and resignation, I turn, knowing the inevitable. Hushed, melodious music vainly strives to calm my racing engine. I recline on a divan of soft and sumptuous fabrics—the finest silks from Damascus and Arabia—strewn with the coolness of fresh-scented rose petals. Above, the dome of a pavilion studded with precious gems—pearls, aquamarine, and rubies—stretches the width of the sky. Shirin is beside me, among the 72 houris attending me. Her body is pearlescent—soft and glowing in the ethereal light—her breasts budding, firm, round and perfectly pointed. We lust for each other's lips as the houris anoint us with heady perfumes—Shirin with jasmine tinged with citrus, me with sandalwood and cypress—and lather every inch of our bodies with precious oils. I pull Shirin close to me and, with the gentle guidance of the houris, we become one. I hear and feel her breathy murmurs of ecstasy. I, too, breathe heavily with pleasure . . .*

Suddenly, I emit a low, deep groan, and I am conscious of my entire body convulsing. I continue to throb as I lie there alone, thrilled but ashamed of what just happened—wishing the pangs of my passion would subside, my pajamas and the sheet would dry, and I could go back to sleep. But the thought of one thing and my obsession to find a way to fulfillment keep me awake for hours.

MONDAY, JANUARY 24, 1966 I wake up, stiffly aware I must go down to the corner of the yard. I painfully peel my crusty pajamas from my manliness, dress, slip into my boots, climb down the stairs, and maneuver through the mud to the little room with its burlap-covered door. On my return, Gholam Husayn's wife, who does my laundry, asks, "Mister, can I wash your clothes today?"

"*Baleh,*" I say nervously and think, *Is my guilt apparent? Or did they hear me groan with passion during the night?*

I gather my laundry bag and take it to her, a look of embarrassment on my face.

In my kitchen, I lock the door and take a mini bath in the few inches of water allotted for such endeavors. Then, hanging my shaving mirror on the nail of the balcony post, I lather my face and begin to shave. Next door, little Ismael, Mulla's son, is crying—something not out of the ordinary. But this morning it is not his mother or Mulla caring for him. It is Shirin trying to calm him.

"Ismael, *negah kon* (look), *Amo* Tom. Ismael, *salaam Amo* Tom."

He stops crying and gives me his usual salute.

I salute back and say, "*Salaam,* Ismael. Ismael, *salaam.*"

He is satisfied, smiles, and babbles, "*Amo* Tom," to Shirin.

"*Baleh, Amo* Tom," she tells him as she carries him back and forth along the porch, keeping a covetous eye on me.

My knees turn to rubber, and I'm not paying attention to my shave. My eyes are fixed not on my image in the mirror, but on the object of my craving desire, who is cradling my little Ismael in her arms.

"Ouch!" I am awakened to reality by the bloody gash I've made on my chin. Quickly I wipe it away so Shirin won't notice my immature, unmanly clumsiness.

"*Khodahafez,* Ismael." I wave to him. He and Shirin wave back.

My gosh, this is getting exciting. I fantasize about my dream and the many ways we could be together—where we could meet in secret, how I would get her a message, what our first kiss would be like . . . my mind whirls. Her audacity beguiles me. I never liked being the hunted, but the forbidden thrill of being sought by this young village girl titillates me.

Every vacant moment throughout the day involves another scheme of how and where we might meet. I am obsessed. I'm addicted, and I haven't even tasted the sweet nectar.

At dinner, Yavar and Ismael want the latest news on how I'm doing. "Fine," I answer, knowing their question is loaded with underlying meaning.

"No, did you sleep well last night? You seem very tired," Yavar pries with a smile.

"*Baleh*, I slept OK," but the flush of my face belies my stab at camouflage. I don't tell them of my near sleepless night and my heavenly dream of Shirin and the houris.

"You got a bad cut on your chin. Did you get that shaving this morning?"

"*Baleh*." I'm reluctant to go into details, but, as if I have been given a truth serum, I blurt out, "Shirin was at Mulla's this morning when I was shaving . . ."

The guys begin to smile, and I see they can't wait to hear what's coming next. "Well, I was shaving and little Ismael was crying. You know how he cries all the time. Well . . . I was shaving, and Shirin was at Mulla's, and she was trying to quiet Ismael. She was walking him back and forth on their porch, telling him to salute *Amo* Tom. He always salutes me, and I am the only one who can calm him. Well, as I was saying, I was shaving, and . . . and, I cut myself."

"And why did you cut yourself? You shave everyday, and you never cut yourself."

"Well, I just cut myself . . . cut myself, you know. I wasn't paying attention, I guess."

"And what were you paying attention to?" The guys can hardly restrain their laughter.

"Well . . . little Ismael, of course!" I know my face is red, and I'm beginning to perspire.

"Ismael!" they repeat, and dissolve into laughter.

"*Baleh*. Well . . . I was really looking at Shirin holding Ismael. And my knees were beginning to shake . . . and . . . I cut my chin."

"So it was your knees that caused you to cut your chin," Yavar guffaws.

I look down and blush more, realizing how ridiculous my story sounds.

Ismael and Yavar are amazed at the boldness of the young girl, and delight in the pronounced effect she is having on me. When I head for home, Yavar again wishes me, "Sweet dreams."

Although I am exhausted, it's hours before I fall asleep. Suddenly, I awake from a powerfully erotic dream. The bed is shaking, and my fresh, clean pajamas and sheets are a mess.

TUESDAY, JANUARY 25, 1966 I gather my soap, towel, clean clothes, and my shaving gear, and bicycle to Kordkuy to take a shower and pick up my mail and groceries. There is no way I am going to shave on my balcony today. I don't need to look like a victim of a foreign war because of my weak knees and palpitating heart.

A letter from my professor Mr. Kingrey takes my mind off the more immediate matters of recent days. He advises me on graduate studies. Until a few days ago, the future after Iran, was all that was preoccupying me—I have already sent my portfolio to one grad school. I read his letter several times, and resolve that I must listen to my rational mind. I have always been pretty good at this, but enticing diversions often make decisions very difficult.

Don Croll's momentary visit is another fortunate interlude that takes my mind off carnal desires. He is being assigned to cover another part of the country, and he introduces me to my new field officer.

Then Peter, the Irish writer, shows up again. He wants some of the villagers and me to climb the mountain behind Alang. We persuade him not to do it in the winter when the weather is unpredictable. Instead I propose we tour the villages of Bala Jaddeh and Ghalandarayesh tomorrow. His stopover is well-timed, and I get a good night's rest. Keeping busy is the best medicine for my wonderfully debilitating malady.

BRILLIANCE, STUPIDITY AND REFLECTION

SATURDAY, JANUARY 29, 1966 Sublime and stirring poetry calms the usual raucous banter of the Sherkat-e Sargardon. Reza agilely and melodiously recites the mystical *ghazals* (love songs) of Hafez as his feet rhythmically measure the staccato of his sewing machine and he mindlessly pushes two pieces of cloth beneath the flying needle. Offered in the manner Hafez intended—spoken spontaneously and elegantly amid companions—and though I only partially understand the graceful rhyming couplets, the shimmering cadence of Reza's deeply modulated voice transports us to the dual realms of worldly ecstasy and spiritual awareness. Again I marvel at the brilliance of this man who labors daily over simple fabric in the dusty hovel of a Persian village.

MONDAY, FEBRUARY 7, 1966 *"Befarmayid. Khoosh amadid"* (Welcome), I greet Ismael and Yavar and their families. "Please come in."

For months we had been debating if it would be permissible for them to bring their wives and children to my room for dinner. We concurred that, since I am at their place so much, no one in Alang would object.

I spent most of the day preparing the sauce for Italian spaghetti, kidney beans, salad, and baked apples. When I bring in the plates of spaghetti, stillness settles upon the room. Everyone looks around, aghast. I realize why there is silence and say, "This is spaghetti. It is a favorite food in Italy, and we like it in America too." Though handmade noodles are not uncommon in Iran, the resemblance of the writhing spaghetti to worms causes all to eat with apprehension, but they politely say it is good.

The women are fascinated with the way I have fixed up my tiny room, and inspect each of the rugs. They ask about the people in the photographs over my desk, the antiques, and the painting of Christ I got in Lebanon. When the children grow tired they depart, but not before Yavar mischievously probes, "Now that we have come, when are you going to invite Shirin?" His wife grins widely. I feel a red glow emitting from my face.

FRIDAY, FEBRUARY 11, 1966 "Tom, we came on the new road. No cars can go on it, but there's enough room for my motor scooter. Let's go to my house that way," Sohrab Jahangery, one of the teachers in Alang, suggests.

"All right," I agree.

His friend Sadiq jumps on the back of Sohrab's scooter. I follow them on my bicycle out of Alang to the new highway being built on the north side of the village. It will soon be completed—asphalt from Tehran to Gorgan. It will cut travel time by hours. Now the roadway is under construction, with loose gravel everywhere and a large berm down the center. I struggle to keep up with them even though they are going slowly.

"Hey, Tom, take off your belt. Sadiq can hold one end and you hold the other. We'll pull you to Kordkuy."

"OK. But don't go too fast."

I grab the belt with my left hand, hang on to the handlebar with my right, and we begin to move along. Gradually Sohrab accelerates. My bike wobbles nearly uncontrollably as I'm pulled over the rough gravel. Suddenly the bike and I somersault, and I find myself twisted in the bicycle frame among the coarse stones. The wind has been knocked out of me, my heart is thumping, and my whole body aches.

"Tom, are you OK?" Sohrab and Sadiq inquire as they extract me.

"Baleh." I wouldn't let them know if I weren't. "Americans are tough guys. We may be stupid, but we're tough," I murmur, with difficulty, under my irregular breath.

"Is my bicycle OK?" Somehow I'm more concerned about it than me. I push it along a bit and it seems fine. However, I feel miserable, definitely shaken. My left hand is slightly abraded, but otherwise I'm in one piece. "Well, I don't think we should do that again," I say, getting back on my bike. Still shaking, I cautiously pedal to Kordkuy. I don't let on I'm sore all over.

A few sheep graze in Sohrab's yard.

"Be careful of the ram over there. He is very ornery. Don't go near him. In fact, Tom, stand behind this post on the porch. Don't move!"

Sohrab goes down near the sheep and makes a quick pass at the ram. The ram stands alert. Sohrab makes another pass at him and runs to the house, the ram in pursuit. Sohrab flies inside, pulling the door closed behind him. Bang! The ram's horns smash into the door. The house shakes. I fear the animal will see me, and my already battered body will be the next target.

"Don't move, Tom," Sohrab calls out. "Stand still."

The ram looks at me. I freeze. It turns and ambles down the stairs to its mates.

Back in Alang, my friends notice the scars on my hand and the smashed wristwatch band. "Oh, I fell off my bicycle on my way to Kordkuy." I don't let on about my stupidity.

SUNDAY, FEBRUARY 13, 1966 Mr. Vahdati's visit lends encouragement to Shaban Ali and the village council over the progress of Alang's new water system—not that the whole village has not been excited. In a few days, they'll be setting the water tower upright.

"How are you doing, Tom?" Mr. Vahdati asks. "I don't see much of you any more."

"*Baleh*, I rarely come to Gorgan now. There's always so much to do in Alang, and my time here is running out. In four months, I'll be leaving. I'm feeling bad about that and want to spend the remaining time with my friends. Would you like to come to my room for tea?"

"Thank you, Tom. I'd like to. I haven't seen your place since you first moved in."

Shaban Ali and one of the men from the village council accompany us.

"Tom, your room is very pleasant. I like what you've done with it. You have an outstanding Turkoman rug on the wall above your bed. It is an appropriate souvenir of this area of Iran."

"Tom bought other rugs too," Shaban Ali interjects. "I told him not to waste his money while he was here, to save it and buy rugs to take home. He also bought many books about Iran."

"Good. His bookcase made out of bricks is an excellent idea."

"*Baleh*, I helped him build it."

"*Baleh*, Shaban Ali helps me a lot. I have learned much from him— things I will remember and use the rest of my life. And he's right—at first, I was wasting my money. I was intent on spending my whole paycheck each month, but I couldn't, living in a village. So I would go to the big cities and waste it frivolously. Here there are no cinemas, restaurants, teahouses, or taxis to spend money on, like there are for the volunteers in Gorgan or large cities. Shaban Ali advised me to open an account in the Bank-e Sadrat. Even though Shaban Ali has encouraged me to save, I have it in my mind to spend all my Iranian money in Iran. I made it here, and I feel I need to spend it here. The books and the objects I'm taking back will help me remember Iran, and especially Alang. My friends in Alang are as important to me as my family. They *are* my family now. I've been very fortunate to be in Alang. Thank you for arranging it."

"You're welcome. The people in Alang are exceptional, and I knew they would take care of you well. Shaban Ali and *Agha*, I have heard Tom's Farsi is the best in his Peace Corps group."

"Oh, I'm not the best. I can barely read and write. One of the guys can speak like a Persian and he reads the newspaper and even takes notes in Farsi. He studies hard. I haven't studied at all. There's too much to do here in Alang. I just finished this drawing for the new village council room that will be built on top of the water reservoir."

"It's noteworthy how you are working with Shaban Ali and the people in Alang, and your drawing is first-rate. Did you do the watercolors on the wall too? I recognize the tomb at Roshanabad. Is the other one from Alang?"

"*Baleh*. I hope I can do more before I depart."

"And, Tom, what do you plan to do when you go home?"

"I intend to go to graduate school. I already have my application in at several places. I want to teach art someday. Being in Iran has really focused me. I found I love teaching. It's exhilarating to see the look on my students' faces when they learn something new. And I love the stimulation of working with people, especially when we're working together on a project bigger than any one of us could do alone—like the water systems and bathhouses we're putting in the villages, or even the little schools built in Ghalandarayesh and Ghalayesh."

Shaban Ali smiles in agreement.

"Living in Alang has made me realize what's most important in life. I love being with and working with people. I guess that's why I want to become a teacher. I never wanted to be a teacher before I came here. I have even thought of coming back to Iran to study Persian art, but I would need to know the language much better to do that."

"And what about military service?" Mr. Vahdati inquires.

"I may be called to serve in the military. As you know, America is sending many men to Vietnam. I may have to go, but after being in Iran and experiencing the good in human beings, I don't think I could survive the hate and killing that are taking place. Oh, I mean . . . my body would survive, perhaps, but my mind wouldn't. Not after being here. Not after being in Iran."

MONDAY, FEBRUARY 14, 1966 With shy smiles, Yavar and Ismael pull an egg out of each of their coat pockets.

"Tom, four eggs—can you make dinner for us tonight? Our wives are invited out, and we are left alone."

I laugh. "You guys don't know how to cook! See, you couldn't live without your women. Of course I'll make dinner. It won't be much—not like the good dinners I get at your house. I'll fry some potatoes and make an omelet. I wish you had told me earlier. I would have prepared something nice."

"Oh, our wives will be out tomorrow night again."

I laugh some more. "Well, then we'll have dinner here again. I'll invite others, and we can have a party. I'll buy some lamb tomorrow and make a stew. You liked the baked apples I made? I'll make them too."

At dinner Yavar facetiously asks, "Is your Persian romance blossoming? We need an update. Have you had Shirin up to your room yet?"

Ismael chuckles.

"Up to my room! Fat chance," I say smiling.

"So what's the latest? Tell us."

"Well, I'm trying to put her out of my mind. I'll be going in a few months, and I can't get myself involved and make it even more difficult to leave. I had to force my mind to analyze this rationally. I need to go home and go to graduate school. I have to get on with my career. I can't get involved in something that will get both of us in trouble—serious trouble. It's not reasonable. Besides, thinking about her frustrates me. She *is* very pretty, and I'm intrigued by her audacity—her daring. I wish I could get to know her. She seems to be a very strong-willed young woman—especially for a girl her age, and one from a small village. She's got real courage to be pursuing me."

"*Baleh*, she's so *sheitan* (devilish), but it's good you're having a Persian romance," Yavar interjects delightedly.

"As much as I try to forget her, the problem is, she appears everywhere I go. I keep seeing her, and then I get all fired up again. She persistently teases me with her eyes and smile. It's awful because my mind tells me one thing and then the next minute I get carried away by the excitement I feel inside. There are times I can hardly stand it."

The guys smile. Yavar says, "Tom, you are in love."

"Yes, I'm afraid so. But it's hopeless. It's unattainable love. I wish life were a whole lot easier."

UNEXPECTED VISITORS AND REQUESTS

TUESDAY, FEBRUARY 15, 1966 Anticipation runs high. The structure of the water tower is assembled and is lying on its side across most of the main street. We await the arrival of the crane that will set it upright over the well that gushed forth the day I came.

Midafternoon, the large rig manages to maneuver down the pathway to Alang. Now, as on the day I arrived, everyone is in the central village for possibly the most unsurpassed spectacle in Alang's history. Cables from the crane are attached to the top of the structure. Javad, calling over a bullhorn, advises the onlookers to stand back. The cables tighten, and the gangly top of the tower lifts off the ground. "Stop," Javad yells.

Water tower, Alang

Despite its ominous objections, a sheep that had been tethered in the thickets nearby is brought forward. Two men bind its feet while another quickly slits its throat and someone places a silvered copper bowl below the draining neck. The animal kicks momentarily and then lies motionless. The blood is thrown on the tower while the crowd calls out to Allah and Mohammad to bless the project and Alang.

The crane strains as the tower rises skyward. Under the weight, the back of the tractor lifts off the ground. "Oh, my gosh—it's too heavy," I exclaim.

Guys instantly jump on the cab, and the wheels again meet the earth. Gradually the crane's laboring struggle brings the structure upright. The sound of creaking metal signals the tower's placement on its footings. Another call to Allah and Mohammad thunders through the village.

LITTLE ISMAEL IS CRYING as we assemble at Mulla's for a lamb dinner to celebrate the new water tower. His mother, grandmothers, and aunts unsuccessfully endeavor to calm him as they work together to prepare the dinner. Shirin is there too, often carrying Ismael past the door, furtively glancing in at me, aware that I notice her too, and telling Ismael, "*Amo* Tom is here." In exasperation, Ismael's mother calls to Mulla to care for his son. Mulla steps outside, and I hear him trying to deal with the screaming child.

He tells Ismael, "*Amo* Tom is here. Let's go see *Amo* Tom." Mulla brings his son to the door. "See, Ismael, there's *Amo* Tom. *Amo* Tom is here to see you. Ismael, *salaam Amo* Tom."

Mulla sets him down. I receive the customary salute with a hesitant smile from a tear-stained face. I return the salute and hold out my arms.

"Ismael, *beah* (come). *Beah beh Amo* Tom" (Come to Uncle Tom). I pat my lap, motioning he should come. "*Beah inja* (Come here), Ismael."

Smiling, he walks to me. I grab him, take him in my lap, and talk to him softly. The tears disappear, and a contented calm overcomes him. The men in the room marvel at the transformation and the power I seem to have over the child. Mulla tells them, "Tom is the only one who can stop him from crying. Every morning he waits outside on our porch to see his *Amo* Tom, and if Tom doesn't appear when Ismael expects him, he begins to cry. The week Tom went to Tehran for the conference was awful. Ismael cried almost constantly for his *Amo* Tom."

"Cheh ajib" (Unbelievable). The men look at each other in disbelief. Ismael falls asleep beside me, his head on my lap.

THURSDAY, FEBRUARY 17, 1966   The rosy picture of how good everything is in Alang is beginning to erode. As I become truly "Tom of Alang," I learn the real social and political structure of the village. I am no longer the stranger—the outsider looking in. When I came, I was told the "official story," because they didn't know why I was really here. They knew I sent monthly reports to Tehran. Who knew what I wrote and where the reports might go?

"Tom, everything is not as we told you at first," a friend confides. "We told you that because that is what we wanted you to know. It is what we say—what we tell strangers—that so-and-so is honorable, that he helps the poor, and that the poor love and respect him. But, Tom, he is very rich and he knows how to get richer. Before, another man was very rich—not as rich as the new guy—but he was kind. You have seen the choice old rugs and objects he has in his house, but his house is old and humble. Well, the new guy grew more powerful, and he acquired more and more land, even land from the former rich man. Now that old man strives to keep his family honor. The new rich man has about 325 hectares (800 acres)—and that is just what he owns near Alang. He has land elsewhere as well, and he has factories, homes in Gorgan and Tehran, tractors, a Mercedes-Benz, and a fleet of jeeps. He buys the poor peoples' cotton and wheat when the price is low, and stores it in his warehouses. Then he sells it in the spring when the price is at least double what he paid."

"How much is a hectare of land worth?"

"A man can make about 3000 tomans ($400) a year on a hectare of land. He can live quite comfortably on that if he has no wife and children. If he has a family, it might be a little tough, but they can manage. So you see how rich this man is. This time of the year he pays his workers three tomans (about 40¢) a day. However, if the weather is bad, his workers will have no work. When the days get longer and there is more work, he will pay them five tomans, and at peak season—about two weeks during the harvest—seven tomans (90¢) a day."

He continues, "My father has about 32 hectares, so we do quite well, especially since our family spends only about 7500 tomans ($1000) a year on food, clothing, and other things. I must help my father with the bookkeeping, but contrary to you in America, I can never get a job. It would be an insult to my father. That's why we have the Sherkat-e Sargardon. It is indeed the 'Do Nothing Company.' The guys that gather there have fathers who are rich, but not so rich the sons don't have to live in the village. The sons of the very rich live in nice houses in Tehran, have servants, drive expensive cars, and go to exciting places."

"What about the poor? Will they ever have a chance for a better life?"

"Probably not. They just become poorer. If they have a little land, often they sell parts of it to survive . . . and the rich man buys it. The rich get richer and the poor get poorer."

"But isn't the Shah trying to stop this? Isn't that what his White Revolution is all about?"

"*Baleh*, it did help. He has helped millions of poor farmers. The Shah gave much of his own land to the poor people, but he also took land away from the rich to give to the impoverished. The rich, of course, don't like this, so they hate the Shah. Worst of all is the corruption. People under the Shah have turned the revolution into personal profit. They have found many devious ways of becoming rich."

FRIDAY, FEBRUARY 18, 1966 Fridays invariably begin as quiet days in Alang. Men go to the mosque; I cherish the solitude, normally writing letters. Today is unusually warm, so I have kept the windows and door closed to prevent the cool night air from escaping. Voices below alert me guests are arriving. I hear *Haji* Noorallah's little daughter say, "Mister is upstairs."

Six young men are at the door. Two of them are familiar from my excursions to Kordkuy—some of the young guys I do my best to avoid.

"*Befarmayid.*" I welcome them in, quickly closing the door behind them to prevent the late morning heat from entering. I learn their first names and then go to the kitchen to prepare tea and snacks. *Well, there goes my undisturbed morning by myself,* I mumble. *So much for writing letters home.*

As I enter with the tray of refreshments, I am aware they have been assessing the contents of the room.

"Mister, you have a very fine Turkoman rug. Is it part silk?"

"*Baleh.* I got it in Gonbad-e Kavus."

"I'm sure it was very expensive."

"No, not too much. My friends in Alang say I did well on it."

"Mister, it is very warm in here. Don't you open the windows?"

"It *was* very cool in here before you came. I was trying to keep the heat out by not opening the windows."

We sit in the closed-up room, drinking hot tea, me answering their questions. I am hoping the heat will encourage them to leave. Eventually, not even I can stand it. I open the windows and door. When I turn around, one of the guys stands up and shows me his fist arrayed with brass knuckles. Although I had never seen knuckles that close, instinctively I know what they are. *OK, Tom, act cool,* I tell myself.

"Do you know what these are?" he asks me.

"Of course, but they are rarely used in America—only in the movies."

There is silence.

"Why do you have them?"

There is no reply.

"Maybe you should put them away and we talk awhile. I'm interested in knowing about you guys and you might want to know about America."

Our conversation continues, strained as it is, while I politely offer more tea and cookies. As noon approaches, I look at my watch and lie, "I'm sorry. I've been invited to lunch today and must get going. Thank you for coming all the way from Kordkuy for a visit. I'll go downstairs with you now."

I take them to the street, bid them *khodahafez,* and walk to Mulla's house.

"Tom, don't ever invite those guys into your room again," Mulla's wife Noor Jahan tells me as I enter their courtyard. "Never." Her face is pained.

Then Mulla's mothers* and *Haji* Torfeh join in emphasizing how bad those guys from Kordkuy are. "Don't ever let them in your house again.

---

* See Wednesday, October 28, 1964 for an explanation of Mulla's mothers.

Fahmidi" (Did you understand)? All are shouting at the top of their lungs.

"*Baleh,*" I answer sheepishly.

"We have been worried about you all morning and have kept a watchful eye on you from our porch. Those boys are bad," Mulla's mother says.

"I was worried too, and kept my eyes on Mister's door," *Haji* Noorallah's wife, my landlady, calls over the wall from her porch. She had heard the commotion next door. "But *Haji Agha* and Ghorbon weren't home."

Oh, my gosh. I have everybody worked up in Alang. I sigh resignedly.

"Where's Mulla?"

"Mulla went to Gorgan with Jafar to get some medicine for Jafar's mother. They will be back soon. If Mulla had been here, I would have sent him over, but we were alone."

I tell them about the brass knuckles.

"See, those Kordkuy boys are bad, not like the boys from Alang," *Haji* Torfeh chimes in.

"This is not good," Noor Jahan says. "They have seen what you have in your room. It's not good."

"But I didn't know who they were when they came to the door," I say apologetically.

"*Baleh*, but don't let anybody in whom you don't know. Anyone from Alang is OK, but no one else. Do you understand?"

"*Baleh.*"

"*Salaam*, Tom. What's going on?" It is Mulla. His wife, mothers, *Haji* Torfeh, and my landlady relate what transpired.

"Mulla, if you had been here, I would have sent you over to be with Tom," his wife tells him.

"Mulla, I am sorry. I didn't know who they were, and I was being polite, like Iranians."

"Tom, the problem is you have become too Iranian, but it doesn't sink in," he looks at me in resignation over my hopelessness. "Tom, come. Stay for lunch. We need to talk."

"Mulla, actually I got rid of them by saying I was invited to a friend's house for lunch," I tell him with snickering embarrassment.

"So, if I sent you home, I would make you a liar. Come."

SATURDAY, FEBRUARY 19, 1966 "Tom, I saw Mister Jim in Gorgan and I didn't recognize him," Ismael Mirsalehi tells me. "He has grown a beard. I asked him why; he told me his sister is getting married, and it is the custom in America to grow a beard when your sister gets married. That's very strange. I never heard of it."

"Oh." I look at him, puzzled. Then I realize my opportunity. "Oh, *baleh*. You never heard of that? It is bad luck if her brothers don't grow a beard. We do it all the time in America." He spots my amused expression. "It's to make sure she will have a boy baby," I continue, but my face betrays my attempted cover-up.

"Tom, you are very *sheitan* (devilish)." As I try to stop him, he quickly grabs and yanks out a wad of chest hair poking from the top of my shirt.

"Me? *Sheitan*?" My eyes glisten. "Not me," I insist innocently. "Mister Jim maybe, but not me."

"*Na*. Both of you are *sheitan*," Yavar agrees.

"Mister Jim was pulling your leg," I tell Ismael.

"Pulling my leg? What's 'pulling my leg'?"

"It's when someone pulls one of your legs and makes it longer so you walk around like this." I demonstrate, trying hard not to laugh. However, the guys are wise to my shenanigans. I know I'm in trouble now.

FRIDAY, FEBRUARY 25, 1966 Footsteps on the balcony indicate the arrival of visitors on this balmy late-winter afternoon.

"Tom, we haven't seen you in over five weeks, so Kathy and I thought we would check if you are still alive. Are you doing OK?" Jim asks.

"Hey, thanks for coming. I heard you grew a beard, Jim. Looks good. What a trick to play on my friends, making up American customs to fool them." His sparkling eyes reveal his delight. "I've been thinking about you all in Gorgan, but never get the chance to come in. There's too much happening here. Well, really, it's more like I'm already missing Alang and don't want to leave. There's not much time left for us, is there, Kathy?"

"Yeah, less than four months. It seems unreal."

News of the appearance of fun Mister Jim, and particularly the enticing Miss Kathy, spreads through the quiet village. Instantly my room is filled with men, including Jafar, who has zealously been awaiting his introduction. He is on his best and usual charming behavior—definitely prospecting, and here to impress.

Jim suggests, "Let's go to Gonbad-e Kavus next Friday to see Barkley and the new volunteers there. Kathy and I also want to go out on the Jurjan plain to see the city Genghis Khan destroyed."

"Yeah, I'll go. I'd like to explore the plain again and pick up more glass fragments. I may make a window out of them someday."

"Hey, I'll take you," Jafar enthusiastically volunteers. "Mulla will come too. We can go in my jeep. It will be fun."

FRIDAY, MARCH 4, 1966   We spend a long and enjoyable day in Gonbad, first briefly with Barkley and the new volunteers, and then poking around the vast plain on which the city met its demise when Genghis and his men plundered through. I fill my Pan Am bag with fragments of glass, and when a little boy from a nearby village asks if I want to buy a small broken glass bowl and shards, I inquire about the cost of the bowl. "Two and a half tomans," he answers.

That's only pennies, I think, *but there are thousands of broken pieces all around.* Nevertheless, the boy is so cute and shy, and the bowl is more complete than anything I've found.

"I'll give you two tomans (20¢) for it." He hands me the bowl with the fragments in it. I only wanted the bowl, not what was inside. *Oh, well,* I tell myself, *he'll scramble through the ruins another day and find more. Besides, he's satisfied, and two tomans is a lot of money for him; as much as his father makes in a whole day this time of year.*

Jafar looks at me with incredulity, as if to say, *You'll buy junk like this when it's lying everywhere!*

I inspect some of the mud-covered fragments in the broken bowl, and discover two unglazed terra cotta animal heads, a bone chess piece, and two tiny, fragile glass bottles. I give the bottles to Kathy.

Jafar picks out the chess piece, inspects it, and crushes it between his fingers. I am devastated that, having survived this long, it could be destroyed with so little thought.

TUESDAY, MARCH 8, 1966 "Tom, I need to talk to you. I need your help." Jafar has arrived at my room alone.

"*Baleh,*" I respond apprehensively. I'm never quite sure what Jafar has up his sleeve.

"Well, Tom, I want you to do me a favor."

"*Baleh.*"

"I want to take Miss Kathy for my wife, and I want you to go *khastegari* (be a go-between) for me."

"But . . . Jafar, you are already married . . . and you have two children." I try to say it calmly, without expression—without betraying the concealed shock I am afraid my face registers. The idea is too preposterous for me even to consider bursting out in laughter.

"*Baleh,* but Miss Kathy would be my play wife—my just-for-fun wife. We would do things and travel together. Will you ask her for me? Please."

"Jafar, I can't do that. That is not what American women do. Miss Kathy wouldn't do that."

"How do you know? I have enough money. She will like it. She won't have to work. My other wife will do all the work. We will just have fun together. Tom, you must do it for me. Please ask her."

"Jafar, I can't ask her. She would be insulted, because American women . . . well . . . they wouldn't do it. You already have a wife. We cannot have two wives or two husbands in America. She would not say yes."

"You could at least ask her. She might like it."

"Jafar, you don't understand. It's not proper in America."

"Maybe she will not want to go back to America if she has me."

I do all I can to stifle a laugh. Such confidence. Such arrogance. *It's pathetic when a guy knows he's good-looking and thinks he's a man of the world,* I muse.

"Jafar, I'm sorry, I can't ask her. It's not right. She would be very upset."

"Tom, we are friends and you won't help me? You won't ask her?"

"Jafar, yes, we are friends, but I can't do this. I'm sorry."

FRIDAY, MARCH 11, 1966 I hear the shuffle of feet on the planks of the balcony leading to my room. From the window, I see *Haji* Torfeh.

"Salaam, Haji, hale shoma khoobeh" (How are you)?

"Alhamdulillah. Hale shoma khoobeh, Aghaye Mister Tom?*"*

"Alhamdulillah. Khoobam. Moteshakeram."

Haji holds a small photograph. She hands it to me and explains, "I want you to have this as a remembrance of me. It is my passport photo. I am going to Mecca in a few days. But I will not return. I am going to join my husband who died on our pilgrimage to Mecca many years ago."

I sigh trying hard to suppress my emotions.

"Oh, *Haji*, thank you. I will always treasure it. I will never forget you. But you must return. You have to come back to Alang."

"No. I am an old woman. The trip to Mecca is very difficult. I will not come back to Alang. I have come to say goodbye to you."

My eyes water as I look at her kind, wrinkled face. What she tells me I cannot accept.

"No, *Haji*, you must come back."

"Mister, can I have a photo of you? I want a remembrance of you to take to Mecca."

I step into my room, shaking with emotion, and return with my passport photo. I hand it to her. She takes it in her hand, looks at it, and then kisses it. *"Moteshakeram. Khodahafez, Aghaye* Mister." She turns and shuffles to the ladder-like stairs. I watch with tears streaming down my face as her head disappears below the wooden deck.

SUNDAY, MARCH 13, 1966 Though we were up late celebrating at farewell dinners, everyone is awake early, gathering near the new water tower in the center of the village. A chartered bus is being loaded with baggage, and all are bidding each other goodbye. Eighteen people from Alang are departing today for Tehran and, in a few days, will be getting on a flight to Mecca. With a heavy heart I watch as *Haji* Torfeh boards the bus, agonizing over what she told me. Knowing I am going to forbidden Mecca, if only vicariously with *Haji*, calms me.

REASONS TO CELEBRATE

SUNDAY, MARCH 20, 1966—NEW YEAR'S EVE Although the Peace Corps gave us several days off for Iranian New Year, I cannot miss the excitement of celebrating this traditional holiday in Alang. Today is especially momentous—the new asphalt highway opened all the way to Gorgan, and Alang's water system is inaugurated. We now have running water to central locations throughout the village. The next step is to get it to individual courtyards. Amid the enthusiasm, I reflect on what has transpired since I arrived in Alang on that auspicious day when they struck water a year and a half ago. Maybe, just maybe, I *was* a "good omen." Still, doubt plagues me about the value of any contributions I might have made as a Peace Corps Volunteer to the advancements in any of the villages around here. They did it on their own. Inwardly I am proud of that, but really, why am I here?

Nevertheless, I would never give up any of this. It will forever be the defining moment of my life.

MONDAY, MARCH 21, 1966 "Tom, *Eid Mobarak*—Happy New Year."

It's Shaban Ali calling from below. I go to the edge of the balcony, shade my eyes as light breaks the horizon, and return the greeting.

"Tom, hurry and get ready. We must go see our friends."

Today, and for nearly two weeks, Iranians sport new clothes and visit family and acquaintances. It is a festive time in Iran of celebrating spring and the New Year. I prepared for several days, buying a hundred oranges, cookies and candy, and having a dishful of coins ready to give to children.

We make the annual joyful pilgrimage from house to house. Our hands are sprinkled with rose water that we gently rub on our face and arms. We enjoy each other's company around a cloth spread with the *haft seen* (Seven S's) of food and objects with names that begin with the Persian letter *seen* that promise good fortune in the New Year. The objects vary among families; however, everywhere there is a plate of *sabzeh* (sprouting wheat or barley) that symbolizes rebirth. We are offered a small dish of *samanu* (a sweet pudding made from ground germinated wheat) sprinkled with green, slivered pistachios. It assures wealth. There is also the *seeb* (apple) that represents beauty and health and a dish of *seer* (garlic) signifying medicine. Of course, there is the container of *sekkeh* (coins) for the children. Often there are dishes of ground *sumagh* (the popular deep-red Persian spice) signifying the color of sunrise and birth, and *serkeh* (vinegar) symbolizing old age and patience. Some homes have a vase of *sombol* (hyacinths) or *senjed* (dried wild olives) representing love, along with painted eggs, a symbol of fertility. Occasionally a goldfish, a sign of life, swims in a clear bowl. In the center, beside the Koran, is a marriage mirror and lit candles. Wherever I see it, I think of Shirin—our eternal vision of each other seemingly etched in the glass.

Shirin is still tormenting me, making my days—and nights—an emotional roller coaster of unrestricted fantasy and terrifying imagined reality, of wanting to find a way to stay in Iran—any way—and rationalizing that I must go home and get on with my life and career. She tantalizingly appears at many of my friends' and I am distracted to the point where I don't hear them talking to me. They repeat their words and seem to wake me as if I were in a dream.

Friends come to my place, but they eat little. I am disappointed. They scold me when I give a few coins to their children and press an orange in their hands. Later, in the street, I overhear an old man tell someone, "Don't eat up all of Mister's things. He will go out and buy more. He should save his money."

THURSDAY, MARCH 24, 1966 With my bag and some of the oranges, I head for Gorgan on Hajireza's decrepit vehicle.

"Tom, the new road is first-rate—tarmac, the whole way to Gorgan. No more of that muddy pot-holed mess for *Mashini Mashti Mamdali.*" Hajireza smiles with his gleaming golden grin and I concur wholeheartedly. "Now we can be in Gorgan in 15 or 20 minutes."

My knock on the door of the Mirsalehi courtyard elicits excited greetings. I chat with Ismael's parents and brother as the family gathers their things. We are going to the Khanpoors at Meti Kola.

A YOUNG VILLAGE GIRL DISEMBARKS with us when the bus stops at Meti Kola. Ismael tells her, "Carry Mister's bag."

"No, I can carry my own bag," I insist to no avail.

The girl hoists the heavy bag on her head. To have a young woman carry my luggage is disconcerting. In America, if I were any kind of gentleman, I would be carrying *her* luggage.

"Take it to *Aghaye* Khanpoor's house," Ismael commands, "and tell them the Mirsalehis and Mister are coming."

The Khanpoors are at the gateway door as we approach. *"Eid Mobarak. Khoosh amadid"* (We are happy you came). In animated conversation, we saunter to the house, where Yavar's smiling parents await us.

The next three days are joyous reunions, strolls in the village and the countryside where the trees are awakening from their short winter slumber, volleyball, romping with the children, and playing bingo in the evenings.

Ismael Mirsalehi, Tom Klobe, Yavar Khanpoor in Meti Kola

SATURDAY, APRIL 2, 1966 "Shaban Ali, tell me about Sizdah Bedar."

We have found a spot near the edge of the fields to have a picnic. Shaban Ali's wife tries to calm fussy baby Sayeed. The other children enjoy the grand outdoors, away from the confines of their muddy courtyard.

"It is the thirteenth day of the new year. Nou Ruz lasts for twelve days. On the thirteenth day, it is bad luck if you don't go outside for a picnic with your family. So we go to our gardens or the forest to celebrate. Today we

Shaban Ali Rahemi with his wife and family and brother

throw away the *sabzeh* from the *haft seen*. It collected all the bad luck, so we throw it into running water to banish the *divs* (demons) for the rest of the year. Young girls who wish to be married before next year's Sizdah Bedar tie the leaves together before it is thrown away."

My mind strays, imagining Shirin has tied the leaves of the budding wheat together—and that if I stayed in Iran, we would be celebrating Sizdah Bedar together next year.

THURSDAY, APRIL 7, 1966 The realization I am leaving Alang is foremost in my mind, and the minds of the entire village. With my impending departure, we all recognize I have truly become part of their families. My friends' wives and mothers talk with me, and I am included in family events. Tonight I wait with nervous anticipation for the visit of Reza and Javad with their mother, wives, and families. Reza and Javad have not come to my place since the terrible fight with my landlord a year ago. Other than the teachers' wives, no village women have ever been in my room. We have carefully planned this to include their mother. Neither my landlord nor anyone in the village, we think, could object if a respected old lady came with her sons and their families to my house—to the home of a single man.

My little room is crowded with so many people. The women are intrigued by what I have done with it and by the rugs and artifacts I have collected. With my limited supply of teacups and glasses, we take turns drinking tea. My stash of cookies and fruit is sufficient, even for Rozy and Abdullah and their brothers and sisters.

FRIDAY, APRIL 8, 1966 *"Aghaye* Mister," my landlord soberly stops me.

"Baleh." I fear for the worst—that he will reprimand me for having Reza and Javad and their families over.

"Mister Tom, my wife and I think you should bring your rugs to our house while you go on vacation. We don't want anything to happen to them while you are gone, especially now that you are so near the end of your stay with us. Of course, we always keep a watchful eye on your place, but many people know you have valuable rugs now. The people in Alang are no problem. We don't worry about them. But those hoodlums from Kordkuy know what you have. That is not good."

"OK, *Haji.* I will bring them over sometime today. *Moteshakeram."*

"You call my son Ghorbon. He will help you."

SATURDAY, APRIL 9, 1966 "Tom, be sure you are back before the Shah comes to Gorgan. It will be a memorable day. We want you to meet the Shah. He might come to Alang. His agenda includes a visit to a village near Gorgan and the Rahemis have extended an invitation to him."

"Baleh, I'll be back by then," I assure my friends. "I wouldn't miss it."

MEMORIES AND THINGS

MONDAY, APRIL 11, 1966 "Hey, guys, come on in." Bill greets us at the door to his compound in Hamadan. "Hi, Jim, how are you doing? Glad you came. And," he looks at me with a smile, "how's the rug dealer? Have you bought any more lately? My co-worker can't wait to see you. He wants to take you to the bazaar."

"How's he doing? No, I haven't bought any more rugs. What do you two think—that's all I came to Iran for?"

"Just checking. Just checking. Make yourselves right at home. This place isn't much, but you're welcome to hang out here. Hamadan is a pleasant city this time of year—but not in winter. It was bitter cold. It's one of the coldest places in Iran—definitely not the kind of place for a thin-blooded guy from Hawaii." Bill always has a way of lightly rubbing it in, with a sparkle in his eyes and a broad, mischievous smile.

"Hey, can I get you guys an *abe jou* (beer)? It's my basic nourishment."

"Yeah, I could go for one," Jim accepts. "I need to wet my whistle."

"Not for me. I don't like the stuff—at least since I grew up. My parents say I liked beer as a little kid. Guess I thought I was being big. But once I could drink it legally I had no interest in it. It's strange. It's always the forbidden fruit that entices me. I'm satisfied with some tea. *Kam rang*, please. No sugar."

"*Kam rang?*"

"*Baleh, kam rang*, weak. It means little color."

"There's not a lot to see here in Hamadan, even though it's the oldest continually inhabited city in Iran. You must see the Sang-e Shir (Stone

Lion) on the edge of town, overlooking the city—a colossal lump of rock that looks vaguely like a lion. Oh, possibly it was a lion in its day. It's at least 2400 years old, and may have been one of the lions guarding the seven gates of the ancient city. Hamadan was originally Ecbatana from the Bible. Well, don't be surprised if you see a few young girls there rubbing the lion's face with grease and kissing its nose. Supposedly that will guarantee they find a husband soon. So, unless they're really attractive, you should maybe run the other way when they start rubbing." He laughs. "And if they're really hot, you can tell them about me. I live here, you know."

"Does rubbing the lion work for guys as well?" I inquire, refraining from hinting why I'm asking.

"I don't know. Remember you have to kiss the nose too."

"Oh, well, I'm not Irish—not into kissing stones."

"Also, you shouldn't miss the tomb of Esther and Mordecai off the central Meydan-e Shah (Shah's Square). You know, Esther from the Old Testament? Well, reputedly it's her tomb, but the building dates from the Middle Ages. Nevertheless, whether it's Esther and Mordecai who are there or someone else, it's likely the tomb of Jews. Hamadan was a prominent Jewish center in Iran."

"We saw the *meydan* with the statue of the Shah on horseback when we came into town. It's spectacular—with the colonial style buildings and their cupolas on every corner and the snow-capped mountain beyond."

"Yeah, that's Mt. Alvand—nearly 12,000 feet high. The snows seem to blow constantly on its summit—like a giant, silent, preening bird."

TUESDAY, APRIL 12, 1966 Jim and I take Bill's suggestions of sights to see in Hamadan. First, the Sang-e Shir; however, we're disappointed not to find any young Hamadani girls kissing the lion's nose and looking for eligible young bachelors. Instead, we have to settle for a grand view of the city framed by the majestic Zagros Mountains.

The city is grandly laid out, with six wide boulevards radiating from the central square. The dismal tomb of Esther and Mordecai momentarily holds our attention. Briefly we pass through the bazaar on our way to meet Bill and his co-worker for lunch.

"Tom, it's been a while since Bill and I saw you in Tehran. He tells me you haven't gotten any more rugs. You'll be getting out of practice," his co-worker chides with a grin.

"*Baleh*—but we just walked through the bazaar, and I want to go back. Who knows what I'll uncover?"

"If you find something, I'll help you bargain. I know most of the rug merchants in Hamadan."

In the afternoon I wander through the bazaar on my own—my favorite way of exploring—rummaging in junk shops and seeing what rug dealers have available. In one shop I spot an old brass *manqal* (brazier).

"How much is this?"

The shopkeeper responds, "One hundred tomans" (about $13.00).

"It's very heavy, and I'm traveling by bus. If you reduce the price, I might consider it."

"OK, 90 tomans."

"That's only ten tomans less. Not enough. I was thinking 50 tomans."

"*Na*, give me 85 tomans and you can have it."

"*Na*, it's still too much. OK, I'll come up to 65 tomans. How about it?"

"*Na*. Can't do it."

"*Kheili khoob* (Very well). *Khodahafez, Agha. Moteshakeram.*"

In another tiny nook, an old man sells used housewares—much of it plastic, copper pots, shards of old ceramics, and corroded pieces of bronze. Some look like the Luristan bronzes in the Musée Iran Bastan in Tehran.

"Are these old?" I ask.

"*Baleh*. Very old," the tired-eyed old man in rags responds. "They've been under the ground for many years."

I look through the objects, many of which are broken, and select two bronze arrowheads, four pins, and an armband. "How much do you want for these?"

"Twenty tomans" ($2.60).

"Oh, that's a bit much. I thought you would tell me a better price than that. How about it? Couldn't you do better?"

"*Kheili khoob*, 15 tomans."

"Oh, I was hoping it would be less."

"What do you want to pay?"

"Seven tomans. Maybe I would give you eight."

"OK, *Agha*, give me 12 tomans and they are yours."

"*Na*, I'll give you nine. Will you take nine tomans?"

"*Na*, they have value. They are old. I need 11 tomans for them."

"They're still too expensive. *Moteshakeram, Agha. Khodahafez.*" I turn to leave.

"*Agha, beah* (come), *dah toman.* Give me ten tomans."

I give him the ten tomans and he wraps the pieces in scraps of old newspaper. He hands them to me with a gentle smile and gestures with his hand, "Is there anything else here you would like?"

"*Moteshakeram, Agha.* I don't think so." But I look around some more. "*Agha*, how much is this bowl?"

"That is very old—very important. For you, *Agha*, it is 75 tomans."

"Seventy-five! That's a lot of money. And it's broken. Seventy-five tomans is very much for a broken bowl."

"*Agha*, it is old. Hundreds of years old. Seventy-five tomans is very little for something that old."

"But it's broken. *Agha*, I bought the other things from you. Certainly you can give me a better deal on this broken bowl."

"Seventy tomans."

"Thank you, but it's still too much. Won't you come down for me?"

"OK, 65 tomans for you," he says with a smile.

"Oh, too bad. I don't have a lot of money. How about 45 tomans?"

"Oh, no, 45 is too little! It's an exceptional bowl."

"But, *Agha*, it is broken. See."

"If you were that old you would be broken too."

"*Baleh*," I say grinning. "I am still young. And I like your bowl. I would like to look at it all my life and think of you. Won't you go lower?"

"OK, 60 tomans."

"*Agha*, you are hurting me very much. How about if I give you 55 tomans ($7.30)? Please." I show him the money as enticement.

"*Kheili khoob*, for you, *Agha*, 55 tomans." He wraps it in newspaper. "Come back again."

"*Enshahallah* (If God is willing). *Khodahafez, Agha. Moteshakeram.*"

My treasures stashed in my Pan Am bag, on the way out of the bazaar I spy a beautiful little rug on the gleaming white wall of a shop. It is alone, darkly radiant and magnificent in the bright solitary lamp of the shop. I stop, transfixed by it.

"*Salaam, Agha,*" I say as I step inside.

"*Salaam, hale shoma khoobeh?*"

"*Alhamdulillah, hale shoma khoobeh?*" I say perfunctorily, amazed by the vision before me. "How much is the rug?"

"One hundred tomans."

"It's very nice—very nice—but it is not very big. Would you take less?"

"*Na.* It's first-rate, worth even more."

That is not what I wanted to hear, and I struggle to find something wrong with it to use as a bargaining point. "Fifty tomans," I offer sheepishly, hoping he won't be insulted.

"Never! It is worth much more. But I'll consider 95 tomans."

"Ninety-five! That's hardly any less! You can do better than that."

"You make another offer. How much will you give me?"

"I told you 50 tomans. The rug is very little and it's very dark."

"*Kheili khoob*, the lowest I can go is 90 tomans."

"Sorry, *Agha*, that is too much for me. *Khodahafez.*"

As I walk away he calls out, "80 tomans."

It is nearly dark when I reach Bill's house. He and Jim have already had a couple of *abe jou*.

"Hey, Tom, I'd offer you an *abe jou*, but I know you don't care for it. I'll put on some water for tea. Where are the rugs you bought?"

"I didn't get any. But I saw a little one I really liked—about so by so." I indicate 16" × 20". "We couldn't agree on a price."

"That little! Well, my co-worker is coming later. He wants to help you."

"Oh, I don't think we can agree on a price. There is too much of a separation between us. But I got some other treasures." I pull the bowl and bronzes out of my bag.

"How much did you pay for this broken bowl?" Bill asks.

"Fifty-five tomans."

"Fifty-five tomans! Tom, you're crazy—totally out of your mind! I don't believe it—just crazy! Fifty-five tomans for a broken bowl! All I can think of is all the *abe jou* I could get for that!"

"Yes, Bill, and all you'd do is piss it out and have a monstrous hangover the next day. I'll enjoy the bowl the rest of my life."

He shakes his head and mumbles, "I don't even want to know how much you paid for the bronzes."

Bill's co-worker arrives. "*Salaam.* Hey, Tom, did you see any rugs?"

"Rugs!" Bill exclaims. "Rugs! Yeah, he saw a little one he likes. Come look at the junk he got—that he spent good money on—a broken bowl and some old corroded bronzes. He's out of his mind."

"Bill, I may be different from other volunteers. Maybe it's because I'm an artist and I look at and feel things in a different way. The visual has always been important to me—a striking sunset, a beautiful face—or even one weathered by the crags of time, like the man I bought this broken bowl and crusty bronzes from. I'll be leaving Iran soon. You just came. I'm feeling very bad about leaving Iran and its people. I've come to love this place as much as anything I have ever loved. And I feel sad I'll never be able to return—to see my friends, to see this place again. My family has always struggled to live, and I wanted to see the world, but I knew I would never be able to do it. That's part of the reason I joined the Peace Corps. Well . . . now I'm halfway around the world and I love this place as if it were my own home, but when I leave, that will be it. I'll have a few photographs and some objects to help me remember. Oh, I'll have my memories, but I fear they'll fade like an old drawing . . . slowly, time will erase even them. Only the photographs and these things will serve as the bridge to the other side of the world . . . the bridge I'll never be able to cross again. So whatever I take back from Iran will endow my home and life in America with some of the symbolic and even physical attributes of Iran. For me, these objects will create a mental and physical association with Alang—with Iran and its people. I must never forget. Iran will forever be part of my life."

There is prolonged silence. Then Bill's co-worker ventures, "Tom, that little rug Bill says you saw—how much was it?"

"He wanted 100 tomans. He came down to 80. I offered him 50."

"How big is the rug?"

"About so by so."

"Very small—even 50 tomans is too much for a rug that size. He thinks because you're a foreigner you have lots of money and you'll pay anything. Tomorrow evening we'll go and I'll tell him to sell it to you for less than 50 tomans."

WEDNESDAY, APRIL 13, 1966   The picturesque, ramshackle Kermanshah bazaar hangs atop a cliff in the central city. Shy Kurds, with their stringy headdresses, and sometimes a few white pigeons, guard tiny shops no bigger than closets. One sells bells, locks, and chains—another handmade tools. The sound of metal hitting metal rings in the air. Two men alternately heave heavy sledgehammers onto a glowing strip of iron, while another, with long pincers, holds it on the anvil. Elsewhere, sheep carcasses hang from hooks. The butcher hacks a hunk of flesh off one, weighs it, slaps it in some old newspaper, and gives it to the *chador*-covered purchaser. She hands him a few tomans, and he returns a bit of change. She ambles on, stopping to pick out some shriveled potatoes from a huge mound piled beside a squatting vendor. Farther along, Jim and I fortify ourselves with fresh kebab on *sangak*, the delicious flat bread baked on stones. Down a short, dark alley, daylight unveils a worn cobblestone courtyard. To the side, an emaciated old gray horse patiently waits for duty and two men converse on a bright bed of flowers as they repair a colorful Persian carpet, the wall of the building behind them patched together with tar paper and reed mats.

Our eyes smart in the bright overcast light when, reluctantly, we leave the labyrinth of dark, intriguing passageways. We hail a black-and-white taxi, but before we get in, I haggle over the price to Taq-e Bustan at the northern edge of town.

At the base of a cliff, stupendous Sassanian reliefs face a reflecting pool fed by a spring. Two arched niches cut into the mountain preserve some of the finest Sassanian art. Although I have seen so much in my nearly two years in the Peace Corps, my knees quiver when I realize I'm standing before carvings that commemorate celebrated men and events in history.

Jim and I doze on the two-and-a-half-hour bus ride to Hamadan. I had a miserable night thinking about the rug and the *manqal*. To preserve my health, I conclude, I'd better get the *manqal*, even if it is heavy to lug around. And Bill's co-worker wants to help me with the rug. He's there when we reach Bill's.

"Tom, let's go to the bazaar now. We need to get that rug."

"I saw a *manqal* I would like to buy too."

"Kheili khoob, let's go. How much did he want for the *manqal?"*

"He wanted 100 tomans, but I got him down to 85. I said I would give him 65. We should see if we could meet each other halfway—75 tomans."

Soon the *manqal* is mine. We head off to see the rug.

"Tom, it's very dark and small. Are you sure you want it? He's asking too much for it."

"Yes, I like it."

"Kheili khoob. I'll see what I can do."

They begin arguing vociferously in Kurdi, or a dialect. *Oh, this is so unnerving. If only I understood what they're saying.*

Finally he tells me, "Give him 50 tomans."

"Is he happy with 50 tomans? I don't want it if he is not happy."

"I told him that's all you'll pay. He will sell it to you. It's not worth even that, but he thinks it is, and that you are a rich foreigner."

"My friend, I don't want him to feel bad. I won't get the rug."

"Kheili khoob. Let's go then." He's plainly disgusted with me. He obviously drove a hard bargain.

I apologize to the shopkeeper, and we leave.

"Tom, why didn't you buy the rug? You said you would pay 50 tomans. I tried to get it for 35, but he said 'no,' so we settled on 50. You should have given him the 50 tomans."

"I'm sorry, but I don't want the man to be unhappy. I don't want him to lose money on it."

"Iranians will never lose money. We are too clever. He would not sell it if he were to lose money. He is Iranian! You should have bought it if you wanted it."

Now I feel awful I have upset Bill's co-worker. That's why I like to do my own bargaining. However, to buy it without his help would have undermined his ego too.

"Tomorrow, before Jim and I depart for Isfahan, I will buy the rug," I say, as a way to appease him. But I'm doubtful anything I say now will remedy the insult.

FRIDAY, APRIL 15, 1966 In Isfahan, Jim has one objective—to pick up the large engraved tray he ordered.

After Jim leaves for Gorgan, I begin my exploration of the city. The splendid Safavid palaces and the serenity of the mosques captivate me. However, the plain exterior of the Islamic-looking Armenian cathedral in the Julfa quarter of Isfahan belies the brilliance inside. Persian floral tiles adorn the domes and upper spandrels. Below, Christian frescoes vividly portray scenes from the Old and New Testaments. In a huge scene of the Last Judgment, a placid, seemingly boring Heaven with its staid and proper residents is presided over by Jesus and his mother. Below, in the middle, St. Michael divides the people on earth. The lowest register, Hell, with its horrific demons and tortured souls—stripped of their clothes—holds my undivided attention. Such excitation! Such tempestuous fervor! What a thrill to quicken the pulse! Imagine whom one would meet there—all the most interesting people of this earth.

SATURDAY, APRIL 16, 1966 It is dark as the bus rolls out of Isfahan at 5am. A faint glow in the east signals the coming dawn. I look back at the city with its twinkling lights as we cross one of the 17th century Safavid bridges and head south across the desert.

SMASH! I quickly look up. A web of tiny crystals obscures the road ahead. Then, suddenly, the windshield limply drops into the bus, on top of the driver and his assistant. The sudden gush of wind causes the emergency door I'm leaning against to fly open. I grab the seat and doorframe to keep from lunging out. The passengers gasp as the driver halts the bus. Evidently a rock, kicked up by an approaching truck, hit the windshield. With no alternatives, the bus limps to Shiraz like an injured dragon with its gaping mouth gobbling the wind.

By midmorning we near the little road that leads to Pasargadae—the capital of Cyrus the Great and his tomb. "Can you let me off here?" I ask the bus driver.

"But your ticket is to Shiraz. It is a long way to Shiraz. And Pasargadae is nine kilometers from here. It is dangerous out here alone."

"It's OK. I will walk to Pasargadae. Then I will catch another bus to Naqsh-e Rostam and Takht-e Jamshid (Persepolis)."

He looks at me strangely, but stops and lets me out. I'm sure he and everyone on the bus think I'm a crazy foreigner. They don't understand my unwavering trust of Iranians. Immediately somebody happens along and gives me a ride.

The massive tomb isolated on the vast plain is singularly austere. Except for a few columns, not much survives of the 6th century BC city built by the founder of the Achaemenid dynasty. Reflectively I wander among the ruins, contemplating the 2500 years of history that have unfolded since Cyrus walked on this very ground. Lost in my reverie, I return to the road to begin my trek to the highway. A colorful local bus stops. "*Agha*, where are you going?" the driver inquires.

"Naqsh-e Rostam."

"*Beah, bala*" (Come aboard).

I pile into the bus and a man offers me a seat near the front. I refuse it, but he is adamant. "*Moteshakeram,*" I thank him, and *salaam* the men around me. They are Qashqai, all with dark, weathered complexions and wearing their signature beige hemispherical felt caps with tall, upturned rims. The women are in the back, aglitter with their immense, colorful skirts and heavy makeup.

"*Agha*, where in Iran are you from?" someone asks.

"From the north—near Gorgan."

"Of course," a man says to the others, "everyone in the north has blond hair and blue eyes."

I gulp. *Oh, my gosh. I don't dare let on now I'm not Iranian. I can't make a fool of this man.* So, for the next 60 kilometers to Naqsh-e Rostam, I guardedly answer their questions about northern Iran.

Naqsh-e Rostam, the royal necropolis of four Achaemenid kings imposingly hewn out of a cliff high above the ground, staggers the imagination. Below, seven Sassanian reliefs depict scenes of imperial conquests and royal ceremonies. The Sassanian rulers, as Shah Mohammad Reza Pahlavi aspires to, wanted to associate themselves both historically and visually with their Achaemenid predecessors. Nearby are some Zoroastrian fire altars, and in front of the towering rock wall a curious cubic structure, though now dug out to the original ground level, appears half-submerged in the sand. It dates from the 5th century BC, and may have been built by Darius I as a fire temple, though there are no smoke vents, or it may have held royal archives or served as a mortuary chamber. I am genuinely pleased to see a modest modern structure—powerfully simple and somewhat reminiscent of its 2500-year-old predecessor. A sign indicates it is a school built by the Sepah-e Danesh. How wonderful that a school would be built here in the 20th century, representing one of the finest achievements of the Pahlavi dynasty—education for the poor. Here are monuments from three illustrious periods in Persian history—the Achaemenids, the Sassanians, and the Pahlavis.

"Mister, do you want a ride?" a young man stops and asks.

"*Na, moteshakeram*, I can walk. I am only going to Takht-e Jamshid."

"*Na*, get on. I'll give you a ride." He motions for me to get on the back of his bicycle. So I straddle the back wheel and we talk as he struggles to transport his additional load.

"*Moteshakeram,*" I say when he drops me off at the base of the imposing staircase at Persepolis.

"The pleasure was mine. Enjoy the rest of your time in Iran. *Khodahafez.*"

This is Iran, I think as I ascend the steps to the ancient city. Iranians are always there, welcoming total strangers. What a tradition! We talk about "aloha spirit" in Hawaii; but we have no corner on aloha. Iran is truly a place of aloha.

SUNDAY, APRIL 17, 1966 In Shiraz, I head for the bazaar—always a favorite destination. In a shop I see something strange near the bottom of a four-foot high pile of folded rugs.

"Could I see that?"

"Mister, it isn't good. Not for you. It is dirty. Ugly! I have many other better rugs for you. Let me show you."

"No, I would like to see that one."

"Mister, I am telling you it is not good. You will not like it."

I sense he may be reluctant to unpile all the rugs to get to it, only to have me run off and leave him to restack them. "*Agha*, I will help you put the rugs back. I promise. I would like to see that rug."

Unenthusiastically, he unpiles the rugs and spreads out a most unconventional specimen. He is right. I nearly retch on the smell of urine and vomit caked into the rug, along with rice and the remains of other meals. Notwithstanding, the rug is extraordinary—a huge, gangly orange lion stretches across a red field, and four little lions, each holding up a *shamshir* (the sword of the Iranian coat-of-arms), surround it.

"Qashqai?" I ask.

"*Baleh.*" He volunteers nothing else. He seems decidedly irritated I have given him this unnecessary work.

"How much is it?"

"Three hundred tomans" ($40.00).

"*Agha*, that is a bit much for a rug in such poor condition. It's dirty, and it smells terrible."

"I told you it was bad, but you wanted to see it."

"*Agha*, can't you lower the price on a rug that is so poor?"

"*Na*, but I can wash it for you if you want it."

"I'm going to Isfahan tomorrow. I can't take a wet rug with me. I will get it washed in Gorgan, where I live. Will you sell it to me for 250 tomans, and I will get it washed?"

"*Na*. I will wash it."

"*Agha*, that won't work. I told you I'm leaving Shiraz early tomorrow morning. Here—take the 250 tomans," I insist, handing him the money. "I won't pay more."

With a show of presumed reluctance, he takes the money.

"*Kheili khoob.* Let's repile the rugs."

"*Na*, Mister. I can do it. It's not your work."

"*Agha*, I said I would help you."

I grab one side of a portion of the pile. He takes the other side, and together we restack the rugs.

"*Agha*, do you have a sack to put the rug in?"

"*Baleh*, Mister." He finds a sack and cord, binds up the rug, and hands it to me. "*Khodahafez*, Mister," he says with a smile.

"*Khodahafez.*" We shake hands.

MONDAY, APRIL 18, 1966 By noon we are in Isfahan.

"*Salaam, Aghaye* Mister, did you buy a rug in Shiraz?" the attendant at the hotel desk asks.

"*Baleh*, a Qashqai rug."

"Qashqai rugs are not of high quality. You should buy an Isfahan rug. They are the best."

"*Baleh*, but they are too expensive." I don't tell him that I dislike the ornate rugs made in Isfahan—that the tribal rugs of Iran are more my taste.

Everybody in Alang recommended I not miss the Shaking Minarets—for them, one of the greatest marvels in Isfahan. I climb one of the minarets, begin to shake it, stop, and look at the other one. Yes, it's swaying too. Logical. Funny this is so fascinating to my friends in Alang.

I lose myself in the Grand Bazaar, savoring the sounds and smells and buying old brass bowls for a few tomans each. A large brass tray attracts my attention. It is Russian. The seal stamped on it is TK—my initials. I can hardly contain my astonishment.

"How much is it?" I ask the man.

"Twenty tomans." We agree on sixteen ($2.10).

On the way to the hotel, a shop owner in one of the tourist shops on the Meydan-e Shah invites me in. "Would you be interested in Persian miniatures?"

"No. They are all fakes here in Iran, and I don't like the new ones painted on bone or ivory."

"I have one that isn't a fake. Would you like to see it?"

"*Baleh,*" I reply skeptically.

He sets it on the counter. It is like none I have seen in any shop—as magnificent as those in museums. The individual strands of the men's beards and the woman's tresses were unmistakably painted with a brush with a single hair.

"May I pick it up?"

"*Befarmayid*. Nice, isn't it?"

"*Baleh,*" I answer casually, not wanting to appear too excited. I hold it to the light to see if the miniature was painted over text on an old page from a book. *My gosh,* I say to myself, *there's writing on only one side of the paper. This is incredible.* Tentatively I ask, "How much is it?"

"One hundred ninety tomans" ($25.00).

"Do you know what it is about?"

"It is the story of Siyavush's ordeal by fire from Ferdowsi's *Shahnameh.*"

"Oh, yes, down here in the corner is written Siyavush in pencil."

"You can read Farsi too? How did you learn Farsi?"

"I can only read a little. It's too hard for me to read a lot. I only learned to speak Farsi. I'm an American Peace Corps Volunteer, and live in a village in the north near Gorgan. I've been here over a year and half, and in two months I'll be going home. I'm sad to be leaving Iran. I love Iran as much as I love America. I'm heartbroken I'll never be able to come back. My family is rather poor . . . well, not *poor* poor, but not rich. So when I go home, I'll be leaving my new home, my adopted home—Iran—and I'll never be able to return." My voice cracks with emotion. "So I'm trying to find things from Iran that will ensure I remember this place I love so much."

I stop, a bit ashamed to reveal all this to a complete stranger. We both are silent for a while.

"*Enshahallah* (If God is willing), you will be able to come back to Iran," he says kindly.

"*Enshahallah.*" Attentively, I inspect the miniature. *Can it be real at that price?* I conjecture. Even if it is a fake, the painting is so refined and of outstanding quality.

Finally I venture, "Would you sell it to me for less?"

He comes down in the price much more than I anticipated. I counter his request, buying it for half of what he originally quoted.

WEDNESDAY, APRIL 20, 1966 Laden with a heavy suitcase, a box, and the bundle containing the unwashed rug, it would be impossible to lug all my stuff from the new road into Alang, even if it is now closer to the village. I take the bus to Gorgan planning to catch Hajireza's mobile contraption directly to Alang. However, Jafar and Mulla see me on the street as they drive by.

"Tom! You're here! Welcome back. We weren't expecting you for another six days. You told us your vacation was two weeks."

"*Baleh*, I couldn't wait to get back to Alang. I missed all of you. There is not much time left. I want to be with you. Also, I bought too much. I couldn't carry it around."

We speed off down the new highway to Alang.

"Tom," Jafar tells me, "Alang is like Paris now. It's wonderful. We have electric lights out to the new highway. You will see."

"Wow! That's terrific. I can't wait to see it."

Although I've never been to Paris, I can't help but think the analogy is unique, even if it is a bit preposterous. I say to myself, *Poor Paris, the City of Light, being compared to Alang.* But for me, Alang will always be better than Paris. *My Alang will always be home.*

STILL MUCH TO LEARN

THURSDAY, APRIL 21, 1966 "Tom, you have seen much more of Iran than any of us."

"*Baleh*, and I have seen more of Iran than I have seen of America. *Enshahallah*, someday you will see Iran like I have seen it. Iran is a spectacular country." I describe the fantastic places I saw, and show my friends pictures in my art books so they can share my enthusiasm in experiencing Iran's glorious history.

"Show us what you got. You bought another rug?"

"*Baleh*. It is Qashqai. I need to wash it. It is very dirty and it smells awful." I pull it out of the sack and the guys look in horror.

"I'll say. It stinks," Shaban Ali declares. "Put it out on the balcony. You can't keep it in here."

"I know. I want to wash it today."

"How much did you pay for it, Tom?" Mulla asks caringly.

I was hoping nobody would ask, but I knew otherwise. "Two hundred and fifty tomans," I respond with apprehension. "But he wanted three hundred," I say quickly.

"Oh, Tom, you haven't learned. Iranians are too crafty for you. Iranians have swindled you again."

"But the rug is big, over two meters by about a meter and a half. And I bargained. He wanted 300 tomans. And . . . I like it."

"Tom, it's ugly and it's dirty. Awful! Filthy! What are you going to do with it?"

"I will wash it—today."

"And once you wash it, what will you do with it?" someone else joins in. "It's bad. It's sinful to have a rug with a lion in it. It's against Islam. The persons who made it were not respectful Muslims. They should not make rugs with living beings in them. A lion breathes. The Koran forbids making images of living, breathing things. Only God can do that. The weavers will go to Hell for doing it. On the Day of Judgment, God will ask them to breathe life into the images they created on Earth, and since they will not be able to do it, He will banish them to Hell."

"But the lion doesn't look like a lion," Mr. Kucheek volunteers. "The artist couldn't draw well; so it isn't a real lion. Maybe the weavers won't go to Hell."

Oh, my heavens, I say to myself, *I've bought a rug that offends their religion.*

"Tom, what are you going to do with it when you go to America?" Mr. Kucheek continues. "It's not well-made. It's not a fine weave like Turkoman rugs."

"That's why I like it. I want to use it in my children's room someday."

"Ah-hah—see he is married, and has a wife and children," I hear one of the guys whisper to the others. "He's been lying to us all along. He has kids in America."

"Well, if you are going to use it in your children's room, it's OK," Mulla counters. "It would be colorful in a child's room. Children would like it. But you must clean it very well. What else did you get, Tom?"

With that analysis of my purchasing savvy, I am even more reluctant to show them what else I bought. However, there's no point in trying to hide my sins; they'll find out anyway. And I have found it's better to be entirely forthright with them. Besides, I want them to know my interest in Iran, even if it is unconventional to them.

"What's in the box?"

"A *manqal*." I see Shaban Ali's face drop. "I got it in Hamadan." I pull it out. "I've wanted one ever since I saw them used in Alang."

"And, how much did you pay for it?"

"Seventy-five tomans."

Several pick it up to determine its weight. An argument ensues over whether I was over-charged or if I at least paid a fair price for brass. Next,

I gingerly dig out the broken bowl from Hamadan and hand it to Mulla. I already know the verdict, but I'm resigned to facing the music.

The chorus begins. "Tom, how much did you pay for this broken bowl?"

"Oh, be careful. It's old," I caution one of my friends who seems about to break it in half. "I paid 55 tomans."

"Fifty-five tomans!" The refrain undoubtedly reverberated through half of Alang.

"*Baleh*. In Tehran it would have been 550 tomans," I say sheepishly.

"Tom, we're sorry. Leaving Iran is making you crazy. Don't spend your money on junk like this. This is old and broken. You paid way too much."

"But he wanted 75 tomans at first, and I like it. There are old, broken bowls in the Musée Iran Bastan. I want it as a memory of Iran. I will treasure it as long as I live."

Shaban Ali thoughtfully reminds them, "Tom sees Iran differently from us. He sees Iran's history in these objects. He sees our culture . . . and he sees us in them. He knows Iran is good. We look at Iran today, and wish we were like America. We want the things from America because we feel they are superior to those made in Iran. Tom truly loves the things of Iran. We should be proud he's taking them back to America."

"But this is a broken bowl. It's not good to take this back to America. Americans will think we're poor."

"Tom is an artist. He has studied Iran's history. He knows their value."

"I did not buy them because they have value. I bought them because I like them and they will help me remember Iran and you. I feel very bad about leaving Alang and Iran. Probably I will never be able to return. In America, most artists are very poor, so I will struggle to live and I will never be able to come back to Iran. However, I'll have these things, and the memories of you and Iran, forever."

There is silence.

I get out the bronze arrowheads, pins, and armband; the brass bowls and trays; the miniature; and the small rug. There is little discussion of whether I paid too much for them.

Someone says, "There must be gold in the large tray—the one that has his initials on it. He knows. He is too clever for us."

SOMEBODY CALLS FROM BELOW, "Tom, *beah*, *zud bosh*" (come quickly)!

We look out my window.

"Bring your camera. The *Hajis* have returned from Mecca."

People are scurrying through town, excited at the news. I grab my camera, and we run through the village to the new highway. Hundreds of people are already there, joyfully greeting the pilgrims as the orange-and-white Iran Payma bus is unloaded. I scan the crowd, searching for *Haji* Torfeh. Finally I see her, momentarily close my eyes in gratitude, and make my way nearby. Politely and reservedly we greet each other. *She did return!*

The euphoric crowd wends its way back to the village. The rest of the day is a series of joyous reunions. At the home of *Haji* Tofigh, I congratulate him on becoming a *haji* and he modestly recounts the pilgrimage and trip.

Return from Mecca—Alang's *mullah* (turban) and Mulla's father (white skullcap)

FRIDAY, APRIL 22, 1966 Reza invites me to a quiet lunch with him and Rozy. Her cousin Abdullah is there before he is called to his own home. I love being with the children, watching them play, listening to their cheerful chatter, and talking with them—laughing.

"Tom, we are becoming very sad. Soon you will be leaving Alang. Alang will never be the same."

"Reza, I am the saddest. I will be leaving all of you. You have become my brothers—my family. When I left America, I knew I would be going home to see my parents and my brother. Now I am leaving you . . . and Rozy, and all my friends who are my family . . . my home . . . and I will never see you again." My eyes water. "I will miss Rozy and Abdullah, Mulla's little Ismael, Shaban Ali's children, and Mirsalehi's and Khanpoor's children. In America, I don't have little children around me. Life will not be the same without them."

"Tom, you must get married and make children of your own."

"*Baleh*, but I don't know when. My life will be very different when I go home. I will become 'American Tom' again. I can no longer be carefree 'Tom of Iran' . . . the Tom I like more than 'American Tom.' I will have responsibilities. I will have to do what I need to do . . . what everyone expects of me. I will go to the university to study. I will have to work to live and to pay for the university. I will have no money to get married and have children. Besides, I have to find the right woman first."

"But what about Miss Lily or Miss Del?"

"Reza, if I go to school in another state, I won't see them for at least two years. That's a long time. I may find another girl and want to marry her. Besides, Del is in Africa. She won't be coming home until next year. I may never see her again. And she may have found a guy she likes more than me. Lily will still be in Hawaii. She has one more year to study before she will become a nurse. She wants to go into the Peace Corps too. And I want her to do that. Being in Alang has been so meaningful for me, I want her to have this kind of opportunity. I would be selfish to deny her this experience. So it will be three years before we see each other again. She, too, may find another man. So going back to America is like starting over. There, I'll have to prepare for the future. It won't be like the two years of my life here.

"Sometimes I think I would like to stay here . . . and never go back to America. That's my heart speaking to me. My mind tells me I must go back. It's very hard. I have come to love Alang and Iran too much."

THE DOOR OPENS. A young girl enters, gathers the teacups and pot, and spreads the oilcloth upon the floor.

"What do you think of her, Tom?" Reza asks in English.

"Nice." Knowing Reza, I wonder what he has on his mind. Is he interested in her, or is he inquiring if I might be interested? After all, it would be a way of keeping me in Alang, and I would be able to have children of my own like Rozy and Abdullah."

"My father wants to take her as his wife," he confides in English.

With excruciating difficulty I attempt to conceal my shock. "Your father is an old man."

"Yes, I know. He is 62, but he wants to marry her."

"What does your mother say?"

"She will consent. She is an old woman, but she is always his first wife."

The door opens again. I study the beauty of this fresh young girl more earnestly as she brings in a tray with plates, silverware, and food. I can't believe what I just heard. Although our conversation reverts to Farsi and other topics, my mind lurches at the thought of what I have learned.

SATURDAY, APRIL 23, 1966 With the warming weather, Ghorbon has moved into the large unfurnished room next to mine. Tonight when I return, he follows me to my door.

"*Befarmayid*, Ghorbon." I light the kerosene lamp and go to make tea.

"Mister Tom, my family is becoming very sad you are leaving us. Tom, don't go. Don't go to America. Stay with us. Stay in Alang."

"Ghorbon, I have to go to America. It is my home. *Baleh*, Alang is now my home too, but I must go to America."

"Mister Tom, I want you to stay in Alang. I want you to be here for my wedding."

"Your wedding? You didn't tell me you were getting married when you visited me previously. When is your wedding?"

"I don't know. But I want you to be here for it."

"Thank you, Ghorbon. I would like to be here for your wedding. Your family is like my family now. Who are you marrying?"

"My father has not told me yet." My mind cartwheels, imagining a young man anticipating a forthcoming marriage, not concerned who his wife will be.

"If you don't know the girl, how do you know you will love her?"

"Whomever my father selects will be fine. He knows. He will choose a good wife for me."

Although I have been here over a year and a half, I'm still baffled by traditions totally out of my cultural context. I *am* more American than I am Iranian, I conclude.

SUNDAY, APRIL 24, 1966 "Tom, friends of yours—Americans—are *lokhteh lokht* (naked naked)! Between here and Gorgan!" Jafar incredulously informs me upon his return from Gorgan.

"*Lokhteh lokht!*" I exclaim. "They didn't have anything on?"

"*Baleh. Lokhteh lokht*—your friends." (For Iranians, all foreigners are friends of each other, no matter what country they are from.) "They are wearing shorts and the men have no shirts on. They are *lokhteh lokht!* The women are wearing shorts too!"

I am amused that "naked naked" is distinguishable from naked and that "naked naked" means you are wearing shorts. I am curious about what being absolutely nude would be called. Nevertheless, I am disgusted that foreigners would travel in any country in attire offensive to the their hosts— even if they are in a remote area—and that they would not be mindful of local customs and observe appropriate mores of attire and conduct.

TUESDAY, APRIL 26, 1966 A somber, heavy sky signals dawn. It's still raining, but the deluge from which the noisy tin roof spared me during the long dark night has diminished. With umbrella in one hand and *aftabeh* (ewer) in the other, I shuffle to the *mostarah,* careful my rubber boots don't get stuck in the knee-deep mud.

Courtyards are filled with water. The street is a swill of debris gathering against walls and any obstruction. Fortunately, houses in Alang are built off the ground, and the surrounding fields have adequate drainage. The water rushes to the low-lying desert to the north.

I wade to the Sherkat-e Sargardon, the best place to gather local news.

"*Salaam*, Tom, did you sleep well?"

"No. The rain was too strong. It peppered the roof all night. I thought the roof would collapse."

They agree they did not sleep well either.

"We are lucky here in Alang. The water is draining away. But between here and Gorgan, many villages and fields are badly flooded. When you look to the north from the highway, all you can see is water—straight to the Soviet Union. It's shocking."

"Oh, my gosh—are Ghalayesh and the Turkoman villages OK?"

"I'm afraid not," Reza says. "There is water everywhere. *Enshahallah*, the water will subside rapidly."

WEDNESDAY, MAY 4, 1966 "Tom, I went to Ghalayesh yesterday. That's why I wasn't in class," Shaban Ali apprises me. "I didn't tell you I was going because I didn't want you to see what might be there. It is very bad. The entire village is under water. The people have moved to a little mound nearby, but they are out in the open—no tents, not much food. It may be a long time before the water subsides."

"Oooh, and it's raining again today. Those poor people."

"*Baleh*, their homes and crops are destroyed. The flood stretches nearly 80 kilometers east of the Caspian, almost to Gonbad-e Kavus. CARE and USAID brought in food and tents for the people, but rich men shove the poor people aside and haul the supplies away in their jeeps and fancy cars."

"Shaban Ali, how can this be? The food and tents are for the flood victims. How can anyone take that away from them? The Shah is trying to stop this kind of corruption. Can't somebody stop them? Can't something be done?"

"It's the way it's always been. No one, not even the Shah, can stop the rich and powerful when they are ruthless."

TUESDAY, MAY 10, 1966 Shortly before 5am, bright sunlight steams in my transom windows. Perfect. How providential—the rain has stopped.

"Tom, come quickly—the tractor parade has begun. Bring your camera," a friend calls to me.

We run to the new highway. Much of Alang, including the *mullahs*, is already there, cheering as hundreds of tractors draped and waving the Iranian flag head to Gorgan.

Jafar arrives with his jeep. "Tom, get in. We have to go to Gorgan now. You must see the Shah."

Many of us pile into the little jeep, some even hanging out the sides. Jafar speeds down the highway on another of his daily trips to the city. We pass the seemingly endless line of tractors heading to Gorgan to celebrate Mazandaran's agricultural might. I scan the plain to the north. Water everywhere—as far as the eye can see. I lament the misery this catastrophe has wrought.

"*Baleh*, Tom, this is the worst flood we have ever had. The people are suffering. Entire villages are inundated. Hopefully the rains have stopped and the waters will recede. But today is a day of joy. The sun is out, and the Shah is here. Tom, Gorgan is beautiful. The shops have been repainted, and forty triumphal arches span the streets."

It has been weeks since I've been to Gorgan, and I'm enthralled by the transformation. We pass under arch after arch, each more elaborate than

Ismael Gilani, Gorgan

the previous; the most spectacular is a huge red tractor, near the Shah's palace, where vehicles pass under the engine. Iranian flags are everywhere.

Crowds surge to find the best spot along the streets to glimpse the Shah and see the parade. We maneuver to a prime location to hear the Shah's speech. Recalling the assassination attempt of a little more than a year ago, I fear for the Shah's safety, and am apprehensive about being close. However, it's exciting to see him and observe the awe and adulation of his people. This is a proud moment for Gorgan and the people of Mazandaran—a time when Iranians come together as one, a country united behind their king. I am pleased by the intensity of this display of nationalism. Though there are risks, the Shah understands the necessity of being among his people. In gazing at their king, they validate him as king, and acquiesce to their position as his subjects. The Shah, in being before them, becomes the focal point of his kingdom. There is a quasi-religious dimension here—the Shah surveys his people and cares for them, much as God provides for the faithful.

At night I reflect further on the day. The announcement of his visit to Gorgan and the preparations attendant to it made it appear as if his subjects were the orchestrators of the event, but, foremost, the Shah is the event and its initiator. As in ancient times, an occasion such as this is staged to demonstrate the political fact of hierarchy and to ensure the cooperation of the people in the institution of monarchy. It's an opportunity to survey the economic base of the province—one that gives pride to the populous; but for them, it also proclaims the power of the Shah. Here, agricultural cultivation is used to embody the legitimacy of his rule. His presence proclaims Mazandaran a bountiful region, and his concern for the land and his people. His palace in Gorgan serves as an expression of his sphere of influence and his interest in the province. The city's public garden that surrounds the palace, where people from all walks of life stroll, symbolizes his munificence, his love for his subjects.

A NEW REALITY

WEDNESDAY, MAY 11, 1966 The actuality of leaving Alang and Iran is no longer illusory. The Peace Corps has scheduled my lab tests, x-rays, and language exam tomorrow; the termination conference is next week, through Wednesday, while my dental appointment is not until Saturday, May 21. That means ten days in the big city at a time when spending every moment in Alang is of utmost significance. *Why couldn't they schedule more efficiently?* I grumble.

I marvel at the geological formations as the bus ascends the narrow two-lane highway through the rugged valley of the Haraz River. It won't be much longer, and I'll never see this again.

Suddenly, dust rises from the cliff above. Pebbles begin to rain upon the road and pelt the bus. Rocks the size of a person's head narrowly miss us. *"Zelzeleh"* (Earthquake), someone shouts. At once a united call of *Bismillah-e Rahman-e Raheem* seeks God's mercy. The driver pushes on. What else can he do? To stop may be more dangerous. The cascading rubble subsides and I contemplate, *Another near miss! Still . . . being in Iran has been worth all the risks.*

THURSDAY, MAY 12, 1966 Hell-bent on getting to the hospital in Shemiran in record time, the taxi driver speeds up Khiaban-e Pahlavi, swerving in and out of traffic, often driving in the left-hand lane. Horns blare angrily. I hang on to the seat in front of me, cowering as approaching traffic descends directly toward us. Somehow, each time, the oncoming driver and mine veer away moments before imminent impact.

SCREEEECH! CRASH! The taxi is thrown about, and glass flies around me. Cautiously I open my eyes. My driver and another are standing in the street, shouting, swearing, and threatening each other. The driver sides of their vehicles are liberally scraped, mirrors broken. *Oh, my gosh. I need to get out of here.* I recall someone advised us to disappear if a taxi we hired was ever in an accident. "You could be responsible for the accident," he warned. I deposit the fare on the seat and slip out, run to the next block, and catch another taxi to my destination. I'm shaken, thankful I'm not arriving on a gurney at the hospital for my lab tests.

SUNDAY, MAY 15, 1966 It's good to see the other PCVs. Some I haven't seen since we parted in Tehran twenty months ago. Most look forward to going home. But a pall hangs over us. Several guys have received word to report to their draft board within two weeks of their termination. The reality of going home to America and of Vietnam stuns us. It's as if returning is not as exciting and important as coming to Iran was two years ago. What's happened to us in these two years? Most of us are too naive to ask what's happened to *America* in these two years?

The Peace Corps tries to prepare us for reverse culture shock, of having to face American culture when we get home. Knowing how I love Alang and its people, I now recognize the likelihood of the difficulties I might go through. It seems more real than the obscure nature of what we had been told in training about culture shock when we arrived in Iran.

There is ample time for individuals to report on the highlights of their work in Iran, on the difficulties they encountered, and how they overcame adversities. Some express frustration over their feelings of failure—that they had not achieved the three big projects we were mandated to accomplish. I sit and listen, overcome that many had given two years of their life to a cause they sincerely believed in and now they are going home with the psychological burden of not having effectively fulfilled their duties. Anger that America, a country I love so much, has encumbered its own young citizens with such anguish, consumes me.

"Big projects are not what the Peace Corps is all about," I blurt out. "It's not the physical accomplishments that are important—the schools, libraries, or bathhouses that were built, the water systems that were put in, the agricultural improvements that occurred. That's what USAID did for years. Often the people we did these things for saw it as *our* project, not *their* project. They had no sense of ownership. Our success must be measured in another way, one closer to the Kennedy ideal that inspired the Peace Corps. That is in the areas of love, honesty, sincerity, and understanding." My voice begins to shake. "I came here nearly two years ago to help . . . but I found Iranians are capable of helping themselves. However, I could offer inspiration and encouragement. So what was achieved in Alang and the four other villages I worked in, I am proud to say, was done by them. Maybe sometimes it came about a little faster because I was there, but always, it was their achievement." I take a deep breath. "Now I'm leaving Alang and Iran, . . . not because I want to, . . . but because that was the deal. I have one more thing to say. That is: Thank you, America. Thank you, Peace Corps. And thank you, Iran. Being here has been and always will be the greatest experience of my life, so great that in these two years I realized if I didn't return home alive, I was not going to sit down and cry about it."

Regardless of my impromptu, heartfelt speech, Peace Corps officials cajole us into writing glowing reports of what we accomplished in the two years we were here. "It's critical you make these reports positive. They will be submitted to Washington and used to show Congress the commendable work of the Peace Corps in order to maintain funding."

In my political naiveté, I am incensed. This, clearly, is as bad as or worse than the corruption we criticize in Iran. I fume silently. America should be above this, but here it is at the highest level—right in Washington.

At the end of the day, disgusted and deeply troubled, I go to the hotel room I share with an Iranian near the Meydan-e Toopkhaneh in south Tehran. I have to think this out myself, away from the other volunteers. With resolve, I begin my report.

> This isn't easy for me to write a report of what I've done in these two years because if you went to Alang, you would find no physical changes that could be attributed to my staying there. I built no schools or bridges,

paved no roads, or brought about no great agricultural changes. You might call me the volunteer who did nothing, for what improvements that were made in Alang were instigated and carried out entirely by the people.

You may ask then, "What did you do in these two years?" I can only say I had a wonderful time and I must thank the Peace Corps and the US Government for giving me something which I could never have gotten if it had not been for them. These two years, I'm sure, will always be the two most meaningful years of my life, and I would not trade them or change them in any way. I lived them to their fullest, and of this I cannot be sorry.

Yet you say, "What did you do?" What can I say, for what I did cannot be measured like bridges, or schools, or roads, or English classes? I simply loved and let love. And what more should I have done?

What I have done could only begin to be measured in leaving, and suffice it to say this day need not come so soon. I will only leave because this was expected when I came, and not because I want to leave. In a way, I will never leave Alang, and I hope the day is soon when I will be able to return.

But you still may ask, "Just what have you done?" I will be happy to be known as "the volunteer who has done nothing."

Tom Klobe

TUESDAY, MAY 17, 1966 The chill of my reception at the Peace Corps office when I show up for my repeatedly postponed language exam is palpable—because of my report, I presume. I perform miserably in the oral, although I have thought and dreamed in Farsi for over a year. Unconsciously I pepper my speech with Gilaki or the Alangi dialect, making what I say unacceptable to the Tehran examiners. I decline to take the written exam.

SALTS OF ANGUISH

TUESDAY, MAY 24, 1966 Nervously, very late in the day, I sit in the doctor's waiting room in Tehran. I want to hear what the doctor says, but I don't know what I want to hear. Mainly, I want him to tell me the truth. Either way, it's going to be painful.

After nearly an hour of anxiety I hear, "Mr. Klobe." My heart sinks. I sigh. Trembling, I enter the doctor's office.

"*Salaam, Aghaye* Doctor . . . my name is Tom Klobe. I am an American Peace Corps Volunteer," I introduce myself in Farsi, taking deep, uneasy breaths between sentences. "I live and work in Alang, where little Mahmood lives. I have come about Mahmood. . . . I know he has had a heart operation here in Tehran. I have been told you have done what can be done here in Iran . . . that he may live only a year or two . . . but in Europe or America, there is the capability to do surgery that might allow him to live a normal life. I am going home in a few weeks . . . and I have thought of taking Mahmood with me for an operation in America."

A few hours before, Peace Corps officials recommended I not consider this. They told me, "It's very risky—very difficult to raise the money. Two volunteers tried something like this. They ended up in a big mess, and had to bear the costs themselves. Pan Am would not pay for air transportation, and the operation in the United States was very expensive. Also, regulations on Iranians departing the country for any reason are very difficult and prohibitively expensive, so it would be a problem even getting an exit visa."

In my mind, though, I have to resolve this in my own way.

"Doctor, please tell me about Mahmood."

"Mr. Klobe, we have done what we can for Mahmood. Yes, he may only live a few years, but he could also live a very long life. I appreciate your concern for Mahmood. Now it is better that he is in the care of his parents. It would be very expensive to take him to America, and another operation there may not be that beneficial to him. It is best he stays in Iran."

"But, Doctor, what will happen to him?"

"We don't know. We will do what we can. Mahmood is in God's hands."

With a mixture of agony and grateful relief I tell the doctor, "Thank you for giving me your time and talking about Mahmood. I pray he will be fine. *Moteshakeram. Khodahafez.*"

It's now dark as I wander down the street, lost in anxious reflection. Abruptly I stop, struck by a horrible thought. I run back to the doctor's office and barge in the door.

"I need to see the doctor. Can I see the doctor again?" I tell the attendant.

The doctor hears my request to see him one more time and comes out. "Yes, Mr. Klobe?"

"Doctor, what do I owe you? I took your time. I don't want Mahmood's parents to be charged."

"Mr. Klobe, there is no charge. Please put your mind at rest and have a safe journey back to America. Thank you for coming to Iran. I hope you enjoyed our country."

"Oh, thank you, Doctor. I love Iran . . . as much as I love America."

WEDNESDAY, MAY 25, 1966 My third trip over the mountains in four days! Sunday I got back to Alang, heard about Mahmood, asked Reza to find out the name of Mahmood's doctor, told Reza to keep the purpose of my immediate return to Tehran secret, spent Monday night in Gorgan with Jack and Dave (it would be my final visit with them and Kathy, Jim, and Noel), and Tuesday morning took another bus to Tehran.

Today I convince the bus driver to let me off at Alang and somberly walk into the village. Reza and I go for a stroll together, and I explain my discussion with the doctor. Distraught, fearful of what will become of Mahmood, Reza nevertheless reassures me.

"Tom, don't worry about Mahmood. Go home. You must resume your life in America. Get married and make some children of your own. *Enshahallah*, you will come back to Alang someday. We will never forget you."

Pained, I look at him. *"Baleh*, Reza, I will never forget Alang. I will never forget all of you."

We walk in silence for a long time.

"Tom, Rozy and I want you to come to dinner tonight. Will you please come? Let's go to my house for tea now. It will be good for you."

I don't answer. We turn and head for his house.

Rozy's playful antics and her excitement over seeing me help lift the weight that burdens me. When I look at her and realize in three weeks I will never see her again—I will never see her grow up—I taste the salt of sadness in my mouth.

"Rozy," her father says, "get the gift you are going to give *Amo* Tom."

Rozy runs off and returns, her hands outstretched toward me, holding a little packet. I accept it, barely able to utter a *moteshakeram*. She throws her arms around me and I hug her closely so she won't see my tears. Somehow I don't want her to know that our time together is ending, that her *Amo* Tom is leaving her.

I open the packet. Inside is a beautiful gold chain and pendant of the Blessed Virgin. I look at Reza, unable to articulate a thank you.

"It is from Rozy for you to give your wife on your wedding day."

I purse my lips, holding back my emotions. With difficulty, I thank him.

Why is the process of leaving so difficult? We sit there silently. Rozy chatters blithely.

THURSDAY, MAY 26, 1966 The round of farewell meals begins—lunch at someone's house, dinner at another. None is easy. The carefree joy of being "Tom of Iran" is encumbered with an awareness of an irreversible ending.

My students gather for the usual tea and easy conversation. Afterwards, Ismael, Yavar, and I retreat to their house for dinner. They and their families will also be leaving Alang for the summer holidays.

"Tom, this is for you," Ismael says, handing me a rug. "It is small, but it is a thank you from us for teaching us English."

I unroll it. It's old and beautiful.

"Ismael and Yavar, I can't accept this. It's too nice, and I don't have anything for you."

"You have given us something more valuable than any rug. You have become our friend, and you have taught us English. What we have learned and experienced can never be taken from us. They are ours forever."

"Thank you, but this is too much."

"No, it is yours for you to take home to America—a remembrance of us. The rug is special to your memories of Alang because I got it from my aunt," Ismael explains. "Many years ago, she bought two Hamadan rugs from Tofigh Rahemi. This is one of them. So the rug is also part of Alang."

Their wives smile approvingly. The children stand there with quizzical expressions on their faces, obviously not comprehending the significance of this moment.

"Thank you. I will always remember you. You know how I feel. I will miss you and the joy of your families very much. If only Iran and America were not so far apart."

FRIDAY, MAY 27, 1966 Shaban Ali and Nemetollah Savarsofla arrive at my door carrying the *manqal* I had seen at the Savarsofla house. "*Aghaye* Savarsofla wants to give you this to take back to America." Now I realize why Shaban Ali's face fell when I said I bought a *manqal* in Hamadan.

"*Agha, moteshakeram.* I cannot accept it. It is yours. It belongs to your family—your history. You must keep it."

"No, *Aghaye* Mister Tom, we want you to have it. I have two more at my house. We do not need three. One is yours as a memory of Alang."

"Oh, *Agha*, thank you. I will always cherish it. Forever I will remember you and Alang. I will never forget."

SATURDAY, MAY 28, 1966 "Tom, I wish you weren't going away. I wish you would stay in Alang."

"Mulla, I wish I could stay in Alang too. I don't want to leave."

"Tom, Noor Jahan and I are going to have another baby. I want you to be *Amo* Tom to our new baby as you are for Ismael."

"Mulla, that's fantastic. I wish I could be here to be *Amo* Tom again."

"Tom, what name should we give the baby? What are your favorite names—if it is a boy . . . and if it is a girl?

"Mulla, I don't know. That is for you and your wife to decide."

"But what are your favorite names?"

"Mulla, I have always liked the name Michael. It's my middle name. When I have a son, I would like to call him Michael. I have never thought about a girl's name. My wife will have to decide that." *

SUNDAY, MAY 29, 1966   We all attempt to maintain a semblance of continuity—a denial of the inevitable transience of time. My classes give structure to life. There is little point in going to village council meetings except to say goodbye in each of the villages. I can't return to endure the grief of parting another time.

Everything is collapsing around me. Shaban Ali helps me take down the Turkoman rug over my bed and we roll it with my other rugs in one large torpedo-like roll.

"I will get some burlap sacks and we'll stitch them around the rugs to send to America." Shaban Ali's voice conveys sadness and finality. "We also need to have a wooden box made for your bronze pot and the *manqals*. Let's determine the measurements, and I will have a carpenter make it."

MONDAY, MAY 30, 1966   This is a proud day for me. Shaban Ali and I attend a ceremony in Kordkuy to honor seven young men of the Sepah-e Danesh who are completing their two years of service working in villages in the district. They have taken exams that qualify them to become teachers. As they are honored, I think about the work they have achieved in the past two years—the schools they have built and the children they have taught and given hope to—and the enlightened intellect behind the establishment of the Sepah-e Danesh. How valuable this is to Iran—that these youthful Iranians who have a high school education can contribute constructively to the future of their country by teaching in lieu of fulfilling military service. This is a superb example for the rest of the world to follow.

---

* Mulla wrote that they had another son, and his name is Michael.

I'm especially proud of two of them—the two who worked in the villages of Ghalandarayesh and Ghalayesh. Each has asked to be posted in his respective village—a request that eloquently demonstrates the caliber of these two young men. That they would choose to return to the hardships of village life is inspiring, for they could have accepted positions in a larger town or city.

Sepah-e Danesh (second left from Ghalandarayesh, second right from Ghalayesh)

WEDNESDAY, JUNE 1, 1966 The past week has brought a steam of visitors, most bearing gifts: aged ceramic pots—even beautiful shards they found in the fields—hand-woven towels, a coin from the time of Reza Shah, a small glass vase from the Qajar dynasty, an old brass spoon, and a brass candlestick. Many are family heirlooms. They know I'm packing to go home. Mulla comes with a beautiful Russian samovar.

"Tom, this is from us—my wife, Ismael, and me. Remember, you wanted to buy a samovar in Gorgan, and I wouldn't let you? It was because Noor Jahan and I decided we would give you this one. It has been in our family for many years and we don't use it any more. We use the new kerosene one. This one is too old. It needs coals. We want you to have it."

"Mulla, thank you. You're right. I did want an old brass samovar because the samovar is so much a part of life in Alang—how we sit as friends and drink tea together. It will be a wonderful memory of you and your family . . . and of Alang."

Another day, *Haji* Torfeh climbs the stairs with great difficulty to see me.

"*Aghaye* Mister Tom, this is for you." She hands me a plain oblong piece of ceramic with a hole in one end. "It is old."

"*Kheili moteshakeram. Haji*, what was it for? How was it used?"

"It was a cover for a water jar in ancient times. A string went through the hole and it was tied around the handle of the jar. The cover kept dirt from getting inside."

"Oh, *Haji*, this is so remarkable. *Moteshakeram*. I will always appreciate it because you gave it to me. *Kheili moteshakeram*."

"*Aghaye* Mister, have a safe trip home to America. Be careful." Her eyes are watering. "Say *salaam* to your mother from me . . . and thank you for coming to Alang, *Aghaye* Mister."

"*Moteshakeram, Haji*. I will tell my mother *salaam* from you. I will tell her about you and your kindness. You take care of yourself, *Haji*. I will miss you."

She turns and shuffles to the stairs. I watch her descend one last time.

THIS EVENING, ISMAEL AND YAVAR invite me to share our final family meal together. On Friday they will leave Alang for the summer, the Khanpoors going to Meti Kola and the Mirsalehis to Gorgan. I despair at the thought of not seeing the children again—not seeing them grow up.

Ismael hands me the Chinese-looking pot I had seen in their *mostarah* in Gorgan.

"Tom, this is for you. I know you will care for it forever. The children will break it someday if we keep it."

"Ismael, thank you. You have already given me the rug and the little Qajar vase. You should not give me so much."

"As I have told you before, you have given me more. Thanks to you I can read and speak English without translating into Farsi. Now I can think in English."

"Ismael, it is not I who taught you. It is you who learned. You are a very diligent student. You worked very hard and you learned well. It is you who did the work, not me. You will do very well in the university entrance exams. You must write to me when I get home."

I turn the pot in my hands examining the free brushwork of the blue-and-white design that is unmistakably Chinese—a Chinese landscape. Then I turn it over.

"Ismael, this *is* Chinese. Look, Chinese characters! What do you know about it—how your family acquired it?"

"Only that it has been in our family for years."

"Ismael, yes, I will take good care of it . . . and recall our time together when I look at it. Thank you so much."

When the lights blink, we rise.

"Ismael, Yavar, I will see you at the picnic tomorrow." Then the difficult moment of saying goodbye to the families begins.

"Say *khodahafez* to Mister," their mothers prod the children. I bend down. They each put their arms around me. I grab and hug them deeply. I suspect they think I'm saying goodbye to them because they're going away for the summer—they think we will be together in the fall. They don't understand we will never see each other again. It is just as well that way. It's not as hard.

As I try to conceal the emotion that fills my mouth and head with the heavy salts of anguish, I long for the children's refreshing innocence. My friends' wives see the distress that wracks my face. We bid each other a difficult farewell. I walk into the night carrying the Chinese pot, barely able to see through the tears that now flow freely.

THURSDAY, JUNE 2, 1966 An outing at Nahar Khoran, an isolated summer picnic area in the mountain foothills a few kilometers from Gorgan, is fun, but the thought of parting preoccupies me, and it's on the minds of my friends as well. *It's strange—when I left Hawaii two years ago, I felt bad, but not like this. I wonder if it's because I knew I'd be returning in two years. My family and friends would still be there. Now I'm leaving my friends—my family—and I will never see them again.*

I strive to project my upbeat "Tom of Iran" nature, but I fear the serious "American Tom" is rearing its head—regaining control.

THURSDAY, JUNE 9, 1966 As if it were preordained, like striking water the day I arrived in Alang, this week, my last, work begins on the construction of a new bathhouse with showers. Similar construction has also started in Chahardeh and Bala Jaddeh. Plus, each village now has running water to individual courtyards. Tremendous progress has been made in the twenty months I've been here, but it's all because of them. In Alang, Shaban Ali and other young men had to argue hard at village council meetings for a bathhouse with showers. "Mister Tom won't take a bath in our common pool because it is too unsanitary—too dangerous. He bicycles to Kordkuy to take a shower," I heard them say. I am proud of what they have done, and am confident the momentum will continue.

SUNDAY, JUNE 12, 1966 I begin packing my suitcase for my trip home. Shaban Ali comes to help. He notices the photographs have been removed from the wall above my desk. We say very little—certainly our inability to articulate is a sign of the finality of our endeavor.

Finished, we sit quietly amid the boxes, glancing at the room and forlornly at each other. Nearly all the familiar signs of my existence are now stripped away.

"Tom," Shaban Ali says slowly, "I will miss you . . . thank you for coming to Iran." He hesitates longer. "You know . . . your being here has made me love my country more . . . *moteshakeram*."

"Shaban Ali, you are welcome. *Kheili moteshakeram.* That is the most beautiful thing you ever could have told me. I know you know I love Iran. Now I know you love Iran even more. I will never forget that. I will always love Iran, and I will always love you and the people of Alang. You truly are my family . . . my brother."

I wipe my eyes with my handkerchief.

MONDAY, JUNE 13, 1966 Many watch my desk, cabinets, and Peace Corps book locker hoisted over the balcony onto the top of Hajireza's bus. Next, my stove and tank of gas, kitchen table, and boxes of dishes are handed over the railing. My bicycle is heaved up to rest with everything else. My landlady and her children look on vacantly. Ghorbon, her oldest son, helps.

"Tom, don't go to America. Stay in Alang. Stay with us." Ghorbon says.

"Tom, sit here—right next to me." Hajireza points to the honored wooden stool beside him. "There is not much time for us to be together." Shaban Ali and Mulla take the seat behind us.

"Tom, don't go home. Stay here." As we head for Gorgan, Hajireza repeats the constant refrain, and others join in. "Alang is your home now."

"*Baleh*, Alang is my home, but I have to go back to America. I am sorry. I must go."

"Tom, we will take your things directly to Mister Jim's and Mister Noel's house. We can unload them there."

"*Moteshakeram*. Yes, they will be there to assist us."

I say goodbye to my Peace Corps friends and wish them well over the next year. "In a year, you'll be packing up too."

"Have a great trip home," they call out.

Soon, Shaban Ali, Mulla, and I are on another bus, heading to Alang. We go to my room. The kitchen is empty. My room is strangely disarrayed—already not mine. Mulla brings a wheelbarrow, and we transport to his house the huge roll of rugs, the crate with the bronze pot and other treasures, my air and sea freight containers, and my suitcase. All that is left are the three chairs and bed from Mr. Vahdati. When he comes to Alang later today for a farewell ceremony hosted by the village council, he will take the bed and chairs back to Gorgan.

That will be it—essentially the end of "Tom of Iran."

IN CONTRAST TO MY FIRST DAY IN ALANG, I prepare more properly for this ceremony. I wear a white shirt without a tie—as the men in Alang do—my dark suit pants, and best shoes. Words of appreciation and regret that I am leaving are exchanged; however, today I am so choked with emotion I can hardly voice what my heart and mind speak so clearly. *Haji* Tofigh presents me with a beautiful blue cloisonné vase on behalf of the village council.

The bed frame and chairs are loaded into the back of Mr. Vahdati's jeep. I thank him for all he has done for me. We shake hands. We wave goodbye.

Forlornly I trudge to my room. Somehow Shaban Ali, Mulla, and my friends know I have to do this alone. I look around at what had been home for nearly two years—the dung-covered walls with faded traces of where my rug and pictures hung, the plank floor, my curtains still at the windows, and the shade covering the bare bulb that hangs in the middle of the room. *That's all—only memories now.*

I lock the door and descend the stairs one last time. *Haji* Noorallah and his wife have been watching me silently, as have Ghorbon and his little sisters and brothers. I hand *Haji* the keys and manage a *moteshakeram.* Tears well in the eyes of *Haji*—this immutable man. Distressed, his wife leaves the porch for the comforting shelter of their house, her *chador* pulled over her face. I hear her sobbing within. Ghorbon and the children say nothing.

"Khodahafez," I say with a slight bow, my hands to my chest. I hear their *khodahafez* as I turn toward the courtyard gate. Everyone grimly watches as I walk alone along the street to Mulla's house.

TUESDAY, JUNE 14, 1966   The entire day is painful as was dinner last evening. Knowing this is the end of my stay in Alang, everybody comes to be with me. I am grateful to see them, but the intensity of my feelings is crushing. Though I don't want to go, I can hardly wait to be released from this misery. Dinner is again a heavy, somber occasion. All the joys of earlier days are gone.

When the party is over and the lights are out, very much alone I reflect on the past two years—what I have learned, who I was, how I have changed, and who I have become. I arrived as an idealist, positive in my conviction that I, a young American, could change the world . . . and I still am an idealist. But now my idealism is tempered by pragmatism, a realization of my own limitations, and that societies and individuals behave in ways that I cannot control or change. I can only hope that by enthusiasm and example others will be charged with a vision of the possibilities of a new world.

Although I tried to belong and they accepted me, I was always the odd one—the outsider. While I became "Tom of Iran," I used my American self whenever I saw it would work to my advantage. There was duplicity in my existence here. In some ways I regret that, but I suppose it can't be avoided. I am a person of two cultures now—not quite one and not quite the other.

I thought I had nothing in common with these people; I had lived in an entirely different world, with very different values. Now I see we aren't so different. There are certain basic human values we all cherish: love, peace, and understanding. We are more alike than we are different. I had to live out of my own cultural construct to see this clearly. It's strange. You can go through all kinds of higher education, but in the end, it comes down to opening yourself up to knowledge that comes from having your feet on the ground and being receptive to the words and feelings of others. Being here, I learned about a salient source of wisdom that has brought new meaning to my life. I learned to listen and be more open. This is undoubtedly a crossroad in my life where I embrace choices that will distance me from some American values. Above all, I gained new knowledge, new values—a form of understanding not aligned with objective reasoning, one filled with human and spiritual awareness.

It's ironic—while I was almost always with others, for the first time in my life I was alone. I had time to think, to determine what was important to me, and how I wanted to dream. I will be going back to America a different person, but I'm not sure whom this "American Tom" will be.

Most of all, being in the Peace Corps has given me confidence. I survived this, and it has taught me to be fearless in whatever I choose to do. Yet I know Iran will never be far from me.

WHAT A WAY TO GO

WEDNESDAY, JUNE 15, 1966 I lie there awake long before I hear the familiar and comforting sound of the pre-dawn call to prayer. In the next room, Mulla and his wife get up, so I, too, rise.

Mulla and I have breakfast together. We don't say much. Words are not necessary today. I remove the high school graduation ring from my finger.

"Mulla, I want you to have this . . . as a memory of me. You wanted to complete high school. With this ring, you will finish it."

"Tom, this is your ring. You need to keep it." He hands it back to me.

"No, Mulla, it's yours. I want you to have it. Please."

"Thank you, Tom. I *will* finish high school. Thank you for helping me." *

Someone calls Mulla. He goes to the door. "Tom, I have to take care of something," he calls back. "You finish breakfast. I'll return soon."

I hear him speaking with his wife. She enters and kneels politely near the door. "Tom, why did you empty your hand for Mulla?"

"Because Mulla is my very good friend. I want him to have my ring as a memory of me and to encourage him to finish high school."

"Tom, it is your ring. You must keep it—not give it to Mulla."

"No, I want him to have it. He is one of the best friends I have ever had. He is my brother. It is for him."

Others come to say *khodahafez* and we have tea together. Mulla tells somebody to take my things to the highway. Then the sad, final leave-taking begins—my friends and their children, their wives standing in the

---

* Mulla received his high school diploma in 1975. His son Ismael became a physician in 1997.

background but coming forward to say goodbye. Almost half of Alang is at Mulla's place. I cannot hold back—this is the saddest day of my life. Slowly, a nearly silent mass of men moves me toward the courtyard gate. There I glimpse Shirin, the object of my unfulfilled desire, standing to the side. She attempts a smile. I see her tears too. She pulls her *chador* over her face, turns, and heads alone down the street. I begin to cry even harder.

The walk to the highway is excruciating. More villagers come to say *khodahafez* and join the procession. At the roadside, as we wait for a bus, I look back at Alang—forever my home. A lone woman stands respectfully away from the men, her *chador* pulled tightly to her face. It is *Haji* Noorallah's wife, my landlady. Mulla recognizes her too and says, "She came by herself. You are truly her son."

Jafar hails an oncoming bus. My baggage is loaded while the passengers look on at the crowd of men embracing me and bestowing the traditional Iranian departing kiss on each cheek. Mulla boards and pulls me in. Shaban Ali, Reza, and Jafar follow. Mulla takes a seat in the half empty bus and indicates I should sit beside him. The others take seats across the aisle and behind. However, I go to the back, looking at my friends and Alang through the streams of tears that flow down my face. We wave. I strain to look until they and Alang are out of sight. Then I watch and watch until the fondly familiar peak of the Alborz behind Alang fades in the haze of the bright morning sky. I tremble in silence, unable to contain my feelings of intense and unyielding loss.

Much later, I join my friends. They say nothing, but Mulla gently puts an arm around me. My tears flow anew.

THE BUS STAGGERS IN ITS ASCENT into the valley of the Haraz. Ultimately, like an old and overworked donkey, it gives up, unable to budge. We wait beside the road, squinting in the bright, high-altitude sun. Another bus stops, eager to take on additional passengers and baggage.

In Tehran we quickly take my freight to Peace Corps headquarters. Then we catch a taxi to see Ismael Mirsalehi who is in Tehran for the summer to study English at the Iran-America Society. He is living with other guys who are also studying there. Our short visit is extended when one of Ismael's roommates brings a plump, *chador*-covered young woman upstairs. They go into an adjoining room. I look around, seeking to confirm my suspicions. The guy comes out and inquires, "Would anyone else like her? She's waiting."

"How was she?" someone asks.

"A little sweaty, but this is Tehran this time of year."

There is another taker. When he returns looking like a contented cat after having his mouse, he asks me, "Next?"

"*Na*," I say embarrassed. Somehow sloshing around in a well-trodden path seems too much like wading to the *mostarah* in Alang with all the rain we had recently—without my rubber boots!

"He's holding himself for tonight," Jafar volunteers. "Tom wants to go to Shahr-e Nou."

Following a little more delay and the eventual departure of the well-worked woman, we go to the hotel before dinner and the evening's entertainment. We all strip down to our underwear and lie on the beds, desperately trying to remain cool in the early summer heat.

"Tonight, we will sleep on the roof. It will be cool there," Jafar informs me. "These rooms are hot all night long. But first, Tom, before we go to Shahr-e Nou, we need proof you are circumcised."

I'm startled. As if that was going to make any difference at Shahr-e Nou. And if I weren't, would that stop us from going? Or would they immediately rush me out to have the necessary surgery performed? But I respond, "I've told you many times I'm circumcised."

"Yes, but we have no verification. We've heard most American men aren't circumcised." They are looking at my package, trying to determine my status through my briefs. "Tom, we need to see. Pull down your underwear. We need to be sure."

"No! I've told you, and I don't have to show you anything to prove it," I reply, decidedly irritated.

Jafar grabs a glass of water. "Then I'm going to dump this water on you unless you show us."

I kick the glass out of his hands, but not before the contents soak my crotch and reveal my condition through the white cotton fabric.

Satisfied I would make an acceptable Muslim, he says, "Tom, you broke the glass. You'll have to go out and buy a new one."

"You'll have to go buy one," I reproach him.

UNDER THE COVER OF DARKNESS, we head for our destination—a lot more discreet than the red-light district in Beirut, and much like any other Tehran neighborhood, with houses behind a courtyard gate.

Men ring buzzers and are let inside. Many seem to know where the preferred merchandise is. They must be regulars. We ring doorbells too, enter, and check out the *ab o hava* (weather, literally water and air, a euphemism for the wares). If the stock isn't up to par in one place, we investigate another source. It's sort of like going to the bazaar; you check out all the goods before you buy.

"Tom, do you see anything here you like?" I'm often asked.

"Na." We head for another place. Occasionally I notice someone missing from our group. I surmise he went back to make a discriminating purchase. After a while, with a satiated look, he hooks up with us again.

Often the women sit on a raised dais with the light intentionally directed so prospective customers get an unobstructed view of what they are procuring. Like in a waiting room, chairs are provided for clients. At one establishment, two rather enticing specimens sit nonchalantly showing their provisions. One is heavily made-up—rather hard; the other is softly delectable. She languidly raises an arm behind her head, running her fingers through her hair, causing her dress to hike up. I'm intrigued at how short the dress is—mini skirts and dresses had not yet been invented when I left America. She squirms so we can get a more advantageous view of her unpackaged commodity. My reaction is conspicuous.

"Tom, this is the one for you," one of my friends announces.

With contained difficulty I say, *"Na, befarmayid.* You go." It is obvious he is having a hard time holding in his reins. He rises, forks over his cash to the madam, and designates his preference.

"Leili."

The girl rises and coquettishly ambles off. Our friend follows. We wait, watching rapturously the beguiling movements of her workmate.

"Tom, go for it. She wants you," another of my companions encourages. "Leili," the madam calls again. We look at each other with disgust. "He only got in there," one of them says.

Leili reappears, sashays to her chair on the dais, and spreads herself out. We breathe heavily.

Our friend also returns looking a bit harried, but satisfied. "Was it OK?" somebody asks.

"*Baleh*, she is good. Tom, you will like her. It's your turn."

"*Baleh*, Tom, go for it. See, she's looking at you. She's yours. Come on. Do it," my cohorts goad me.

"*Na, nemekham*" (No, I don't want). The guys are greatly disappointed by my disinclination to partake.

My mind recoils. This all seems too public for me. There's no privacy. I might as well do it out in the street so everyone can see. In Hawaii, my friends and I never talked about what we did. We didn't discuss private matters. We'd tell the priest—in confession—and hope we wouldn't get a lecture and that the penance would only be a few Our Fathers and Hail Marys—not a whole rosary. We would promise not to do it again and we truly intended to be virtuous—at least while we were still in the confessional. That's the advantage of being Catholic. You can go to confession and get rid of all the sins and pray that if your time is coming it will be right after you say your penance, because you know the contrition won't last too long.

And this seems a bit dangerous—like playing Russian roulette. I didn't bring the necessary precaution, and to do it *bi lebas* (without clothes—condom) my last night in Iran would worry me all the way home, even though the girls are supposed to have a medical check each month. Still, you don't know what sort of social malady they might have contracted in the meantime. I don't want to be like one of the PCVs who tarried in Shahr-e Nou without the essential safeguard and was tormented for months about what might show up on his medical exams. Also, knowing myself, once I've gone down that easy rabbit hole, there's no turning back. I'll be looking for that ready Wonderland in every city I pass through, and God knows there are plenty of cheap enticements all along the way—Delhi, the infamous

Cages of Bombay, Calcutta, notorious Bangkok, Phnom Penh, the China dolls in old Hong Kong, Taipei, and, if I have any money left, the geisha houses of Tokyo. *Tom, this is one night you have to control yourself,* I resolve.

"No, not tonight," I tell the guys.

"But we came here just for you."

I inwardly laugh and think, *Just for me!*

"It's getting late. We ought to get back to the hotel," one finally suggests.

"I need to have a massage. I know a madam who gives me the best massages," another says. "Let's go there first."

Together we follow him to a run-down house in a seedy section of Shahr-e Nou. The grossly overweight and flabby madam clearly knows him well. They go off, and my friends and I look around at the environment. Obviously we were in a high-class neighborhood earlier. We hear noises from an upstairs room that plainly announce he is getting more than a massage, or at least a certain kind of massage. Eventually they emerge.

"Tom, she wants to give you a massage too."

"Na, nemekham," I decline.

"Chera? She's very good. She wants you. No charge."

"Na, nemekham," I repeat.

"Show him your boobs. I hear Americans like breasts. That will turn him on."

She obliges and instantly I'm sitting there with the biggest pair of knockers I ever experienced right in my face. I'm beginning to perspire and wonder when this is going to end and to what extreme it will go. I try to ignore the blatant natural scenery before me. Finally she puts them away.

"Ya Allah," one of the guys says. "It's time we get back to the hotel."

We hail a taxi. I remain silent, somewhat dismayed, but appreciative of our nocturnal escapade. Certainly it is a night to remember—my last in Iran. What a way to go!

JAFAR IS RIGHT. The room is still hot. The roof is a reprieve, but we need the blankets. For a while, we gaze out across the vastness of the city with its millions of lights. The snoring of others around us competes with the hum of traffic, punctuated by blaring horns. Though this is beautiful, my mind drifts to Alang and, again, I taste the salty sadness of my departure. "I'm putting the key here beside my bed in case anybody needs to go down to the room," Jafar says.

Soon I detect the guys are already asleep, but it's going to be a long time before I drift off. The day and night have been too highly charged for my mind to settle down quickly. I smile at the thought of the evening's entertainment and am relieved I was able to resist. But it's Alang that swells through my head. Vividly I see my friends as they were when I last walked through the village, the crowd at the highway, my last sight of Alang, and then the dimming mountain behind. My pillow is drenched from the tears that stream from my eyes and nose. Thoughts of Alang never go away. Alang will forever be drawn exquisitely in my memory, yet I fear it will be recalled only in memory. *My grief is in parting. What will there be to lean on when the drawing fades?* I cry and exhaust myself in sorrow.

. . . The bus stops at the highway. Everyone is there with me. We hug and kiss and I'm carried effortlessly, as if I am floating, into the village—my Alang, my home. My excitement is intense; I can hardly breathe. I am here forever, my friends—my family—all around. At Mulla's gate, my beautiful Shirin looks on, smiling. My heart quickens. There I lie on the street, as everybody watches. The enticing Leili unbuttons my shirt and rubs her fingers through the hair on my heaving chest. Her hands wander down into my pants. She gently touches my throbbing manliness. Despite my embarrassed objections, the massive madam with the huge boobs removes my pants and underwear. Completely naked and ashamed of my condition, I grab for my clothes. But she hands them to a horrific-looking witch who drops them in a nearby fire.

"No," I call out.

"You won't need them any more," she heckles. "It's always scorching here. You're sweating already. Poor Tom. Bring some of that soothing lather for him," she orders her noisy, ugly, well-toasted cohorts with long, stringy hair and bulging eyes. They wade into the stinking, stagnant, sewage-riddled puddle beside the road. Slimy goo oozes between their gnarled fingers as they bring the repugnant stench to lather me—every part of my naked white body. I see the radiant Shirin still looking on. I try to cover my extended nakedness, but now Shirin is crying. She pulls her

chador over her face, turns, and walks away. I fidget in an impossible attempt to escape, but my tormentors jeeringly hold me down. "Tom, don't fret, no shame, you'll be in this condition forever. We're all waiting for you. We want you. You are ours now. Though you may become tired, we won't. When you have finished all 72 of us, we'll start all over." One particularly eager shrew pulls me on top of her wretched naked body, grabs my head, and penetrates my mouth with her warty tongue. I nearly gag with the stench of her breath—not unlike that of a long-used mostarah. Her harsh nails dig into my back. Ugly companions roughly guide me inside her. It feels like I'm entering a tunnel lined with coarse sandpaper. The massive madam sits on my butt and starts pumping up and down; her pendulous breasts smash against my back. Humongous waves of sweaty, flabby fat surround me with each thrust, and my instrument aches from its rugged treatment. One of the nags grabs my exposed parts and yanks . . .

"Arrgh." My body heaves and convulses. My heart pounds violently and I breathe heavily. The bed is wet from perspiration, and my pajamas and the sheets are a mess from my explosion. I wait with anxiety for the inflamed swelling to subside and hope my cold, wet pajamas will dry before daybreak. They don't. As the first light of dawn signals the beginning of this sad day, and while it's still dark, so no one sees what happened, I grab the keys and go down to the room to clean up.

THURSDAY, JUNE 16, 1966 "I need to get my tickets from Pan Am, go to the Peace Corps office for my mail, and get travelers checks. I'll be busy all morning. Let's meet here at the hotel in the afternoon. By then, Javad will be here. Then tonight we're all going out to dinner on me. My flight to New Delhi departs at 10:05, so we have to be at the airport well before that."

I suspect where at least some of the guys will be going while I'm away; however, not one mentions intentions and destinations.

The Peace Corps covers the cost of our airfare home by the least expensive route—that being through Europe. I opted to return via the Orient to see the places and art I had studied. Brent is the other volunteer going home through Asia, so we planned to travel together for the first several weeks. He did not want to go to Nepal. Consequently, I changed my itinerary to travel with him through India. Then I discover he changed his mind and is going to Nepal.

Barkley is staying another year to complete some projects; however, he is returning home for a few weeks to see his parents. We sit down together to read our mail. Mom's letter includes a newspaper clipping about Barkley.

"Wow, Barkley, this is outstanding! Why didn't you tell us?"

"What?"

I show him the clipping about how the city of Gonbad-e Kavus built a monument to him. Barkley registers considerable agitation.

"This is all false. I don't know anything about this. Can I take this upstairs to show the director? I want an explanation."

I sit there, even more disillusioned with the Peace Corps and America than I was at our termination conference a month ago, when we were coerced to write glowing reports to send to Washington. And now this! The big news stories about Peace Corps Iran are all false. First there was the useless bridge at Pol-e Bihajat that hit *The Dinah Shore Show*. Then the international incident, when an Iran PCV crossed the Soviet border on a dare, was seized by the Soviet border patrol, and it took weeks of negotiation between Washington and the Kremlin to secure the volunteer's release. Meanwhile, US papers ranted that Soviet soldiers had crossed the border into Iran, kidnapped him, and the USSR was holding him illegally. There was also the story of the school a PCV built with funds from America. That's fine, but the Iranians called it the "American school." It was not *their* school. Now this, about Barkley. So much could be told—truthfully— about Barkley. Why do they make something up? Lies! Why can't America just tell the truth? And we were critical of Iran's subtle control of thought when they censored the song about Officer Krupke in *West Side Story*.

I'm going home to a country I have always loved so much—and I still love America—but America is not the pure and sacred place I thought it was. Has something happened to me, or is it America? Being in the Peace Corps has taught me never to believe what comes out in the media. It's made me a terrible skeptic. Worse, it's reinforced my distrust of officials and authority. The seeds of constant questioning my parents implanted as a kid, now based on my new reality, have deeper meaning and relevance.

OUR DINNER AT PAPRIKA, a little Hungarian restaurant that is a favorite of foreigners, is painful—our final meal together, forever—the seven of us: Shaban Ali, Mulla, Reza, Javad, Ismael, Jafar, and me. I can barely eat.

Brent is already at the airport when we arrive. He takes a picture of my friends and me. *I'm holding up pretty well,* I compliment myself. However, when the flight is called, I totally break down. *This is it—forever.*

I hug each of them, board the plane, and sink into my seat in uncontrollable anguish.

Mehrabad Airport: Javad, Shaban Ali, Reza, Tom, Jafar, Mulla, Ismael

FRIDAY, JUNE 17, 1966 It's already sweltering when we arrive in New Delhi in the early morning—the temperature is well over 100°. It makes the nearly unbearable heat of Tehran seem cool by comparison. Brent and I go to the Peace Corps hostel. My gut is rebelling, causing me to spend the next three days in two places—in bed and in the bathroom. But my mind is somewhere else—in Alang. Alang rarely leaves me. I realize I am incredibly homesick. Maybe that's causing my upset stomach, just as I took culture shock out on my stomach the first months I was in Iran. Often, in my despair, I resolve to get on a plane and return to Iran—forever, for good. Then my rational mind counters, *Tom, you fool, you can't do that. You're going home to America. Get Alang out of your mind. You are an American, and you need to take responsibility for your life. You are going to graduate school. You have a career to pursue.* But the pull of Alang plays on my emotions, and I want to return. Slowly I force my pragmatic mind to dominate; the cramps dissipate, I begin to eat again, and Brent and I go on nearby excursions before he departs for Nepal.

Alone, and with resignation that I am reverting to serious "American Tom," I head south across the staggeringly hot Indian subcontinent by train and bus.

THE DISTANCE REMAINS

FRIDAY, AUGUST 26, 1966 With thoughtful trepidation, I board the aircraft in Tokyo. *I made it this far; I guess I can make it the rest of the way.* A training flight had crashed on the Haneda runway six hours earlier, killing all five of the flight crew.

Trembling with excitement, I momentarily stand at the open door of the parked Pan Am Clipper, surveying the glaringly bright island sky. Once familiar cool, heavy trade winds salute my arrival in Honolulu. *I am home—back in America,* I tell myself with near disbelief. However, the thrill of being home is tempered with apprehension, a feeling that I no longer belong here. I have experienced so much since I walked upon this ground nearly two years ago; it seems anticlimactic to return. I am now a citizen of the world.

"Welcome home." The passport official looks up and smiles as he confirms my identity with the document's photo. "Peace Corps?" he asks. He had seen the NO FEE and Dean Rusk-stamped signature inside the cover.

"Yes." I had almost responded *baleh.*

"Thank you for representing America abroad." He stamps the page containing my photo.

IMM. & NATZ. SERVICE
HONOLULU, HAWAII 379
ADMITTED
AUG 26, 1966

SOON I'M ON A BUS to friends' in downtown Honolulu.

"Can I call my brother?" I ask. "It's my parent's 27th anniversary. They don't know I was coming home today. I told them it would be sometime in early September."

When my brother answers I say, "Alan. This is Tom."

"Tom! Are you *here*? In *Hawaii*?"

"Yeah, I got in from Japan a couple hours ago. I'm at Les and Jo's. Can you pick me up here? I can't wait to see you and Mom and Dad."

"Gosh, welcome back. I'll be there as soon as I finish work. It will be terrific to see you."

When Alan arrives I suggest, "Let's get Mom and Dad some flowers for their anniversary." We stop at a local mom-and-pop store on Nuuanu Avenue and buy torch ginger.

Outside on the sidewalk, Alan bursts into laughter. "You've been away too long! You're completely out of it."

"What do you mean?"

"The way you came out of that shop—you're so funny."

"Funny? Why? How did I come out?"

"You backed out. And you bowed and nodded all the way as you thanked them. You're really weird!" he scoffs.

"Gee, Alan, I didn't even know I did that."

Riding home, I wonder if I really have changed in these two years.

Alan turns off the engine and we coast into the driveway. I glimpse Mom and Dad sitting at the table. Mom heard the car anyway and looks out the kitchen window. "Ooooh, ooooh, ooooh," she squeals as she rushes out the door. She grabs me and hugs me as I get out of the car. All the while she utters, "Ooooh, ooooh, ooooh." Dad stands at the door, smiling.

"That's it. I can't eat anything," Mom says, sobbing. She sits in her chair, looks at me, and continues crying. "Today's our wedding anniversary. Oh, this couldn't be better. This couldn't be better," she constantly repeats. "It's so good to have you home." More tears flow. "You have letters from Alang." Though I want to read them, being home with family is more important now.

Still crying, Mom calls her sister. "Tom is home. . . . Yes, he's home."

Soon my cousins Debbie and Denise fly in the door and give me their hugs and kisses. The girls have grown a bit; otherwise, everything seems the same. It's hard to believe I'm home with my family.

As I lie in bed, I ponder how different I feel. They're all the same, but I don't quite relate. *If I was an anomaly in Iran, why am I an anomaly here? I love them, but somehow I feel like an outsider—removed from them.* They ask me questions, but they seem only half-interested. Maybe it's just that they—or I—can't grasp that I am home.

LATE 1966—SUMMER 1971 The distance remains for a very long time. I am home but not at home. No longer can I relate to America. The unbridled consumption and waste are disgusting. The first time I take my mother to the supermarket, I walk out and sit in the car to wait for her. The abundance and the packaged consumerism are more than I can handle. I left one kind of America, and I have come back to another. Has it changed that much, or is it me? Yes—now there's the Vietnam War, turbulent anti-war protests, hippies, and LSD.

I spend weeks in the library, devouring back issues of *Time* magazine, striving to fathom the country and culture that proceeded along at breakneck speed while I remained calmly immersed in nearly a different century. America and I had both passed the Age of Innocence.

In a conversation with my mother and her sister about Iran and Islam, I mention, "We all believe in one God; so we aren't that different. Muslims have a high regard for Jesus and Mary; however, for them, Jesus is not God. I see the practice of religion as cultural, and if I had stayed in Iran I would have become a Muslim because it would have been the most appropriate way of expressing my belief within that culture."

My mother listens thoughtfully.

"Have you lost your faith because you lived in Iran?" my Aunt Dodo exclaims. She is appalled I would utter such a statement.

Graduate studies at the University of Hawaii present greater possibilities than other schools for building on the understanding I had gained in Iran. At the core of my graduate work are perceptions of space and the spiritual that stem from my life in the Middle East.

It's exciting to exchange stories with Del when she returns from Africa after New Year's. She is heading off to southern California for graduate school, so our days together are brief.

Lily and I enjoy each other's company until she graduates with her nursing degree and heads to Hilo for Peace Corps training. Painfully I see her depart for Thailand almost exactly three years after I left for Iran.

LETTERS FROM IRAN tell of the loss they feel without my presence and the difficulty children have in comprehending that I don't visit them any more. "Rozy called out in her sleep, '*Amo* Tom, *koja-i* (Uncle Tom, where are you)? *Chera dar manzel neesti* (Why aren't you at your house)? *Manzele tu khalieh* (Your house is empty). *Amo* Tom, *beah*'" (come). Reza continues, "The light went from my village when you left." Little do they know the loss I feel being separated from them. In my mind, I resolve I will return.

Ismael Mirsalehi writes that he attained the highest score in the English exam, but dropped out of the course at the Iran-America Society because the class was too easy. Later he was accepted at the university, passing the entrance exam in sixth place out of nearly 500 applicants. His scores in English were the highest.

I frame the drawing of *Haji* Torfeh's husband and photograph myself with it. At Christmas, I write to *Haji* and enclose the photo. Mulla writes, "Your letter arrived on your New Year's Day. *Haji* was weak, but I read her the letter and showed her your picture. Slowly *Haji* said, 'Say goodbye to him.' She closed her eyes, her head sunk into the pillow, and she died."

Other letters I receive in the first year I am back trouble me deeply. Somehow my name has been placed on the rosters of subversive domestic groups soliciting money to overthrow the government of the United States by any means. With each letter, I shudder at the thought of anyone wanting to bring about the demise of our great country. Yes, I would like America to be perfect, and there is much that needs to be improved, but having lived and traveled in other countries, I know America is the best there is. I am convinced that the way to bring about change is to be involved in initiating change within the system—not getting rid of the system. Nevertheless, how my name and address were obtained perplexes me. I have done nothing since I got home to warrant this; I've joined no anti-war protests, nor written any letters criticizing the government. I ask other returned volunteers if they have had similar letters. None has. I wonder if my critical Peace Corps termination letter sent up a red flag and the Peace Corps fed my name and address to subversive groups to see how far I would go. Nothing would surprise me. The many false media accounts about the Peace Corps in Iran and the stories about foreign students being duped into subversive activities by CIA operatives concern me. Again I lament that the country I love so much is not unblemished.

THOUGH I OBTAIN A MFA in June 1968, my search for a teaching position bears no fruit. My desire to return to Iran seems remote. A move to southern California in August 1969 to teach within the state college system provides some hope. Meanwhile, my interest in living Iranian culture, one truly Islamic, grows. When I was there, my attention centered on ancient Iran. As I learn, I become more convinced I must return to see and document much of what I ignored when I lived there.

On New Year's Eve 1969, alone, in a little rented cottage ten houses away from the birthplace of our presiding president, Richard Nixon, I make a New Year's resolution: *I am going to Iran.* Not this summer—I couldn't save enough by then—but the summer of 1971. I'll set up a special Iran account to save for the trip.

My friends in Alang beg me to come back, but I don't apprise them of my intent. I would hate to disappoint them if I can't go.

MEMORIES, MEMORIES

TUESDAY, JUNE 1, 1971 As the flight from Rome to Tehran enters Iranian airspace, I run from side to side within the near-empty aircraft, straining to see all I can of the land I have missed so intensely for so long. The endless, barren, tan-colored landscape below is hardly forbidding—only accepting. Even from this height one can distinguish the life-giving dots of the *qanats* (underground aqueducts) that march in file like soldiers for miles across the desert.

We begin our descent into Tehran. As passengers disembark, I momentarily sit in stunned silence, unable to imagine I am back in Iran.

"You want to go here?" the taxi driver exclaims when I hand him Ismael Mirsalehi's address. "This is not a hotel. This is a small alley in an old part of Tehran."

"It is my friend's house."

"Your friend?"

"*Baleh*, my friend lives there. He goes to the university. He and his family are from Gorgan. I was an American Peace Corps Volunteer in a village near Gorgan from 1964 to 1966. He was a teacher in the village. I have wanted to return to Iran ever since I left five years ago."

The taxi driver is enthralled with his unusual passenger—an American who speaks Farsi and who is being delivered to a poor section of Tehran.

He stops at the entry to a tiny street. "Wait. I'll see if the house is here."

He probably finds it inconceivable that an American would venture into this part of Tehran. After a while he returns. "*Baleh*, this is the place. Your friend is not at home. He is at the university this evening, but his little boy is home. He said he knows Mister." The driver maneuvers down the narrow alley and stops at a large blue metal gate; except for the number 159, it is indistinguishable from any other.

"Davood." I smile at Ismael's son. He greets me shyly. "*Agha*, thank you for bringing me here," I say gratefully to the driver, who seems reassured his perseverance was not in vain.

Davood closes the gateway door. A loud clang echoes through the neighborhood.

"Davood, you have gotten big. How old are you now?

"Eight years old." He leads me across the courtyard to the house.

"Where are your mother and sisters, Davood?"

"They are in Gorgan. Tomorrow my father and I are going to Gorgan. He has his final exam tonight."

"When will your father come home?"

"About nine o'clock."

"Davood, have you and your father had dinner?"

"*Baleh*, we had dinner before he went to his class."

"And what were you doing, Davood?"

"I was upstairs watching TV at my friend's house."

"Oh, I'm sure you like TV. Well, you go and watch TV. I'm going to get some dinner. I will ring the doorbell when I come back."

I savor the nearly forgotten authentic taste of *chelo khoresht* (rice and stew) and think about how great it is to be back in Iran—a place I love so much. Even walking the path back to the house seems real: the smells, the sounds—except for the TVs—and the children playing, looking at me curiously, and shouting, "Hello *Meesteer*. Hello."

Davood politely leads me across the courtyard to the house. "You go back upstairs and watch TV," I tell him. "I will stay here until your father comes."

When the gate opens I hear Davood flying down the stairs.

"*Baba*, Mister *amad*" (Papa, Mister came)!

Ismael greets me with a kiss on each cheek, in the Persian manner of friends who have long been separated. "Tom," he says with a grand smile, "you have a *bist-o-noh sibeel*" (twenty-nine mustache).

"A *bist-o-noh sibeel?*"

"*Baleh*. Twenty-nine is a nearly maximum mustache in Iran, as the word for thirty in Farsi is *si* and the word for mustache is *sibeel*. So your twenty-nine mustache is a very big *sibeel*. And your hair is longer now. You are almost a hippie."

"*Baleh*, almost a hippie," I repeat, grinning.

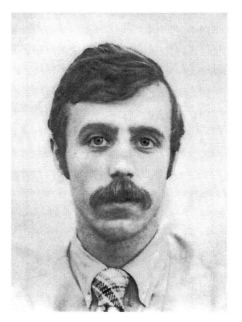

Tom with *bist-o-noh sibeel*, 1971

We spend the evening catching up on our lives since we saw each other at the airport five years ago.

"Tom, tomorrow you must come to Gorgan with us. My wife will be happy to see you. Vida and Sima too."

"It will be super to see them and your parents and brother again. I have never seen Sima."

"*Baleh*, but she knows you from your pictures. And she talks about Mister. Khanpoor is living in Gorgan now. He will be very glad to see you. Why didn't you tell us you were coming?"

"Ismael, I didn't want to disappoint you in case I didn't make it. I have been saving my money since New Year's Day 1970 so I could come back to see all of you."

WEDNESDAY, JUNE 2, 1971 Memories, memories—the journey across the mountains, through the wondrous valley of the Haraz, the familiar, nearly unchanged towns along the Caspian, the sight of the identifying peak behind Alang, and then Alang. I look out longingly as we pass. It is all I can do to resist requesting to get out here.

"Tomorrow I will be home," I tell Ismael and Davood. They witness the dampness in my eyes.

"Tom, stand here—right in front of the door," Ismael tells me when we reach their courtyard. He knocks on the door.

"Baba?" I hear Vida respond and the sound of footsteps advancing.

"Baleh," Ismael answers.

The door opens. Vida's eyes grow large. "Mister!" Sima looks on cautiously.

"Mama, Mister *amad*," Vida calls back.

"Mister?" I hear her mother's voice from the house.

"Baleh, Mister, with *Baba* and Davood."

Her mother comes running. Ismael's parents and Taghi are right behind. Ismael and Davood are thrilled to be in on the surprise.

After exchanging greetings, I say, "It's wonderful to be with family again. Better than returning home to America five years ago. It was good to see my parents and brother, but I felt very strange being home. It was home, but it was no longer home. I felt like I didn't belong there any more. Here, I have come home to being 'Tom of Iran,' if only for a while. I have missed Iran and all of you."

"We're happy you are back. Let's go surprise the Khanpoors too."

"Walking the streets of Gorgan is like a time warp, Ismael. It's like I never left."

The excitement of seeing the Khanpoors is overwhelming. They find it hard to believe I'm here and my *bist-o-noh sibeel* is a topic of much teasing.

THURSDAY, JUNE 3, 1971 *"Aghaye* Mister Tom!" Hajireza shouts, his golden countenance filled with elation when I show up at the bus station. He bestows the typical Persian greeting. "Tom, when did you come? *Bah, bah, bah.* Let's go to Alang right now. We can't wait for the bus to fill. Let's go."

Now older, Hajireza's bus, *Mashini Mashti Mamdali*, rattles more than ever as we sail at full throttle along the highway to Alang.

With horn blaring, we bump through the main street, pass the Sherkat-e Sargardon, and stop near the water tower. Reza and company saw me as we passed. They come running, and the joy of seeing each other is intense. Mulla takes me and my bags to his house. Little Ismael has grown; he is shy—no longer the toddler that cried for his *Amo* Tom. Reza's Rozy, too, is shy and reserved. Shaban Ali's children, also, have gotten big—it's amazing what five years have done. But my friends and, importantly, the Sherkat-e Sargardon have not changed. The day is one grand reunion. Soon my lagging Farsi is entirely restored.

"Shaban Ali, let's visit *Haji* Tofigh and Ezetollah. I can't wait to see them."

Our reception is warm and filled with gentle memories of my arrival in Alang on the day water surged from the bountiful earth and of the two years in which I became an Alangi. *Haji* is proud I now teach at a university in America. He gathers the letters I sent him and thanks me for remembering him.

"*Haji*, thank you for your letters. I, too, have kept them."

The following days are filled with the joy of catching up on five years of separation and visiting nearby Islamic buildings. But our visit to the Imamzadeh Ibrahim and the cemetery at the edge of Alang is disturbing.

"Where are the tombstones?" I ask.

"We got rid of them. They were a problem when we cut the grass."

"Cut the grass? The sheep always cut the grass."

"*Baleh*, but we have a lawn mower now. The stones were a bother, so we dug them up and threw them away."

"Threw them away! Where did you throw them?"

"In a ravine."

My heart sinks. I had intended to photograph and make a rubbing of the stone with the ancient calligraphic inscription I admired on my first visit to the cemetery. What a waste. Something so old—so beautiful—gone forever. If I had known they were going to throw it away I might have shipped it home. Now there isn't even a photographic record of it—nothing!

SUSPICIONS AND DECEPTIONS

MONDAY, JUNE 28, 1971 The bus heads southwest from Tehran to Saveh on the first leg of my journey across Iran to study and photograph Islamic architecture. Late in the day, I reach the holy city of Qom and relinquish my passport at the hotel desk as we did when we traveled in Iran as PCVs. It will be returned as soon as it is registered with SAVAK. As I open the door to my room, the deep and sublime call to prayer pervades the air. "*Allahu Akbar...Ash-had an-la ilaha illa Allah...*" The call is soothing and peaceful—a reminder of the religion that garners my respect, if not my adherence. Though the room is hot—it faces west and the setting sun—my body quivers at the sound and the sight from the window. The golden dome and tiled minarets of the shrine of Masumeh are silhouetted against the gloriously pink evening sky. As the sun disappears, the domes and minarets are bathed in lights. How could anything in this world be more resplendent—more spectacular?

TUESDAY, JUNE 29, 1971 "Why do you want that? Are you going to make a rug?" The vendor clearly finds it peculiar a foreigner wants to buy a rug design. "You should buy a rug."

"No, I'm not going to make a rug, and I cannot afford a rug from Qom, but I would like to buy a drawing from you. I am an art professor, and I want to show my students in America how designs for rugs are made on graph paper and then the weavers make a rug from it."

"Oh, you plan to teach your students how to make Persian rugs?" His fear a clever American will take over the Persian carpet industry is apparent.

"No, I'm not going to teach them how to make carpets. I want them to know how carpets are made so they will have an appreciation for the rugs that come from Iran. Perhaps they will want to buy Persian rugs."

"How do you know Farsi?" His wariness is still evident.

"I was an American Peace Corps Volunteer in Iran for two years. This summer I returned to see my Iranian friends and to study Islamic art. Will you sell me the drawing you made?"

"I've never had anyone buy one of my patterns just for the design. Only people who make rugs buy from me."

"Well, you are an artist and I am an artist too. I would like to have one of your art works as a memory of you."

His apprehension turns to well-deserved pride, and he sells me the drawing.

AS SHADOWS STRETCH across the square fronting the shrine, pilgrims file past, oblivious to me. Beggars patiently wait for their alms and humbly thank the pious for their charity. While I watch, I calculate that a beggar collects more than a full-day salary in less than an hour if everyone gives only the smallest coin. I'm reminded of my friend Gholam Husayn, the *kargar*, who works hard under the burning sun all day to receive much less.

WEDNESDAY, JUNE 30, 1971 Dressed in a black long-sleeve shirt with a tiny gray floral pattern, dark gray low-rise flared trousers, and my good shoes, I approach the office of the shrine of Masumeh. With my *bist-o-noh sibeel* (twenty-nine moustache) and longish hair, I look like a restrained hippie, hopefully, conservative enough to allow me into the shrine, especially with the official letter of introduction from my dean.

As a professor from California, I am greeted with respectful courtesy. "Please show him the entire shrine and the museum," my escort is instructed. "And let him take pictures too."

I remove my shoes and reverently enter as hundreds of pilgrims stream past. The chamber under the golden dome that contains the cenotaph of Fatimah—Hazrat-e Masumeh—the sister of Imam Reza whose burial place I visited in Mashhad on that ignoble New Year's Eve with Shaban Ali, dazzles with its infinitely reflecting mirror work. A sort of Westminster

Abbey of Iran, the complex houses the tombs of four Safavid and two Qajar shahs, Qajar princes, and many court officials.

IN KASHAN I GREET THE PROPRIETOR and his clients as I step inside a local *chai khaneh* (café) at the entrance to the bazaar.

"*Chelo khoresht-e badenjan, lotfan*" (Rice and eggplant stew, please).

Conversation momentarily ceases. All eyes are upon me. I nod and greet each man as we make eye contact. Suddenly the place is abuzz.

"Where are you from? How do you know Farsi? Why did you come to Kashan?"

The questions go on and on. The shop remains busy long after everybody finishes eating.

"*Agha*, can I leave my bag with you? I want to see Bagh-e Fin and the bazaar, and then go to Natanz. I am told it is cooler there at night than it is in Kashan."

"*Baleh, befarmayid.*" He takes my suitcase and puts it behind the counter. "Natanz is very pleasant. You will like it."

A leisurely stroll in the quiet, lush garden of Bagh-e Fin,* with its refreshing murmur of water channels and bubbling fountains protected by the cooling shade of cypress and plane trees, is a welcome respite from the unrelenting heat of the vast desert landscape beyond the city. The soft, sweet smell of roses fills the air; their bushes line the stone pathways.

Back in town, I'm consumed by the excitement of the 19th century covered bazaar, its grand domes a honeycomb of tiny *muqarna* (niches). Nearly everyone greets me with familiarity—many were in the café at lunch—and they quickly introduce me to their friends. Instantly I become the curiosity and the entertainment. Persian hospitality demands we have tea together.

At the edge of the steps of a narrow passageway, an old man has staked out a few feet of selling space—mostly junk, but also blue-and-white tiles splattered with dried mortar. "They're old," he tells me when I pick one up.

---

* Built in the Safavid period and fed by a spring on a hillside behind, the garden is a Persian vision of paradise. It garnered the special interest of Shah Abbas I (1571–1629) who constructed at its center a two-story pavilion over the watercourses. In the 19th century the Qajars, especially Fath Ali Shah, added to the garden.

"How old, *Agha*?"

"Old! A hundred years! They are Qajar—from an old house in Natanz."
A modern renovation and the old tiles are no longer wanted, I suspect.

"How much, *Agha*?"

"For one or all of them?"

"One. I can't buy all of them. They are too heavy for me to carry."

"Sixty tomans ($8.00) for one."

We settle on half that, and I stuff the tile into the bag with my camera.
Old ceramic pots lure me into another shop. *"Salaam, Agha,"* I warily greet
the owner. I have heard Persians are experts in making fake old pots, and I
don't know the field well enough to be able to detect their artistry. *The way
I am going to learn is to look and talk with shopkeepers,* I rationalize.

"Agha, how much is this?" I ask as I clean the grime from a tile. I don't
need to ask about its date or where it is from. It is a fragment from a *mihrab*
(prayer niche) from Kashan—13th century.

"Seven hundred tomans" ($93.00).

I haggle over the price and we agree on 400 tomans ($53.00).

"Aghaye Mister, would you like to see the ceramics at my house?"

With unease, I agree to go with him, leaving the glazed tile in his shop.
Together we walk to the edge of the bazaar and get in his plush automobile.
In a short time we are at his house somewhere in Kashan. I feel like a little
boy in a candy shop. I decide I may be interested in a 13th century turquoise
ceramic tile. We agree on a price of 400 tomans. It may not be real, but it's
so beautiful—and $53.00 isn't that much.

"Agha, I had planned to go to Natanz today. Now the banks are closed so
I won't be able to cash a travelers check until tomorrow morning. Do you
know of an inexpensive hotel where I could stay tonight? Then tomorrow
I will meet you at your shop and I'll give you the 800 tomans."

"Fine. We'll get your bag and I'll take you to a hotel near the bazaar."

The hotel is truly local—up a stairs, with tiny rooms, and a sign out
front I can barely read.

They didn't even take my passport. In all likelihood, they've never had
a foreign guest before, I surmise as I settle into my room. I run off to find
dinner, fully aware of every turn I make so I can retrace my steps to the

hotel. A *chai khaneh* has a big pot of *ab gusht* (lamb soup)—one of my favorite peasant foods. I enjoy a serving with the traditional bread, *sangak*, and return to my room to admire and clean the four-dollar Qajar tile.

THURSDAY, JULY 1, 1971 *"Sobh bekheyr,"* I greet the man at the *chai khaneh.*

"Sobh bekheyr," he smiles, happy I returned for breakfast.

I'm soon entertaining the morning crowd with my ability to converse in Farsi. I am inevitably a boon for business.

When the bank opens, I cash my travelers check and head for the bazaar. Kashan's fabled summer heat is already debilitating. In a nearby café, I stop to drink a Pepsi. A man approaches.

"Salaam," he greets me. Then he shows me a card, and the hair on the back of my neck stands on end. SAVAK!

"Salaam," I respond. "Can I offer you a Pepsi?"

"Na, moteshakeram (No, thank you). I need to ask you some questions," he goes on in Farsi as he takes a chair on the other side of the table.

"Baleh," I say cautiously, my mind careening.

"Can I see your passport?" I hand it to him. He inspects it. "Thomas Michael Klobe." He looks at me.

"Baleh. I go by Tom. You can call me Tom." My friendliness is deliberate.

"How do you know Farsi?"

"I learned Farsi as an American Peace Corps Volunteer in Iran from 1964 to 1966."

"Where were you in Iran? Where were you stationed?"

"In a village near Gorgan in the north."

"What is the name of the village?"

"Alang," I reply with external ease and casualness but internal reluctance.

"Alang." He takes notes in a little book.

"Baleh."

"And what is your profession?"

"I am a teacher."

"Where do you teach?"

"In California, at one of the state colleges near Los Angeles."

"Why did you come back to Iran?"

"To see my friends and to research Islamic art and architecture. Someday I hope to teach Islamic art."

He fingers my passport and inspects the Iran visa. "I notice you entered Iran on June 1st."

"Baleh."

"Today is July 1st. Where have you been the last month?"

"I was visiting friends in the north."

"And anywhere else?"

"In Tehran. I wanted to see the museums and mosques in Tehran. As I said, someday I intend to teach Islamic art, so I need to see and study as much as I can. I have become very interested in the art of Islamic Iran."

"Have you been anywhere else?"

"I went to Saveh to photograph the Masjid-e Jomeh (Friday Mosque). Then Qom. Qom was incredible. I was given a tour of the shrine of Masumeh. It is very beautiful."

"You came to Kashan yesterday. How is it you seem to know everyone in Kashan? Have you been here before?"

He knows I came here yesterday. And he thinks I know everyone in Kashan.

"Oh, I don't know everyone in Kashan. This is my first visit to Kashan."

"But many people in Kashan know you."

"Oh, I talk to anyone who wants to talk to me. I love Iran and Iranians. I guess people like to talk with me because I know Farsi. I like to speak Farsi too."

"Where did you stay last night?"

"In a little hotel on the other side of the bazaar."

"What was the name of the hotel?"

"I don't know. You go this way, and then that way, and then that way, and a little farther on is the hotel," I tell him, motioning with my hands.

"You shouldn't stay in places like that. You should stay at the hotel where the tourists go. It is better."

"This hotel is fine. It is good enough for me. Besides I don't like hotels where tourists are. I would rather be with Iranians. I didn't come all the way to Iran to be with other tourists."

"Where did you have dinner last night?"

"At a little *chai khaneh*. It was near the hotel."

"What did you eat?"

"Ab gusht."

"Ab gusht! That is bad!"

"I like *ab gusht*. It's very good."

"No, it is bad. It is peasant food. It is not healthy. You should have eaten at the hotel where all the foreigners eat."

"No, *ab gusht* is very healthy. I always eat at places where Iranians eat because the food is safer. The food will be freshly made and the ingredients will not have sat around before they are prepared. In the hotels where Westerners go often the food is spoiled before it is cooked. It is very dangerous because those places don't have adequate business. I know. That is why I always eat where Iranians are eating."

"No, in the future you should eat at the hotels where tourists eat."

I think, *This guy just doesn't get it.*

More questions continue. Then, "When are you leaving Kashan?"

"Today."

"Where are you going?"

"To Natanz."

"Why are you going to Natanz? There is nothing there."

"Oh, there are very important Islamic monuments at Natanz. The Masjid-e Jomeh is from the early 14th century. And there's the Khaneqah and the Imamzadeh Abd al-Samad."

"Where are you staying tonight?"

"In Natanz."

"There is no place to stay in Natanz. There is no hotel there."

"I find that hard to believe. Everybody tells me I should stay in Natanz—that it is cool there, that it's very nice. People from Kashan even go to Natanz during the summer to get away from the heat here. They say it's very pleasant there."

"No, there is no hotel in Natanz. There is no place to stay. You can go there during the day and then come back to Kashan."

"No, from Natanz I am going to Ardestan and Na'in.

"What time do you expect to go to Natanz?"

"Very soon. There is a bus to Natanz from Kashan every fifteen minutes. It takes an hour to get there."

"No, there is only one bus a day to Natanz. It departs at 2:30 in the afternoon. You can go on that bus only. There are no other buses."

"I was told there is a bus to Natanz every fifteen minutes."

"No, there is just one bus every day—at 2:30. That is the one you take."

I don't answer.

"Excuse me." He goes to the café desk and asks to use the telephone. I look at my watch. Nearly an hour has passed. I decide it is time to be on my way. I rise and start to the door. The agent abruptly stops me. "Sit down," he commands. Despite the heat a chill sidles down my back. He hangs up the receiver. "Come with me."

Outside he hails a taxi and I am whisked off to a building somewhere. I am ushered upstairs. The agent introduces me to another man who speaks English. I am asked the same questions in English and given the same advice. The first agent is writing in an adjacent room—no doubt a report on his interview with me. I contradict the same directives about hotels, eating, and traveling to Natanz that shortly before I argued in Farsi. I have little time to think—just answer the questions as rapidly as possible. Another hour passes quickly. Then the first interviewer comes in. The two confer briefly and the first then reads his report in Farsi to the second interviewer. When I detect mistakes I rebut, "That's not what I said. It was this way…"

"Well, Mr. Klobe, you go back to your hotel. At 2:30 you can take the bus to Natanz. However, there is no place to stay in Natanz so you will have to return to Kashan tonight. You must stay in the tourist hotel. Do you understand?"

"*Baleh.*"

They conduct me downstairs and hail a taxi. I instruct the driver to take me to the entrance to the bazaar so I can find my hotel from there. Calmly at first, I sit on the bed. Then I start thinking. My mind races and my heart begins pounding so clamorously I'm sure it can be heard over half of Kashan. The loudness nearly bursts my eardrums. I am wet with perspiration, not only from the unbearable heat of Kashan, but from the anxiety of what I just endured and what I have heard SAVAK can do.

Funny—I was so calm all the while I was interrogated. However, now my angst is reaching a point where I can hardly breathe. I feel I am going to explode any moment.

I look at my watch—almost 11 o'clock. If I hurry, I may be able to catch the 11am bus to Natanz. I take out my money for the room and gather my bags. As I pass the desk, I quickly give the money to the owner and race down the stairs. I hail a taxi.

"The bus station to Natanz."

Within minutes, we are there. A bus sets off imminently, and I am on it—a mess, but I am out of Kashan. The farther away we get, the more I calm down.

THE BUS MOMENTARILY STOPS beside the road near Natanz. The town is visible to the left. Mountains are to the south. It is cooler here. Little tables are scattered beneath scrawny trees. I wander over to a small shack—the local roadside *chai khaneh.*

"*Agha*, can you direct me to a hotel in Natanz?"

He looks at me aghast. "*Agha*, there is no hotel in Natanz. This is the hotel." He points to rows of bed frames beneath the trees.

SAVAK was right. There is no hotel in Natanz, I tell myself.

"*Agha*, how much is a bed?"

"Three tomans."

"Fine. I'll spend the night here. Will you take care of my suitcase? I want to see Natanz."

I order lunch and go to photograph the buildings I came to see. As the sun lowers and streaks of pink and purple paint the sky, the little tables under the trees blossom as oases of quiet conversation and laughter. The nightly crowd from Kashan is descending upon refreshing Natanz.

"Hello," a man at a nearby table ventures. "Where are you from?"

"Hello," I respond. "I'm from America—from California." I indicate I know Farsi and our conversation quickly develops. He and his family are from Kashan and they often journey to Natanz to escape the dreadful, sleepless heat of the city.

"I was in Kashan yesterday. It's very hot there. It's much cooler here."

"What did you see in Kashan? Did you go to Bagh-e Fin?"

"*Baleh*, it's very beautiful, and I also spent a lot of time in the bazaar. It is one of the best in Iran."

"Did you see Khaneh Borujerdiyeh?"

"No, I never heard of it."

"Go back to Kashan to see it. It is magnificent—a private home from the Qajar period. The family still lives there. Tell them you are a professor and you are studying Islamic art. They will let you in. Be sure to go."

"Unfortunately, I don't have time. I'm going on to Ardestan, Na'in, Yazd, and Kerman—then Isfahan and Shiraz."

We talk until darkness envelops the encampment. Scattered lanterns cast eerie shadows among the nighttime companions. I take my suitcase, stash it under a bed, unroll the mattress, and lie there taking in the magic of the night—the sound of crickets and sight of stars, so many I imagine there truly is a dome of pearls, aquamarine, and rubies above.

Sleep does not come easily—too much to think about: SAVAK, not getting the tiles, and that I missed the Khaneh Borujerdiyeh. I replay the interviews in my mind, trying to establish the motive—what SAVAK was alarmed about.

Obviously they were following me the day before. They knew when I arrived and that all the merchants in the bazaar seemed to know me. Then they lost me—probably when I went off with the shopkeeper to his house. Then the hotel didn't take my passport and submit it to SAVAK. That's why they insisted I go to the tourist hotel. This morning, when I showed up on the street, red flags went up. I was nabbed.

They were also perplexed about where I'd been for one month. I arrived in the country, then vanished because I didn't stay in a hotel until the two nights I was in Qom. Then I disappeared in Kashan, and I seemed to know everyone there. Very suspicious—especially since I know Farsi so well. But they must have been satisfied with my answers or I'd be sitting in prison right now, being tortured until I said what they wanted me to say—even if it weren't true.

I wish I had been able to get those tiles. They're outstanding, but it is just as well I wasn't carrying them when the agent picked me up. Yet they made no mention that I had bought the Qajar tile. Certainly they were aware of that, as they knew nearly everything else I did in Kashan, and the shop I bought it at was right out in the open in the bazaar. Oh, well—the two other tiles weren't meant to be. Something I like but can't have.

I wonder if I should return to Kashan on my way to Tehran? I could stay in Qom overnight, take an early morning bus to Kashan, go to the man's shop, and tell him I want the tiles and that I'm going to see the Khaneh Borujerdiyeh. Maybe he would even bring the tiles to me in Qom so I wouldn't have to lug them around Kashan. If SAVAK picks me up again, I could explain a man recommended I see the Khaneh Borujerdiyeh. That's why I returned. I could get a haircut so I look different, and SAVAK wouldn't recognize me.

I rehash everything and my strategy to get the tiles countless times. I'm losing sleep. This is not good for my health.

TUESDAY, JULY 6, 1971   The bus pushes across the blinding whiteness of the vast salt desert. Heat waves shimmer above sandy, desiccated hills. The bus and its human content bake under the murderous summer sun. Insufferably dry heat blows ceaselessly in the windows. Punishing hours pass. Only sheer determination mitigates the grueling full-day journey from Kerman, again through Yadz and Na'in, then west.

As we approach Isfahan I ask a fellow passenger, "What are those?" pointing to large, strange, circular structures.

"They are *kabutar khaneh.*"

Kabutar is pigeon and *khaneh* is house, I decipher. *"Kabutar khaneh?"*

"Baleh. Kabutar khaneh. They were built so the pigeons would go inside to roost, and then the droppings were used to fertilize the orchards and gardens surrounding Isfahan. One building holds thousands of pigeons."

"Amazing! There are hundreds of towers everywhere."

"Baleh. Iranians figured this out a long time ago," he says with pride.

THE STUNNING ISLAMIC MONUMENTS of Isfahan become the focus of hundreds of photographs over the next three days—among them, the quietly majestic Masjid-e Jomeh that chronicles over 800 years of the finest Persian architecture, the brilliant Masjid-e Shah, and the modest, but restrained Masjid-e Shaykh Lotfallah. Though it is in restoration, I'm seduced by the intimate beauty of Hasht-e Behesht, a 17th century Safavid palace—its very name means eight heavens.

Late each day, little shops in the bazaar and along Chahar Bagh Avenue supply a wealth of wonders to thwart a night's rest unless I succumb to them. Fortunately my ability to bargain has not diminished.

"What is that?" I ask, pointing to a rag piled in a dark corner of a shop on Chahar Bagh.

"It's an old rug. Actually, it's two. Half of one is missing entirely and the other is in very bad condition."

"Could I see them?"

"*Baleh*, but they are in bad shape. You are the second person to notice them. The other is a curator from the British Museum. He wants the museum to buy them."

I figure this is all part of his spiel to lower my abilities to bargain. His perceived plan has a reverse effect. *How can I compete with the British Museum? And it's better it go to a major museum,* I rationalize.

He is absolutely right. Both are in very bad condition, almost threadbare.

"Who is depicted in the rugs?"

"Fath Ali Shah. He was one of the first Qajar shahs, very famous for his long black beard and wasp waist. He had many wives and fathered over a hundred children."

"I saw his tomb at the shrine in Qom about a week ago and I've seen pictures of him. Where did you get the rugs?"

"They were found in an old house in Gilan province. They had gotten wet and when they were pulled off the floor this is what was left of them."

"It's a shame. Too bad they aren't in better condition."

During an extended conversation, he asks, "Mister, could you help me? Some Americans bought a rug in my shop. They promised they would send me the balance of the money. I trusted them and sent them the rug, but they never sent me the money. It is nearly a year now. I don't know English well, so I can't write to them. Could you write the letter for me if I tell you what to write?"

I'm disgusted Americans would take advantage of a trusting Iranian.

"*Baleh*, I'm happy to help."

After I write the letter, we resume conversing casually. Intermittently I glance at the remnants on the floor. Finally I ask, "*Agha*, you mentioned the British Museum is interested in these rugs."

"*Baleh*, but it is a long time since I have heard from them. They probably decided not to get them."

"*Agha*, how much are the rugs?"

"One thousand five hundred tomans ($200) for both."

I am surprised by the low price. "*Agha*, I might be interested in the more complete one. What would your price be on it?"

He immediately comes down. I counter with 650 tomans.

"I need to get 850 tomans" ($113).

"How about 700 tomans?"

"I can't do that. However, if you have travelers checks, I would take a $100 check."

I agree to the strange request. He folds up the disintegrating carcass and hands it to me.

"Come back whenever you are in Isfahan," he says warmly. "Thank you for writing the letter for me."

"You're welcome. I hope you get the money from those Americans. I'm sorry they would do this to you. I wish I could come back to Iran and Isfahan more often, but it's very far away."

SATURDAY, JULY 10, 1971   I gaze at Persepolis as the bus speeds along on its way to Shiraz. The tent city being built near the base of the staircase to the great terrace holds everyone's attention. It will be the site of the 2500th anniversary celebrations of the Persian Empire in October, when dignitaries from 50 nations will gather with the Shah to commemorate the event. My friends are talking about it with pride and excitement and insist I stay for the occasion. They don't want to admit I have a job in America. For them, I'm still part of the Sherkat-e Sargardon, and they cannot conceive I'm no longer "Tom of Iran"—that I have become "American Tom" again.

Nevertheless, my love of Iran and respect for Iranian culture is ceaseless.

I, too, am carried away with the splendor of the anniversary preparations, and proud Iran has risen to the center stage of world attention—that the Shah is able to garner the respect of world leaders and bring them together on Iranian soil for one of the most august gatherings in human history. I see the tremendous value in the Shah's desire to use this event to build nationalism. Iranians are truly beginning to believe in themselves, and Iran is becoming a vital force in the international community. I, like my friends, am especially proud the Shah's campaign to build 2500 schools in commemoration of the anniversary is enthusiastically becoming a reality.[*]

The highway between Persepolis and Shiraz is being prepared, the airport enlarged, and accommodations in Shiraz upgraded; all are key improvements to the infrastructure that will contribute to tourism in one of the world's most historic locations.

Rather than revisiting Persepolis, instead the Islamic buildings in Shiraz warrant my attention—specifically the 18th century Masjid-e Vakil with its colorful tiles and serene prayer hall, and the massive Zand fortress. With my letter of introduction, Iranian officials graciously invite me to see and photograph Shah Cheragh, the mausoleum of the martyred brother of Imam Reza, with its bulbous blue-tiled dome and glittering interior constructed with thousands of minute mirror tiles that reflect the passion of the pilgrims within.

MONDAY, JULY 12, 1971 From Qom, camouflaged with a fresh haircut, I board a bus for Kashan to implement my scheme.

"Salaam, Agha," I greet the shop vendor. Immediately I notice both tiles I now am placing myself at tremendous risk to acquire.

"*Salaam*, you were going to come two weeks ago. I thought you decided not to get the ceramic pieces."

"I'm sorry. I didn't want to haul around those heavy tiles as I traveled in the south. So I made up my mind to pick them up on my way to Tehran. Besides, a man I met in Natanz told me to see the Khaneh Borujerdiyeh."

"Khaneh Borujerdiyeh! It is wonderful. I will take you there."

---

[*] Anyone who wanted a school built in his name was asked to give $4000. Because fervor marking the celebrations was so great 3200 schools were actually built.

"Excellent. Also, could you bring the tiles to my hotel in Qom and I will pay you there? They are so heavy and I don't want to carry them. The bus for Tehran departs at 4 o'clock, so you need to bring them before that."

He looks at me curiously, possibly wondering why I am willing to cart them from Qom to Tehran and not from Kashan to Qom.

Uneasily I pass through the bazaar with him to the Khaneh Borujerdiyeh. Its domed reception halls, polychrome stuccowork, and frescos of Qajar princes are remarkable, even in their weathered condition.

As we leave I tell him, "It's getting warm. I want to get a taxi so I can take the next bus back to Qom. You bring the tiles to me before 4 o'clock."

"Mister, come with me to my shop. I will put the tiles in a box and take you to the bus for Qom."

Reluctantly I agree, and with trepidation follow him through the bazaar.

"Mister, I'm going to get a box. You stay here in my shop. I will be right back. Here's a chair."

With delusive calmness, I move the chair to the back of the shop and sit down. I wait—nervously I wait. I look at my watch. *He's been gone fifteen minutes already. How long does it take to get a box?* I wait some more. I look at my watch. Twenty minutes now . . . I get up to look cautiously out the front of the shop to see if he is coming or if any SAVAK agents have their eyes on me. My quick glance registers no one. I anxiously sit on the edge of the chair. I hear my heart pounding and it's becoming hard to breathe. I'm sweating now. *Twenty-five minutes and he hasn't returned. Could he be a SAVAK agent and has gone to their office?* My mind races. *Should I split, get a taxi to the bus station, and get out of Kashan? What if he doesn't bring the tiles to the hotel? Then what?* Desperately I try to remain calm, but my thoughts are driving me crazy.

After more than a half hour, he reappears.

"Where's the box?" I ask with agitation.

"Mister, because the piece that is a portion of a *mihrab* has writing on it from the Koran, I went to the Ayatollah for permission to sell it to you. He said no."

"*Agha*," I look at him sternly, "I wish you had not done that. You said you were going to get a box, not go to the Ayatollah. I trusted you. *Agha*, although Islam is not my religion, I am a friend of Islam. My very best friends are Muslims. They are so important to me I traveled a long way from California to Iran to see them this summer. They are like my own family . . . they *are* my family. I love them very much. Also, I am studying Islamic art and architecture because someday I plan to teach Islamic art in America. I want to use art as a way of telling Americans about Islam and Iran and its people. *Agha*, I found that portion of the *mihrab* covered with dust in a corner of your shop. I cleaned it off. *Agha*, I would always care for it and show it the utmost respect because it is an object from your religion. I am very disappointed you did this. I want to go now. You bring the other tile to Qom before 4 o'clock if you want to sell it to me."

"Mister, I am sorry. Forgive me. I want you to tell the Ayatollah what you told me. Maybe he will change his mind."

"No, *Agha*, I don't want to go. I am tired, and I am perturbed by what you have done. I want to go to Qom."

"Mister, please come with me. I want you to talk to the Ayatollah."

I acquiesce. In his car I won't be seen by SAVAK, and maybe the Ayatollah will be influenced by my story as the shopkeeper is.

My betrayer puts the tile in a sack and we walk to the edge of the bazaar. He hands me the sack and says, "Get on." It's his motor scooter!

My shirt becomes soaked with a flood of sweat. I get on. Off we go—me hanging on to him and the sack. Horror of horrors, he passes directly in front of the SAVAK headquarters. I look the other way, hoping with my new haircut I won't be detected.

It is now lunchtime, and the Ayatollah is humbly sitting with colleagues around an oilcloth, breaking bread. My Judas introduces me and tells the Ayatollah he wants him to hear my story. I relate it to an outwardly impassive individual. When I finish, the Ayatollah looks at me intensely and declares, "If you will go to the shrine at Qom, study Islam for the rest of the summer, and become a Muslim, I will give you the tile."

I sit there momentarily, stunned, and sweat pouring from every pore in my body. Deliberately, looking straight at him, I say, "*Agha*, I am sorry. I could never do that. That is bribery, and for me that is unethical—immoral. It is an insult to your religion—a religion I have the utmost regard for—the religion of my very best friends. I could never do it out of respect for them. I am sorry." I look down at the floor. There is no response. I look at Judas and signal we should go. The tile remains on the floor.

Outside I order my companion, "Take me to the bus station for Qom. If you want to sell me the turquoise tile, bring it to me by 4 o'clock."

Hurriedly we speed to the treeless wasteland at the west of town. A bus is leaving in fifteen minutes. Disgustedly, I say goodbye to my deceiver.

"Mister, if I brought the tile before the bus leaves would you take it?"

Soberly I look at him, "*Baleh*, but you must put it in a box."

Fuming, I get into the baking bus, and with intense effort attempt to calm my frayed nerves. Sometime later, the bus begins to pull away from the unshaded desert meeting area. With a glance back I see a lone motor scooter approaching. "*Agha*, wait," I tell the bus driver. He stops. I get off and my so-called friend hands me a box. I peer inside. The tile is there. I hand over the 400 tomans, mumble a *moteshakeram*, and turn to get on the bus.

"Are you coming back to Kashan, Mister?" Judas calls to me.

I turn and look at him, "No, *Agha*, I'm never coming back to Kashan."

As the bus wends its way to Qom I wonder, *Does he really want me to have the mihrab fragment?*

ADRENALINE ADDICTION

SUNDAY, AUGUST 1, 1971 Hot, dry air blows in the open windows of the worn-out bus as it rumbles southeast to Tayabad over rough gravel roads. Intermittently we stop near sun-baked villages to pick up and drop off passengers.

"What is that?" I exclaim. Huge and mysterious open towers, like the rib cages of giant raven-picked skeletons, loom ominously behind the rounded mud hovels of a monochromatic hamlet.

"They are windmills." The travelers delight in my naiveté.

"Windmills!"

"Baleh."

"But the blades are vertical. They don't go around in a circle."

"Baleh. The first windmills were built here in Khorasan. This is how we invented them," they proudly tell me.

In Tayabad, I find a room that I share with two guys and a woman. They are European "freaks" traveling on the cheap and eager to smoke their way along the Hippie Trail through Afghanistan, India, and Nepal.

MONDAY, AUGUST 2, 1971 "Khargird in over there."

The driver points to the ruins of a 15th century *madreseh* (theological school) following a fifty-kilometer bus ride southwest into the desert.

"Be back at the road by one o'clock. That's when a bus comes on its way to Tayabad. Don't miss it. It's the only bus. Do you understand? It's the only bus."

"Baleh. Moteshakeram. Khodahafez."

I wave goodbye. The driver and passengers look on in disbelief that anyone would get out in such a godforsaken location. I watch as a cloud of dust rises behind the disappearing vehicle. I look at my watch. Almost 10:30. I better drink some water. It's already broiling out here in the sun.

I wander along a seldom-used path to the *madreseh*. The gateway door is securely padlocked. As I roam around the isolated structure, I discover a hole under the wall at the side, obviously dug by animals. I squeeze through, smug that nothing can halt this determined researcher. Inside I marvel at the harmony of proportions, the symmetry of the four *iwans*, commanding even in their deteriorated state—one on each side of the courtyard—framed by arcades and galleries with superb tilework. Single-mindedly I photograph the exquisite tiles and the crumbling *muqarna* (niches) of the domes. It's hot, but here at least I'm often out of the direct sun.

Hmmm, it's almost noon. I better get out to the road in case the bus is early. I don't want to miss it. I squeeze under the wall, take more photos of the exterior, and trudge to the dirt highway to wait. There is no shade, just scorching sun. I eat the bit of bread and the apples I brought, and drink my water. It's intolerably hot out here, and in a few hours I'll be back in Tayabad anyway.

One o'clock arrives. There is no bus. *Well, I really didn't expect it on time. This is Iran. Being here taught me to be patient.*

Two o'clock comes. No bus yet. *Gee, I sure could use some water. Too bad I drank it all.*

Two-thirty. No bus.

About 2:50, I detect dust on the horizon—a jeep. The driver stops.

"What are you doing here? Where are you from? Where are you going?"

"I'm an American. I came to see the *madreseh* at Khargird. I'm waiting for the bus to Tayabad. It was supposed to come at one o'clock. I have been waiting here since noon. You're the first person to come by."

"I'm not going to Tayabad, but get in. There is a place along the way where the road forks, and if you wait there, you will have a better chance of getting a ride. I'll be heading out into the desert there, to a little village where we're making a film. You shouldn't be out here all by yourself. It's too dangerous."

He lets me off . . . somewhere.

"Stay here," he says. "Something should come from either direction that will take you to Tayabad. All the best. *Khodahafez.*"

"Moteshakeram. Khodahafez."

It is now going on 3:30. The sky is turning a menacing gray. Hearing a dull roar, I watch a baleful dark cloud approach. A strong wind swiftly engulfs me, the blowing desert sand biting at my skin. I crouch down, leaning against the post of the highway sign for support, desperately trying to guard my face and eyes from the stinging granules. However, determined not to miss any mode of transportation, I watchfully squint, keeping an eye on the forsaken road.

Four o'clock. Nothing. Four-thirty. No bus. Nothing. Quarter to five. Nothing! I can't walk to Tayabad. I don't remember if there were any villages along the way. Now I'm so confused, I'm not even sure which of these roads leads to Tayabad. I have no idea where I am. I shouldn't have drunk all my water. I shouldn't have eaten all the apples. *What if nothing ever comes? Will I be left out here all night? Will wolves come down out of the hills? Will they circle me, constantly coming in closer and closer? Will I become their long-awaited dinner?*

Close to five o'clock, I notice a far-off speck on the road. I stand up, still leaning against the post of the highway sign so I won't be blown over by the unremitting wind. I close my eyes, say a momentary prayer of thanks, and wait. I open my eyes.

There is no bus. Nothing! Am I going crazy? Was it a mirage?

I look again. There's the bus! It's left the road—going across the desert.

I run toward it, screaming at the top of my lungs, "Stop, stop," waving my camera bag over my head. I fly like an antelope on the wings of the wind. But the bus keeps going . . . and going. I practically pass out from exhaustion and terror. Frantically, my body gasps for air.

All I can do is return to the highway. As I look up, I see another trail of dust issuing along the road. It's a transport truck. I need to get back to the highway before the truck gets to the sign. I try to run, but now I'm running against the wind. My aching legs move, but I seem to be getting nowhere. I scream, "Stop, stop!" I wave my bag over my head.

Mercifully, the truck stops. A man calls, *"Zud bosh. Zud"* (Hurry up. Hurry), his voice, traveling on the wind.

"Wait. Wait," I scream. I don't give thought that the wind is carrying my voice in the opposite direction and he can't hear me over the sound of the motor. I strain to run against the relentless whipping wind.

"Hurry," he keeps calling.

"Baleh, I'm trying. Wait."

I reach the truck and virtually collapse, my body heaving for air.

"Beah bala" (Come aboard).

I thrust out my hand for him to pull me up into the cab. I slump into the seat beside him, gasping for breath. My eyes seem to turn inside my head. He reaches across and pulls the door closed.

"He's stoned!" he exclaims to the driver. "Totally out of it."

Writhing and gulping for air, I imagine they have seen other foreign "freaks" who have crossed the border from Afghanistan. However, they've probably never seen one in as bad a shape as this.

"Where do you want to go?" the driver's assistant asks.

I gasp, "Taya . . ." I gulp for more air. "Taya . . . Taya . . . bad."

He indicates they are headed there. Slowly I regain a semblance of composure and relate the story of how I went to Khargird, waited for the bus that never came, got the ride from the Iranian film person, saw the bus take a shortcut across the desert, and then they came along.

"Moteshakeram. Kheili mamnunam," I thank them when they let me out in Tayabad. The thanks is an understatement.

In the hotel, I lie in bed, contemplating the day and how I could still be out in the desert—tasty bait for wolves, and of the goodness of Iranians; the guys in the truck could have taken my Nikon camera and telephoto lens, passport, and money, and ditched me somewhere where I would have become wolf fodder anyway. Now that I'm still here, the adrenaline rush of survival is intoxicating—seductive. *What else can I do for a little excitement?*

WEDNESDAY, AUGUST 4, 1971 Seeking more adventure, I board a village bus that bumps along over unpaved roads across the desert to Qadamgah.

The tiny octagonal 17th century shrine at Qadamgah is set amid cooling gardens fed by a subterranean spring believed to have been miraculously created by Imam Reza. On Fridays and holidays, pilgrims flock here to revere the black stone slab bearing the imprint of the feet of the Imam. Today, in the heat of summer, almost nothing stirs. A tired gray donkey and a few sheep keep watchful eyes on me from their shaded posts in a nearby caravanserai. Mud-brick houses with flat roofs silently climb the hill behind the shrine. Beyond nearby fields, the desert melts in the burning haze.

Late in the day, the driver of another bus points across the desert, "Sangbast is over there. You can't get there from here. There's a river below. You will have to go to that village and then walk on the other side."

I look at him curiously. The early 11th century tomb of Arslan Jadhib is not far away. When the bus is out of sight, I start across the desert. I'm stopped at the edge of a deep canyon. The bus driver was right. Even if the river is dried up, there is no way I can scale the walls of this ravine to get to the other side. As the sun bakes the parched land and me, I trudge to the village and pick my way to the isolated tomb and lonely minaret. All around, intermittent tufts of dried scrub patiently wait for life-giving water.

Etched against the blue sky, the tomb is powerful in its stark severity. Inside, the herringbone pattern of bricks in the grand dome and the brick calligraphic inscription at its base provide a humanizing element to the tomb's guileless, restored simplicity. As I wend my way back to the highway and wait for a bus to Mashhad, far across the empty horizon, the sun languidly dyes a vast celestial canvas.

THURSDAY, AUGUST 5, 1971 In contrast to my illicit Nou Ruz eve entry with Shaban Ali to the shrine of Imam Reza in Mashhad, my official letter yields access to the shrine—even to the roofs, where I obtain detailed photographs of the elaborately cut tiles on the domes. Furthermore, shrine officials show me the restoration workshops and explain how the colorful and intricate tilework is done—pieces fit together like a giant jigsaw puzzle.

SATURDAY, AUGUST 7, 1971 For the last two days I have searched for the shop that had the embroidery I didn't buy at Nou Ruz in 1965. This morning I continue my perambulations of the streets. *Hmmm, that looks like it may be the old hardware store over there.* I cross the street and look in the window.

The embroidery is hanging in the same place it was six years before.

"Salaam, Agha," I say as I enter, trying to contain my excitement.

"Salaam," the shopkeeper answers.

"How much is this old piece of cloth?"

"Three hundred rials."

Exactly the same price he started at six years ago. I was willing to pay almost anything for it now, but as a matter of principle, I need to bargain.

I tell him, "Too much."

"How much do you want to pay?"

"It's in very poor condition. It has holes, and some of the embroidery is worn away. I'll give you 150 rials."

"No, too little. But you can have it for 200 rials."

Wow, just like before, I say to myself. "No, still too much," I tell him. "Look, it's damaged, not good. I will give you 150 rials. That's the highest I will go."

"Give me 175 rials and you can have it."

An exact repeat. I should hold out for the 150 rials to see if he will do it.

I plead, "No, *Agha*, for me 150 rials. I would like to take it back to America as a memory of Mashhad and you."

"Where in America are you from?"

"California."

"My nephew is attending the University of Southern California."

"He is! My friend is studying at the University of Southern California. See, we have something in common. You should let me have the embroidery for 150 rials."

Ultimately he agrees. I am proud of the fact I can bargain so effectively, but also ashamed I would be so ruthless over a mere 25 rials (33¢).

PAINFUL PARTINGS

SUNDAY, AUGUST 15, 1971 Again I board a bus in Tehran heading toward Mashhad, this time going only as far as Damghan—340 kilometers east—to visit Gholam Husayn and his family, who now live in the little mountain village of Chordeh. Chordeh is 40 kilometers south of Alang, but no direct roads cross the intervening Alborz Mountains.

"Mister Tom!" I am greeted as I wait in Damghan for a bus to Chordeh. I look up, surprised I would be recognized in a place I have never been.

"*Salaam,*" I respond with a bit of puzzlement. "Ziah?"

"*Baleh. Salaam,* Tom. You recognized me," he says gleefully. "How are you? Did you finish the rug I showed you how to make?" Ziah Isaree, an expert rug repairer, who, on a visit to see his brother in Alang, had made me a loom and taught me how to weave a rug shortly before I left five years ago.

"No, Ziah. I haven't finished it. How are you? It's great to see you."

"What are you doing here? Why are you going to Chordeh?"

"I'm going to see Gholam Husayn and his family. I came to Iran this summer to see my friends and study Islamic art. I saw the Tarik Khaneh here in Damghan. It's the oldest mosque in Iran—from the late 8th century. It's impressive."

Ziah beams.

"And the 11th century Seljuk tombs and minarets with their intricate brickwork are equally outstanding."

"I am glad you saw them. But Tom . . . I have bad news. You should not go to Chordeh."

"Why?"

"Gholam Husayn is not there."

My heart sinks.

"Gholam Husayn is in prison. He did something bad for a rich man. It was not his fault, but he was put in jail. The rich man is still free."

I nearly cry.

"And the family? Musa, Isa, and Ruholla? And their mother?"

"They are in Chordeh."

"I must go to see them." Ziah sees my eyes watering.

"Tom, I will take you to see them. But tonight you must stay with me."

"*Moteshakeram*, Ziah. I received letters from Gholam Husayn and the boys. I am so proud of them. Gholam Husayn and his wife were so honest and he was so determined his boys would get an education. Gholam Husayn is one of the most honorable men I have ever known."

I recall when I lived in Alang, and one morning before dawn, Gholam Husayn cautiously called at my door to ask if he could borrow ten tomans. Musa was sick and they needed to take him to the doctor. He carefully reminded me his wife would do my laundry to repay me.

"Tom, I am sorry. I know how bad you feel. I'm sorry I had to tell you."

"Ziah, don't be sorry. It is best I know now. I am so sad for Gholam Husayn and the family."

In Chordeh, Ziah takes me to the home of Gholam Husayn. His wife and children are as pleased to see me as I am to see them.

"Gholam Husayn is not here," his wife tells me, "but you must stay for dinner."

As a single man, I am unsure of the proper etiquette of having dinner at a friend's house when he isn't home, even if his young sons are present.

"*Moteshakeram*. Ziah Isaree has invited me to dinner at his house. I will be staying with him tonight."

"No, you must have dinner with us. Gholam Husayn and the boys will be disappointed if you don't stay. Ruholla, run along and tell *Aghaye* Isaree Mister Tom is having dinner with us."

We have an enjoyable, if strained, evening together. Musa is a Boy Scout now, and he is learning English in school. I ask if Gholam Husayn is OK. They assure me he is, but no one alludes to where he is.

"Give my *salaam* to Gholam Husayn," I say when I leave. "Musa, Isa, and Ruholla, you study hard in school so someday you will each have a good job and do things to benefit Iran." I shake hands with the boys, happy I've seen them, but very downhearted as well.

THURSDAY, SEPTEMBER 2, 1971   Somehow I thought this departure from Alang would not be as difficult as the one so painfully etched in my memory. But this summer has proven that my connection with Alang and my friends runs very deep; plus, the uncertainty of being able to return—though I intend to—weighs heavily on me. The vicissitudes of life . . . I am going back to America; anything could change life's course, and I could never see my friends again.

As five years previously, in the morning, everyone gathers at Mulla's. Again, the process is not easy. Slowly, like before, we proceed together through the village to the highway. As the bus and onlooking passengers wait, saying goodbye is excruciating. I board the bus, press my face against the window so other passengers will not witness my embarrassing grief, and stare until Alang and the mountain disappear in haze.

At Babol I catch a bus to Meti Kola to bid farewell to the Khanpoors. They are visiting their family before school starts. Departure the next day is tough, but I bravely tell them I will be back. Nevertheless, doubt plagues my mind.

SUNDAY, SEPTEMBER 5, 1971   Javad with his son Abdullah, Mulla, and Mr. Kucheek arrive early at the Mirsalehis in Tehran. They had driven from Alang yesterday to take me to the bus station this morning and say a final *khodahafez*. Now, as I part from the Mirsalehis, the impending emptiness and loneliness of saying goodbye crushes me. It is almost impossible to look into their faces. The silence of our parting speaks more profoundly than words.

There is little said at the bus station as well. I hug each of my friends and young Abdullah, board the bus, and mutely gaze from the window as it pulls away. We wave. Again, unrestrainedly, tears flow. *Will we ever see each other again? When? Why does parting have to be so painful?*

The man sitting next to me remains silent, compassionately letting me overcome the bewildering loss I experience. It is a long time before I gain a semblance of composure and we introduce ourselves. His name is Iraj. He, too, is going to Tabriz. I tell him about my friends and my love of Iran. We stop for lunch at a small roadside restaurant.

"Mister, pay ten tomans now," I am told when I enter with Iraj.

I get out my wallet.

"Put it away," Iraj says. He is annoyed and the two men argue in a dialect.

"Come," Iraj tells me. We sit at a table.

"What is the matter?"

"He wanted you to pay before you eat and then he would give you money back when you finish. That is their policy with foreigners."

"That's OK. I can pay him now."

"No. I told him, 'Not with Mister.'"

"It would be all right for me to pay before I eat."

"No. I told him it is insulting for Iranians to treat guests like that. He said after they have eaten, many foreigners say they don't have money. Now they make them pay before they eat."

"Iraj, don't feel bad. The man is doing what he needs to do. I heard many stories about foreign travelers who stay in a hotel and eat meals there and then say they have no money to pay. They pull out their empty pockets. Sometimes the hotel owners even buy them bus tickets to the Afghan border so they won't prey on any other innocent Iranians. It is deplorable. I am sorry. Iran is on the Hippie Trail. The hippies want to travel across Iran cheaply so they will have more money to spend on hash in Afghanistan and Nepal."

TUESDAY, SEPTEMBER 7, 1971 "Mister, this is not the border," the driver insists when I request to get off the bus in Maku. "It is another 22 kilometers to the border."

"I know; I want to see a friend at the army garrison."

"A friend? At the army garrison?"

"*Baleh*, Captain Manouchehr Housaini. His family asked me to stop and see him."

Reluctantly he lets me off. He and all the passengers look on quizzically at the unusual American who disembarks at this lonely outpost near the edge of godforsaken Maku. I nervously gaze at the dusty brown village tucked among crumbling boulders beneath a soaring rocky cliff overhang. *Why would anyone settle here? And this is earthquake country!*

"*Salaam*, Tom," Captain Housaini says with a smile as I'm shown into his office. "My family told me you would be coming. You're on your way to Turkey?"

"*Baleh*, I'm on my way home. It's sad to leave Iran and my friends. I had a wonderful summer, but I have to go back to work. It was good to see your family in Gorgan. Little Reza has grown up. I remember the days when your wife taught in Alang and I would spend evenings with her and your son and the Mirsalehis and Khanpoors. Those were the best two years of my life."

He smiles. "But Tom, life was difficult for you living in the village."

"*Na*, not so difficult. I learned a lot of important lessons during those two years. Alang was good for me. It taught me how to live—what is most essential. Alang is my home—forever. My family is there—always. I only wish Iran and America were not so far away from each other."

"Tom, I see you love Iran very much."

"*Baleh*, very much."

"My family said you bought many things this summer to take back to America."

"*Baleh*, I sent a big crate to Los Angeles. My house in California is a little bit of Iran. It is memories—memories of a place I love very much—a place I never want to forget. The objects are an expression of my loyalty to Iran. The search for them, acquiring them, and then enjoying them bring me much pleasure. It is like a search for my roots—my Iranian identity and the meaning it imparts. Also, they help me tell Americans about Iran and its people."

"Tom, your interest in Iran is truly amazing."

"*Moteshakeram*. But foremost, Captain Housaini, the things I got help me learn about Iran, its history, and its culture. They force me to study and learn more. I am thinking about going back to school to study Islamic art—especially the art of Iran. This summer I took at least a thousand photographs of Islamic art and architecture in Iran, Afghanistan, and Uzbekistan. I plan to use them in my teaching. Americans need to know more about Iran and Islam."

We talk awhile longer over tea, and Captain Housaini offers, "Tom, I'll take you to the border at Bazargan. I'm glad you took the time to stop and see me."

He summons his chauffeur, and soon we are at the border crossing. The bus I was on and its passengers are still passing through immigration and customs. Captain Housaini takes me to the front of the line. My passport is stamped, and Iran is left behind.

DIVERSION

FALL 1971–SUMMER 1978 Although I am back in the familiar environment of my little rented cottage in Yorba Linda and enjoy being with students, life seems empty after the intensity of my summer. Disenchantment with the stymieing politics of academe and its disregard for student aspirations where I am teaching reinforces my resolve to enter a graduate program in Islamic art history.

The satisfaction of being on the receiving end of the classroom is worth the hundred-mile round trip to UCLA. The 12th century ceiling of the Cappella Palatina in the Norman palace in Palermo becomes my topic of research in a seminar on the Fatimids. Lily is now married to Roger, a Peace Corps Volunteer she met in Kathmandu, who is vice consul at the American Consulate in Palermo. They suggest I come to Sicily to research and photograph the intricate ceiling constructed and painted by Muslim artists, now the topic of my dissertation. Roger negotiates permission for me to do this in the summer of 1973.

While stimulated by the complexity of my research, I feel like a traitor to my beloved Iran. How easy it is for me to be diverted. It's been this way all my life. I find everything too interesting.

DEL AND I ARE MARRIED in her hometown of Hilo in 1975. Rozy's gift— the pendant of the Blessed Virgin to be given to my wife on our wedding day—becomes the symbol of my distant friends' presence on this joyous occasion. Letters express their accord with my choice of a life partner. I resolve someday I will take Del to meet them.

In July 1977 we pack to move to Hawaii, where I will be gallery director at the university and teach design and Islamic and medieval art history.

BEFORE WE LEAVE CALIFORNIA, a letter arrives from Javad. It's written in script. I can't read it. We spend an evening with Farjad, a brilliant young Iranian I met at UCLA, and his wife. I have him read the letter.

"Tom, this letter is very funny. Your friend is writing about the death of his brother."

My heart sinks. "Reza?"

"Yes."

"Reza was my best friend. He was like my brother. His little girl, Rozy, was the first to call me *Amo* Tom."

Tears moisten my eyes. Del reaches for my arm to comfort me. I think of Rozy and her little sister and brothers, and that I will never see Reza again. Never. Never.

"Tom, I'm sorry," Farjad says with sudden sympathy.

"Read me the whole letter, Farjad. Please."

The letter is devastating. Reza died of a heart attack. Farjad helps me compose a letter of sympathy to Javad and Reza's family. I am consumed with grief. My fears that "my Alang" will not be the same when and if I return are being realized.

AT THE UNIVERSITY OF HAWAII, I'm excited to work in an environment with people of various ethnicities and on projects of international significance—where I'm learning about other cultures and applying the knowledge gained as a community development volunteer in the Peace Corps.

In the summer of 1978, with our entire savings in travelers checks, Del and I lock the house to venture off, with Iran our ultimate destination. We disingenuously promise our parents we won't enter Iran if turmoil is brewing—revolutionary unrest has already been reported in our papers. Initially we head for Palermo and the Cappella Palatina. By late June we begin our four-week journey on local buses and overcrowded trains through remote central and eastern Turkey, researching and photographing Seljuk art and architecture.

OMINOUS OMENS

SATURDAY, JULY 22, 1978 A battered, run-down bus maneuvers the treacherous gravel roads across mountains to the lonely border outpost in southeast Turkey. Passengers—mostly Kurds—board near tiny villages and are let off somewhere along the way. We left Van early in the morning, but it's late afternoon when the bus stops at the border. We are the last passengers remaining, and the driver motions that Iran is ahead. We pass through the Turkish checkpoint and lug our baggage to the Iranian side.

"Would you like a ride to Rezaiyeh?" we are asked as we clear Iranian immigration.

"No, thank you. We will take a bus."

"There is no bus out here. We'll give you a ride."

"No, thank you," I decline again. I had noticed the Germans clearing customs, and suspected the two fancy Mercedes-Benzes were the booty of a clandestine auto smuggling ring. Instinctively I don't want to be involved in anything illegal in Iran. Besides, why would they be crossing the border in this secluded and difficult location when the roads to the crossing at Bazargan are so much better?

An Iranian asks, "Rezaiyeh?"

"Baleh," I respond smiling. "How much?"

"Four hundred rials" ($5.70).

"Geran. Kheili geran. (Expensive. Very expensive.) Rezaiyeh is only 50 kilometers away." I heard about Iranian inflation, but this is outrageous.

"Meleh shoma (Whatever you want). There are no buses. I'm going to Rezaiyeh. You can ride in the back of my truck."

I attempt to bargain, but the scarcity of transportation and the time of day are distinctly at my disadvantage. Irked, I agree to 370 rials. Del and I pile in the back and our driver heads off—away from the setting sun—eastward to Rezaiyeh, I hope. We keep our eyes closed as dust swirls around us. I momentarily peer at Del. She is entirely white with dust, and the luggage and I are covered with white powder too. Then I realize we are riding in the back of a chalk truck. I regret that my wife's introduction to Iran—a place I love so much—is so formidable.

It's dark when we're let off in central Rezaiyeh—two ghosts. We brush each other off, but it's hopeless. The chalk clings to our sweaty skin and clothes. I search for a hotel, but at every place I'm told, "We have no rooms." I'm unsure if they are telling the truth or if it's our appearance that signals not to deal with us. At last I find a hotel that accepts us—but the room is microscopic, with a single bed and two feet of space at the side. The price is an exorbitant 565 rials ($8.00) a night.

"Del, this has to be OK. I'll sleep on the floor."

We tuck the suitcases under the bed and are thankful to find a bathroom down the hall.

Quietly, I consider that we may run out of money long before we leave Iran. And ominously, there were riots in Tabriz a few days ago. We must pass through there to get to Tehran.

MONDAY, JULY 24, 1978 On the way to Tabriz, we stop at Maragheh to walk among the indistinct remnants of the famous observatory founded by Hulagu Khan in the 13ᵗʰ century for the astronomer/scholar Nasir al-Din al-Tusi. The sun-parched hamlet barely stirs. However, as Del and I wend our way along mud walls to the bus station at the edge of town, a car approaches, jumps the gutter, and heads directly toward us. Quickly we dodge out of the way and watch with trepidation. Was it after us because the driver saw we're foreigners?

The car hits the wall. It reverses, hits a tree, proceeds forward once more, rams a parked car, backs up, and skidders along the street, striking whatever is unfortunate enough to be in its erratic path.

"It's curious what has happened in this technological century in this little town, when back in the 13th century Maragheh was the foremost center of astronomical research in the world," I say to Del.

In Tabriz we find a room in the basement of a hotel. It seems comfortably secure in light of the recent disturbances. Outwardly the city is calm and peaceful.

THURSDAY, JULY 27, 1978 "Del, you stay here. We can easily get to Alang before dark if we get a bus now."

I stand in line at the TBT bus station in Tehran. Savvy travelers, we've worked out a system—she serves as guard of our luggage, while I run errands.

"*Salaam, Agha,* two tickets to Gorgan," I request after waiting in line for fifteen minutes.

"What day?"

"Now. Today. As soon as possible."

"*Agha*, there are no seats available on any buses today. There are two on the 8am bus tomorrow. That's it until Saturday. Do you want them?"

I'm taken aback. "*Moteshakeram, Agha.* I will try another bus company."

"*Meleh shoma*, but all buses are completely booked days in advance."

I return to Del frustrated. "There are no more seats on any buses today. Tomorrow morning is the earliest we can go. Back in 1971, all you had to do was come here and get on a bus and off you went. You stay here. I'm going to another station to see if I can get tickets for today."

Lines at Iran Payma are interminably long too, and when I reach the desk, the first available bus to Gorgan is on Saturday. I run back to Del and get in line again, hoping the two tickets to Gorgan tomorrow morning are still available.

The man looks at me. "I told you there are no seats on any buses today."

"*Baleh*. Can I have the two tickets to Gorgan on the bus tomorrow?"

"*Baleh*. They are the only ones left, in the back on top of the motor."

That's the hottest spot on the bus, and in the July Iranian heat it won't be pleasant—but my objective is to get to Alang.

FRIDAY, JULY 28, 1978 "Mister Tom." I hear a soft voice behind me as we wait to board the bus for Gorgan.

I turn around. A young man in a soldier's uniform smiles.

"Shoma Alangi hastid" (Are you from Alang)?

"Baleh," he says smiling. "I'm a Rahemi. I thought you might be Mister Tom since you were getting on the bus to Gorgan. That's why I called your name quietly. If you weren't Mister Tom, you wouldn't respond. I was a little boy when you lived in Alang."

"Baleh, it is twelve years ago that I left Alang. You must have been six years old. This is my wife, Del. I am taking her to Alang to meet my friends."

He politely acknowledges her, and exchanges his seat near the front for one next to us on the motor. We spend hours talking as the bus crosses the mountains and zips down the valley of the Haraz River and along the Caspian littoral.

"Mister Tom, we will get off in Kordkuy and catch a taxi to Alang," he says. "You have too much luggage to carry from the highway."

I can hardly contain my excitement as I distinguish the familiar mountain behind Alang.

"Del, we're almost there."

The dusty main street of Alang has barely changed in the past seven years, or even twelve. *Alang is still "my Alang,"* I contentedly tell myself. But as we pass the closed doors of the Sherkat-e Sargardon, the lump in my throat and dampness of my eyes remind me Alang is not the same. I will not see my good friend Reza this time.

The taxi pulls into Mulla's courtyard, and the jubilation begins. Everybody is overjoyed to meet Del. The women are especially animated and greet her with, *"Salaam, hale shoma khoobeh?"*

She replies, *"Salaam."* They all giggle. Mulla and some of the young men speak to her in English.

"I must see Shaban Ali," I tell Mulla. Quickly we rush across the squalid square in front of the water tower and round the corner to Shaban Ali's gateway.

"Shaban Ali, Tom *amad"* (Tom arrived), Mulla calls.

"Bah, bah, bah, Aghaye Mister Tom and Del," I hear him.

He appears on his doorstep, his wife and children behind him. They run to greet us. His oldest, Halimeh, is married and will soon make Shaban

Ali and his wife grandparents. She and her sister are not wearing *chadors*. Halimeh's husband, Heydar Savarsofla, is from Alang. He is a brilliant young man who is a pilot in the Iranian Air Force. His English is excellent. I think back to the years I lived in Alang, and how Iran has changed.

"I was hoping to come to America," Heydar tells me. "They told us we could go to America for training if our English was good enough. So I studied very hard. I wanted to go. I wanted to visit you. In the end, they said my English was so proficient, I didn't need to go to America."

I can plainly see his disappointment.[*]

Back on the street, we excitedly talk with friends. Javad arrives. He grabs me and pulls me along to his house. His head is buried on my shoulder as he sobs and rancorously calls out, "Allah. Why? Why have you taken my brother Reza from us? Tom came all the way from America to see us— to be with Reza and you have taken Reza away. Why God? Why? Why did you do this? Why did you take Reza away? Tom is our brother—our brother."

With my arms around him, I, too, am overcome with profound sadness, but also a strange feeling akin to fear. I had never witnessed such overwhelming grief. I look back to see if Del is there. She is following respectfully behind. I cannot introduce her now, and I hope she is not frightened. I regret that she is experiencing this so soon after her arrival in the village.

At the Abtahi compound, the women wail uncontrollably. I am ardently distressed I'm causing this intense sorrow. Rozy's smiling face I so fondly remember is drawn and cheerless, that of a woman robbed of being a teenager. In the emotion I am speechless, in agony that my presence has renewed the family's loss of Reza. Eventually I am able to introduce Del. Javad and I and the family gain a measure of composure, but memories of Reza burden the joy of the evening meal.

SUNDAY, JULY 30, 1978   As we lie on the floor late at night I ask, "Del, tell me about the festivities in the women's quarter. It sounded like you

---

[*] Heydar was killed when his F-16 was shot down in the Iran-Iraq War of 1980–1988.

were having so much fun." We had been at the first evening of wedding celebrations for *Haji* Tofigh's daughter. "All we did was sit around the edge of the room and stand up and greet each other when someone new came in. It's the way it always is. The best was to be with *Haji* Tofigh and Ezetollah and to see everyone again. They had a little more to talk about tonight because I was there, but it was really quite dismal."

"Oh, we had a lot of fun. The women sang and danced and we laughed a lot. We had a lively time. It was even more festive because I was there, I'm sure. Even though I don't know Farsi, we found ways of communicating. I had the place of honor right next to the bride. They even boiled water for me to drink because Mulla's wife, Noor Jahan, insisted."

FRIDAY, AUGUST 4, 1978 The Mirsalehis now live in Gonbad-e Kavus. Ismael is principal of one of the schools. A picnic in the stippled shade of a nearby park is filled with the tender joy of being with family. Vida, Davood, and Sima have grown up. Davood has a trim mustache like his father's. A new little girl, Sepideh, has been added to the family. Obviously spoiled, she has the curiosity and mischievousness of Davood when I first met him in 1964. Ismael indicates the children are doing well in school.

"Ismael, have you ever considered sending Davood to a university in the United States? If he came to Hawaii he would have us to help him. He could get a job to pay his way through the university."

"No, my son won't work when he goes to the university," his mother exclaims.

"That's how Del and I got our education. We always had part-time jobs. It's the way it's done in America." I drop the subject.*

SUNDAY, AUGUST 6, 1978 "*Aghaye* Dooshgeeri," Yavar Khanpoor shouts as he opens the family's courtyard gate in Babol. *Dooshgeeri* (Showertaker) was his favorite name for me. "Mister *va* Del *amadand*," he announces our arrival.

He hugs me as the family runs toward us. I introduce Del. It is a most

---

* I never hear from Ismael Mirsalehi after 1978. In 1992 Mulla informed me that Davood had become a martyr in the Iran-Iraq War. My grief is equal to that at the loss of my friend Reza.

tender reunion, filled with laughter and joy. Yavar is handsomely gray, and Farsheed and Fereshteh are now young adults. Two more daughters have been added to the family. The easy informality of our visit brings back memories of the gentle years we lived in Alang.

"Let's go to Meti Kola. My father and brother's family are waiting to see you and meet Del."

I'm thrilled to show Del the picturesque sweetness of Meti Kola with its green lawns, orchards, and whitewashed walls.

TUESDAY, AUGUST 8, 1978 "Be sure to return before you leave for America," the Khanpoors insist as we board the bus for Tehran.

"*Baleh*, we will," I assure them.

Del and I visit museums in Tehran, including the shockingly surprising collection of Pop Art the Queen assembled in the Museum of Contemporary Art. Nowhere in our travels had we ever seen such a comprehensive collection of high quality contemporary art. Even the catalogue is a work of art, packaged with three suckers in a traditional Iranian plastic sweetmeats gift container. My adopted country has certainly advanced in the short time I have been away.

WEDNESDAY, AUGUST 9, 1978 An evening in the company of the eminent yet humble Mr. and Mrs. Karimi at their understated, contemporary home in Shemiran is an uncommon occasion. The yard, with its fruit trees and pool, extends from one block to another. Mr. Karimi is the retired Minister of Education. Their daughter is one of my students at the University of Hawaii. They had been to our house when they visited her in Hawaii, and they immediately perceived my abiding love for Iran. Mr. Karimi urges, "When you return to Tehran from your journey to Isfahan and Shiraz, stay with us."

"Thank you, but my friends from Alang will be picking us up at the hotel near the bus stations in south Tehran, so we will need to be there."

"It would be better for you to be with us. You are always welcome here."

"Thank you, Mr. Karimi. It is much appreciated."

"No, Tom, this is not *taroof*. We want you to stay with us."

FRIDAY, AUGUST 11, 1978 We arrived in Isfahan yesterday after a long, hot journey across the western edge of the great desert. The minimal sensuousness of the landscape and the memories it conjured were a meditative peregrination into the past. We found a hotel on Chahar Bagh Avenue, but following an uncomfortable night in less than clean surroundings, we move to another hotel this morning.

I can't wait to show Del the magnificent Meydan-e Shah, with its grand mosques and palace, but first we stop at Chehel Sotun, the Palace of Forty Columns. It is noon, the moment of the call to prayer on a Friday, as we approach the Masjid-e Shah.

"Del, let's go to the hotel now and come back after lunch."

Following a nourishing Persian meal, we venture out to the street. Gun-toting soldiers with bayonets unsheathed stationed about twenty feet apart line both sides of the street. I grab Del's arm and hesitate. As we cross, I look north to the nearest intersection. A tank with its gun lowered points in our direction. Now across from the hotel, we debate what we should do. We determine it may be prudent to return to the hotel. As we turn to the street, a shopkeeper nods his head, indicating his agreement with our decision.

"What is the matter?" I inquire at the hotel desk.

"Oh, there was a scuffle at the prison this morning and some inmates escaped. Everything will be fine."

"Del, I suggest we wait in the lobby until the ruckus dies down."

A military vehicle with a bullhorn rambles down the street, proclaiming a curfew from 8pm to 6am. I ask someone what it said to confirm I heard correctly, "What happened?"

"There was a riot in Isfahan this morning. That's why the military is out. It is better you don't go outside. The airport has been closed."

"Is it only in Isfahan?"

"*Baleh*, only Isfahan. The rest of the country is calm."

Hiding my concern, I look at Del. We go to our room to confer, and decide there is little point in remaining in Isfahan. We might as well go to Shiraz so Del can see Persepolis. Supposedly it is quiet there.

We slip out and cautiously pick our way up the street, past the soldiers with their intimidating rifles to the intersection where the menacing tank's powerful gun ominously projects down Chahar Bagh. We slip around the corner until we are opposite the bus station. I grab Del's arm as we wait for a break in the maddening traffic. Suddenly I see our opportunity to dart across the street.

"Don't run," a man shouts as we sprint across. "They'll shoot you."

We make it in one mad dash. The men at the bus station reprimand me and tell us not to run when we go back.

"Is everything calm in Shiraz?"

"Yes, Shiraz is peaceful. Do you want tickets for Shiraz?"*

"*Baleh*, two tickets for tomorrow."

I purchase the tickets and am reminded, "Don't run."

"*Baleh. Moteshakeram.*"

As we near our hotel, a commotion impedes us. We carefully approach and discover the windows of the Bank-e Sadrat, two buildings away from our anticipated haven, had been smashed in the short time we were gone.

"Stay in the hotel. Don't go anywhere," we are advised when we return.

SATURDAY, AUGUST 12, 1978 Del and I gaze at Persepolis and the glorious tent city, remnants of the 2500th anniversary celebration in 1971, as the bus speeds by on its way to Shiraz. I look at her, elated she will see this tomorrow—something she has taught about for years—and now she will be able to talk about it firsthand.

In Shiraz we quickly find a hotel.

"Del, let's go to the bazaar. It's one of the best in Iran. They may have some Qashqai things. This is where I got our lion rug."

When we get there, however, mammoth doors cover the entrance—it's locked.

"Undoubtedly there were problems in Shiraz too, so they closed the bazaar," I tell Del. "We better return to the hotel."

---

* In actuality 89 people, with estimates up to 150 or more, had been killed by government forces in a massacre in the New Mosque in Shiraz on August 10, 1978. See Mary Elaine Hegland, *Days of Revolution: Political Unrest in an Iranian Village* (Stanford: Stanford University Press, 2014), 126–128 and Charles Kurzman, *The Unthinkable Revolution in Iran* (Cambridge: Harvard University Press, 2005), 60–61.

SUNDAY, AUGUST 13, 1978 "What are these?" Del wakes me. "Bugs!"

I look. "Ewww, bed bugs!"

We get up, shake out our clothes, and shower. Fortunately, we close our suitcase at night. Nevertheless, we pound it out and check our shoes, descend to the lobby, pay our bill, and search for another hotel, hoping that it won't have bed bugs too, and that we don't bring any with us.

We catch a bus to Persepolis and wander among the imposing ancient ruins. Del is spellbound. In Shiraz, we visit the tombs of Hafez and Saadi. In our hotel room, Del starts our daily laundry. Suddenly the lights go out.

"Del, it's just in this area. I can see lights down the block. Hopefully they'll come back on."

We finish the laundry by flashlight and go to sleep, imagining bed bugs. When dawn breaks, there are none.

MONDAY, AUGUST 14, 1978 On the long, hot bus ride back to Isfahan, we fantasize about a cooling shower and a delicious dinner at the hotel topped off by large hunks of refreshing watermelon—the perfect way to end a grueling trip.

It is near curfew when the bus rolls into Isfahan. We had already decided we would stay at the hotel directly across from the bus station, thereby eliminating the need to walk on the streets of a city seemingly under siege.

"These sheets are dirty—filthy," Del announces, inspecting the bed.

I call the desk and ask for clean sheets. Promptly they are delivered. I take the new sheets and hand the young man the dirty ones. Del is already in the shower, so I tell him that we will make the bed. When we check the new sheets, they aren't much cleaner than the previous ones.

"I wonder if they washed them in the river?" Del ponders with disgust.

Clean and refreshed after our showers, we go to the dining room for dinner. We are the lone guests. The staff stares at us blankly.

"Do you have a menu?" I inquire.

They look at us in dismay. "*Agha*, we don't have any food. We can't go out to shop because of the curfew," one of the staff explains.

"Well, so much for our dreams of a scrumptious dinner and the restorative pleasures of cool watermelon," I mumble to Del.

She sits there, irritated. "Well, Tom, what are you going to do now?"

"*Agha*, do you have anything to eat? We need to eat and we can't go outside to find a restaurant that might be open. Do you have any bread? And tea? Anything else?"

He leaves. I hear talking in a back room. He returns. "*Agha*, we have a little bread and one egg. We can make tea. How would you like the egg?"

"Boiled, please. *Moteshakeram.*"

After a while he returns with the boiled egg, pieces of stale bread, and tea. To the side, the staff watches us share the egg and gnaw on the rubbery bread. The waiter brings us more tea to wash it down.

"*Moteshakeram, Agha.*" I express my gratitude for almost miraculously producing a meal, even if it wasn't of Biblical quantity or quality.

TUESDAY, AUGUST 15, 1978 "Del, the city seems to have settled down since Friday. I want to get some *gaz* (nougat) to take to Alang. Isfahan is famous for it. Also, I want you to see the Masjid-e Shah and Ali Qapu palace."

The stately Safavid mosque is forever exalted in its angled orientation, vast courtyard, soaring dome and minarets, and spectacular tilework.

"I recall my first visit, Del, when a man was praying under the colossal dome across the courtyard, but his whispered supplication was clearly audible as I stood beneath the entrance *iwan*. The acoustics within this building are sublime."

WHEN OUR BUS ARRIVES in south Tehran from Isfahan, I call the Karimis. The incidents in Isfahan and Shiraz have provoked a sense of urgency in us to accept his invitation to stay with them.

"Tom, I'm glad you called," Mr. Karimi tells me. "Are you and Del OK? My wife and I worried about you when we heard that riots broke out in Isfahan. Get a taxi and come here immediately. Don't stay in south Tehran. It's too dangerous."

During a quiet dinner in the peaceful enclosure of their garden, we tell them about our trip. Del relates her excitement over seeing Persepolis and how she will use the slides in her classes. We witness their pride over our enthusiasm for Iran.

"Tom and Del, my wife and I want you to take the Qajar painting home with you," Mr. Karimi tells us.

"No, we can't do that. It's yours." I had commented on the painting the evening we were with them, and told them we had gone to the Negarestan Museum that day. It contains the Queen's collection of Qajar paintings. Disappointingly, it was closed for restoration.

"No, Mrs. Karimi and I discussed this and we want you to take the painting with you."

"Oh, thank you, but the painting is yours. You said you got it in Mashhad many years ago. You should give it to one of your daughters."

"No, Tom, we want you and Del to have it. This is not *taroof*. It will be perfect in your Persian house in Hawaii," he says with a smile.

"Thank you, Mr. and Mrs. Karimi. But you need to keep the painting."

"No, Tom, we insist you accept it and take it to America."

In the confines of our room Del tells me, "Tom, the Karimis want you to have the painting. You need to be gracious about accepting it."

"No, Del, you don't understand Iranian *taroof*."

"I don't think it is *taroof*. They truly want you to have the painting. If they bring up the painting in the morning you ought to accept it."

I don't answer her.

WEDNESDAY, AUGUST 16, 1978 Together we enjoy a casual Iranian breakfast of freshly baked bread, smooth white goat cheese, jams, and fruit with tea under the shade of a plane tree in the garden. The gentle sounds of the bubbling fountain and the singing birds seem a world away from the hustle and bustle of the city below.

"Tom, Mrs. Karimi and I want you to take the painting with you to America. We will be pleased it is part of your collection of Persian art. It is a gift from us—a thank you for taking care of our daughter Shaharazade."

Del looks at me.

"Mr. and Mrs. Karimi, the painting is yours. However, I have thought about this and I am happy to accept it. Thank you. Forever it will be a memory of you and our time together here in Iran. Del and I will call it Shaharazade, in honor of your daughter. We must take it off the stretcher and carefully roll it up. We should get a tube to put it in so it doesn't get damaged on our way home. It's a long way to Hawaii."

They smile. "*Moteshakeram*, Tom.* Our chauffeur will take us downtown to the fabric bazaar to get a tube."

When we leave for the hotel where we have arranged to meet our friends from Alang, the Karimis ask, "Can you come to see us one more time?"

"We will be in Tehran one day before we depart on August 22nd. Our flight is early in the morning."

"Then can you have lunch with us on the 21st?"

"Yes, that would be nice. But I do want Del to see the Crown Jewels that day. Today, before our friends pick us up, we are going to Shahyad. I left Iran before it was completed in 1971."

"Yes, Del needs to see the Crown Jewels. You can see them after our lunch. And, Tom, you will like the exhibits at Shahyad."

The Karimis are right. First, the monumental grandeur of the Shahyad tower is humbling. The underground exhibits, and the audio/visual presentation with its 20 movie and 120 slide projectors operated by five computers, are world-class. It presents a cavalcade of Iranian history from ancient times to today's smiling schoolchildren.

WE CATCH A TAXI for the return to the hotel, and I note the amount on the meter. When other passengers get out, the driver turns off the meter.

"*Agha*, why did you turn off the meter?"

"For you, sir, it is a flat fee."

"I'm sorry, *Agha*, I pay what the meter says. Please turn on the meter."

"Sir, it is a flat fee."

"*Agha*, stop here. I don't want to ride with you."

He argues, but when he stops for a light, Del and I get out. The driver angrily swears at me. I ignore him, check my map, and calculate we have gone about a third of the way to the hotel. I hail another taxi, check his

---

* Following the revolution, Mr. Karimi sent his wife to stay with their daughter in the US while he remained behind to sell the house. Almost weekly, he lowered the price. On the morning of November 4, 1979, with the house still unsold, he locked the doors and went to the airport with only the clothes he was wearing. When he arrived in San Francisco, his family informed him that militants had taken the US Embassy in Tehran. Another daughter in Iran, regularly checked the house, but discovered its contents were disappearing and all the trees were being cut down.

meter, and confirm his route on my map as he drives. I'm adamant about not being conned by another taxi driver. However, when we reach the hotel, I discover that somewhere along the way he turned off the meter and he is demanding an amount many times what we paid when we went to Shahyad. I object and throw some money on the seat, more than we paid going, and walk away. He screams and swears at me. I answer back with a litany of swear words as well and run up the little alley to the hotel.

JAFAR AND MULLA ARE WAITING for us. We get our bags and make a reservation for our two last nights in Iran. Jafar takes us down several nearby streets that were firebombed while we were away. It looks like a war zone, with burned-out shops and gaping holes in charred apartments above. For a long time, as we navigate the gridlocked traffic of Tehran, I wonder what is happening to my cherished Iran. I hope it won't get worse and that the airport won't be closed. However, I'm determined not to let Del and my friends see my uneasiness—the silence of love. If the airport is shut, our friends will certainly drive us to the Turkish border, and we will get a bus to Ankara, I conclude.

"Can we stop at the Khanpoors to let them know we are safe?" I ask as we near Babol. "They knew we were in Isfahan the day of the riot."

"Sure, Tom," Jafar agrees.

Yavar and the family are relieved to see us. "Stop by one more time on your way back to Tehran," they urge.

Jafar assures them we will.

THE NEXT SEVERAL DAYS are excruciating. People come with gifts—humble scarves and pieces of embroidery. Mulla and Noor Jahan give Del a Turkoman rug. "I'm sorry it's torn," Mulla says. "The dog destroyed it."

"*Moteshakeram*. We'll have it fixed in America."

Our impending departure and the draining thoughts of an indefinite reunion weigh on me as if I were carrying a marble slab on my back. The news on television each evening adds to the burden. Almost daily the Shah appeals to his people to use restraint and asks for calmness and their support. But I see, and my friends do too, that he is a man severely weakened and not well. But we don't speak about Iran's future. We can't imagine anything different from what we know.

SATURDAY, AUGUST 19, 1978 Our last day in Alang. My anguish is evident whenever I see someone. I worry about Iran and them, and am tortured by thoughts of not knowing when I will see them again.

Then someone turns on the television. Chills run up and down my spine. The news report is calamitous. Somebody locked the doors of the Cinema Rex in Abadan and lit it on fire. At least 400 people perished. The Shah looks drawn and weaker than ever. Now I clearly see my friends' concern for him and themselves.

Our dinner at Mulla's house is nearly silent. The women are present to be with Del. The coming together of our departure, the terrible and senseless loss of life in Abadan, and the future of Iran are more than our human minds can bear.

SUNDAY, AUGUST 20, 1978 The morning is like two others I have lived through—only worse. *It is the future I fear,* I tell myself. *Will I ever return? Will I ever be able to sit with my friends again? Or will they and Alang forever be only a remembrance?*

We take pictures—all final memories. Jafar comes with the jeep. Our baggage is loaded. Del says a tearful farewell to Noor Jahan, and Mulla's sister and her daughter. She gives her straw hat to the daughter.

I look at Shaban Ali and know deep within me I am leaving my brother in a land far from my own.

Javad jumps in the jeep, hangs on to me, and entreats, "Allah. Why? Why did you take Reza from us? Why? Why? Tom came to Alang. Now he is leaving, but you took Reza before they could see each other. Why? Oh, God, why did you do this?"

With our heads pressed together, we cry all the way to the highway. Jafar stops. Javad gets out. He crouches down beside the road, covers his face, and I see his body shaking in distress as we drive away. It is a long time before I can say anything.

As promised, we stop in Babol to say goodbye to Yavar Khanpoor and his family. Only briefly we mention the horrific events of yesterday in Abadan. Goodbyes are never easy, but my heart tells me this one seems absolute.

TUESDAY, AUGUST 22, 1978 Jafar and Mulla speed us to Mehrabad airport. Yesterday morning we spent quiet time together—mainly listening to the news from Abadan. Lunch with the Karimis was also somber. Leaving, they wished us a safe trip home. The Crown Jewels were the sole touch of splendor in an otherwise dark day. Now we say a sad farewell.

Jafar and Mulla wait as we clear passport control, Del in one line, I in another. She has the tube with the painting. Assuming she is a Persian leaving the country not wearing a *chador*, the immigration official gruffly speaks to her in Farsi. She presents her American passport. Flustered, he switches to English. In our travels in Iran, she was often mistaken for Persian, and when people spoke to her, they were aghast when I was the one to answer in Farsi.

"What is in the tube?" he repeats, now in English.

"A picture," she replies.

"Fine. Have a safe trip home."

We look back at Mulla and Jafar and sadly wave to them. Tears well as I realize this is truly my last physical connection with Alang.

THE BRITISH AIRWAYS PLANE smoothly lifts off the ground. For me, it is Iranian ground, almost sacred to my very being. I press my head against the window, but can't see through the water that floods my eyes. It is a while before I'm able to glimpse the vast desert and mountains below. Eventually, looking out, I see a large body of water.

"Del, we are over Lake Van in eastern Turkey. If there's a problem now, we will head for an emergency landing in Ankara. We are out of Iran."

I breathe a sigh of relief. It is the first she knows of my anxiety. But that relief is mingled with fear—of what will happen to Iran, and to my friends.

EPILOGUE

HOPING THE SITUATION IN IRAN will get better, I put off writing to thank my friends for our summer together. But the revolution we experienced in its infancy escalates and on January 17, 1979, the Shah leaves Iran. America is vilified, and I'm afraid to write. I fear for my friends because of their association with an American.

On November 4, 1979, Islamist students and militants take over the American Embassy in Tehran, and America becomes the "Great Satan." I agonize over my allegiance to the two countries I love while the American media shows angry Iranians shouting, *"Marg bar Amrika"* (Death to America), and Americans shout hatred at Iranians.

I pray for a letter from Alang—a letter that will signal it is all right for me to write. Nothing comes. My friends have never wanted me informed of the unpleasant; they want my life in Iran to remain vivid and beautiful in my memory—unspoiled. For me, there is always a sense of helplessness—certain sadness. Years later, I find out about the death of a friend or other disturbing news, and the pain of having lived in dubious hope stabs at my heart.

In the summer of 1982, while traveling in France, I send several letters in which I make no reference to America, my work, or that I ever was in Iran. I don't include my last name or a return address. Finally, in 1983, letters arrive from Shaban Ali and Mulla. This is the signal for which I've waited five long years. Our correspondence resumes, and Javad Abtahi writes as well. Shaban Ali calls me one Christmas Day, and on other occasions we also hear each other's voices on the phone. Each time, his wife insists on speaking with Del. *"Salaam, hale shoma khoobeh?"* they say to each other, and then laugh with joy.

Shaban Ali sends pictures of the building I called home as a Peace Corps Volunteer. It is a skeleton in decay—weathered—the windows of my room broken. In ruin, my house seems only a romantic metaphor for the passage of time. Its neglect is a symbol of loss and absence—a by-gone season, like a love that drifts away. I pause and weep for a love at the edge of the sands of the desert—the traces of mud and sticks erased by the dimming winds of time.

Shaban Ali, Mulla, Ezetollah, and children of friends who are gone now send emails and beg me to return to Iran; however, no one can assure I will be able to spend quality time with my friends—*if* a visa is granted.

But hope never diminishes. Often I do return . . .

. . . *Gorgan, but all vanishes before I reach Alang* . . .

Or,

. . . *I hover over the village, seeing my friends, hearing them laugh and talk* . . .

And I wake . . . and lie there in the stillness of a Hawaiian night.

THE MEANING I GIVE ALANG has shaped me. It has both imposed limits on and extended the possibilities of my existence.

Alang is both a living presence and a memory, a palimpsest of the real and the collected remembered images of it—a merger of past and present, the present always slowly erasing the exquisite drawing of the past. Now only remembrance substitutes for the actual past, to which I cannot return.

Memory is but a momentary breath—a lingering fragrance. It is the trace of something gone and irretrievable. I savor the view of the village to which my memory is attached, but the dew of my tired eyes weighs heavily on my soul. Will the village forever only be a place left behind?

GLOSSARY

abe jou	beer
aftabeh	ewer
Agha, Aghaye	Mr.
Ahvalet?	How are you?
Alhamdulillah	Praise to God
amad	came
Amo	Uncle
Amrika	America
ast	is
baba	papa
bah, bah, bah	expression of approval
baleh	yes
beah	come
befarmayid	polite expression, welcome, you first
behbakhsheed	excuse me
chador	woman's body covering
chai khaneh	teahouse, café
Chashmeh shoma mesle koone merg khoorus memoneh.	Your eyes look like a rooster's ass.
chera	why
dehyar	community development worker
Enshahallah	If God is willing.
Hale shoma chetoreh(i)?	How are you?
Hale shoma khoobeh(i)?	Are you well?

Hale shoma khoob hast?	How are you?
hast, hastid	it is, you are
hammam	bathhouse
inja	here
In ketab ast.	This is a book.
iwan	large vaulted chamber open on one side
jub	gutter, open drainage ditch
kalle pache	sheep's head
kargar	laborer
kheili	very
khiaban	street, avenue
Khanoome	Mrs.
khoobam	I am well.
khoob(eh)(i)	good, well
khodahafez	goodbye
madreseh	school, historically a theological school
Majles	Parliament
mamnunam	I thank you
Man qalam doram.	I have a pen.
manqal	brazier
meleh shoma	whatever you wish
meydan	square
merci	thank you
mihrab	prayer niche
moallem	teacher
mostarah	toilet, outhouse
moteshakeram	thank you
mobarak	greetings, blessings
na	no
Nemekham.	I don't want.
rafti	you went, you left
salaam	hello
Salaam allekum.	Peace be with you.
sangak	flatbread baked on hot pebbles

Sepah-e Danesh	Literacy Corps
Sepah-e Solh	Peace Corps
Shab bekheyr	Goodnight
Sobh bekheyr	Good morning
Shemiran	exclusive section of north Tehran
Sherkat-e Sargardon	Do Nothing Company
shoma	you
Shoma qalam dorid?	You have a pen?
taroof	politeness, protocol
Un ketab ast.	That is a book.
Ya Allah	With the will of Allah

AS A PEACE CORPS VOLUNTEER in Iran, Tom Klobe learned the persuasive qualities of quiet leadership that enlightened his 29-year career as Director of the University of Hawaii Art Gallery. He organized and designed over 200 exhibitions, five of which received the prestigious Print Casebooks: Best in Exhibition Design award. His book *Exhibitions: Concept, Planning and Design* was published by the American Association of Museums Press in 2012. He has authored or edited over 35 publications.

Klobe was named a Living Treasure of Hawaii in 2005 and was the recipient of the University of Hawaii Robert W. Clopton Award for Distinguished Community Service in 2003. In 1999 he was honored by the Republic of France as a Chevalier de l'Ordre des Arts et des Lettres for his contributions to the arts in France and Hawaii.